Your Baby's First Year

week by week

Other books by Glade B. Curtis, M.D., and Judith Schuler, M.S.

Your Pregnancy Week by Week, 4th Edition
Your Pregnancy: Every Woman's Guide
Your Pregnancy After 30
Your Pregnancy Questions & Answers
Your Pregnancy Recovery Guide

Your Baby's First Year
week by week

Glade B. Curtis, M.D.

Judith Schuler, M.S.

Lori Eining, R.N., technical assistant

FISHER

BOOKS™

Library of Congress Cataloging-in-Publication Data
Curtis, Glade B.
      Your baby's first year week by week/ Glade B. Curtis, Judith Schuler.
          p. cm.
      Includes index.
      ISBN 1-55561-232-5 (pbk.) - ISBN 1-55561-257-1 (hc)
        1. Infants-Care. 2. Infants-Care and hygiene. I. Schuler, Judith. II. Title.

RJ61 .C967 2000
649'.122-dc21   00-037601

Fisher Books
5225 W. Massingale Road
Tucson, Arizona 85743-8416
(520) 744-6110

Fisher Books is a member of the Perseus Books Group.
Find us on the World Wide Web at http://www.fisherbooks.com

Fisher Books' titles are available at special discounts for bulk purchases in the United States by corporations, institutions, and other organizations.

Text design by Gary Smith, Performance Design
Production: Randy Schultz
Illustration: Leslie Sinclair
Illustrations on pages xxxiii, 3, 84, 102, 111,
  120, 235, 435, 443, 483: Gary Smith, Performance Design
Illustration on page 319: David Fischer
All photos from New Family Photo CD© Eyewire, Inc.

First printing, September 2000

     5 6 7 8 9 10—03 02 01

Contents

Acknowledgments

This book, as with others I have written, is a result of my interactions with many pregnant women and their partners. Their excitement and inquiring minds produce many questions about the miracle of birth and the development of the resulting infant. It is my privilege to participate in this wondrous process on a daily (and often nightly!) basis. Those who speak the words following the birth—"It's finally over!"—learn rather quickly that it has just begun! My thanks are sincere to these couples and families for allowing me to share some of this joy.

Lori Eining, R.N., has proved to be a key ingredient to the completion of this project. Patients in my office over the years have been touched by her caring and compassionate nursing skills and genuine dedication to their care. Her friendship and support bless my patients daily.

My five children and two grandchildren have given me "on-the-job training" with babies week by week during the first year (and beyond), and I thank them for this opportunity. My wife, Debbie, and family offer support and understanding in professions (doctoring and writing) that require many sacrifices on a daily basis. My parents continue as shining examples to me and give me unconditional love and support.

My special thanks go to Megan and Hailey Harbertson for their dedication. Also, the always-available assistance of David Stevens has been invaluable to me. Without their help, this project would not be completed!

—**Glade B. Curtis, M.D.**

I want to thank my parents and my son, Ian, for their love and support. Special thanks to Bob Rucinski, who set up my new computer and got it up and running for this book. He also checked every website to be sure they still existed and were what they said they were. No pornographic sites slipped by his eagle eye! Bob, your help is always valuable to me. Somehow, saying thank you just doesn't seem adequate.

—**Judith Schuler, M.S.**

A Letter to New Parents

Dear New Parents,

After your baby's birth, as you hold this new life that has been entrusted to you, you may have many questions about the future. What will baby be like? Will she be smart? Will he be athletic? How quickly will she grow? When will he walk and talk?

Every parent looks ahead with hope and maybe a little uncertainty. All parents want their baby to excel and be the best she possibly can be. When we are around others with babies who are close in age, we often compare our baby to theirs. It's not unusual—we all do it. (We know—as parents, we've both been there!) But our advice is to avoid such comparisons as much as possible. Your baby is like no other. Like you, she will function on her own schedule. She'll eat or sleep when it's right for her. The best thing you can do for everyone concerned is to get to know your baby. Her development is geared to her personality and focus. Learn what's normal for her, and the rest will take care of itself.

In this book, we've included a great deal of information in each weekly discussion about a baby's mental, physical and social development. However, when these developmental changes occur (that is, the weeks we put them in) are *estimates* of your baby's developmental stage at a given time. Each developmental step represents an average; a baby's own development could occur anywhere from 6 to 10 weeks on either side of the week in which our discussion falls and be perfectly normal. Don't worry if your baby doesn't do something exactly at the time it's discussed in the book. Every baby develops in her own way. That's what makes her unique.

> **Each developmental step represents an average; a baby's own development could occur anywhere from 6 to 10 weeks on *either side* of the week in which our discussion falls and be perfectly normal.**

What's most important is that baby's development progresses in a *sequential* way. By this we mean that baby uses skills she has mastered to develop other skills. As your baby develops, she may focus on one task at a time. If she's learning to walk and concentrating her efforts on balance and movement, her language development may slow for a while. When she becomes adept at walking, you may discover her babbling more and making new sounds.

Baby's Personality and Temperament

Your baby's personality and temperament can influence how he develops. Researchers once believed the environment and parental child-rearing practices influenced a baby's personality more than anything else. Now they believe that babies are born with definite personality characteristics shaped by many factors, including genetics and experiences in the womb and during birth.

> **As your baby develops, she may focus on one task at a time.**

To assess personality, researchers study baby's activity levels, eating and sleeping patterns, and how he interacts with his environment, among other traits. Some babies move around a lot; others are quiet and move little. Babies who move around a lot may achieve muscle control more quickly than a baby who is less active.

Some babies are more adaptable than others. An adaptable baby often has few problems when his environment changes, even drastically. A baby who does not adjust as easily may be cautious in his approach to a new situation. This may seem to affect his ability to learn quickly but really isn't a problem if he learns something well.

Another area researchers look at is baby's digestive system. Some babies have no problems with digestion from birth, while others may have digestive difficulties for months after birth. If a baby isn't bothered by digestive upsets, physical, mental and social development may progress more smoothly because energy is not diverted to dealing with stomach distress.

It's worth making an effort to understand your baby's personality, because you will be more open to the way he develops if you understand him. If your baby is easy to get along with, not fussing or crying a great deal, he will probably adjust easily to various situations. Babies with this type of personality usually reach the various developmental milestones at about the time we discuss in each week, given a few weeks on either side as discussed earlier. A more-active infant may be more easily overstimulated, which can make it harder for him to focus on various developmental tasks. But don't worry; many babies with this personality type learn to settle themselves in a short time, after which they progress more quickly.

However, development may not be evenly paced, with quicker gains in one area and slower progress in others.

A third personality type might be described as "shy." Some babies are more withdrawn than others. They may resist new experiences and stimulation. These babies require more attention than other babies in the first few months of life. It's a good idea to introduce new situations carefully to enhance this baby's ability to deal with it. As time passes and you know your baby better, if you believe your baby is more inclined to this personality type, you may want to ask your pediatrician for advice on ways to help your child progress.

How Can You Help Your Baby?

You are the key to your baby's development. You provide stimulation in many areas, an environment that promotes growth, and the love and encouragement every baby needs to motivate her. Provide your baby with activities, games and play that help her

> **You are the key to your baby's development.**

develop. Provide stimulating experiences. In each weekly discussion of this book, we give you games to play and things to do with baby that will help you both grow into your new environment.

A Note to Parents of a Premature Infant

You may be the parent of a "preemie," a baby born before he was fully developed in the womb. It's not an uncommon occurrence—about 6% of all babies are born before 37 weeks of gestation. Their growth is measured a little differently from a full-term baby's. However, they should develop in the same sequence as a baby born at full term; just the timing will be different.

If your baby is premature, subtract the number of weeks he was premature from his actual birth age to get his "developmental age." For example, if your son was born 8 weeks premature (before his due date), subtract 8 weeks from his chronological age. If he is now 12 weeks old (from his actual date of birth), his developmental age is only 4 weeks. He has used the time from his birthdate to his expected date of birth to finish developing as a full-term baby. After he reaches his full-term due date, he will begin to grow as if he were full term. Your doctor will chart his growth to make sure he is healthy. The most important thing your physician will watch for is evidence of the baby's steady growth. Research has shown that by the time a premature infant reaches 2 years, his weight is average, and by the time he reaches 3-1/2 years, his height will also be average.

Don't be alarmed if your premature baby seems to be slower to develop and to progress than other babies his age. If they are full-term infants, they've had a head start on development. Within a short time, your baby will be making similar strides. Studies have shown that babies born as early as 32 weeks have often caught up completely with their peers by age 2 (if they were spared serious complications of prematurity). If your son is consistently achieving developmental milestones, even at a slower pace than full-term babies, relax and enjoy him. Try not to compare his progress with other babies' . . . however, if you do, compare his progress to babies born when he was due!

A Well-Baby Book

This is a well-baby book. We do not attempt to cover problems or situations that occur when a baby is born very ill or with a major health problem. Parents who face a grave health problem with their baby do well to rely on their pediatrician and other healthcare providers to help them find the information and solutions they seek.

We chose not to cover topics in such a brief fashion that you might feel we were not serious about them. However, we do provide suggestions in the Resources section, page 492, about where to find answers about serious health issues.

When You Adopt a Baby

You may become new parents as a result of adopting a baby. What an exciting time this is for you! Your baby may not have grown under your heart, but he or she will quickly grow in your heart. We congratulate you on the arrival of your baby.

Adopting a baby can happen after you have been informed about the upcoming event months before baby's birth. Or you may be waiting to adopt a child, and the arrival of your little one happens almost overnight.

We hope this book will supply you with the confidence most new parents need with a baby. If you have not had a great deal of time to prepare for the arrival of your baby, read the chapters that deal with preparing for baby's birth (Before Baby's Birth), what occurs while baby is in the hospital (Baby's First 48 Hours) and the first few days of baby's life (Week 1). They provide insights into many aspects of baby's development.

Enjoy Your Baby and This Book!

We hope the information we provide is helpful to you as you watch your little one grow. This first year is one of tremendous growth and change for your baby, and a year of great joy for you, too. You will be amazed, as almost all parents are, at how quickly your child becomes a person in his or her own right.

With our very best wishes,

Glade Curtis, M.D., and Judith Schuler, M.S.

P.S. In this book, we alternate the use of "he" and "she" each week when referring to the baby. In the even-numbered weeks, all references to the baby will be "he." In odd-numbered weeks, references will be to "she."

Before Baby's Birth

Preparing for a new baby is a lot of fun, but it takes a lot of effort, too. You want to be prepared to take good care of your new baby—from buying the right nursery items to choosing a pediatrician. Here's a plan of action that will get you ready for one of the most exciting days of your lives.

This chapter contains a fairly comprehensive discussion of things baby may need. We include information on your baby's layette, swings, cribs and bassinets, and various nursery items. We discuss car seats because you'll need to have one available for baby's first car ride—home from the hospital. Finding a pediatrician may be one of the most important decisions you make, so we discuss this first.

Finding a Pediatrician

You may want to select the physician who is going to care for your baby before your baby's birth, so you can get to know him or her before you meet in the hospital, after your baby's birth. If you don't have a physician in mind, ask around for a referral (see box below).

Choices for the type of physician to care for your baby include a pediatrician, a family physician or a general practitioner. A family physician or general practitioner may be the only type of medical practice available in some areas.

How Do I Get a Referral?

- **Ask your OB/GYN for a reference.**
- **Ask family members, friends and co-workers the names of doctors they know and trust.**
- **Call your local or county medical society.**
- **Check with your insurance provider to see if they have a list of pre-approved physicians you must use.**
- **If you are a member of a health-maintenance organization, contact the patient advocate for information on which pediatricians are accepting new patients in the HMO.**

Meeting the Doctor

Some parents-to-be choose a pediatrician ahead of time. If you decide to do this, call for an appointment 3 to 4 weeks ahead of your baby's due date. Tell the person you speak with that you are interviewing pediatricians for your expected baby. Some practices hold individual meetings; others have group sessions with several couples. Ask about the cost of this meeting. Some doctors will meet with you for free; others charge a fee.

If problems arise in dealing with this physician after your baby is born, you can choose another healthcare provider. Your choice is not permanent.

Preparing the Nursery

Your baby's nursery may be a separate bedroom, an alcove or a corner of your bedroom. The essential things you'll need when you bring baby home are a place for her to sleep and a designated changing area. The other pieces we discuss are not essential, but they might make your life easier.

> **A Word of Caution:**
>
> **Be careful about buying secondhand nursery equipment or borrowing someone else's. Some items might not meet current safety standards. Refer to the safety features described below for various pieces of equipment.**

Baby can sleep just about anywhere—in a cradle, a bassinet or a crib. If the nursery isn't ready when your baby is born, even a basket or drawer will do for a short time. Your baby won't need a crib until she can sit up. (Crib design and safety are discussed below.)

Consider purchasing these nursery items: some sort of bed (crib, bassinet), a changing table, a rocking chair, chest of drawers, diaper pail, baby monitor, small lamp, mobile, vaporizer or humidifier, and a smoke detector. A rocking chair is a wonderful place to nurse your baby and to comfort her, too. New designs of diaper pails keep diaper smells inside. Monitors make it easy for you to keep tabs on baby without going into her room and waking her up. You can listen to her and, with some models, also talk to her. Choose a small lamp with a low-watt bulb to light the room softly. A colorful mobile

> **When you bring baby home you'll need a place for her to sleep and a designated changing area.**

will delight and entertain baby for a long time; keep it out of baby's reach by suspending it from the ceiling. A vaporizer or humidifier will keep the air in baby's room moist and can help make breathing easier, especially when she has a cold.

Paint. Don't overlook the issue of paint in baby's room. Be sure the room is painted in nontoxic paint; if you're unsure, repaint the walls.

For baby's entertainment. You might want to consider including a swing and a bouncer chair. Both are great when you need to put baby in a safe place that will keep her happy. These items keep baby entertained and occupied.

Cribs, Cradles and Bassinets

Your baby needs a comfortable, safe place to sleep. Some parents decide they want their baby to sleep in a bassinet in their room for a while. Others put baby in her own room, in a crib or bassinet, from the first day home. Other parents have a "family bed," in which parents and baby sleep together in one large bed. (See the discussion in Week 5.)

Bassinet. This is a small, portable bed for baby. She can sleep in it until she gets too big, after which she can be moved to a crib. The bassinet mattress should fit snugly, and sheets must not pull up. A wide base is suggested so the bed does not tip easily.

Crib. This furniture is more permanent than a bassinet. Some cribs are designed to grow with your child and can be converted into a juvenile bed. Before you purchase, check out various safety features as established by the Juvenile Products Manufacturing Association (JPMA), the Consumer Product Safety Commission and the American Academy of Pediatrics.

Crib safety features. Keep in mind these safety features when you shop.

- Bars no farther apart than 2-3/8 inches. If you can pass a soft-drink can through the bars, they're too far apart.
- Mattress should fit snugly–you shouldn't be able to fit more than two fingers between the side of the crib and the mattress.
- The mattress should be firm and supportive.
- Railings should be 26 inches higher than the lowest level of mattress support or at least 4 inches above the mattress at its highest level.
- Corner posts should not be higher than end panels to prevent catching clothing when baby tries to climb out (when she's older).

- Nontoxic finish used on crib.
- If you're using a secondhand crib, be sure paint is lead-free. New cribs must be painted with lead-free paint.
- There should be no cutouts on the head- or footboard so baby's head can't get caught in them.
- The foot release/latching mechanism should be childproof.
- Be sure the teething rail (around the crib) and all hardware are sturdy and securely fastened to the crib.
- Never use cleaning bags or garbage bags as a waterproof cover for the mattress.

Sheets. In addition to the crib, you'll need three or four fitted sheets. Fitted sheets should wrap at least 2 inches under the mattress on all sides. Discard sheets if they shrink. Straps that fit under the mattress to hold sheets in place can be used. Never use a top sheet or waterproof pads on top of the fitted sheet. Some researchers now believe the crib should be free of all items except a fitted sheet and baby to reduce the risk of SIDS—no bumper pads, pillows, comforters or blankets while baby is sleeping. (See the discussion in Week 8.) If baby is chilly, put her in a zip-up sleeper to keep her warm. A crib wedge is a piece of foam that elevates baby's body while she sleeps and may keep her from rolling onto her stomach. (See Baby and Sleep in Week 1.)

Be sure the bars or slats of the crib are no farther than 2-3/8 inches apart.

Crib placement. Crib placement is important, too. Don't put it against an outside wall. Keep it away from radiators and air ducts (hot or cold). Keep the crib away from window-blind cords or drapery cords. Don't attach mobiles or anything else to the crib that baby could get tangled in.

Baby's Layette

Buying baby clothes is something parents and grandparents enjoy. It's fun to dress baby in the cutest or the sweetest outfits. But let's be practical: Most babies don't need all those things. They get by just fine with some basic styles for the first year. A few cute outfits are fine, but don't spend money on them if you don't need to. (You may receive many clothing items as shower and baby gifts.)

Basics for baby. A baby doesn't need very much. Diapers, T-shirts, gowns that open at the bottom, footed sleepers, socks, bibs, a hat, a warm cover-up, one-piece short- or long-legged "onesies," blankets and towels are the items you'll need to stock up on. How many of each you need depends on your personal situation. The list below should get you started.

- *6 to 8 T-shirts*
- *4 or 5 gowns*
- *4 lightweight footed sleepers*
- *2 blanket-weight footed sleepers*
- *6 pairs of socks*
- *6 bibs*
- *1 or 2 hats*
- *1 warm cover-up for going outside in chilly weather*
- *6 one-piece short- or long-legged "onesies"*
- *6 cotton receiving blankets (look for ones that are square–it's easier to swaddle baby)*
- *3 hooded baby towels*
- *3 washcloths*

Follow safety guidelines when choosing your baby's crib.

How Many Diapers

- **Where diapers are concerned, more is usually better!**

- **Have about 8 dozen diapers on hand (order 100 a week for a newborn if you have a diaper service).**

- **A combination of cloth and disposable diapers may help you meet all your needs.**

Toiletries. In addition to clothes, you'll need some toiletries for baby. A brush and comb, nail clippers or scissors, nasal bulb syringe, an ear-type or rectal thermometer, baby shampoo, diaper-rash ointment, baby oil, baby powder, baby wipes, cotton balls and petroleum jelly may all come in handy. Keep them together so you'll be able to reach them quickly.

Find the Best Deals

Outfitting a nursery can be stressful, especially if you start from scratch. Costs add up, and there is considerable variety to choose from also. Comparing prices can be tedious, but prices vary a great deal from product to product and store to store, so this task is probably worth your effort. To find the best deals for various baby items:

- Compare prices of an item at different stores, such as a discount store, a specialty store, an outlet store, a warehouse store and a secondhand store. You may be surprised how much you can save buying from the least-expensive place compared to the most expensive!
- Check out the Internet for on-line shopping, if you have a computer. (See the Resource section, page 492.)
- Try out some items for comfort of use before you buy. For example, if you're thinking of getting a backpack or front carrier for your baby, your build can make a difference in how comfortable one is over another. It isn't a bargain if you won't use it.
- Keep an eye out for sales. If you are in a baby store or department, ask the sales associate if a sale is coming up soon—many are glad to tell you if items are about to go on sale.

It's easy to spend more than $7,500 the first year on baby's necessities and other basics (this includes setting up the nursery with crib, changing table and other items). By comparison shopping, you can bring down costs somewhat. Avoid last-minute shopping and look around–your savings could be substantial.

Ear thermometer. One item you might want to have on hand is an ear thermometer. These devices are fairly new on the market. The thermometer uses infrared sensor technology to measure baby's temperature in her ear. Developed by the Jet Propulsion Laboratory to study stars in our galaxy and beyond, the technology was adapted to serve as a thermometer that measures body temperature in the ear in a matter of seconds.

The greatest advantage about this thermometer is its speed of measurement—1 or 2 seconds.

Easy to use: Place the tip of the thermometer in the ear, and

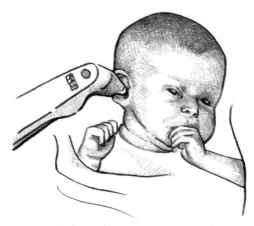

An ear thermometer can measure baby's body temperature in seconds.

hold it for a couple of seconds. The thermometer analyzes and averages from five to 32 separate measurements (the number measured depends on the brand you buy), and the readout is in Fahrenheit or Celsius. Some thermometers display the temperature in oral or rectal equivalents.

If you have a sick baby who is already uncomfortable, taking her temperature in a few seconds, as compared to 3 minutes rectally, may make everyone in the family happier.

Changing Table Set-Up

You can set up a changing table in baby's room or some other part of the house. If you have a two- or three-story house, you might want to have a place to change baby on each floor. Above all, the changing table must be sturdy. A safety strap that prevents baby from rolling is also advisable to use. Be sure you can store all the items you'll need safely out of baby's way. Before long, she'll be curious and active—and reaching and grabbing.

Your changing table should be the right height for you to change diapers comfortably—no higher than your breastbone, no lower than your hips. A pad with a raised edge is a good choice.

Caution:

Never leave baby unattended on a changing table.

Place the changing table away from windows to keep baby safe and warm. Put it in an area away from the crib so baby can't get items off it while she's in her crib. Don't place it near anything that dangles, such as window-blind cords, to keep baby from entangling herself. Consider putting a bright-colored poster on the wall or a mobile above her head to catch her attention and keep her occupied while you change her.

Have at hand clean diapers, diaper-rash cream, baby wipes, powder (use cornstarch powder because talc can cause problems if it's inhaled), lotions (fragrance-free), cotton balls, petroleum jelly, some clean clothes and clean blankets. Add anything else you think you might need for your situation. Keep items close at hand in a basket or on a shelf (out of baby's reach).

Have diaper bag, will travel! Pack some changing items in a bag so you can have them ready when you're on the go. A rubber-lined bag makes a good diaper bag. Fill it with four to six diapers, a bib, a spare outfit, a pacifier, formula, a couple of bottles, wipes and a toy or two.

Cloth or disposable diapers? Parents want to know which is best. It all depends on you and your situation. Disposable diapers are convenient to use. They save on utilities because you don't have to wash or dry them. You can take them when you go out, and you don't have to worry about disposal. You don't have to use rubber pants or diaper pins. However, when your baby has wet pants, you may not know it. The outer lining prevents you from knowing she's wet.

Cloth diapers need to be washed—by you or by a diaper service. This can be an inconvenience or an expense that you don't want. You may have to rinse diapers twice to get out all the detergent, if you wash them at home. Baby will also have to wear rubber pants, so you'll need to wash those, too. A diaper service is great but they can be a little costly.

Many parents use a combination of both cloth and disposable diapers and find it works well for them. If your baby is going to go to day care, you may be asked to bring only disposable diapers. Whatever you choose, you'll change thousands of diapers this first year!

Car Seats

The most important piece of baby equipment you can buy is a car seat. Your baby needs to ride in a car seat every time she rides in a car—it's the law in all 50 states. One report found that an average of 35 babies a year die in auto accidents on the way home from the hospital.

A car seat provides the best protection for your baby in case of an accident. Some parents mistakenly believe they can safely hold their baby in a crash. It can't be done. Crash tests have proved that a 10-pound baby would be torn from an adult's arms with great force in an accident at only 30 miles per hour! We also caution you not to take your baby out of her car seat to feed her, change her or comfort her while the car is moving.

From the time your baby goes home from the hospital, she should be placed in a car seat. Until 1 year of age and 20 pounds, the car seat should face the rear of the vehicle. The safest place for her is the middle of the back seat. After that, the seat can be turned forward, but keep it in the back seat. See the discussion in Week 52.

A car seat is an absolute necessity. Even newborns and low-birthweight babies need to be properly secured in a car seat, starting with their very first car ride.

When choosing a car seat for your baby, be certain it meets the safety standards of the JPMA, the Consumer Product Safety Commission and the American Academy of Pediatrics. You may choose from an infant-only seat, good until your baby reaches 20 pounds, or a convertible seat, which can be used until your child reaches 40 pounds. The infant-only seat is more comfortable for a young baby because of its semireclining position.

If your baby is low-birthweight. Parents who have a very small baby at birth may hesitate to put her in a car seat designed for larger babies. Car seats are designed for average-sized babies. A small baby may be uncomfortable in one. A small baby may have trouble breathing in a semireclined infant seat. One study showed a small baby may have decreased oxygen levels and increased episodes of apnea (baby stops breathing briefly) in a larger car seat. The solution may be to choose an infant car bed that meets federal safety standards, if your baby seems to have trouble breathing in a regular infant car seat. Baby lies flat, which allows her to breathe more easily. She will be protected in case of an accident.

If she has no breathing problems, an infant-only car seat is a good choice. For her comfort, use a rolled headrest pillow made especially for car seats to cradle her head. If you can't find one, a tightly rolled blanket will do the trick. To help keep baby from slumping, you can also place a receiving

Caution!

Never put a car seat in the front passenger seat, especially if it has an air bag. If your car has side-impact air bags in the back seat, as some newer models do, be sure baby's car seat is placed in the middle of the back seat or ask your dealer to disable those air bags.

blanket on either side of her and between the crotch and crotch strap of the seat.

Common car-seat mistakes. While many parents use car seats, some use them incorrectly. The most common mistakes include

- the car-seat harness is attached incorrectly, too loosely or not at all
- a rear-facing car seat is reclined improperly
- the seat-belt system is improperly locked or not locked at all
- the car seat is not fastened tightly in the seat
- the car seat is too big for baby
- the baby's harness, which keeps her securely in the seat, doesn't fit correctly
- the harness straps do not go over her shoulders and lie flat against her chest

We are often asked, if a baby is growing up in a city and the parents do not have a car, if a car-safety seat is necessary. The answer is an emphatic yes! Even if a baby rides in a taxi, she should be placed in a safety-restraint system. Many parents in this situation choose to invest in a convertible "travel system." It's really three products in one—a car seat, an infant carrier and a stroller. You can use it from birth until baby is a toddler. And it's convenient for you—one product can fulfill many needs.

We cannot overemphasize the importance of providing a car seat for your baby. If you can't afford a car seat, many organizations provide reduced-cost or free car seats to a family. Some hospitals let you borrow a car seat until you can get one of your own. Ask at your local hospital or call your local police department for information. You might also want to check with your car insurance company—some offer discounts on car seats.

The final word is: Keep your baby safe. Never let her ride in any vehicle without being buckled up and belted in.

Baby's First 48 Hours

Your baby has just been through one of the toughest battles he will ever face. It's a big job to be pushed down the birth canal and out into the world. Sometimes mother and baby need help, and baby must be delivered with a vacuum extractor or forceps, or by Cesarean section. No matter how your baby arrives, it is wonderful to meet him!

Your newborn is amazing. When he enters the world, all his major organs are functioning. He can see, hear, smell, taste and feel. He may look as though he has no awareness of what's going on, but he is sensitive to events taking place around him. (We discuss this in depth in Week 1.)

What Does Baby Look Like?

If you're like most new parents, the first thing you do when you see your baby is to examine him from head to foot. What does he look like? Does he have hair? Does he have 10 fingers and 10 toes? Is he all right? These concerns are universal–we felt the same way when our children were born.

If your baby is average size, he'll weigh between 7 and 8 pounds, and be between 18 and 22 inches long.

His Head and His Face

You may notice that your newborn's face is puffy, and his head is slightly misshapen and has a "mashed" or "conehead" look. It's common for a baby's head to look like this because the skull, which is actually made up of several bones, had to change shape (mold) to move through the birth canal. You may think his head looks enormous—it is! At this time, his head accounts for 25% of his body, which is one reason his skull had to reshape to fit through the birth canal.

Your baby's face might look a little askew, as if he'd been in a fight or slid down a slippery slide on his face. His nose may be flat, and his chin a little out of place. He may have some bruises on his face. The skin over his brow may be wrinkled and loose, and his eyes may be swollen and bloodshot. As with his misshapen head, this is due to the exertion of birth. A misshapen head may take a little

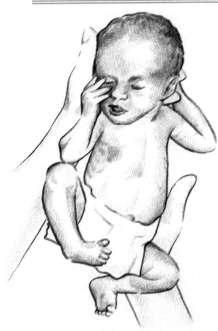

A newborn baby usually shows the stresses of childbirth for a little while, but soon he'll be round and rosy!

longer but should be normal-looking in a few days.

His eyes will appear blue or be dark. However, his true eye color won't be evident until he's about 6 months old.

The two soft spots on the top of his head are called *fontanels*. One is close to the crown; you'll be able to see and feel his pulse there. The other is above his brow on his forehead. These spots decrease in size as his bones grow together. It's OK to touch them gently; they're covered with a thick, protective membrane.

You may also notice the crown of baby's head is lumpy, swollen and/or discolored. This is called a *caput* and results from his head pushing against his mother's cervix and the birth canal. The caput quickly disappears; it will look better every hour and often appears normal by the time you go home in a few days.

If he has hair, you may be surprised by the color. This hair is usually temporary. His real hair (the permanent kind) will begin to grow soon, although some babies don't get permanent hair until they're close to a year old (or older!).

You may notice a few blisters in your baby's mouth. Check his thumbs and fingers for any thickened or callused areas. Most babies suck their thumbs or fingers in utero; your baby probably did, too. Your baby may have a *nursing tubercle* on his upper lip, which stiffens the lip and makes grasping your nipple or a bottle nipple easier for him. If his chin quivers or his legs and arms seem shaky, it just means that more electrical impulses are being sent to muscles than are necessary, which results in these movements. This is normal, and movements decrease over the next few months.

Baby's Skin

Next you may examine the skin on his body. Most babies are covered with a thick, white, waxy coating when they're born, called *vernix.* Vernix protected baby's skin while he was in the uterus. When he's cleaned up, you may be able to see the veins through his skin, which is still thin. His hands and feet may peel. He may have birthmarks.

A Caucasian baby's skin color can range from purplish to pinkish gray. The pigmentation of babies of color may not be evident for hours or even a few days after birth. Many are born with light skin that darkens. If baby's a little blue in color, it may be caused by mucus in his air passages. Most mucus is suctioned out, and he coughs out the rest.

His skin may appear yellow- or orange-tinged by the second or third day—about half of all newborns experience *jaundice.* The color is caused by the inability of baby's liver to remove breakdown products of blood cells, and the buildup causes the skin to look yellowish or orangish. A mild case of jaundice goes away in about a week or 10 days: It may last slightly longer if your baby breastfeeds. See the discussion in Week 1.

Delivery marks. Delivery marks occur in almost every delivery. They can occur while the baby is in the uterus, during the descent through the birth canal and during delivery. The use of forceps or a vacuum extractor to assist with delivery may increase the chance of delivery marks. Marks can vary, from a misshapen head (nothing to worry about; it will change rapidly after birth) or a flattened ear or nose, to bumps and bruises. Forceps may leave marks on the side of the head, in front of the ears. A vacuum extractor may leave a mark on the back or crown of the head. These marks fade within a few hours to a few days. Lotion may be helpful in some situations.

Call the doctor if any of the marks get bigger or if they don't fade within the first few days. If they become warm to the touch, or hard, let your doctor know.

Birthmarks. A baby may show many types of marks after birth. These include salmon patches, stork bites, hemangiomas, strawberry marks, Mongolian spots, café au lait spots, port-wine stains, spider veins (nevi) and pigmented nevi (beauty marks). All are discolorations or marks on the skin.

- *Salmon patches,* also called *stork bites,* are pinkish areas usually found on the head or face caused by blood vessels in the skin. Some are temporary; some are permanent.

- *Hemangiomas*, also called *strawberry marks*, are fairly common birthmarks. About one in 10 babies has them. They are often red or pinkish and may not appear until a few weeks after birth; most disappear by age 10.
- *Mongolian spots* are flat, blue-colored marks, which look like bruises, found on the back and buttocks. They are seen most often in dark-skinned and Asian babies. These spots are not a sign of disease and should fade by age 3, but they may never disappear completely.
- *Café au lait spots* are usually tan to light brown in color, can be seen anywhere on the body and are usually permanent.
- *Port-wine stains* are purple to red in color and often permanent. They may fade somewhat, or they may be removed by laser surgery when baby is older.
- *Spider nevi* are dilated blood vessels that look like a spider web; they usually fade by 1 or 2 years of age.
- *Moles* or *pigmented nevi* come in several colors, from light brown to black.

Keep an eye on any birthmarks your child has. Call the doctor if a birthmark grows or changes color. If a mark is close to the eye or on baby's face, your pediatrician will check it. If baby has six or more café au lait spots on his body, have them checked by your doctor. If port-wine stains appear on any part of the face, they should be checked regularly. The doctor should check moles that bleed, change color or get bigger.

In most instances, birthmarks are watched to see if they fade or go away on their own. Laser surgery is used in many instances to remove birthmarks and moles. Other treatments may be possible in specific cases.

It's interesting to note as you examine your baby that his skin is the most developed sensory organ he has right now. He'll love it when you gently rub and stroke him.

Examining Other Parts of His Body

Baby's hands and feet are so small they may amaze you. He'll probably hold his hands in tight fists. His fingernails may be paper-thin; don't be surprised if they already need trimming! Often his legs are drawn up against his tummy—this is called the *fetal position*. If you gently pull them out, his legs may appear short. And when you let them go, it's almost as if they were on rubber bands—they pull right up again against his body. His feet have only a heel bone at this time. The cartilage that makes up the rest of his foot will become bone later. His peanut-shaped feet may turn inward.

His tummy may be prominent. This isn't fat; it's caused by a lack of muscle tone. This disappears as he becomes more mobile in the next few months.

Your baby's genitals may appear swollen and enlarged; this can happen with either sex. A girl may have a vaginal discharge. See the discussion in Week 1. Don't worry—this is normal and will clear up in a few days. The mother's hormones crossing the placenta causes these symptoms.

In a few cases, a baby may experience a bone break, fracture or a dislocation during delivery. These conditions heal well, with no lasting result, and are usually treated with bandaging. If your baby experiences any of these problems, use great care when lifting him. Dressing must be done carefully; bathing may have to wait awhile.

Your baby's heel is usually pricked for a blood sample, so it may look sore or inflamed. His hips may seem loose-jointed and crack when they move. This is normal and caused by hormones from his mother. Your pediatrician will examine your baby for signs of a dislocated hip, which can be treated.

If you notice a hard lump between baby's ribs, it's a bone called the *xiphoid process.* Soon it will be covered with muscle and fat as baby develops, so don't be concerned about it. Your baby may also have a hollow vertical area running down his tummy. This is caused by the two muscle bundles on either side of the abdomen—they haven't grown together yet but will as baby grows older.

Baby's bowels. Even though you probably never imagined it, you will be concerned about your baby's bowels. It doesn't only mean changing diapers; your baby's stools can be an indication of health.

Your baby's first bowel movement is called *meconium.* It consists of cellular material and other substances from his digestive tract as it developed in the womb and looks yellow-green, brown or like black tar. Your baby must get rid of this material in the 48 hours after birth before normal digestion can begin. If he doesn't, you doctor may be concerned about intestinal obstruction.

Once your baby passes the meconium, his stools will be yellow-green and look like birdseed. If you breastfeed your baby, his stools will look different than a baby's who is fed formula.

Baby's Senses

It may seem incredible, but soon after birth, a baby can recognize his mother's voice *and* her scent. Before your baby is born, he is already sensitive to sounds, light and temperature. His senses develop quickly once outside the womb. As we've already mentioned, he can hear, see, feel and taste when he is born. Let's examine what his senses are like at this time.

Taste. Your baby is born with a desire for sweet things, which is suited to the flavor of formula or breast milk. His taste for bitter, salty and sour develops later. At this time, he can distinguish bitter and sour tastes.

Hearing. Baby's hearing is not fully developed at birth. Parts of the ear are immature, so your baby can't hear the range of sounds you can. Low-frequency sounds can be heard by baby at birth, including the human voice. Studies have shown that babies prefer the sound of the human voice to any other sound. To help baby develop his hearing, speak to him often in a slow, exaggerated voice. You'll both enjoy the interaction, and you'll help him develop his hearing.

Sense of smell. Researchers believe that your baby's sense of smell is well developed at birth. Within hours of birth, a breastfeeding baby will use his nose to find his mother's nipple. Amazingly, your baby's sense of smell may be developed in utero— certain food flavors and odors, such as garlic, cross the placenta to the baby. If you love garlic and onion flavors, baby may already be familiar with them! If you breastfeed, exposure continues because flavors pass into your breast milk.

Your baby will learn about some smells as he grows. He will learn which smells are "good," such as those associated with foods, and which smells are unpleasant.

Touch. A baby is sensitive to touch from birth; his skin is the largest organ of his body. It doesn't take long for him to become familiar with the touch of those close to him. Your touch will soothe him or stimulate him.

It's important to know how to touch your baby. A baby likes a firm touch. It makes him feel secure. He also likes to be stroked and massaged—that's why we include different massage techniques in the first 6 weeks of discussions. Massaging your baby has benefits for him and you. Studies show that babies who are massaged for

10 to 15 minutes before bedtime or napping may sleep better and be less irritable.

Sight. Eyes may be quite developed by birth and capable of seeing many things. However, the baby's brain isn't as fully developed, so he doesn't see as well as an adult. That's one reason you'll have to hold an object very close to baby for him to see it, about 8 to 12 inches away. He can distinguish light from dark and prefers black-and-white patterns. If you move an object farther away from him, his eyes may cross. He can't focus both eyes on the same thing just yet.

Vision and hearing tests. Today, many hospitals and physicians are testing a baby's hearing and vision *before* he leaves the hospital. A baby's eyes are usually tested shortly after birth for eye disease and proper function, especially if there is a family history of problems. If a problem is discovered, your baby may need to see an ear, nose and throat specialist (ENT) or an ophthalmologist.

Hearing is tested by recording electrical brain activity in response to various sounds or by listening for an echo in the inner ear. If your baby has a hearing loss, it could affect the way his speech develops.

Baby Tests
Immediately and again shortly after birth, your baby will be subjected to a variety of tests to assess his health and to provide his physician with information about any potential problems. The chart on page xxx shows the major tests your baby may be given.

Baby Functioning after Birth
Parents frequently exult, "It's over!" after a baby's birth, when in reality it has just begun. Baby's functioning after birth includes his first attempts at breathing, coughing fluid from the lungs, sneezing, movement of legs and arms, and often passage of urine or a bowel movement.

With those first breaths, your baby goes from being totally dependent on blood flow from the placenta to using his own lungs and airways to breathe. The blood flow in the heart changes—blood that was diverted from the lungs directly to the body before birth now flows through the chambers of the heart into the lungs, then into the body.

Baby Tests
Name of Test and Purpose

Apgar Score

This test is used to assess your newborn's overall condition immediately after birth. The Apgar score is used to determine the baby's current health following delivery but is not used to predict future health.

The baby is evaluated at 1 minute and 5 minutes after birth; a score of 0, 1 or 2 is possible in five areas—heart rate, color, muscle tone, respiratory effort and reflex irritability. Each time the test is given, scores from the five criteria are added together, for a maximum total of 10. An average score for most babies is 7 to 9.

Blood Tests

Tests are done on the blood to check for hyperphenylketonuria, anemia, hypothyroidism, sickle-cell anemia and blood-glucose levels. Results often indicate whether baby needs further evaluation.

Blood is taken from baby's heel for a blood screen.

Coombs Test

This test detects whether Rh-antibodies have been formed. Blood is taken from the umbilical cord for testing if the mother's blood is Rh-negative or Type O, or if she has not been tested for antibodies.

Reflex Assessment

This assessment tests for several specific reflexes in baby, including the rooting and grasp reflexes. If a particular reflex is not observed, further evaluation will be done.

Neonatal Maturity Assessment

Various characteristics of baby are assessed to evaluate his neuromuscular and physical maturity. Like the Apgar test, each characteristic is assigned a score, and the sum indicates baby's maturity.

Brazelton Neonatal Behavioral Assessment Scale

The test covers a broad range of newborn behavior and provides information about how a newborn responds to his environment. It is usually used when a problem is suspected, but some hospitals test all babies.

New parents are often concerned about baby's color. "Are babies always so blue?" they ask. The answer is, "Yes," but the baby soon turns pink. Hands and feet are the last areas to turn pink.

Following delivery, baby is often quiet but is soon crying and moving. The nurses weigh, measure and evaluate your baby in the moments after birth. During this time, he becomes more alert.

Your baby will exhibit several reflexes. The *grasping reflex* causes baby's hand to become a fist when his fingers or palm are touched. When you touch or rub his cheek, his mouth will open and he will make a sucking motion; this is the *rooting reflex*. The baby will throw his arms and legs out, then quickly draw them in when startled. This is the *Moro reflex*.

Baby's Birth Weight

"How much does he weigh?" is one of the first questions new parents ask. What a baby weighs is influenced by many factors, including your health during pregnancy, medications, smoking, nutrition, diet, length of the pregnancy (early or late) and the size of your partner. The average weight at term is 7 pounds, 2 ounces, but this can vary widely. In addition to weight, other measurements are made, including length (average is between 18 and 22 inches), head circumference and abdomen circumference.

Baby's weight may fall a little in the days following delivery. Most babies lose a few ounces and many become shorter if the birth was vaginal and the head was pointed.

Baby's Care in the Hospital

Your baby's pediatrician will visit him in the hospital, and any follow-up care will be arranged. The pediatrician will examine the baby, perform a circumcision, if you request it, and get acquainted with you and your partner. The pediatrician will establish a schedule of follow-up visits in his or her office. Be sure you know how to contact the pediatrician or the pediatrician's office if you have any problems.

Circumcision

Circumcision is the surgical removal of the foreskin on the penis of a baby boy. It is usually performed in the hospital or the doctor's office by a pediatrician, obstetrician or family doctor within a few days of delivery. If circumcision is part of your religious ritual, it is performed

Baby's Milestones and Important Dates

Record some of baby's "firsts" and other important milestones on these pages.

Date of birth _____

Weight _____

Height _____

Apgar scores _____

First day home _____

_____

First outing _____

_____

First doctor's visit _____

_____

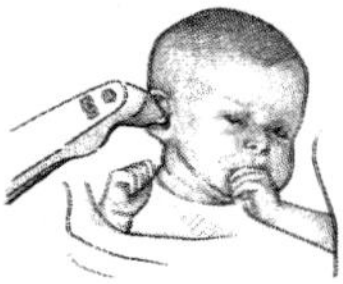

First bath _____

_____

First haircut _____

_____

First holiday _____

_____

First playmate _____

_____

Smiles _____

Lifts head _____

Laughs out loud _____

Tracks a moving object _____

Discovers hands _____

Bats at a toy _____

Favorite toy_____

_____

Reaches for an object _____

Sleeps through the night_____

Eats solid food _____

Favorite food _____

_____

Says "ma" or "ga" _____

Sits supported _____

Rolls over _____

Shakes a rattle _____

Discovers feet_____

Holds a bottle_____

Drinks from a cup_____

Sits alone _____

Stands with support_____

Waves bye-bye _____

Plays peekaboo _____

Claps hands _____

Rolls a ball_____

Cuts a tooth _____

Crawls _____

Climbs stairs _____

Walks assisted_____

Stands alone_____

Takes a step _____

Says "dada" _____

Says "mama"_____

Uses a spoon _____

Feeds self _____

Walks alone _____

Weight at first checkup
   (approximately 2 weeks)

_____

Height at first checkup
   (approximately 2 weeks)

_____

by someone in your religion who is trained to do it, and it is done outside the hospital in a religious ceremony.

The decision to circumcise your son should be made by you as a couple. If you have questions, discuss them with your pediatrician. A surgical consent is required before a circumcision is performed, so you can ask questions about the procedure. Local anesthesia is used, and the procedure takes about 5 minutes. See the discussion in Week 1 for care after circumcision.

Dislocated Hips

Dislocation of a baby's hip(s) occurs more often in baby girls and in babies delivered in the breech position. About one in 60 newborns is affected; 85% of these are girls.

When your baby is examined by the pediatrician in the hospital, his hips are checked to see that the upper leg bone (femur) fits in the hip socket (pelvic bone). A "hip click" (a clicking sound) may be heard when the legs are pulled apart. Skin folds on the buttocks may not be symmetrical or one leg may appear shorter than the other. If left uncorrected, he may have a limp when he begins to walk.

> **If you have questions, be sure to ask your pediatrician or obstetrician. No question is "dumb," so ask! You may want to make sure your partner is present when you ask a question. It's always good to have two sets of ears at an exciting time such as this.**

Today, surgery is rarely required to correct the problem. Splints are usually used for a few months, sometimes called *pillow* or *diaper splints*. They keep the hips widely separated. It's like wearing three or four diapers at one time. In some cases, plaster splints (like a cast) or braces are used. In most cases, the problem is corrected before the end of the first year.

Weekly Milestones at a Glance

Week 1

Physical Development

- responds to sudden changes with entire body
- can lift head
- moves head from side to side
- controls arm, leg and hand movements by reflex
- sleeps and wakes on a continuum
- head flops forward or backward when held in sitting position
- controls swallowing and rooting by reflex
- sleeps between 19 and 20 hours/day
- moves bowels often and sporadically
- feeds 7 to 8 times/day

Senses and Reflexes

- blinks at bright lights
- focuses between 8 and 10 inches away
- eyes tend to turn outward
- is sensitive to direction of sound
- hands remain fisted much of time due to reflex grasp
- distinguishes volume and pitch of sounds; prefers high-toned voices
- lifts head when placed on stomach or at someone's shoulder
- moves head from side to side
- distinguishes tastes: likes sweet already
- will grasp and grip something if hand accidentally strikes it

Mental Development

- quiets when picked up or in response to any firm, steady pressure
- stops sucking to look at something
- shuts out disturbing stimuli by going to sleep
- makes animal-like sounds
- learns to expect food at certain times
- looks at person briefly

Social Development

- shows excitement and distress
- seems to respond positively to soft human voice
- becomes alert to and tries to focus on human face or voice

Week 2

Physical Development

- arm, leg and hand movement still reflexive
- startles spontaneously (Moro reflex)
- hands usually fisted or only slightly open

Senses and Reflexes

- stares at objects 8 to 18 inches away
- roots for breast, even if not breastfeeding
- is soothed more easily by higher, female voice than by a male voice

Mental Development

- alert about 1 in every 10 hours
- cries for assistance
- quiets when held or when he sees faces

Social Development

- eyes fix on mother's face in response to her smile
- stares at faces
- responds to human voice

Week 3

Physical Development

- thrusts out arms and legs in play
- can lift head briefly when lying on stomach
- may dig heels into mattress then thrust with legs (this moves her body)

Senses and Reflexes

- coordinates eyes sideways when looking at light or an object

Mental Development

- has vague and impassive expression during waking hours
- prefers patterns
- may calm when you speak gently to her and hold her upright against your shoulder

Social Development

- makes eye contact
- adjusts posture to body of person holding her

Week 4

Physical Development

- rolls partway to side from back
- when pulled to sitting position, may hold head in line with back

Senses and Reflexes

- can grasp object when fingers are pried open, but quickly drops it

Mental Development

- remembers object when it reappears within a couple of seconds
- may make an "ah" sound when he sees parents or hears parents' voices

Social Development

- may clutch at person holding him
- may make throaty sounds

Week 1

How Big Is Your Baby This First Week?

The information we provide in this section each week is based on average expected growth for a baby. Growth changes we cite here are based on a full-term baby weighing 7 pounds who is 20 inches long. Your baby may grow a little more or a little less in a given week. If your baby is born small, growth may be less than what we indicate. The same holds true if your baby is large; her growth may be faster or she may gain more weight. There's also a difference in size (and sometimes the rate of growth) between boys and girls.

The object of providing this information is to help you determine if your baby is growing and gaining weight at a steady pace. It's important to remember that if your baby is born prematurely, her weight gain and growth may be delayed for a time but usually catches up.

Baby Care and Equipment

Umbilical-Cord Care

Almost every baby goes home from the hospital with a stump of umbilical cord still attached. It takes from 7 to 10 days for it to heal and fall off. Until then, keep the area clean and dry to promote healing.

You don't have much to do in the way of care. When you change baby's diaper, wipe the cord with a cotton ball dipped in alcohol. Fold down the diaper top so it will not rub against the stump. Change baby as soon as she is wet to reduce irritation further.

Penis Care for Circumcised and Uncircumcised Boys

Circumcision. As parents, you may decide to have your son *circumcised,* which means the foreskin of his penis is removed by a surgical technique. This is usually done in the hospital, unless it is part of your religious observance and done in a religious ceremony a short time after your baby leaves the hospital. You will be shown how to care for the circumcision while you are in the hospital.

Care. After the circumcision, you may notice your son's penis is a little red, and there may be a yellow secretion. Both are signs the incision is healing. Keep the area clean; put a little petroleum jelly on the tip of the penis each time you change his diaper.

The incision should heal within a week; however, if you notice swelling or sores, call your doctor. He or she may suggest using mild antibiotic gels on the spot or advise you to clean the area more often. Sometimes ice or a cold pack is used, but do this *only* when directed to do so by your doctor.

Care when no circumcision is performed. If your son is not circumcised, gently pull back the foreskin of his penis each time you change his diaper. Using warm water and mild baby soap, wash the area thoroughly.

Feeding Your Baby

Feeding your baby is one of the most important things you do for her. You'll know when she's hungry; she'll exhibit definite signs of hunger, including fussing, putting her hands in her mouth and turning her head and opening her mouth when her cheek is touched.

How often to feed. Most newborns eat every 3 to 4 hours, although some feed as often as every 2 hours. You may feed at regular intervals to help your baby get on a schedule. Or you may decide to let your baby set her own schedule—some babies need to eat more often than others. At times a baby needs to feed more often than usual, such as during periods of growth.

> **A baby is usually the best judge of how much she needs at each feeding.**

A baby is usually the best judge of how much she needs at each feeding. She'll usually turn away from the nipple (mother or bottle) when she's full.

It's a good idea to burp your baby after each feeding. Some babies need to be burped during a feeding. (See the discussion of Burping in Week 2.)

Spitting up. Babies frequently spit up some breast milk or formula after a feeding. It's common in the early months because the muscle at the top of the stomach is not fully developed. When a baby spits up enough to propel the stomach contents several inches, it is called *vomiting*. If your baby vomits after a feeding, don't feed her again immediately. Her tummy may be upset. Wait until the next feeding.

Breast or bottle? Many believe that breastfeeding is the best way to feed baby. Breast milk contains every nutrient a baby needs, and it's easily digested. Research has found that breastfed babies have lower rates of infection because of the immunological content of breast milk. Breastfeeding provides the baby a sense of security and the mother a sense of self-esteem. (See the discussion of Breastfeeding in Week 2.)

If there are reasons you cannot or choose not to breastfeed your baby, be assured she will do well on formula. It won't harm her if you don't breastfeed. No mother should feel guilty if she doesn't breastfeed her baby. An infant can still get all the love, attention and nutrition she needs if breastfeeding is not possible. (See the discussion of Bottle-feeding in Week 3.)

Picking Up and Handling Baby

If you're like most first-time parents, the thought of handling your baby fills you with trepidation. She's such a tiny, delicate being! You want to pick her up correctly, and you don't want to drop her. Rest easy—she's not as fragile as you think. There are ways to handle her so you'll both feel confident.

What to do. Always support her head with your hand or arm, and keep an arm or hand under her back. You may hold her close or a little more loosely. Use smooth motions when moving her, and always protect her head with your arm or hand.

When you hold her or if you wear her in a sling or front carrier, do so *only* when you are doing something that could not harm her. *Never* cook over a hot stove or handle hot or caustic liquids while holding baby.

Diapering Baby

Changing your baby's diapers is a necessary task you'll do thousands of times. Once you get the hang of it, you'll be able to do it quickly and efficiently. Men are capable of learning this skill also! Change baby's diapers whenever she's wet or soiled to prevent irritation and diaper rash. A newborn wets between six and 10 times a day. Bowel movements are more variable. Some babies poop two or three times a day, others only every few days. Whether your baby is breastfed or bottle-fed may also make a difference in her bowel movements.

You don't need to clean baby with baby wipes if she has only a wet diaper. Urine is germ-free; using a baby wipe every time you change her could irritate her skin. If possible, let her "air out" (go without a diaper for a while) between diaper changes. It helps reduce the risk of diaper rash.

Diapering Your Baby

This method for changing baby is quick and easy!

1. Lay baby on the changing table; strap her in or keep your hand on her tummy.
2. Undo pins or diaper tabs on soiled diapers, and gently lift her ankles. (You can do this with one hand.)
3. With your other hand, wipe any feces into the dirty diaper and put it to the side.
4. Using baby wipes or wet cotton balls, clean the genitals. With a girl, wipe from front to back to avoid contaminating the vaginal area, which could cause a urinary-tract infection.
5. Let her air dry or dry her with a soft washcloth.
6. Slide a clean diaper under her as you again lift her ankles. (See illustrations A through H, opposite, for folding diapers.)
7. Fasten diaper with pins or tabs, and adjust leg openings so there are no gaps. You're done!

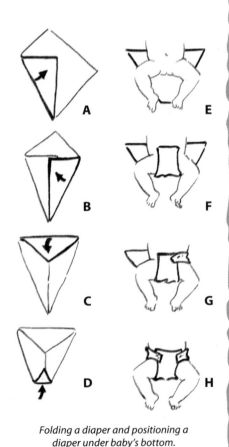

Folding a diaper and positioning a diaper under baby's bottom.

Dressing Your Baby

Dressing baby is a challenging task for a new parent. It's not like dressing a baby doll—baby dolls don't wiggle and squirm! We know a few tricks to help make your first attempts a little easier. Our best advice is to take it slow, and don't get frustrated. With practice, you'll soon be an expert.

Tops. After you've diapered baby, put on her undershirt. Hold the shirt neck open with your thumbs, and slip it over her head. Reach into the end of one sleeve, grasp her hand and gently pull it through. Adjust the body of the shirt once you've got both arms in.

Bottoms and "onesies." When you put her pants on, first reach through the bottom leg opening and grasp one foot. Slide it through the opening, then do the same for her other foot. Once both feet are through the leg openings, pull pants up to her waist. If you're putting on overalls, we've found sliding them on from the bottom works best. Adjust them, snap the legs, then hook the straps.

With a sleeper or one-piece outfit that opens down the front, lay it down on the changing table, then lay baby on top of it. Slide baby's arms, one at a time, through the sleeves, adjust, then slip baby's feet through the openings. When everything's in place, snap the snaps or zip up.

Keep the room warm. When changing your newborn, keep the room warm. A small baby gets cold quite quickly when undressed.

Swaddling Your Infant

Before her birth, your baby was in a pretty tight environment, with little room to move. When she's born, the lack of confinement may make her feel a little insecure. *Swaddling,* wrapping her snugly in a soft blanket, may help if she seems discontented. It may help make her feel secure and comforted. (See the box on page 8.)

Milestones This First Week

During the first year of life, your baby grows and changes according to stages of development. These are the four most important developmental categories:

Motor development. *This refers to your baby's ability to control voluntary body movements. Your baby's large and small muscle groups develop dramatically this first year. At this time she moves*

How to Swaddle Your Baby

1. **Lay a blanket (a square receiving blanket works well) on a flat surface in a diamond shape. You can fold down the top and tuck it inside or leave it up, if you want to protect baby's head.**
2. **Lay baby on the blanket, and place her arms by her side. Fold the top-left edge of the blanket across her body, pulling it taut. Tuck excess material under her back.**
3. **Bring the bottom corner of the blanket up over her body. Some babies like their legs tucked into a fetal position; others don't.**
4. **Fold the top-right edge of the blanket across her body**
5. **Tuck excess material under her back.**

She can be laid in her crib in this manner, or you can hold her.

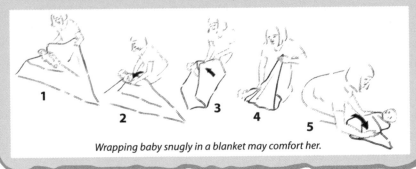

Wrapping baby snugly in a blanket may comfort her.

very little, yet by the end of 12 months, she will be walking or ready to walk!

Language development. *Development of language includes her speech, and also her attempts to listen and to understand language around her.*

Mental development. *As your baby's brain grows, her thinking skills develop.*

Social development. *Social skills she learns help your baby relate to the world around her.*

As the weeks and months pass, your baby will move from one learning task to another, and her focus will shift. Don't worry if she seems to be slow in one area for a while; it's her overall development you are concerned with.

At birth, your baby's brain is not fully developed, and a great deal of growth must still occur. A baby's brain grows most rapidly from the last trimester of pregnancy through the first 3 months of life.

Baby's Sight

From the moment your newborn opens her eyes after birth, she can see her world, although it is a bit fuzzy. She is nearsighted, and her best field of vision is about 8 to 12 inches away from her. She will stare at objects placed in this range of her vision. She can also tell the difference between a human face and other objects— she prefers faces. (If the baby is smiling at you at this point, it's probably gas.)

A Newborn's Hearing

Your baby hears most noises in the first few weeks as echoes, not distinct sounds. However, she hears voices; she recognizes her mother's voice at or shortly after birth and will soon recognize the voices of other people around her. Speak to her often, about everything, and you will help her develop her hearing and begin to relate to language. A baby can't learn to talk or begin to understand the subtle nuances of language if she doesn't hear a lot of conversation.

Other Newborn Development

Calming baby. Soothing a fussy baby takes experimentation on your part. After all, you don't know each other very well yet, so you may need to try different tactics to help her settle. You may find your baby calms when she is swaddled. (See the discussion above.) Swaddling helps her feel secure and may help her focus. Rocking and patting her or offering her a pacifier are other options. Some babies calm down when they listen to monotonous "white" sounds, such as a vacuum cleaner running. Try different things when baby needs to be comforted.

When you snuggle or feed your baby, your skin-to-skin contact makes her feel secure and safe. It also provides gentle stimulation. Offer her this contact as much as possible.

Early reflexes. Two reflex actions you may notice in baby right now are the *rooting reflex* and *reflexive smiling*. When your baby roots, she is searching for food. She will open her mouth and turn her head toward that side if you stroke her cheek. When your baby is sleeping or drowsy, you may notice her smiling. She's in a dream state—her eyes may be moving at the same time. Enjoy watching her. It's a beautiful sight—soon she'll be smiling at you!

Note: See also the box on page 10, *Milestones This Week*.

Milestones This First Week

Changes in Baby You May See Now

Physical Development

- responds to sudden changes with entire body
- when startled, arches her back, kicks her legs and flails out arms *(Moro reflex)*
- can lift head
- moves head from side to side
- controls arm, leg and hand movements by reflex
- when baby's palms are pressed, she will open her mouth and slightly lift head up *(Babkin reflex)*
- sleeps and wakes on a continuum
- head flops forward or backward when held in sitting position
- controls swallowing and rooting by reflex
- stroking bottom of baby's foot from heel to toes causes toes to flare up and out *(Babinski reflex)*
- sleeps between 19 and 20 hours a day
- moves bowels often and sporadically
- feeds 7 to 8 times a day

Senses and Reflexes

- blinks at bright lights
- focuses between 8 and 12 inches away
- eyes tend to turn outward
- is sensitive to direction of sound
- hands remain fisted much of time due to reflex grasp
- distinguishes volume and pitch of sounds; prefers high-toned voices

- lifts head when placed on stomach or at someone's shoulder
- moves head from side to side
- distinguishes tastes—likes sweet already
- will grasp and grip something if hand accidentally strikes it

Mental Development

- quiets when picked up or in response to any firm, steady pressure
- stops sucking to look at something
- shuts out disturbing stimuli by going to sleep
- makes animal-like sounds
- learns to expect food at certain times
- looks at person briefly

Social Development

- shows excitement and distress
- seems to respond positively to soft human voice
- becomes alert to and tries to focus on human face or voice

Every baby is an individual, and your baby may do some of these things more quickly or more slowly than another baby. If you are concerned about your baby's progress, discuss it with your healthcare provider. Also see page viii.

What's Happening This First Week?

Changes You May See in Baby

Incredible as it may seem, infants often enjoy a growth spurt soon after birth. At 7 to 10 days after birth, your baby may grow in length. When you take her for her first checkup, she may have grown more than you realized.

Your baby's heart rate is faster than yours; her heart beats between 100 and 150 beats a minute. When she yawns, hiccups or has a bowel movement, her heart rate may decrease. She also breathes quite rapidly—up to 50 breaths a minute. This is normal.

When she cries, you may not see tears. A newborn's tear ducts are not yet mature enough to produce tears. This will change soon.

Some babies don't like to cuddle; it's normal. If she stiffens and arches her back when you hold her close, hold her with her back to you. This may be better for her.

Baby and Sleep

You'll notice your baby sleeps at least 18 hours a day in these first weeks. She'll slip between waking and sleeping with little regard for day or night and will eat every 2 to 4 hours. She won't sleep longer at night and be awake more during the day for another 6 to 8 weeks. Exposing her to daylight during the day and putting her in a dark room at night to sleep helps establish this pattern.

"Back is better." A relative, friend or someone else may advise you to put baby on her tummy so she'll sleep better. We now know that "back is better." Put your baby to sleep on her back *every* time you put her down. Why? Research has shown that with a healthy, full-term baby, sleeping on her back lowers the chance she will have problems, especially

Put your baby to sleep on her back *every* time you put her down for a nap or at bedtime.

with sudden infant death syndrome (SIDS). (See the discussion of SIDS in Week 8.) Research also shows that a normal baby doesn't usually have problems choking or aspirating vomit if she spits up while lying on her back because she has a well-developed gag reflex. Some babies sleep better on their stomachs, but don't be tempted to put your baby to bed on her tummy.

Exceptions. Exceptions to the sleep-on-back rule include premature babies who have breathing problems, babies with certain upper-airway problems, babies with birth defects of the nose, throat or mouth, and babies with swallowing or vomiting problems. If your baby experiences any of these, discuss the situation with her doctor.

What Baby's Crying Can Mean

Crying is one of the few ways your baby has to communicate with you. It's her way of telling you she's uncomfortable, hungry or needs attention. As you get to know your baby better, you'll be able to understand what her crying means.

> **When you listen closely, you may be able to hear a difference in her crying.**

Don't worry about picking her up when she cries—you won't spoil her. You'll be building a stronger bond with her. You are teaching her that you will take care of her, and she will feel secure with you.

It may seem like baby cries a lot, but on average, she cries only about 4 hours out of every day this first week. By the second week, she'll only be crying about 2-1/2 hours a day, and by week 3, it'll be down to about an hour and a half. For ways to comfort a fussy baby, see the discussion in Week 4.

Cradle Cap

What it is. Cradle cap is a yellow or brown waxy buildup on baby's head. Also called *seborrheic dermatitis of the scalp*, it is common among newborns and infants. It usually occurs from 1 to 12 weeks following birth; half of all infants get it. If your baby has cradle cap, you'll notice patches of scaly skin on the scalp. They may also appear

Home Treatment of Cradle Cap

You can treat the symptoms of cradle cap at home with mineral oil or olive oil.

1. Dampen your baby's scalp with water.
2. Apply the oil to your baby's scalp to loosen the scaly material enough so you can shampoo it off the scalp.
3. Shampoo.
4. Gently dry the scalp.
5. Keep the area clean and dry.
6. Don't pick at the patches because you might irritate or infect them.

in other areas of the face or at the hairline. It's not painful or itchy, but it looks bad. This form of dermatitis is usually treated by your physician with a corticosteroid lotion. It's OK to use a soft brush to remove skin patches gently after rubbing the scalp with lotion.

When to call the doctor. There should be no signs of infection on the scalp. Call the doctor if the area shows signs of oozing or pus, if the cradle cap fails to respond to the measures listed above, if the skin becomes red or scaly, or if the area becomes inflamed. If there are signs of inflammation or redness on other parts of the body, it could indicate another problem, so be sure to call your pediatrician.

Jaundice

What it is. Two to 5 days after birth, your baby may show signs of jaundice, also called *hyperbilirubinemia.* Symptoms include a yellow appearance of the skin (caused by excessive amounts of bilirubin, a breakdown product of blood cells), which is often first seen in the face. The whites of the eyes may also appear yellow. The yellowness of the skin spreads to the rest of the body. Even the nail beds may appear yellow; pinch the fingernail gently and release to check for yellow discoloration. Your healthcare practitioner will test the baby's blood to determine the level of bilirubin in your baby's system.

To date, determining the bilirubin level in your baby's blood involved doing a blood test. The test could be uncomfortable for baby and her parents because it had to be done repeatedly. However, a new test has been developed that doesn't involve pricking baby with a needle. Called the *Colormate LTc BiliTest,* a hand-held device is used to measure the yellow tinge of baby's skin. The test is 95% accurate, and results are available in minutes. If your newborn must be tested for jaundice, ask if this test is available.

What to do. Mild jaundice is not serious; follow your doctor's advice. Bili lights, also called *phototherapy,* may be used. These ultraviolet lights break down bilirubin, making it possible for it to be passed from your baby's bloodstream. It also helps improve the condition if baby is feeding well because bilirubin is excreted in her bowel movements.

> What's normal for one baby may not be normal for another baby.

When to call the doctor. Call your doctor if your baby appears to be getting more yellow, or if she is not feeding well. Your pediatrician wants to know if your baby experiences any problems.

Trouble Signs

As a new parent, you may be unsure what is normal and what is not with your baby. You may not know when to call the doctor. Be alert to the following signs and symptoms, and call your baby's doctor if she shows any of the following signs:

- difficulty breathing—if she sucks her ribs in when she breathes or if her lips look blue

- vomiting after most feedings, especially if it is brown or green, or is ejected with force (projectile vomiting)

- fever of 100.6F (38.1C) or higher, measured rectally

- yellow appearance; it could be jaundice

- looks different or acts differently, such as extreme lethargy or sleepiness, highly irritable or very pale

Don't worry about calling the doctor—your pediatrician and his or her staff are there to help you. Your questions won't sound silly. They've probably heard any question you can think to ask many times before!

Vaginal Discharge in Girls

What it is. After birth, your baby girl may have a vaginal discharge that is clear or white. This is caused by the excessive hormones in her body from her mother. It is rarely a problem.

What to do. To take care of it, gently clean the vaginal area. It should disappear soon.

When to call the doctor. Call your baby's doctor if the discharge seems excessive or if the color is yellow or green.

Toys and Play This First Week

This first week of life is the beginning of a wonderful time of games and play you and your child will share for years to come. As you get to know your baby better, games and opportunities for fun will begin to present themselves naturally. You'll make a game out of something ordinary, and it will be a special time for you both.

Help Stimulate Her Vision

To stimulate her vision, hold boldly patterned objects within 8 to 12 inches of baby, and let her look at them. At present, she prefers bold patterns and the contrast of black and white. She will also enjoy looking at pictures of people's faces. Cut out some large pictures from a magazine to hold in front of her. Let her gaze at them as long as she is interested. When she begins to squirm or look away, it's time to end the game.

Keep Talking to Her

Begin your journey of play and interaction with words and music. Talk to baby as often as you can; just hearing your voice is what matters. Sing to her—even if you can't carry a tune! Tell her what you're doing and what's going on. Play soothing music for her when she's fussy; it may help settle her.

You'll probably have lots of visitors who want to meet your baby. They'll probably want to hold him. That's OK. However, be respectful of baby's needs. If he's sleeping, don't get him up and pass him around. Let people look while you let baby sleep.

Breastfeed with Confidence!

It's not uncommon to encounter a problem or two when you begin to breastfeed. Don't be discouraged if it happens to you. It takes time to discover what works for you and your baby. Try different things to help make breastfeeding a success for you both. Keep in mind the following as you begin nursing.

- **It takes practice!** Although breastfeeding is a natural way to feed baby, it takes time and practice to get the hang of it.
- **Wear the right clothes**. Clothes made for nursing help you feel more comfortable—buy nursing bras and tops that let you feed baby without baring all.
- **Baby must be comfortable**, so change him before you start. Make sure he's warm.
- **Hold him so he can reach your breast easily while nursing.** Hold him across your chest, or lie in bed. His tummy should touch you; tuck his lower arm between your arm and your side (see illustrations, opposite).
- **Help him latch on to your breast.** Brush your nipple across his lips. When he opens his mouth, place your nipple and as much of the areola as possible in his mouth. You should feel him pull the breast while sucking, but it shouldn't hurt. If you experience pain, disengage him by slipping your finger into the corner of his mouth. Gently pull down to break the suction.
- **Nurse baby 5 to 10 minutes on each breast**; he gets most of his milk at the beginning of the feeding. Don't rush him—it can take as long as 30 minutes for him to finish.
- **Add some cover.** A receiving blanket helps add privacy to your nursing experience.
- **Feed your newborn on demand.** This could be as many as 8 to 10 times a day or more. A baby usually cuts back on feedings to 4 to 6 times a day by the age of 4 months.
- **A breastfed baby may not need burping.** As you begin, burp between feedings at each breast and when baby finishes. If he doesn't burp, don't force it. He may not need to burp.
- **If you see a blister on baby's lip, it is probably from sucking**. It isn't painful, and you don't have to do anything for it. It'll disappear on its own.
- **Between 6 weeks and 6 months, baby grows quickly.** He will take in 3 to 4 ounces of milk for each pound of weight during this time.
- Work around baby's feeding schedule. As he gets older, you'll be in tune with his schedule and you can plan outings and activities more easily.

Frequent nursing stimulates milk production.

Different Breastfeeding Positions

Tummy to tummy. In this position, you and baby are tummy to tummy. Baby is tucked close to you. You can use this position sitting cross-legged on the floor or seated in a chair.

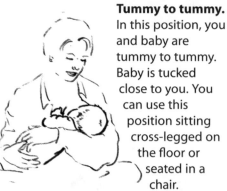

Side position. You may use a side position for breastfeeding, especially if you had a Cesarean delivery. You can breastfeed while

lying on your side in bed. Baby will be tucked in close to you. You can offer either the breast closest to the bed or the upper breast if you lean forward a little. Baby should not have to turn his head to reach the nipple. You may want the support of a pillow at your back.

Football hold. Here, baby is positioned so that his body and legs are at your side, with his feet pointed behind you, rather than across your tummy. You support the back of his head with your hand while he feeds at the breast. You will want to support his back with your arm also. This position is often chosen when feeding twins.

Breastfeeding More than One Baby

If you have more than one baby, you should be able to breastfeed them. You may find it a little more challenging, but many mothers have done it. You may have to be creative in your approach, but with time, you'll probably work it out quite well.

You have many options. You may choose to pump your breasts and divide the breast milk between (or among) your babies, then supplement with formula. You may choose to breastfeed your babies for a short while every time they nurse, then feed them formula. You may try to breastfeed exclusively. Studies have shown that frequent nursing stimulates milk production. Talk with your physician and your pediatrician about what might work best for you.

Is Baby Getting Enough Nourishment?

You may be concerned about whether baby is getting enough to eat. There are clues to look for. Watch his jaws and ears while he eats—is he actively sucking? His jaws will move and his ears may wiggle. At the end of a feeding, does he fall asleep or settle down easily? Can he go 1-1/2 to 3 hours between feedings? Does he have at least six wet diapers a day? Is he gaining weight? These are all indications that the process is working. If you have other concerns, discuss them with your baby's doctor.

Week 2

Baby weighs 7-3/4 pounds and is 20-1/2 inches long this week.

Baby Care and Equipment

Breastfeeding Your Baby

Breastfeeding is a healthy way to feed a baby, and it can help create a close bond between mother and child. (See the discussion of bonding below.) You can usually begin breastfeeding your baby within an hour after birth, provided your delivery is without complications. At this first feeding, you will provide your baby with colostrum, the "premilk" your breasts produce. Colostrum helps boost baby's immune system. Breastfeeding helps you, too, because it stimulates the pituitary gland to release oxytocin, the hormone that causes your uterus to contract to help keep bleeding to a minimum.

Partner's support is important. Whether a woman breastfeeds may depend on what her partner thinks about it. Research has shown that if a woman's partner does not want her to breastfeed, she usually doesn't. If breastfeeding is important to you but not to your partner, explain to him the health benefits for baby. Assure him he'll be able to feed baby expressed breast milk. Often a father will be supportive once he understands how positive an experience it is for the entire family.

It's your right to breastfeed. Some women feel intimidated at the thought of breastfeeding outside the home and possibly offending other people or making them uncomfortable, however unintentionally. Breastfeeding is a natural activity and it is your right to breastfeed. More than 17 states have passed laws making it explicitly legal to breastfeed in public. These laws exist to support breastfeeding mothers.

Breastfeeding benefits. There are lots of good reasons to breastfeed your baby. It's economical—you don't have to buy formula or bottles and nipples. It's easy to travel with baby because you don't have to cart along anything extra. It saves you time; no formula to mix or bottles to sterilize and fill.

Allergies unlikely. It's nearly impossible for a baby to become allergic to his mother's breast milk. If an allergy develops, it's usually to the proteins in the breast milk. If this occurs, a baby can usually continue breastfeeding if his mother avoids certain foods that contain milk proteins.

Breastfeeding may even help prevent milk allergies. This is important if there is a history of allergies in your family or your partner's family. The longer a baby breastfeeds, the less likely he is to be exposed to substances that could cause allergy problems.

Disadvantages. The greatest disadvantage for many mothers is they are tied down so completely to the baby. A woman must be available when her baby is hungry. Breastfeeding can also make other family members who would like to help with feeding feel left out.

Other concerns. If you breastfeed, pay careful attention to your diet. Avoid foods and substances that pass into your breast milk that could cause problems for baby. Some substances you eat or drink (or take orally, as medication) can pass to your baby in your breast milk. Spicy foods and chocolate may cause baby digestive upset. Caffeine in breast milk can cause irritability and sleeplessness in baby. Spicy foods, chocolate and caffeine are just a few things your baby can react to when you consume them.

> You should feel your baby pull the breast while sucking, but it shouldn't hurt. If you experience pain, disengage baby by slipping your finger into the corner of his mouth. Gently pull down to break the suction.

Five Important Reasons to Breastfeed Baby

**We are finding there are many good reasons to nurse your baby.
Here are five of them.**

- **Breast milk offers protection from infection. The incidence
  of ear infections is significantly reduced (by almost 50%) in
  infants who breastfeed longer than 4 months.**
- **Nursing may help prevent diarrhea in infants, and it may inhibit
  the growth of bacteria that cause urinary-tract infections.**
- **Baby's permanent teeth may come in straighter if he
  breastfeeds in infancy.**
- **Breastfeeding may lower the risk of a baby developing juvenile
  diabetes, lymphoma (a type of cancer) and Crohn's disease
  later in life.**
- **Breast milk contains beneficial substances not available from
  other sources. For example, DHA is present in breast milk. DHA
  (decosahexaenoic acid) is the primary structural fatty acid that
  makes up the retina of the eye and the gray matter of the brain.
  During pregnancy, your baby receives this important substance
  through the placenta. After birth, your breast milk continues
  to supply DHA to your baby. Studies have shown that a baby
  with DHA in his diet may have a higher IQ and greater visual
  development than babies fed formula without DHA.**

Medications and breastfeeding. You may be concerned if
you must take medication while nursing. Research shows that
most medications don't affect a mother's ability to breastfeed.
Although they are in breast milk, most medications aren't harmful or
dangerous to baby.

Drugs and medications to avoid include illegal drugs,
chemotherapy drugs, lithium, some drugs that suppress the immune
system and radioactive compounds. Be careful of over-the-counter
medications, too. Many are combinations of several chemicals
or compounds, such as alcohol,
aspirin or caffeine. If you have a
question, call your doctor.

> Spicy foods, chocolate and
> caffeine are just a few things your
> breastfeeding baby can react to
> when you consume them.

What about supplemental feeding? There may be times you have to give baby a supplemental feeding—either expressed breast milk or formula. Try to limit these feedings to only one or two a day. Supplemental feedings can affect your milk supply, decreasing your breast milk production. Even if you must supplement more often, your breast milk is beneficial for baby. He will receive many benefits from nursing.

> Be careful of over-the-counter medications. Select "baby" products when possible. Don't use adult-strength medications unless your pediatrician advises it.

When Baby Spits Up

It's not unusual for a baby to spit up after a feeding, especially for a newborn. Spitting up is not a cause for worry—baby is getting rid of excess breast milk or formula. As he spends more time sitting up, he'll outgrow this. Keep a cloth handy to wipe up any baby spit-up.

Vomiting. Vomiting occurs when a baby forcibly ejects stomach contents, usually in large amounts. Nearly every baby vomits occasionally, and for many different reasons. If your baby vomits more often, contact your doctor.

Different Burping Positions

Whichever way you hold baby, rub or gently pat his back until he burps.

Hold baby seated in your lap, with his head in one of your hands.

Hold him facing you in your arms, against your chest.

Lay him face down on your lap, supporting his head with your hand.

Burping Baby

Some breastfed babies don't need to be burped. Some do. Bottle-fed babies do need to be burped. How should you do it? There are three techniques to use when burping a baby. Try them all, and use what works best for your baby. Whichever way you hold him, rub or gently pat his back until he burps. (See box page 21.)

Sponge-Bathing Baby

Baby's umbilical stump may not have fallen off yet and may still be a little swollen. Continue to clean it by wiping the area with alcohol at every diaper change. At this time, baby needs only an occasional sponge bath. His body isn't dirty. The only area that needs consistent cleaning is his genital area, which you clean after bowel movements.

Sponge-Bath Basics

Have these items ready before you sponge-bathe your baby.

- **large bath towel**
- **baby towel**
- **basin of warm water**
- **cotton balls**
- **baby soap**
- **washcloth**

Bathe in a warm place. Plan to wash baby in a warm area free from drafts. Gather together your supplies before you begin. You'll need a large bath towel, a baby towel, a basin of warm water, cotton balls, baby soap and a washcloth.

Basics for sponge-bathing baby. Undress baby and lay him on the towel. Keep your hand on him at all times. Wash his face first; wipe each eye outward with a damp cotton ball. Use a soft washcloth to wash his face and head, then pat dry with the towel. Put a little soap on a damp washcloth, and clean his neck, torso, legs and arms. Don't overlook his fingers and toes. Wash his genital area. If your son was circumcised, use only plain water until the circumcision has healed completely. You probably don't need to shampoo his hair; cleaning with a washcloth is fine. Rinse him, then dry with a towel. Diaper and dress him.

Outings with Baby

You may want to take your newborn along on errands or out for short visits. If you feel up to it, go ahead. Dress him for the weather—usually only one layer more than you in cold weather, the same number of layers in warm weather. Keep outings short. You'll be surprised how quickly both of you tire or how soon he'll get hungry.

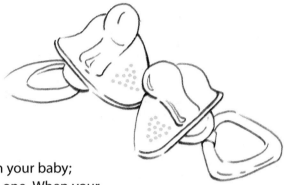

Pacifiers

Pacifiers are OK to use with your baby; however, he may not need one. When your baby fusses, offer him a feeding and comfort him before you give him a pacifier. If your baby needs to suck, a pacifier can help.

Types. You'll find pacifiers in a wide variety of shapes and sizes. Your baby might prefer one kind over another. Be sure the mouth guard has ventilation holes and is wider than baby's mouth. Keep it clean; wash it when it falls on the floor. Don't tie it around baby's neck or his wrist, and don't attach it to his clothes or crib.

Keep several pacifiers handy. Most parents learn by experience that it's a good idea to have more than one pacifier at hand. They tend to get lost or dropped at the most inconvenient times!

If your baby needs a pacifier to help him settle, have one handy. When he's crying, it helps to have one close so he doesn't get too distressed. When the pacifier gets cracked, torn, sticky or shows other signs of wear, replace it—usually after 3 or 4 months.

> **When the pacifier gets cracked, torn, sticky or shows other signs of wear, replace it–usually after 3 or 4 months.**

Baby and House Pets

If this is your first baby, you may be faced with the problem of introducing your new baby to your "old baby;" that is, a dog or cat who shares your life. Sometimes a family pet will react to a new baby the same way a sibling might—with jealousy.

Watch for signs of jealousy. Keep your pet out of the baby's room. Don't leave them alone together. A dog or cat can carry allergies or infections. A dog may be jealous and resent the baby. It might do something you might not expect, so take steps to protect your baby. You'll be protecting your pet, too. See a more-thorough discussion of pets and a new baby in Week 12.

Day-Night Mix-Up

Your baby may have his days and nights mixed up, which can be stressful for you. Try these ideas to help him learn day is the time to be active and night is time for sleep. What works for one baby may not work for another, so you may have to experiment before you find something that works for you and your baby.

- You may notice your baby sleeps for one long period in 24 hours. Encourage him to sleep longer during the night by not letting him sleep more than 4 hours between feedings during the day.
- Allow regular daytime household noises to occur: the sound of a vacuum cleaner running, the radio or stereo playing, the doorbell ringing. This accustoms baby to normal noises, and he will learn to sleep through them.
- When he's up, expose him to family activities. Keep baby near so you can talk to him and interact with him.
- When you put baby to bed at night, keep it low-key. Speak quietly, keep lights low and don't stimulate him with play activities.
- When changing and feeding him in the middle of the night, do it quietly and quickly.
- Don't wake baby to feed him during the night, unless you are told to do so by your baby's doctor. Feed him when he wakes, unless it's been longer than 6 hours since his last feeding.

Milestones This Second Week

Baby's Brain Growth

You have an incredible effect on how your baby's brain grows. Stimulation from you and others who interact with baby helps make his nerves stronger and more efficient. Babies who are not touched often have smaller-than-normal brains for their age. Interacting with his environment develops connections in his brain, so be sure baby receives many different types of stimulation. Just watch for and avoid overstimulation.

Your Baby Sees Clearly only a Short Distance

A baby must learn to do many things that might seem simple to you. This includes seeing objects! At birth, your baby sees clearly for only about 12 inches—this is close to the distance from his eyes to yours during breastfeeding. Looking at him while you feed him gives him a chance to practice focusing. Move your head slowly from side to side to encourage baby's eyes to follow you. This helps build his eye muscles.

> **Move your head slowly from side to side to encourage baby's eyes to follow you.**

Sounds Are Important to a Baby

Your baby can hear, and sounds can be very important. Use his name often, and he will soon recognize it. Speak softly, hum, sing and make other soothing sounds when baby is restless. If those don't work, try "white sounds." Run the vacuum, turn on the radio to static, run water, play nature sounds, run the washing machine or dishwasher. Devices are also available that mimic the sounds baby heard in utero.

Communicate with Baby

Quietly alert. You will notice times when baby is quietly alert. He'll focus his attention on you when you talk to him. He'll follow you with his eyes for a bit. To communicate with him when he is in this state, hold him close and look into his eyes. Or lean over his crib, and talk softly to him. Stroke him softly as you sing to him. Rock him while you pat his back. These activities all help to establish communication between you.

Personality emerges. Baby's personality may begin to appear this week. He may be quiet and happy, or he may be noisy and active. The coming weeks will reveal his personality even more.

> **Use baby's name often, and he will soon recognize it.**

Note: See also the box on page 26, *Milestones This Week.*

What's Happening This Second Week?

Baby's First Checkup

Your pediatrician will probably want to see your baby this week for his first checkup. When you go to this appointment, be sure to bring your insurance card and be ready to fill out various forms. Your baby is a "new patient." You will be asked all sorts of information, such as date, time, place and the name of the doctor for your delivery. You

Milestones This Second Week

Changes in Baby You May See Now

Physical Development
• arm, leg and hand movements still reflexive
• startles spontaneously (Moro reflex)
• hands usually fisted or only slightly open

Senses and Reflexes
• stares at objects 8 to 12 inches away
• roots for breast, even if not breastfeeding
• is soothed more easily by higher, female voice than by a male voice

Mental Development
• alert about 1 in every 10 hours
• cries for assistance
• quiets when held or when he sees faces

Social Development
• eyes fix on mother's face in response to her smile
• stares at faces
• responds to human voice

Every baby is an individual, and your baby may do some of these things more quickly or more slowly than another baby. If you are concerned about your baby's progress, discuss it with your healthcare provider. Also see page viii.

will need to supply the doctor's office with information on problems during pregnancy or delivery, and baby's weight and length at birth. If you have other children, leave them at home for this visit. You have a lot to discuss.

Prepare for the visit. You may be unsure how to prepare for the office visit, especially if this is your first baby. Observe your baby closely and think about what you want to discuss, such as feeding concerns, his sleep habits, health matters and anything else that is important to you. Add any other concerns to your list that you may have. Consider some of the following areas that you may want to discuss—your physician may bring up some of them:

• umbilical-cord healing
• baby's sleep needs
• baby's weight and growth since birth
• eating habits, including breastfeeding concerns
• colic and ways to deal with it
• his personality and any ways to deal with it (fussy or especially active, for example)
• immunization schedule

- circumcision or foreskin concerns
- baby's bowel habits
- developmental landmarks, such as how well the baby is sucking

Schedule next appointments. Your physician will advise you of developmental milestones to watch for and give you a schedule of times for subsequent well-baby appointments, including an immunization schedule.

Vaccination schedule for premature babies. If your baby was premature, you will probably want to discuss his immunizations. The American Academy of Pediatrics advises that premature infants be vaccinated on schedule. Research has shown that by age 4 years, premature infants who were vaccinated on schedule had the same level of antibodies as children of the same age who were full-term infants.

Read the special section about well-baby checkups on page 96.

Milia and Baby Acne

Most parents expect their baby to be born with perfect skin. After all, haven't we heard that someone has "skin as beautiful as a baby's"? The truth is, many babies are born with rashes and other skin problems, which can last through the first few weeks.

Symptoms of *milia* include pinhead-size whiteheads (like very small pimples) on baby's face, particularly the nose, cheeks or forehead. They may also occur on baby's torso. Bumps are caused by a blockage of baby's oil (sebaceous) glands. *Baby acne* is similar to milia in that oil glands are blocked, but hair follicles may also be involved. Baby may have a rash of bumps.

Treatment. There isn't much you can do to treat either of these problems. Time is the best remedy. A baby soon outgrows the rashes. Within a few weeks, he will have beautiful baby skin. Until then, gently clean the affected areas with warm water and mild soap. Be sure baby doesn't scratch the area; it may cause more inflammation. You may have to trim his nails or put mittens or socks on his hands to prevent scratches.

If the pimples or rash spread or appear red and inflamed, contact baby's doctor.

What *not* to do. Don't use strong soaps or alcohol on the areas without first checking with your doctor. Avoid squeezing, pinching, scratching or picking the pimples. It won't make them go away faster, and you might infect them. Don't use ointments, medicated pads or medications without your doctor's advice. If the pimples or rash spread or appear red and inflamed, contact baby's doctor.

Spitting Up

What it is. Baby expels a little of what he consumes after a feeding. Spitting up is common in babies. It takes awhile for a baby's digestive tract to begin working efficiently after birth. It's not a cause for concern.

What to do. Some babies spit up because they eat too much. The stomach can't hold all the breast milk or formula baby ate. If your baby spits up a large amount, feed him less at the next feeding. You may need to burp him more often. Try a gentle burping during and after feedings. Keep baby upright after feeding for 20 to 30 minutes to help reduce how much he spits up.

When to call the doctor. Call the doctor if spitting up persists or becomes projectile. See the discussion of projectile vomiting in Week 3. If baby is bottle-feeding and continues to have problems, you may need to change formulas. Your doctor will advise you.

> **Keep baby upright after feeding for 20 to 30 minutes to help reduce how much your baby spits up.**

Sleep Apnea

Some babies suffer from sleep apnea. It is not a common condition. However, it is good to know the symptoms so you will be aware if baby has a problem.

What it is. *Apnea* refers to a temporary cessation of breathing. With sleep apnea, breathing stops briefly while the individual is asleep. It isn't unusual for healthy babies to hold their breath occasionally for 10 to 15 seconds. Most often a gentle nudge or touch causes baby to "grunt" or snort, and breathing resumes. You probably won't need to worry about this situation with your baby. The problem occurs more often in premature or low-birth weight infants; these babies usually outgrow the condition.

What to do. If you believe your baby is experiencing sleep apnea, make note of the frequency and duration of the episodes.

Discuss the situation with your doctor.

Some parents use intercom systems or sleep (apnea) monitors to alert them to problems. If your doctor believes there is a problem, he or she will suggest a solution.

Bonding with Baby

Like many parents, you have heard the term "bonding" but aren't sure what it means. Bonding refers to the emotional attachment formed between a baby and its parents or someone else. It is a growing process—it doesn't happen immediately—and it deepens over time. Some believe bonding begins even before birth. Parents feeling baby's movements on mom's tummy react to these movements and feel close to their baby.

> It isn't unusual for a healthy baby to hold his breath occasionally for 10 to 15 seconds.

How Can Our Family Bond with Baby?

You have the opportunity to bond with baby whenever you take care of him. Spending time with him, meeting his needs and responding to his needs all strengthen your bond. Hold him close, respond to his needs, cuddle and coo, look into his eyes, make skin-to-skin contact as often as possible. Encourage baby's father to do the same. These suggestions may help family members bond with baby.

- Lie on your side on the bed, with baby facing you. Pull him close so he can feel your breath on his face. Sing or talk to him as you stroke or massage his body.

- Hold your baby so his head snuggles under your chin. Sway together or rock him.

- Lay baby on his stomach along your forearm. Support his head and chin with your hand. Let his legs dangle down on either side of your arm. Protect his head if you carry him like this.

- Lie on the floor or bed with baby on your chest, bare skin to bare skin. Turn his head to the side so he can hear your heartbeat. Enjoy the closeness.

Daily care strengthens the bond. Some women are afraid that if they don't bond with their baby in the delivery room, it will never happen. Not true! Bonding in the delivery room is wonderful and helps both parents connect with baby, but don't worry if delivery complications delay this experience for you. The process can begin hours, even days, after birth, and it will continue for a long time. The daily care you give your baby as parents strengthens the bond between you.

Bonding has a physical aspect. Bonding goes beyond emotional attachment. Researchers have redefined it to include physical bonding as well. It's good for you because it stimulates the production of prolactin and oxytocin, two hormones that help you feel "motherly" toward your baby. The process also helps keep your baby's hormones in balance.

Others can bond with baby. A baby bonds with others besides his parents. Siblings, caregivers, other relatives—baby will bond with them. Love and care create the bond.

Feeding and bonding. If you breastfeed, your bond continues to develop through the feeding process. If you bottle-feed, let your partner feed baby to strengthen their bond. Other family members, such as siblings, can also bond with baby by feeding him.

What if you don't feel an immediate attachment? Some parents don't feel connected with their baby immediately. They fear something may be wrong with them or with baby. Don't worry if this happens to you. It's not uncommon. You may feel overwhelmed after a long or difficult pregnancy, labor or delivery. You may be exhausted. You may experience postpartum distress. Any of these can contribute to your feelings. Take it easy and relax. Within a short time, you will feel closer to your baby.

> When your baby lies on his side, you may notice that the side he was lying on is red, while the other side is somewhat pale. This difference is caused by his immature blood vessels and will soon disappear.

Massaging Baby

Baby soon learns that a gentle touch expresses your love and affection. He'll feel secure when you touch him. Your soothing hands can calm and comfort him. Baby massage is a wonderful way to connect with your baby.

How to massage baby. Find a quiet, warm spot to massage baby. A towel placed on your bed is a good place to start.

Keep lights low. Place baby on the towel on the bed or on the floor. Rub oil on your hands so they'll glide smoothly over baby's skin. With the flattened palm of your hand, rub his feet firmly yet gently, moving up his legs. Continue up his torso, then rub his hands and arms. Make strokes long and smooth. You'll find you both enjoy the interaction.

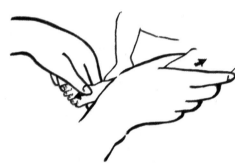

With the flattened palm of your hand, rub baby's feet firmly yet gently. Move up his legs with long, smooth strokes.

Your Newborn Will Cry

It's inevitable—your baby is going to cry. He'll cry when he's hungry, when he's wet and when he's tired. He'll cry when he's bored, and he'll cry when he's overstimulated. It's his only way of communicating with you right now.

What to do. At this time, your baby may fuss and cry for a few hours every day, often in the evenings. Take care of him when he cries, but realize there may be times that you won't be able to settle him. If his needs have been met, and you've cuddled him for a while, you may have to let him cry. Don't feel guilty when this happens. Do burp him after he cries for a time; a crying baby swallows air.

Toys and Play This Second Week

Play is interrelated with your baby's social, mental and physical development. There are many ways to play with him, even when he is this young. You and other people around him are the best "toys" for baby at this time. The interaction between baby and others is the most stimulating experience for him.

Boldly designed mobiles catch baby's attention if they are suspended over his crib.

Look into His Eyes

This game helps develop baby's eye muscles and promotes bonding! Hold baby close, and gaze into his eyes. He will look at you for a bit, then look away. Keep looking at him, and he will soon look back at you. Continue this until he tires.

You're becoming more relaxed with baby as you get to know him better, so trust your instincts. If you feel something may be wrong, call your doctor.

Stimulate His Grasping Reflex

Stimulate his grasp by touching his palm with your finger. He'll grasp your finger by reflex, but it helps strengthen finger muscles. Talk and sing to him as you play this game.

Toys to Entertain Baby

Things baby might enjoy this week include a hanging mobile above his crib or bassinet, a music box, or a tape or CD of soft lullabies to play in his room. Some mobiles are a combination of objects and sound. Colorful figures move slowly as music plays.

Week 3

How Big Is Your Baby This Third Week?

Baby weighs 8-1/2 pounds and is 20-3/4 inches long this week.

Baby Care and Equipment

Bottle-feeding Your Baby
Statistics show that more women choose to bottle-feed their babies than to breastfeed them. Your baby will receive good nutrition if you give her formula.

With bottle-feeding, other family members can enjoy helping to care for the baby.

Bottle-feeding has advantages. Some women enjoy the freedom bottle-feeding gives them compared to breastfeeding. A father can be more involved in caring for his child. Bottle-fed babies often are able to go longer between feedings; formula is usually more slowly digested than breast milk. You can determine exactly how much your baby takes in at each feeding.

How much to feed. Bottle-fed babies take from 2 to 5 ounces of formula at a feeding. They feed about every 3 to 4 hours for the first month (6 to 8 times a day). When baby is older, the number of feedings decreases, but the amount of formula you feed at each feeding increases.

Feeding twins or triplets. Twins or triplets (or even more) are often bottle-fed because it is more difficult and demanding to breastfeed multiples. Some women pump their breast milk and divide it among the babies, then supplement with formula. Other mothers feed only formula if they have more than one baby. Still others try to breastfeed one or two babies at each nursing, feeding other babies formula for that feeding. If you have more than one baby, there are many ways you can provide them with the nutrition they need.

Sterilize the water used for formula. When you bottle-feed, sterilize the water you use until your baby is at least 4 months old or when she starts solids. Do this by boiling it for 1 minute. Do not expect bottled water to be safer than tap water. One recent study showed that nearly 35% of more than 100 brands of bottled water were contaminated with chemicals or bacteria. If you use bottled water, boil it.

Sterilize new equipment. There is no need to sterilize bottles on a regular basis unless you use well water. In that case, boil bottles and nipples for 5 minutes. However, always sterilize new bottles, nipples, caps and rings for 5 minutes before using them for the first time.

> **Bottle-fed babies take from 2 to 5 ounces of formula at a feeding.**

Bottle-feeding and bonding with baby. Some parents fear that if they bottle-feed, they will not bond with baby. There are ways to bottle-feed a baby that can help develop a closer bond between parent and child. Try the following ideas.

- Snuggle baby close to you during feeding. Look into her eyes while you talk or sing to her.
- Find a comfortable place to feed, such as a rocking chair.
- Heat formula to body temperature.
- Remove the bottle during feeding to let baby rest.
- Don't leave the baby alone with the bottle.

Types of formulas available. There isn't much difference among the brands of regular formula available. Most babies do well on milk-based formula. Ask your pediatrician about the type of formula you should feed your baby. Some formulas are iron-fortified. A baby needs iron for normal growth.

More Bottle-feeding Health and Safety Tips

Keep in mind these additional tips when you bottle-feed your baby.

- **Wash your hands before you prepare formula.**
- **Clean feeding equipment thoroughly before use.**
- **Refrigerate any prepared formula or bottles.**
- **Bottles can be given to baby warm or cold, but choose one method and stick to it. A baby likes consistency.**
- **Don't heat formula if it is at room temperature; heat only refrigerated formula.**
- **Never thaw frozen formula by heating it. Let it thaw in the refrigerator.**
- **Before you heat a bottle, remove the nipple and cap.**
- **Heat 4-ounce bottles no longer than 30 seconds in a microwave on high. Heat 8-ounce bottles no longer than 45 seconds.**
- **After heating, replace the cap and nipple, and invert the bottle 8 to 10 times. Don't shake it.**
- **Test the temperature of a heated bottle by dripping a bit on the *top* of your wrist, which is more sensitive than the inside of the wrist.**
- **Don't force baby to finish a bottle.**
- **Be sure formula expiration dates have not expired.**
- **Do not microwave glass bottles; they might crack or explode.**
- **Throw away any leftover formula after a feeding.**
- **Throw out bottle nipples that are hard or stiff.**

In addition, some specialized types of formula are available, but they are for babies with special needs. Use these *only* when your pediatrician advises it. Special formulas available on the market today include

- milk-based, lactose-free formula fed to babies with problems, such as fussiness, gas and diarrhea, caused by lactose intolerance
- soy-based, lactose-free formula for babies with cow's-milk allergies or sensitivity to cow's milk
- hypoallergenic protein formula, called *predigested cow's milk,* which is easier to digest and lactose-free for babies with colic or symptoms of milk-protein allergy

Goat's milk. Some parents ask about goat's milk in an infant's diet—it once was used with fussy babies because we believed it was easier to digest. We now advise parents not to give their baby goat's milk. Similar to cow's milk, goat's milk has a high protein concentration, which may make it harder for baby to digest.

Other bottle-feeding facts. Today we know it's better to feed a baby with a slanted bottle. The slanted design keeps the nipple full of milk, which means baby takes in less air while feeding. Swallowing air can be a cause of discomfort to baby and contribute to gassiness. A slanted bottle also helps ensure baby is sitting up to drink. When a baby drinks lying down, milk can pool in the Eustachian tube in the ear and can cause ear infections.

> Bottle-fed babies often swallow air when feeding, so feed your baby in a semisitting position. This helps prevent air from getting in the stomach.

Burping is necessary. Burp baby after every feeding to help her get rid of excess air. See the discussion of Burping in Week 2. Some babies require burping during a feeding.

Is baby getting enough formula? You'll know baby's getting enough formula if she has six to eight wet diapers a day. She may have one or two bowel movements, too.

Stools of a bottle-fed baby are greener in color than a breastfed baby's and more solid. If your baby poops after a feeding, it's caused by the *gastrocolic reflex*. This reflex causes squeezing of the intestines when the stomach is stretched, as with feeding. It is very pronounced in newborns and usually decreases by 2 or 3 months of age.

If you notice any blood or mucus in baby's stools during these first few weeks, it may be an indication of a milk-protein sensitivity. Usually a little blood in the stools and occasional fussiness are the only symptoms. These symptoms disappear when baby is put on a hypoallergenic formula. Discuss the problem with your baby's doctor if these symptoms appear.

If baby doesn't want a feeding, don't force it. Try again in a couple of hours. However, if she refuses two feedings in a row, contact your pediatrician. She may be ill.

If Baby Chokes on Formula or Breast Milk

Occasionally a baby chokes on formula, breast milk or mucus. It's a common occurrence and one you can handle easily. When it happens, turn baby's head to the side and put her head a little lower than her body. If you need to, use a cloth, your clean finger or a bulb syringe to help clear any fluid from her mouth.

Bathing Baby

By the third week, baby's umbilical cord has fallen off, and it's time to give baby her first real bath. You may be feeling a little apprehensive about it—it's kind of scary holding a slippery little body. With practice, you'll be a pro, and this may become a favorite time with baby.

> When baby is cold, small veins show through her skin, and her feet and hands may look blue. Add some clothes or a blanket for warmth.

How often? You may hear conflicting advice about how often to bathe baby. Some experts suggest 2 or 3 times a week is enough. Others say a daily bath helps keep sensitive skin from drying out. Some suggest once a week! If you have questions about your baby's bathing schedule, discuss them with your pediatrician.

What you'll need. To begin the bath-time ritual, gather everything you'll need in one place. Once you put baby in the water, you can't step away or be distracted for even a second! Have towels, baby shampoo, soap and a washcloth at hand. To help keep baby from slipping, put a large terry towel or foam insert in the tub. Fill the tub (a baby tub or the kitchen sink) with a few inches of warm water. Be sure it's not too hot. Test it with your elbow or the back of your hand.

Putting baby in the bath. Undress baby. Slip your left hand under her shoulder. Place your thumb over her left shoulder and your fingers under her left armpit. Support her bottom with your right hand. Lower her into the water. Begin by washing her face, then work down her little body. Clean her genital area from front to back to avoid infections. Keep wiping warm water over your baby's body as you wash her to keep her warm.

Shampoo. Once you've washed her, it's time to shampoo. You only need to do this once or twice a week, not every time you bathe her. Wash her hair with a small amount of baby shampoo to making rinsing it out easier. Using a small plastic cup or your hand, rinse her head. Pour water from the forehead back to avoid getting it on her face or in her eyes.

Pat her dry. As soon as you've finished, lift her out and wrap her in a towel. Pat her body and her head with the towel to dry her. Patting dry is gentler on her skin than rubbing. Follow with a moisturizer if her skin is dry or if you live in a very dry climate. Diaper and dress her quickly to avoid a chill.

Cleaning Baby's Ears

Your baby's ears will produce earwax, just as yours do. This is a normal bodily process, and you don't need to do much about it. Earwax is a mixture of dead skin cells and glandular secretions. It helps protect baby's eardrum and ear canal from foreign substances.

Earwax usually falls out on its own. Do not stick any type of swab into your baby's ear canal to remove wax buildup. You can clean the outer opening of the ear with a washcloth, but don't try to clean inside the ear.

Don't try to clean inside baby's ear.

Dressing Baby for Outings

You'll be taking your baby out and about more now. Dressing her for the climate might cause you some concern. It's best to judge what she needs by how you feel. Usually in cold weather, add one more layer than you are wearing. In warm or hot weather, she can wear the same number of layers you are. Be aware: When you live in hot climates, you may need to keep a blanket near for colder, indoor air-conditioned temperatures.

"Baby Wearing"

"Baby wearing" is a way of carrying your baby in some type of carrier against the front of your body, close to you. It's a wonderful way to bond with baby because of the physical closeness it provides. It may also encourage brain growth.

A baby can learn a great deal being carried this way. She can see what you see (partially). She can hear conversations. She can feel rhythmic movements when you walk. She can feel your heart beat, which may calm and settle her. It's a wonderful way to expose her safely to the world around her. Also see the discussion in Week 4 of front carriers.

Baby Massage

Your baby will enjoy a relaxing massage—it's tough to be a newborn! Research has shown that massaging your baby every day can improve her digestion and sleep. It can also help muscle development.

Choose a warm spot so baby won't be cold. With baby dressed only in a diaper, place her on a towel or in your lap. Begin by making eye contact; smile and coo at baby. Using firm, gentle strokes, make little circles around her head. Don't use oil on her face or head. Smooth her forehead by placing both hands at the center and gently stroking outward. Make little circles with your fingertips around her jaw.

> A baby's chubbiness is due to the fact she gains weight faster than she grows in length. This pattern changes as she gets older.

Warm some oil in your hands, then stroke her chest. Massage her hands (you'll need to open them), then roll each arm gently between your two hands. Stroke her tummy. Move down to her legs and feet; massage each between your two hands. Turn her onto her stomach, and massage her back. Use long strokes from her shoulders to her buttocks.

Keep your massage to 15 minutes or less. Longer may be too much for a young infant.

Milestones This Third Week

Baby Is Accomplishing Much
Baby is adapting to her place in the family, just as you are adapting to her in your lives. She is accomplishing many things by this third week. She can focus her attention on one quiet activity and shut out other stimuli. She lifts her head for a few seconds, and she turns her head from side to side when she's on her tummy. She adjusts her body posture to cuddle into someone holding her. She may be settling into a regular feeding schedule.

Your Baby Needs to Suck
Sucking is satisfying to baby. Many babies require more sucking than feeding time allows. Sucking is also comforting to her. Because she may not be able to

find her mouth easily to suck on a finger or thumb, offer her a pacifier, if you haven't already done so.

Soothe Your Baby

You may find you can help soothe your baby by providing her with your personal scent. Let her smell something that you have worn or had near you that has your fragrance (it doesn't have to be perfume) on it. Having something close to her with a familiar scent can help calm a fussy baby.

Baby Likes to Watch Faces

Your baby may be making more eye contact with you. When you hold her in your arms and talk or sing to her, you are inviting her to focus on you. You'll find she'll make eye contact for up to 10 seconds, and she'll quiet to stare at a face. She'll gaze at her mother's face longer than anyone else's. In addition to faces, you might introduce new, bold-patterned objects to look at, such as a bull's eye, bold stripes or a checkerboard.

You'll notice that baby is turning her head more from side to side to track a moving object. However, her eyes may cross when she's focusing on something due to lack of good muscle control. Soon this will disappear.

Note: See also the box on page 41, *Milestones This Week*.

What's Happening This Third Week?

Your baby continues to adjust to her new life outside the womb. She sleeps about 16 to 18 hours a day, but her schedule may be erratic. She probably sleeps only 3 to 4 hours before she wakens again. Her periods of sleep and wakefulness follow no pattern, so you can't depend on any time of day when she'll be sleeping. A reason for this is your baby's need to eat. Her stomach is small and can't hold a lot of food. Her tummy's like an alarm clock—she wakes up when she's hungry and she sleeps when she's full.

An Exciting Time for Dad

For a man, attachment to his newborn can be strong and deep. The experience of becoming a father can be emotional. Studies show that when a father is involved with his child's care from birth, he continues to be involved in the child's life as she grows up.

Milestones This Third Week

Changes in Baby You May See Now

Physical Development
- thrusts out arms and legs in play
- can lift head briefly when lying on stomach
- may dig heels into mattress, then thrust with legs (this moves her body a little)

Senses and Reflexes
- coordinates eyes sideways when looking at a light or an object

Mental Development
- has vague and impassive expression during waking hours
- prefers patterns

- may calm when you speak gently to her and hold her upright against your shoulder

Social Development
- makes eye contact
- adjusts posture to body of person holding her

Every baby is an individual, and your baby may do some of these things more quickly or more slowly than another baby. If you are concerned about your baby's progress, discuss it with your healthcare provider. Also see page viii.

Encourage father to care for his baby. Bathing, diapering, feeding, holding, comforting—all are tasks a father can perform. Divide tasks as logically as you can, and work together in caring for your child. Trust in each other's abilities as a parent.

Research has shown that a woman can help her partner become more involved in parenting by sharing her feelings with him and asking for his help. This is a time of great change for the family. A father's involvement means sharing the responsibility and easing a mother's burden.

> Her tummy's like an alarm clock–she wakes up when she's hungry and she sleeps when she's full.

A Common Birthmark

Stork bites, angel kisses or *salmon patches* are all names for a type of birthmark your baby may have. It is usually a flat pink blotch on the forehead near her nose, on her eyelid or at the nape of her neck. No treatment is necessary; it usually disappears by age 1.

What Your Pediatrician Would Like You to Know

Your pediatrician is concerned about your baby's health and welfare. Your doctor realizes and understands you may be concerned about your ability to know what is normal and what is not with a newborn.

Below we discuss common issues that concern parents. These discussions may help you decide what is normal for your baby and help you relax a little. If you are concerned about something in particular, most doctors would have you err on the side of caution and call your pediatrician's office for advice about taking care of baby.

You may be a first-time parent who has never been around newborns before. You may get lots of advice. However, you deal with your baby every day. You know her best. So after you've listened to everyone else, listen to yourself. Trust your instincts!

Babies cry. Your baby will cry—it's natural and expected. A newborn may cry as much as 3 hours a day, or more. It's your baby's only way of communicating with you. Your baby will cry to tell you she's hungry, wet, tired, bored or upset.

As you get to know your baby, you'll know what her crying means because each of her cries is different. You'll be able to tell when something's wrong. Her crying will be different in some way. It may be piercing or uncontrollable or prolonged. Trust your instincts. If you are still concerned about your baby's crying, call your pediatrician.

Your baby will lose some weight. Babies are born with extra fluid to get them through the first 3 to 5 days after birth, whether or not they feed. Your little one will lose some of the fluids she was born with. And after the trauma of birth, she isn't too interested in eating. These two situations contribute to baby's weight loss. A baby loses 10% of her body weight by the third day following birth. If you breastfeed your baby, her weight loss might be a little more because it takes awhile for your breast milk to come in. Within a week after birth, your baby will start gaining weight.

If baby hasn't regained her birth weight by her 2-week checkup or if she loses more than 10% of her body weight in the first 3 days after birth, your doctor may suggest you also offer her formula, if you are breastfeeding.

Spitting up is normal. Don't be surprised or worried if baby spits up. In a newborn, the muscle that closes the opening to the stomach may be underdeveloped. This allows breast milk or formula to come back up. Baby really isn't spitting up a lot, no matter how it looks.

If you're bottle-feeding, be sure baby is sitting semi-upright when you feed her. You might want to use a slanted bottle to reduce the amount of air she takes in.

With bottle-feeding and breastfeeding, burp her several times during a feeding. Hold her or sit her upright after a feeding for a little bit. This helps keep the food down.

Call your pediatrician if baby *vomits* a lot. See the discussion of spitting up in Week 2, and of vomiting in Weeks 3 and 24.

Baby will have some rashes. Most babies have a rash or rashes during their first few weeks of life. Baby acne, milia, cradle cap, bumps and pimples are common. These rashes occur because the mother's estrogen is still circulating through baby's body. Rashes soon disappear, so you don't need to do anything about them. See the discussions of the various skin conditions in Weeks 1 and 2.

If baby has a rash that oozes, call your pediatrician. Call if a rash worsens with simple treatment. These are not common and should be treated by your baby's doctor.

When baby coughs and sneezes. Your baby will cough and sneeze to clear her nasal passages of mucus, dust and other irritants. When she coughs and sneezes, it's probably *not* a sign of illness. It's the only way she has to clear her airways. Don't be concerned unless she also has a fever or is congested and these interfere with her eating or sleeping. If this occurs, call your pediatrician.

Her belly button looks like it hurts. When you bring baby home from the hospital, her belly button probably has a black stump that looks shriveled. You may wonder if you should clean the stump because you believe it will hurt baby. However, the stump of the umbilical cord has no nerve endings. It won't hurt baby if you clean it.

Wipe the belly-button area with alcohol after each diaper change. Give baby a sponge bath until it falls off, within 2 to 4 weeks. If the cord stump doesn't fall off after 4 weeks, contact your pediatrician. He or she will want to know about it.

Baby's bowel movements. What's normal for one baby may not be normal for another baby. It all depends on what your baby eats and how her body processes her food.

If you bottle-feed your baby, she may move her bowels two or three times a day. Her stools may have the consistency of soft ice cream and be brownish in color. As the weeks pass, she may have fewer bowel movements as her system matures.

If you breastfeed baby, she may have loose, yellow, mustardlike stools. She may have a bowel movement after every feeding. Some breastfed babies pass stools less often. It's not unusual for them to go a day or two, or as long as 4 days, without a bowel movement, then have a huge one.

A change in baby's normal bowel routine could be a sign that she has a problem. Call your doctor if you are concerned. Always contact your pediatrician if baby's stools are more watery than normal for more than a couple of bowel movements or if you notice any blood in the stool.

Trust your instincts.

Colic

What is it? *Colic* is a condition in which a baby has episodes of sudden, loud crying and fussiness that often last for hours. About 20% of all infants experience colic, which usually appears about 2 weeks after birth and can last until baby is 3 or 4 months old. A colic attack often occurs at night and can last up to 4 hours. Baby may draw her knees to her chest, pass gas and flail her arms. Her tummy muscles may feel hard. An attack stops as suddenly as it starts. It may help you to know colic is not harmful to your baby.

Why does it happen? Although a great deal of research has been conducted on the cause of colic, we have little understanding of why it occurs. Theories include

- immaturity of the baby's digestive system, also called *gastroesophageal reflux (GER)*
- sensitivity to or intolerance of cow's-milk protein in formula or breast milk
- fatigue in the infant
- some foods a mother eats, if she breastfeeds

What to do. At this time, we can't offer an effective treatment for colic. Don't give baby any type of medication to relieve pain or to stop cramping. They could cause additional problems. You can try the following at home to help ease baby's discomfort during an attack.

- Offer baby the breast or bottle.
- If you bottle-feed, try a formula that is not based on cow's milk. Talk to your pediatrician before making any changes.
- Carry baby in a front sling during an attack. The closeness and motion often help soothe baby.
- Offer baby a pacifier.
- Place baby across your knees on her stomach, and rub her back.
- Swaddle baby.
- Massage baby's tummy.

Try to stay calm and relaxed. If your baby shows signs of colic, discuss the situation with your pediatrician. A baby's incessant crying can cause parents a great deal of stress, so take care of yourself, too.

Take turns staying with baby during an attack. Ask a family member or friend to baby-sit for an evening. Take heart—colic will disappear soon.

Penis Inflammation (Balanitis)

What it is. If your son was circumcised, you may notice redness, swelling, pus or bleeding from the circumcision site. This usually occurs during the first week following circumcision. It indicates the area may be slightly infected, so you may need to take steps to deal with the infection.

What to do. Gently clean the red or inflamed area with a mild soap and warm water. Don't use alcohol because it could sting. Try to keep the area clean and dry. Change baby as soon as he is wet.

When to call the doctor. Contact baby's doctor if bleeding is constant or heavy, or if there is pus or discharge. Your baby's doctor will determine a course of treatment. Antibiotic gels or creams may be prescribed to deal with the infection. Follow the doctor's instructions closely. Clean the area as directed by your doctor.

Projectile Vomiting

What it is. Babies often spit up or vomit a little. It takes time for their digestive tracts to function normally. Spitting up is discussed in Week 2. However, some babies experience recurrent or forceful vomiting, called *projectile vomiting*. Symptoms of the problem include *forceful* ejection of milk, formula, food or medications, water or anything baby swallows. The problem may have several different causes, including illness (flu) or ingestion of food or medication.

What to do. If your baby experiences forceful vomiting, make sure she doesn't choke on the vomit. Discontinue giving her food or any medication.

Call your baby's doctor. Any treatment your doctor recommends will be centered around the symptoms your baby displays, such as gastroenteritis or an allergy to food or medication.

Advisory for parents: Your baby does not have this problem if she spits up a little or vomits once in a while. She must vomit forcefully, projecting stomach contents a fair distance, such as a couple of feet.

Toys and Play This Third Week

You'll find that as baby stays awake longer, you have more time for fun and games. She's beginning to respond a little more. It's enjoyable for you to see her alertness grow and her interaction with you and others become more active.

Note: Watch baby closely when you interact with her. You'll be able to tell she's had enough when she looks away, squirms, gets fussy, kicks, yawns or seems unhappy in some other way.

Talk to Baby in "Parentese" and Call Her by Name

When you play with baby, vary your tone of voice. Talk in "parentese," a high-pitched, singsong tone of voice; she'll love it. Research shows it serves a purpose, too. It helps speed an infant's ability to recognize connections between objects and words.

This week, physical contact continues to be very important. Hold baby in your arms, or sit on the floor and hold her in your lap. Look into her eyes and say her name. Vary the tone you use. Make up rhymes using her name. Use her name in the place of another name while you softly sing a funny song. Say her name often so she'll recognize it.

Say your baby's name often so she'll begin to recognize it.

Play Vision Games

It's never too early to start playing vision games!

Flashlight game. In a dimly lit room, turn on a flashlight, and move its beam back and forth in front of baby. (Never shine the light into her eyes!) Watch her eyes to see if she tracks the light. This exercise helps her develop muscles needed to follow moving objects.

Crib pictures. From magazines or other sources, cut out bright, simple pictures with bold, contrasting colors, like a picture of the sun or a human face. Prop a picture against the side of the crib for a bit. Move it slowly to the other side so she moves her head to see it. (Don't leave the picture in the crib when you leave the room.) Special infant safety mirrors, which can be permanently attached to the side of the crib, can also add excitement as she catches sight of herself.

Help Her Tone Muscles

Bicycle exercise. While baby is lying on her back, grasp her feet and gently move her legs in a circular motion, like riding a bike. This exercise encourages toning of muscles and exposes her to rhythm. A couple of minutes is long enough for this interaction.

> Keep your baby from getting your cold by washing your hands before touching her. Make sure other family members do the same.

Put Baby in the Middle of Things

Although you might not think of it as a game, it's beneficial and fun for baby to be part of the family's interaction every day. Carry her in a front sling as you move around the house, or let her sit in her infant chair as the family eats together. Everyone will enjoy it, including baby.

Week 4

How Big Is Your Baby This Fourth Week?

Baby weighs 9 pounds and is 21 inches long this week.

Baby Care and Equipment

Baby Slings and Front Carriers
Baby slings and front carriers offer parents and others a wonderful, close way to carry baby. It's a piece of baby equipment that can mean a lot; when baby's in a front carrier, you continue bonding.

Sling-style carrier.

Because your baby grows so quickly these first months, you will probably use a front carrier only for about 3 or 4 months. Although probably you'd like to use it longer, your back will say "No!"

Advantages. There are many advantages to carrying baby "kangaroo-style" during the first few months. One study showed babies carried this way cry less. You are close to baby, yet your arms are free. The swaying motion and the wrapped-close feeling may remind baby of the womb, which may help settle him. Slings and carriers are also great for nursing privately in a public area.

How they work. A *sling* is just what it sounds like. Baby is placed on his back in the sling and carried as if he were in a hammock, close to your body. A *front carrier* is like a backpack, only it's on the front. Baby is placed in the carrier part, facing inward when he's very small and facing outward as he gets older (3 months).

Front carrier.

Comfort and safety considerations. Comfort and safety are the most important factors to search for. Check for the following when shopping for a sling or front carrier:

- Straps and snaps are secure so they can't work loose.
- Belts and buckles have some form of backup security, such as double loops or plastic stops.
- Check manufacturer's weight and age recommendations for the carrier.
- Fabric is sturdy and washable. Is it soft enough for baby's skin?
- Seams are reinforced with double stitching at points of stress.
- Shoulder straps and neck straps are cushioned.
- Padded belts make the carrier comfortable for you.
- Product meets the Juvenile Products Manufacturers Association (JPMA) safety standards.

Nail Care

You may be surprised at how quickly baby's nails grow. Sometimes a baby's nails have to be cut soon after birth! You may feel leery about cutting nails that are so tiny, but once you've done it a few times, you'll be a pro.

A baby's nails are thin and very flexible, but they can soon become long enough and sharp enough to scratch him. Trimming them prevents injuries.

How to clip baby's nails. Nail scissors or clippers made for a small child are a good choice. When baby is asleep or relaxed, take one finger in your hand, hold it fingertip-down, away from you. Snip or cut the nail straight across. Don't cut into the quick (the flesh under the nail). Or you can file baby's nails with an emery board. Some parents even nibble them off!

Trim how often? You'll probably need to trim his nails about every 2 weeks. As a rule of thumb, the bigger the finger, the faster the nail grows, so you may have to trim the thumbs more often. (No pun intended.) As baby starts to use his hands more frequently, he'll wear down some of the nails. Be sure to check his nails often. A ragged nail can scratch him.

Toenails. Don't overlook toenails. They are worn down more consistently than fingernails because of contact with socks, booties and footed sleepers. Check his toes at least every few weeks, but he probably won't need toenails trimmed more often than once a month, if that. Once he begins walking, you'll need to check his toenails more often. Long toenails may make walking uncomfortable.

Make gentle little circles with your fingertips around baby's jaw.

Baby Massage—Jaw Area

Your baby is doing a lot of sucking now. That could cause tension around his mouth and jaw. To help relieve some of this tension, massage around his jaw. Make small circles on and around his jawbone with your fingertips. His mouth may open in contentment.

Keeping Baby Warm

A newborn may have a bit of trouble regulating his body temperature. It can take awhile for his body thermostat to begin working. If your baby seems chilled or you live in a cold climate, we have some tips to help keep him warm.

- Cuddle baby close to you when you hold him. This warms him.
- Swaddle him tightly in a receiving blanket.
- Lay him down with a hot-water bottle wrapped in a soft blanket next to him or under him.
- Before he goes to sleep or takes a nap, prewarm his sheets with a heating pad or a hot-water bottle. Be sure sheets are not hot when you put him down. Remove the heat source before you put him down.
- Dress him in a blanket sleeper—you won't need extra blankets.

> When you change your baby's diaper, bend and straighten his legs in a bicycling motion. This activity helps strengthen his leg muscles.

Giving Baby Water

Some parents believe their baby needs more fluid than he takes in at his feedings. Unless advised to do so by your pediatrician, do not give baby water or sugar water between feedings. It will fill his tummy, resulting in him eating less at his next feeding.

Supplemental Feedings

If you must provide your baby with supplemental feedings while you breastfeed, wait until you've been breastfeeding for at least 4 weeks, if possible. This gives your body a chance to adjust and

Well-Baby Checkup

Make your baby's 1-month well-baby checkup now. See page 97 for immunizations he may receive at this next visit.

ensures a good milk supply. It also keeps baby from taking a liking to a bottle (baby finds it's much easier to feed from a bottle than a breast). Some babies refuse to breastfeed after they become used to a bottle. Occasional supplemental feedings shouldn't be a problem after 4 weeks.

Choosing Child Care for Baby

If you and your partner work, child care may be one of the most important decisions you must make for baby. You might find it challenging as you begin your search for child care. Where do you start?

Seek referrals. Ask friends, family members and co-workers for referrals to people or places they know about. Talk to people in your area. Ask at your church, temple or others in the area if they sponsor any programs. Contact Child Care Aware (800-424-2246) or a local referral agency about local resources. If you're interested in hiring a nanny for care in your home, contact a referral agency. See the Resources list, page 492, for some contacts.

Check references carefully. Whomever you choose to provide care for your child, be sure to check references before you make a final decision! This applies to centers as well as in-home caregivers (your home or theirs).

Allow plenty of time to find the right situation. Finding the best situation for your baby can take time. Begin the process several weeks before you need it (maybe several months in special situations like twins). Often this means finding child care before your baby is born. Some places may have a waiting list. There is a shortage of quality child care for children under age 2. If you find a care provider you are comfortable with, but it's not time to leave your baby, ask to put down a deposit and set a date for child care to begin. Keep in touch with the care provider, and plan to meet before you place your child in daily care.

Child-Care Options

You have many decisions to make when choosing someone to care for your baby. You want the best setting and the best caregiver for your child. The way to find that is to know what your options are before you begin looking. You have many choices when it comes to child care. Examine your needs and the needs of your child before you decide which to pursue.

In-home child care. With in-home care, the caregiver can be a relative or nonrelative. It's easier on you to have someone come to your home to take care of your child. You don't have to get the baby ready before you go out in the morning. You never have to take your child out in bad weather. You save time because you don't have to drop off your baby or pick him up somewhere.

In-home care is an excellent choice for a baby or small child because it provides one-on-one attention (if you only have one child at home). The environment is familiar to the child.

Caregiver is a relative. When the caregiver is a relative, such as a grandparent, a sister or someone else in the family, you may find the situation more challenging than you thought it would be. It may be harder to maintain your relationship with your caregiver while asking or telling him or her to do things as you want them done.

Caregiver is not a relative. In-home child care by a nonrelative can be very expensive. You are hiring someone you do not know to come into your home and take care of your child. You must be diligent in asking for references and checking them thoroughly.

A drawback to in-home care is the isolation your child may feel as he grows older. Children need to interact with others, to learn to share and to play. While in-home care can be an excellent choice for your baby, as the child gets older, you may have to arrange opportunities for the child to be with other children.

Care in a caregiver's home. Many parents opt to take their child to someone else's home for child care. Often these homes have small group sizes and offer parents more flexibility, such as keeping the child longer on a day you have a late meeting. They may offer a homelike setting, and your child may receive lots of attention.

However, homes are not regulated in every state, so you must check out each situation very carefully. Contact your state's Department of Social Services and ask about requirements. In some places, local agencies oversee caregivers who are members of their organization. Those who provide care must abide by certain standards, such as the maximum number of children allowed in the home (including their own), and the maximum fees they may charge. They may have to attain certain standards, such as CPR and first-aid certification.

Steps for finding an in-home caregiver. Whether you choose to have someone come to your home or take your child to another person's home, following the suggestions listed below can help you find the best caregiver for your child.

Advertise in local newspapers and church bulletins to find someone to interview. State how many children are to be cared for and their ages. Include information on the days and hours care is needed, experience you are seeking and any other particulars. State that references are required and that you will be checking them.

Talk to people on the telephone first to determine whether you want to interview them. Ask about their experience, qualifications, child-care philosophy and what they are seeking in a position. Then decide if you want to pursue the contact with an in-person interview. Make a list of all your concerns, including days and hours someone is needed, duties to be performed, need for a driver's license and supplying a benefits' policy. Discuss these with the potential caregiver.

Call all references. Have the potential caregiver provide you with the names and phone numbers of people he or she has worked for in the past. Call each family, let them know you are considering this person as a caregiver and discuss the person's strengths and weaknesses with them.

Check out the situation. After you hire someone, drop by unannounced occasionally. Notice how everything appears when you do this. Pay attention to how your child reacts each time you leave or arrive. This can give you a clue as to how your child feels about the caregiver. Do this for *any* type of child care you choose.

Child-care centers. A child-care center is a larger setting in which many children receive care. Centers vary widely in the facilities and activities they provide, the amount of attention they give each child, group sizes and child-care philosophy.

Inquire about training required for each child-care provider or teacher at the center you are interested in. Some facilities expect more from a care provider than others. In some cases, a facility hires only trained, qualified personnel; in other cases, they train the personnel or provide additional training.

Some child-care centers do not accept infants; infants take a great deal of time and attention. If the center accepts infants, the ratio of caregivers to children should be about one adult to every three or four children (up to age 2).

Don't be fooled by appearances. Even the cleanest, brightest place is useless without the right kind of care provider. Check out the center thoroughly. Visit it by appointment, then stop in unannounced a few times. Meet the person in charge and the people who will care for your child. Ask for references of parents whose children are currently being cared for there. Call and talk to these parents before making a final decision.

Care for an infant. Be sure the place you choose for your infant can meet his needs. A baby must be changed and fed, but he also needs to be held and interacted with. He needs to be comforted when he is afraid. He needs to rest at certain times each day.

When searching for a place, keep in mind what care your child will require. Evaluate every situation as to how it can respond to the needs of your baby.

Cost of child care. Paying for child care can be a big-budget item in household expenses. For some families, it can cost as much as 25% of their household budget. Public funding is available for some limited-income families. Title EE is a program paid for with federal funds. Call your local Department of Social Services to see if you are eligible.

> Going to sleep and waking up helps baby bond with parents.

Other programs to help with child-care costs include a federal tax-credit program, the dependent-care assistance program and earned-income tax credit. These programs are regulated by the federal government. Contact the Internal Revenue Service at 800-829-1040 for further information.

Special-care needs. If your baby needs one-on-one care, you may have a harder time finding child care. In these special cases, you may need to allow extra time seeking a qualified care provider.

Contact the hospital where your child has received care. Ask for references, or call your pediatrician. They may be in contact with someone who can help you. It may make sense for the care provider to come to your home if your child has special needs.

Caring for a sick child. All children come down with colds, the flu or diarrhea at times. Today, there are ways to handle an illness if you can't take time off from work to stay home.

In many places, "sick-child" day-care centers are available. They are usually attached to a regular day-care facility, although some are connected with hospitals. A center provides a comfortable place where an ill child can rest or participate in quiet activities, such as story time. Often a registered nurse heads the facility. This person can administer medication when necessary. Fees for this type of service run from about $25 to $55 a day.

Some cities have "on-call" in-home care providers who come to your home when your child is too sick to be taken anywhere. The program is usually run by an agency that deals with child care, and caregivers charge by the hour. Getting a person to come to your home is usually on a first-come, first-served basis, so you may have to wait a day for a provider. However, this can be an excellent way to care for a child who is too ill to be taken away from home.

Milestones This Fourth Week

Sleep and Your Baby

By this time, baby is beginning to adapt to the cycle of day and night, and hopefully, to your schedule. He is developing regular sleep patterns. He may sleep for as long as 6 hours at a time. Your baby's brain affects how he rests. His sleep is different from yours. A baby spends longer time in REM sleep, in which the heart rate and breathing increase, brainwaves intensify and the eyes move under the lids. Dreams occur at this time. REM sleep is lighter than non-REM sleep.

> During the deepest phase of non-REM sleep, growth hormone is released in baby's body and he actually "grows in his sleep."

While your baby is in this state, you may see him sucking, moving his legs and arms, making faces and making sounds. He wakens easily. He won't begin to experience non-REM sleep until he's about 4 months old. During the deepest phase of non-REM sleep, growth hormone is released in baby's body and he actually "grows in his sleep."

REM sleep is essential for brain growth. A great deal of learning and development are occurring in this sleep phase. Research has shown that facial expressions associated with the release of hormones and chemicals important in brain development happen in REM sleep.

Going to sleep and waking up helps baby bond with parents. When he falls asleep, he is separating from you. When he wakens and needs to be comforted and you are there, it reinforces the security of your presence.

Baby can now see faces and objects clearly that are 18 inches away.

Baby's Vision

Your baby's color vision is not fully developed by the fourth week of life. However, don't avoid showing him colorful objects because you've heard baby sees black and white the best. Bold colors in simple shapes can be stimulating. He'll also enjoy toys that include music, movement and color.

Baby can now see faces and objects clearly that are 18 inches away. His eyes are coordinated most of the time, and he'll follow an object with his eyes. His favorite object to look at is still the human face. He may focus on one or two features, often toward the edge of the face, such as the chin or an ear. He loves to watch your expressions change.

Other Changes You May Notice

Grasp reflex. His grasp reflex is developing. He may briefly hold onto anything you put in his hand before he lets it go.

Head movements. He turns his head from side to side to follow an object with his eyes. He may lift his head high enough to clear the area beneath him, but it takes awhile to do it—as long as 30 seconds. He can hold up his head briefly while he's lying on his stomach.

Starting to move. When your baby kicks his legs in the air, he's starting to move. You'll notice he begins to move more as he gets older. That's why it's so important never to leave him alone, even for a second, on a changing table or some other surface he could fall from.

Different types of cries. He may cry loudly if he finds an activity uncomfortable or painful, and he may fuss during a bath. By this week, you may be able to hear a difference in his crying. You may begin to discern whether baby's cry means he's hungry, wet, tired or bored. He may also start making noncrying sounds. By this week, you may be able to hear a difference in his crying.

Mom's voice is special. Your baby can distinguish his mother's voice from a stranger's. Some sounds cause him to quiet down and listen, such as singing, talking or music.

Note: See also the box on page 58, *Milestones This Week*.

What's Happening This Fourth Week?

Regularity of Bowel Movements
About this time, baby's bowel movements begin to fall into a regular pattern. Your baby will have one or two movements a day that look like a mustard puddle or thick green soup.

Feed on Schedule or on Demand?
In the world of child development, some believe that a child should conform to a regular schedule, as an adult does. This is the basis of the "Babywise" philosophy developed by Gary Ezzo and based on his Christian parenting programs. Others in the child development world believe a baby should be fed when he acts hungry; that is, "on demand." The baby is not really "demanding" to be fed; rather, he is expressing his need to be fed in the only way he can—by crying.

Feeding on schedule. The "Babywise" program advises parents to create a routine whereby parents direct a baby's feedings. Babies are not fed on demand when they are hungry. They are fed when the parents determine they should be fed. Parents establish a feeding time, a sleep time and a time when baby is awake. To accomplish this, parents limit their newborn's feedings to only one feeding every 2-1/2 to 3 hours. A breastfed baby must nurse for 30 minutes, even if he doesn't want to. This is supposed to assure him of sufficient calories.

Milestones This Fourth Week

Changes in Baby You May See Now

Physical Development

• rolls partway to side from back
• when pulled to sitting position, may hold head in line with back

Senses and Reflexes

• can grasp object when fingers are are pried open, but quickly drops it

Mental Development

• remembers object when it reappears within a couple of seconds

• may make an "ah" sound when he sees parents or hears parents' voices

Social Development

• may clutch at person holding him
• may make throaty sounds

Every baby is an individual, and your baby may do some of these things more quickly or more slowly than another baby. If you are concerned about your baby's progress, discuss it with your healthcare provider. Also see page viii.

Vitamin Supplements

If your baby was full-term, he probably won't need vitamin supplements, whether you are breastfeeding or bottle-feeding. At one time we believed breast milk didn't provide adequate amounts of vitamin D, but we now know this isn't the case. Talk to baby's doctor if you have questions.

In some special situations, vitamins may be recommended. Premature infants may need additional iron because they didn't store it up before birth. Discuss vitamin supplements with your pediatrician if you are concerned.

After feeding, baby is expected to stay awake for a period, followed by a nap no longer than 1 to 1-1/2 hours. Supporters of the philosophy state that by 8 weeks, parents can stop the night feeding, even if baby wakes up crying.

Feeding on demand. Those who oppose this practice state that many babies, especially newborns, cannot go an entire night without feeding—their tummies are too small. Even by 8 weeks, their stomachs may not be large enough to allow them to go hours without feeding. Dehydration is another concern when babies are not fed frequently throughout the day and night.

Comforting a Fussy Baby

You will need to comfort your fussing baby from time to time. Try the following to calm your baby—these ideas have worked for other parents, and they may work for you, too.

- **Use repetitive, rocking motions, such as swaying, rocking in a chair or just sitting down and rocking back and forth.**
- **Let him suck–whether on a pacifier, his fist, your finger or the breast.**
- **Stroke and massage him.**
- **Carry him in a sling or front carrier.**
- **Bathe him in warm water.**
- **Hold him close against your chest so he can hear your heart beat.**
- **Take him for a ride in his stroller.**
- **Sing to him.**
- **Swaddle him snugly.**
- **Experiment with ways to calm him, such as rubbing his tummy, blowing on his toes, humming softly in his ear.**

Experts say that babies know when they are full and shouldn't be forced to eat more than they want. This could lead to eating problems later in life. They suggest feeding baby on demand. They warn that not feeding baby when he is hungry could lead to insecurity in baby because his needs are not being met.

Crossed Eyes

What it is. Many babies have crossed eyes, also called *strabismus* or *lazy eye*, at this early age. It is normal for baby's eyes not to move in unison because his eye-muscle control has not fully developed. Don't worry that baby has a problem if you notice this condition at this time.

What to do. When this problem does occur, it usually appears in an older baby, around 3 or 4 months of age. If you notice your baby's eyes are crossed then, consult your baby's doctor. Many treatments are available, including an eye patch to cover one eye, glasses, exercises for the eye, medication or surgery.

Failure to Thrive

What it is. If your baby has not gained back enough weight to reach his birth weight by this time, his doctor may be concerned about "failure to thrive." The problem may also be suspected if baby was gaining weight, then stops suddenly for no apparent reason.

What to do. Increase the frequency of the feedings you give baby. Feed him longer, too. Try to get him to take more at each feeding—don't rush him to eat. Setting up a feeding schedule may help increase his caloric intake. Consultation with a dietitian or breastfeeding (lactation) specialist may provide you with additional strategies. If your baby is not getting enough breast milk from nursing, you may be advised to supplement with formula or pumped breast milk.

Contact your pediatrician. He or she will want to know about a failure to thrive because weight gain is extremely important to baby at this time. In addition to additional or supplemental feedings, baby's doctor may advise you to give baby vitamin or nutritional supplements.

Other treatment. When these measures don't solve the problem, baby may need to be admitted to the hospital for further evaluation. Intravenous (IV) therapy may be needed. More serious causes of failure to thrive may also be considered.

How to Take Baby's Temperature
In some situations, your doctor may advise you to take baby's temperature. This can be a little unnerving if you've never done it before. You can take baby's temperature rectally, axillary (under the armpit) or with an ear thermometer.

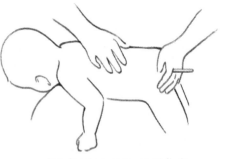

To take a temperature rectally, lay baby on his stomach, across your lap or on a firm surface.

Rectal thermometer. This is probably the most common way of taking a baby's temperature. Rectal thermometers are inexpensive to purchase and easy to use. Follow the suggestions below to make the task easier.

1. Apply a lubricant, such as petroleum jelly, to the tip of the thermometer.
2. Lay baby on his stomach, across your lap or on a firm surface.
3. Hold him steady to prevent sudden movements. Spread his buttocks so you can easily see the anal opening. Gently insert the tip of the thermometer about ½ inch into the

rectum. Hold it in place with your hand to get an accurate reading and to prevent injury.

4. After 2 to 3 minutes, carefully slide out the thermometer and read it.

Axillary thermometer. When you take baby's temperature under his arm, use a rectal thermometer.

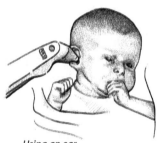

Using an ear thermometer.

1. Make sure your baby's underarm is clean and dry, then place the thermometer in the armpit.
2. Press baby's arm tightly against his side, or hold it across his chest to keep the thermometer in position.
3. After 4 to 5 minutes, remove and read.

Ear thermometer. This type of thermometer is a fairly new addition to a parent's medicine cabinet. See the discussion of ear thermometers on page xviii.

1. Lay your baby on his back on a safe surface, and turn his head away from you.
2. Gently pull back on his ear to straighten the ear canal. Point the thermometer straight into the ear canal.
3. Activate the thermometer while holding the ear canal open.
4. Wait for a beep, and repeat in the other ear. Use the highest number.
5. Because of the difficulty with correct placement in young infant's ears, accuracy may be affected.

What the Temperatures Mean

If taking a baby's temperature is new to you, you may need some interpretation of what various thermometer readings mean. Below is a list of the normal ranges.

- **Rectal temperature–98.2 to 100.4F (36.8 to 38C)**
- **Axillary temperature–95 to 99F (35 to 37.2C)**
- **Ear temperature–97.8 to 99.7F (36.6 to 37.7C)**

Toys and Play This Fourth Week

Choosing Appropriate Toys

When you choose toys for baby, think about his capabilities. Choose those that are safe and appropriate for his age. It's smart to select toys that he'll be able to play with in many different ways as he matures.

It can be tempting to buy toys or games now and in the future that are a little advanced for your child. However, a young child will not enjoy a toy or game that is too difficult.

Make Funny Faces

By this time, your baby may be playing with you. A 4-week-old uses his facial expressions to engage your attention. This is his form of play! You can play with him by holding your face about 12 inches away from his and making funny faces. Or stick out your tongue. He'll enjoy it, and it's a wonderful way to communicate.

> **A 4-week-old uses his facial expressions to engage your attention. This is his form of play!**

Bring your face close to baby's, and slowly move your head from side to side. Make mouth noises. Open and close your eyes in an exaggerated movement. Hold his hands near your eyelashes so he feels the movement. Blow gently on his neck. These silly games help him focus and direct his attention.

Keep Talking to Baby

Your baby can pick up your mood from your voice, so talk to him a lot. You can talk in parentese (see Week 3) and regular speech. You will be helping him begin to understand that communication can express emotion. Read aloud to him, too. Read him books, the paper or anything else you read. Material doesn't matter—it's the sound of your voice he'll enjoy. Talk to him while you stand behind the head of his crib, out of his range of vision. Move into his field of vision as you speak to him, so he makes the connection between your voice and your presence.

Sing nursery rhymes to baby, while you gently clap his hands together. Clap in time with the song you sing. Play music to him when he's awake, but don't leave it on as background noise. You want baby to listen to some sounds, not learn to ignore them.

> **Baby is still sleeping about 15-1/2 hours a day.**

Expose Him to Different Textures

Babies like texture. Let baby experience many different textures by lightly stroking his skin with different types of fabric. Velvet, silk, terry cloth, light wool, corduroy—use any at hand, but try not to tickle him.

Shake a Rattle

Lay baby on the floor on his back. Kneeling behind him, gently shake a rattle about 12 inches above his head until his eyes find it. Move it slowly from side to side while his eyes follow it.

Weekly Milestones at a Glance

Week 5

Physical Development
- actions become more voluntary; reflexes begin to disappear

Senses and Reflexes
- may bat at objects
- more easily calmed by a female voice

Mental Development
- memory for objects continues to grow in length

Social Development
- can quiet self by sucking on fingers or a pacifier
- quiets when held or when she sees faces or hears voices
- prefers to watch a person as compared to an object

Week 6

Physical Development
- can hold head up at 45-degree angle for a few seconds while lying on stomach
- muscle tone improves

Senses and Reflexes
- stares vaguely at surroundings

Mental Development
- studies movement of own hands
- may become excited in anticipation of objects

Social Development
- may smile when you smile
- will stay awake longer if interacting with someone

Week 7

Physical Development
- stays awake for longer periods during the day

Senses and Reflexes
- visually tracks from outer corner of eye past midline of body

Mental Development
- is interested in sounds
- may glance at hand

Social Development
- responds with excitement to a person's presence

Week 8

Physical Development
- head remains fairly erect when he is in the sitting position, but it is still wobbly

Senses and Reflexes
- cycles arms and legs smoothly

Mental Development
- can discriminate among voices, people, tastes and size of objects
- picks out mother's voice from a group of others
- repeats actions for own sake

Social Development
- watches a person alertly and directly

Week 5

Baby weighs 9-1/4 pounds and is 21-1/4 inches long this week.

Baby Care and Equipment

Bathing Baby in a Family Tub

We discussed bathing your baby in Week 3. Some parents enjoy sharing their time in the bathtub with their baby—you might, too. If you bring your baby into the tub with you, take certain precautions to keep her secure. Follow the suggestions below to make family bath time happy, fun and safe.

- Put a rubber mat in the bottom of the tub so you won't slip while you're getting in or out of the tub with baby.
- Have supplies close at hand, such as baby soap and baby shampoo.
- Wear cotton gloves so you can keep a good grip on her.
- Be sure the bathroom is warm but not hot (about 75F/ 23.8C).
- When placing baby in the water, slide her feet-first into the water. If she objects to being in the tub, remove her immediately (the tub may seem too big at this time and make her feel insecure).
- Support baby's head in your arm while you wash her.
- Don't stay in the water too long.
- Keep temperature of your water heater below 120F (48.8C) to prevent accidental scalding.
- Lift baby out of the water first. Wrap her in a towel and lay her on the floor, or give her to your partner before you get out.

Baby Swings

A baby swing can be a wonderful piece of equipment when baby is fussy and you need a rest or a free hand. Some people don't like them because they believe baby is too easily neglected when placed in one. Some refer to swings as "neglect-o-matics." However, others believe swings are heaven-sent.

Features to consider. Be sure any swing you choose has a stable, wide base. With some swings, you place baby in it from the front; other swings are open on the top for ease in getting baby in and out. All swings move in a front-to-back swinging motion. A few also rock her from side to side, in a cradle motion.

To make the swinging mechanism work, you must wind or crank it in some swings. In other swings, the mechanism is battery-operated. Some swings have only one speed, but they can have up to six.

In some swings, the seat that baby sits in reclines in various positions. Some swings are a combination of cradle, swing and infant carrier. These are convenient if you don't want to buy a lot of products, or if you don't have a lot of space in your home. Other features include a timer, a toy bar, music and a washable seat pad.

Baby's Feeding Routine

By the fifth week, your baby is settling into a feeding routine. She's feeding 6 to 8 times a day and taking in 2 to 5 ounces at each feeding. She's probably nursing 5 to 10 minutes on each breast; your milk supply is well established by now. In the next few weeks, you may notice she drops a feeding but increases the amount she takes in at each feeding by about an ounce.

> She's feeding 6 to 8 times a day and taking in 2 to 5 ounces at each feeding.

Ways to determine she's doing well include how many wet diapers she has a day—six is a good sign—and how much she is growing and gaining weight. If your doctor is concerned about her development, he or she will discuss it with you at your next well-baby check.

Milestones This Fifth Week

Baby Enjoys Various Sounds

At about this time, your baby begins to recognize your face and voice. When you talk to her, she may open and close her mouth and bob her head. She is beginning to connect what she hears with what she sees.

> **At about this time, your baby begins to recognize your face and voice.**

She is sensitive to the sound of the human voice. She listens to voices and may respond to the higher-pitched female voice with her own sounds. She may also move her arms and legs. Whenever someone speaks to her, many impulses go through her nerve cells. Repetition of these kinds of interactions help strengthen existing brain connections and build new ones. Baby enjoys many other sounds, too, such as soft music.

Just recently, your baby would stop sucking to listen to a new sound. She still does, briefly, but pays little attention to it unless it's a human voice. She also stops sucking and becomes quiet when studying a person's face. She still doesn't have much of a memory for objects and people, but that is slowly changing.

Milestones This Fifth Week

Changes in Baby You May See Now

Physical Development
- actions become more voluntary; reflexes begin to disappear

Senses and Reflexes
- may bat at objects
- more easily calmed by a female voice

Mental Development
- memory for objects continues to grow in length

Social Development
- can quiet self by sucking on fingers or a pacifier
- quiets when held or when she sees faces or hears voices
- prefers to watch a person as compared to an object

Every baby is an individual, and your baby may do some of these things more quickly or more slowly than another baby. If you are concerned about your baby's progress, discuss it with your healthcare provider. Also see page viii.

Physical Development Continues

When she's in a supported sitting position, your baby can hold her head up briefly. She can also raise her head for a brief moment when she's lying on her tummy. To help her develop and strengthen neck muscles, place her in many different positions throughout the day, such as on her back, on her tummy, in an infant seat, in a stroller, in a front carrier or sling, or in your arms.

> **She's gaining more control of her body.**

As you play with baby, you'll notice she thrusts her legs and arms out and grasps your finger when you put it in her hand. She relaxes her fist to open her hands and fingers. If her hand finds its way to her mouth, she may begin sucking and mouthing her fingers or her fist. It's a way to soothe herself. She's gaining more control of her body.

You may notice her body is uncurling from the fetal position. Her legs are beginning to stretch out a little more. She may arch her back and throw out her arms and legs. She may also stretch her fingers and toes, and twist from side to side.

Vision Continues to Improve

She can now see clearly up to 18 inches, but she doesn't have much control over her muscles, so the best she can do is wave her hand and arm in the direction of what she sees. She may try to push at a hanging toy. She'll even hold a toy in her hand a little longer than she did a week ago.

Note: See also the box on page 67, *Milestones This Week*.

What's Happening This Fifth Week?

Stimulate Baby's Gums

It's never too early to help baby develop strong, healthy gums for the teeth that will soon be breaking through. You can do this by wiping her gums with a clean damp washcloth or a piece of gauze several times during the day and before bedtime. This cleaning stimulates the gums, which keeps them healthy and free of bacteria.

This routine also helps her later. She'll be used to having her mouth cleaned, so when it is time to start brushing her teeth, she won't object.

Baby Cries to Communicate

Crying is baby's only form of verbal communication with you for quite a while. By this time, you are probably beginning to recognize her various cries. Answer her cries as soon as you can. Baby may be overwhelmed by her needs and sensory experiences. Take the following steps to respond to your crying baby.

- Make sure she isn't hungry, wet, cold, hot or hurt.
- Take her in your arms as you sit in a comfortable chair. Look at her face. If her eyes are open, look into them. Hold her calmly; don't bounce her.
- Talk to baby in a quiet voice. Tell her she's safe with you.
- Gently touch her arms and legs to reassure her.
- Hold her until her crying ebbs.

If those measures don't work, try these suggestions.

- Take a shower and place baby in a safe spot in the bathroom with you. The sound of running water may soothe her.
- Put her in the baby swing, crank it up and let her go. Be aware that when the swing stops, you may wake her up if you rewind it.
- A walk might also do the trick, whether in an infant sling or her stroller.
- Massaging can work wonders, so we've included a variety of different massage exercises in discussions these first 6 weeks. See the massage technique described on page 70 to help relieve gas.
- If you cannot console or calm baby, schedule a visit with her pediatrician to rule out a medical problem, such as an ear infection or strep throat.

Responding to your newborn's cry is important.

Responding to cries is important. Responding to her cries immediately during the first 6 months of life doesn't spoil her. It does teach her that you will be there when she needs you. Even at this early age, you are teaching her to trust you. This helps her develop confidence, which in turn makes her more able to learn. She will also be more independent as she grows older.

Baby Massage

Place your hands on one of baby's
arms; put one hand above the other.
Straighten her arm, and gently rotate
your hands back and forth, in opposite
directions, as you move down baby's
arm. Squeeze lightly as you work
toward the wrist. (This is not like the
"Indian burn" you used to give your
brother when you were little!) Do this
with each of baby's arms before going
on to the next move.

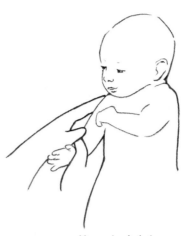

Next, firmly stroke her back,
moving from her neck down to her

Massaging baby's arms.

bottom. Firmly pat her back twice and her bottom once in an
alternating rhythm. Make a game out of it, and sing her a song in
rhythm to your pats.

Massage to relieve gas. If baby has gas, massage her tummy
in circles. Press knees gently into the abdomen to push out the gas.
Repeat the massage and leg presses to relieve gas.

Family Bed

Some parents put baby to bed in her own room from the first day
home from the hospital. Some parents want to keep baby close by,
such as in a bassinet in their room. Other parents want baby in bed
with them—a "family bed" situation.

Advantages. William Sears, M.D., is a pediatrician in favor of
the family bed. In a family bed, parents share their bed with their
baby. Sears believes sharing a bed develops closeness between
the parents and child, and bonding is stronger. There are positive
aspects to it—a breastfeeding mother doesn't have to get up to feed
baby. She can roll over and let baby feed whenever she wants.

What's needed. This situation works only if baby won't disturb
you and you can fall asleep quickly. You must be able to sleep in
any part of the bed, snuggled closely with another person. And you
should have at least a queen-size bed.

Disadvantages. There is a downside to the family bed. Recent
research shows that infants who sleep with their parents may be
at greater risk of suffocating. Evidence suggests that a parent can

inadvertently roll on top of or next to the baby, and smother her. These experts believe the only safe place for a baby is in a crib that meets current federal safety standards.

Alternatives. Manufacturers have recently introduced some new items that might help solve some of the problems discussed above. One item is a minibed that is placed on top of an adult mattress. One side folds down for access to baby and easy nursing. Another product rests next to the bed and is for parents who want baby close but not necessarily in bed with them. The unit is placed next to the adult bed, providing baby with her own space right next to mom and dad. Baby can easily connect to parents in the adult bed for cuddling and nursing.

Dehydration

What it is. Dehydration results when baby doesn't take in enough fluids or loses too much fluid from her body. It can occur if your baby is not breastfeeding properly or if you are not producing enough milk. It may also arise in cases of vomiting and diarrhea. Dehydration occasionally occurs when a baby becomes overheated and does not receive enough fluid to compensate for her overheating. When this occurs, it usually happens in hot summer months.

How to avoid dehydration. To avoid dehydration, keep baby out of the sun so she doesn't get sunburned or overheated. In hot weather, make sure she has plenty of fluids. Give her water only when your pediatrician advises you to. Dress baby appropriately for the weather.

Signs to look for. Dehydration should be a concern if: baby's coloring becomes grayish; her mucous membranes are dry (for example, in her nose); urination has decreased; there is an absence of tearing; her fontanel (the soft spot on the top of her head) is sunken, or she has a rapid pulse and respiration. Your baby should have a wet diaper six to eight times a day, and she should have a normal (for her) number of stools each day. Your baby may also be sluggish if she is dehydrated.

What to do. If you notice these symptoms, and you are breastfeeding, carefully monitor your baby's feeding patterns. Make sure you can see or hear her gulping milk when she feeds. Does she seem satisfied after a nursing session? A full baby will be content.

When to call the doctor. Call your pediatrician immediately if your baby

- hasn't had a wet diaper in 6 to 8 eight hours
- has been vomiting for more than 12 hours
- has passed more than eight diarrheal stools in 8 hours
- has a dry mouth and cries without tears (Note: Newborns may not show tears when they cry.)
- is inconsolable
- seems unusually drowsy or sleepy, or doesn't respond to you
- has a sunken fontanel

Your baby's doctor may recommend oral rehydration in mild to moderate cases. In this situation, baby is given a prepared solution with electrolytes. Small amounts are fed to her frequently over a period of time.

If the situation is severe, a pediatrician may admit the baby to the hospital. Intravenous (IV) fluids are given to replace lost fluids. Accurate measurements of fluid intake and output are also recorded.

Hiccups

What it is. A hiccup is a contraction of baby's diaphragm, which separates the chest and abdominal cavities. It's not uncommon for a baby to have hiccups. Your baby may have had them in the womb. After birth, most babies have frequent episodes of hiccups.

We really don't have any ways to prevent or to stop hiccups. They commonly occur after feeding, particularly after burping. They aren't harmful but may cause baby to fuss or to cry. You won't need to do anything when baby has the hiccups unless they keep her from eating or sleeping. If that happens, call the doctor.

> **No one knows why babies hiccup so frequently.**

Toys and Play This Fifth Week

Nursery Rhymes and Conversations

If you have a recording of nursery rhymes to play for baby, she may enjoy the rhythmic cadence. Or recite some to her from a book. Make a hand puppet out of an old sock, and use it to talk to baby in a high, singsong voice. She'll enjoy the interaction.

Rattles and Rings and Noisy Things

Because she's beginning to develop her grasp, you might choose to let baby play with some safe rattles or rings. They come in all sorts of shapes and sizes. You may offer her rubber or cloth animals or dolls that have squeaks or bells securely fastened inside. Be sure toys don't have small parts, such as eyes, that could come loose.

> Baby may be sleeping for as long as 7 hours a night by this time, if she weighs at least 11 pounds and has no digestive problems.

The Rolling Ball

Choose a brightly colored ball for baby that is big enough for her to see easily. Sit on the floor while she lies next to you, or place her in your lap. Roll the ball on the floor near her. Let her watch it. She may try to reach for it, or she may just enjoy watching it with her eyes.

House Tour

Take baby on a tour of the house while you're holding her. Watch her to see what objects she's attracted to. Point them out, and talk about them as you see them.

When you do routine tasks and chores around the house, keep baby close. Talk about what you're doing; describe your activity. For example, if you're washing the clothes, tell her "This is the washing machine where we wash our clothes." Let her watch you as you put the clothes in and start the machine. Let her watch the water flow in. Describing what you are doing introduces her to household activities, and your conversation stimulates her.

> By this week, you are probably seeing definite signs of baby's personality! She may be quiet and intense, or active and verbal.

Week 6

Baby weighs 9-1/2 pounds and is 21-1/4 inches long this week.

Baby Care and Equipment

Six Good Places to Nurse

If you're like most women, you consider nursing your baby a private interaction between the two of you. However, you may find yourself out and about, with baby screaming at the top of his lungs to be fed *now!* Here are places where you can breastfeed baby with some privacy.

1. **Women's lounge.** This offers some privacy; if someone walks in on you, it's another woman who is probably not offended if you breastfeed your baby.
2. **Women's restroom.** A lounge may not be available, but a restroom usually is. Go into a stall, close the door and nurse your baby.
3. **Fitting room.** If baby's crying is getting on everyone's nerves, including your own, dash into a fitting room for a quick feeding.
4. **Your car.** Park your car in an area that's away from high-traffic areas, and feed baby there.
5. **A local park.** Your park may have picnic tables and benches that are a little removed from the main area. Using your ever-handy baby blanket, drape it over your shoulder and baby's head for added privacy.

6. **In a sling.** When you carry baby in a front sling designed for breastfeeding, it only takes a minute to undo your nursing top and nursing bra. You can feed baby on the go! The head support provided for baby prevents others from seeing that you are breastfeeding.

Keep Baby's Head Covered

A small infant loses a great deal of heat through his head, hands and feet. Before you go out in cool or cold weather, cover baby's head with a cap or warm bonnet. Add a blanket over your carrier for added warmth, if necessary. When you go into a building that is warm, or when the car gets warm, remove the extra cover from baby. He can be just as uncomfortable overheated as he is when he is cold.

Additional Breastfeeding Facts

Feeding is established. By this point in baby's life, your breast-milk supply has come into balance with your baby's demands. You've established a basic routine, and you've discovered what works for you and your baby. You're still feeding him 8 to 10 times in 24 hours, which will continue for the next month or so.

Suddenly, baby is eating more. You may notice that around six weeks of age, your baby wants to feed more often. At about this time many babies go through a growth spurt. Your baby may need to feed more often because he's growing right now. Feed him when he is hungry.

Breastfeeding may help brain development. A recent study of more than a thousand children showed that children who were breastfed as babies scored higher on intelligence tests than children who were bottle-fed. It also revealed that the longer a woman breastfed, the smarter the child was! Why? Breast milk contains over 400 nutrients that infant formula does not. Omega-3 fatty acids, like DHA, found in breast milk may play an important role in how different parts of the brain develop and communicate with each other.

> You're still feeding him 8 to 10 times in 24 hours, which will continue for the next month or so.

Baby may prefer one breast. Your baby may begin to show a preference for one breast over the other about this time. He may even refuse to suck on the other breast. Researchers believe this is an additional effect of the tonic neck reflex, in which turning the baby's head to the side causes him to extend his arm or leg on that side.

Baby's Bowels

Your breastfed baby's bowel movements may become more infrequent. He may poop only once every few days.

Watch for changes. Pay attention to baby's bowel movements. A change can alert you to a problem. If the amount of baby's stool— too much, too little—changes, or the stool differs from your child's normal pattern, you may want to call baby's doctor. If any change in baby's stool is associated with a decrease in appetite or fussiness, contact your pediatrician.

When to contact the doctor. If you notice any blood in the stool, call your doctor or take baby to the emergency room. The most common cause of blood in the stool is an anal fissure (see the discussion in Week 11), which is a tiny cut or tear in the anal opening.

Accidentproof Your Baby Carrier

Nearly 13,000 babies a year are hurt in carrier-seat accidents. Whether you use a car seat or an infant carrier to cart baby around, take precautions to make baby safer. Choose a carrier with a handle that locks securely in place. It should have a seat belt with a crotch-strap restraint. The base must be wide, for stability, and it should have rubber tips or other nonskid material to keep it from sliding.

Precautions you can take when using an infant carrier include the following safety measures.

- Always use the safety restraint. Be sure it holds baby securely.
- Keep baby's hands out of the way when you adjust the handles—you don't want to pinch his fingers.
- Never place the carrier on a counter, table or piece of furniture unless you are holding it. Place it on the floor, away from sharp edges and corners.
- When you carry it, keep one hand on the carrier handle and the other hand under the base.
- Don't leave baby alone in a carrier, even if it is placed safely on the floor.

- Be careful when carrying baby in a carrier—avoid making sharp turns and bumping baby.
- Don't use the carrier when baby is too big or when he begins to squirm and wiggle. He could cause it to fall over.
- If the seat is also a car safety seat, be sure it is correctly installed every time you put it in the car.

Baby Massage—The Back

Place baby on his stomach on the floor or on the bed. Gently turn his head to his right side. Place your right hand on his bottom. With your left hand, move your hand down, in one sweeping motion, from the top of his back to your right hand. Repeat as you cover his entire back.

Is Baby Still Colicky?

Good news—if your baby has been colicky, it often peaks at about this time (6 weeks). It may continue until 10 weeks, but it usually begins to fade gradually this week and will be over soon.

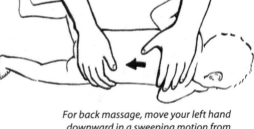

For back massage, move your left hand downward in a sweeping motion from the top of baby's back to your right hand.

Bottle-feeding Preferences

Soon after birth, your bottle-fed baby was able to discriminate between sugar water and milk. By this week, he is able to express his distaste for what he is drinking. If he doesn't like what he's drinking, he will turn his head away from the bottle and may refuse to drink.

Milestones This Sixth Week

Greater Neck and Muscle Control

Baby is gaining more control over his neck muscles. You may notice he shifts his head more often now for a new view of what's around him. He can hold his head up for a few seconds and may extend his legs when he holds his head up.

Is He Really Smiling?

Yes, baby may be smiling on his own! His first smiles were probably not ones of joy or recognition, but by now they are more social in nature. He has been making facial expressions that look like a smile since birth. When you started responding by smiling back at him, you were teaching him one way to interact. Researchers believe one reason that many of baby's facial expressions are smiles is to encourage attachment between parent and child. Baby makes a grimace that looks like a smile. Parent reacts by smiling and cooing at baby. This reinforces in baby that his actions caused a reaction, and he will continue. Soon his smiles will be social, and he'll smile at you (or anyone else) because of the wonderful interaction it brings.

He Expresses Excitement

You may notice that baby becomes excited in anticipation of regular activities, such as bath time or play time. He may demonstrate this by chortling, cooing or making other noises, while he kicks with his legs.

Vision and Hearing Changes

He is more visually alert now when he is in a sitting position. He's beginning to associate lying down with sleeping. Keep him upright, in a semisitting position, for part of his waking hours. He'll enjoy seeing what's going on around him.

Loud noises may startle him. He may also look surprised when he hears a sudden loud noise.

Note: See also the box below, *Milestones This Week.*

Milestones This Sixth Week

Changes in Baby You May See Now

Physical Development
- can hold head up at 45-degree angle for a few seconds while lying on stomach
- muscle tone improves

Senses and Reflexes
- stares vguely at surroundings

Mental Development
- studies movement of his own hands
- may become excited in anticipation of objects

Social Development
- may smile when you smile
- will stay awake longer if interacting with someone

Every baby is an individual, and your baby may do some of these things more quickly or more slowly than another baby. If you are concerned about your baby's progress, discuss it with your healthcare provider. Also see page viii.

What's Happening This Sixth Week?

Introducing the Bottle to a Breastfed Baby

If you find it necessary to feed your breastfed baby from a bottle, keep in mind the following as you help him learn this new skill. It may take time and repeated effort on your part, but you can help baby by using the techniques described below.

- Don't offer a bottle until breastfeeding is well established. Wait as long as you can, at least until 4 weeks, before offering baby a bottle. Introducing one too soon can interfere with your milk supply.
- Let someone else give the baby a bottle. He associates breastfeeding and breast milk with you.
- Offer the first bottle when he's not hungry. If you wait until he's starving, he may be too distressed to eat. If you feed him a bottle when he's only a little hungry, he'll be able to deal with it better.
- Introduce the bottle slowly. Drop a little milk on his lips from the bottle, then wait until he opens his mouth before you put the bottle in.
- Your baby may take to the bottle better if you hold him in a different position than when you nurse him. When bottle-feeding, sit baby in a more upright position.
- Don't lose your cool—be patient. You may need to try feeding by bottle more than once before baby takes to it. If he gets frustrated, angry or upset, take a break and try again later.

Baby Hair Facts

If your baby was born with blond or red hair, he probably had very little of it. With blond and redheaded babies, hair goes into a resting phase and is shed *before* birth. If he had any hair, he'll probably lose it very quickly, and most of it may be gone by this week.

If your baby was born with dark hair, this shedding phase happens later. Your baby will probably have his hair for a while longer, but be aware that he'll shed it before long.

Use What Works to Calm Baby

Experts recommend that for the first 8 weeks of his life, do whatever helps calm and lull your child to encourage good sleep habits in him. Walk him, rock him, sing to him or play "white noise" in the background. Try many different things, and use what works best with your baby.

Babywearing May Make Baby Smarter

Babies who are carried in front slings or carriers appear to cry less. (For more information, see the discussion of front slings in Week 4.) Instead of fussing and crying, researchers believe the babies spend more time in a state of quiet alertness. During this state, an infant is content and receptive to his environment. He may be more ready to learn during these times.

> **Keep baby safe from germs by avoiding crowded areas. Ask people to look but not touch. If family members or friends have a cold, ask them to wash their hands before they hold baby.**

Dermatitis

What it is. *Dermatitis* is a term used to describe several skin conditions. Symptoms of dermatitis include irritation of the skin with itching, mild swelling, redness, oozing with crusting, scaling or thickening of the skin with a shiny surface.

What to do. If your baby has any of these symptoms, try the following measures. Lubricate the affected area with dye-free, perfume-free creams or lotion. Apply cool, wet dressings to relieve itching. Avoid irritants to baby's skin. Don't use soaps or harsh shampoos. Use lukewarm water, not hot water, for bathing. Keep baths short to avoid removing natural oils from skin. Dress baby in light, smooth, soft, loose clothing. Over-the-counter medications may be used to relieve symptoms; check with your pediatrician before using them.

When to call a doctor. Call your pediatrician if the rash is persistent and causes your baby discomfort. Call the doctor immediately if signs of infection appear, such as redness, swelling, the area becomes hot to the touch, or if the baby acts ill.

Your doctor may prescribe a topical steroid preparation and other medications to reduce itching. If a secondary infection

When Baby Has a Fever

A fever may be a sign that the immune system is at work. When your baby has a fever, he may be fighting an infection. Fever is defined as a rectal temperature greater that 101F (38.3C). See the discussion of how to take baby's temperature in Week 4.

You can try some treatments at home to help reduce baby's fever. The following measures are often used with babies.

- Encourage baby's fluid intake.
- Let him rest.
- Don't dress him too warmly.
- Give him acetaminophen, if he seems uncomfortable. Do not exceed the recommended dosage. Follow directions and measurements carefully.
- Pay special attention to other symptoms your baby may have.

When to call the doctor. It's hard not to panic a little when baby has a fever. You are concerned; you want to know what's causing it. If your baby is only 1 or 2 weeks old, call your pediatrician immediately. He or she is likely to want to see baby. Call your doctor at any time if baby

- is less than 3 months old, with a temperature higher than 101F (38.3C)
- has a fever of 104F (40C) and acts ill
- cries inconsolably; cannot be settled
- is lethargic or difficult to wake
- has breathing difficulties
- seems to have abdominal pain
- has a sore throat or difficulty swallowing
- looks or acts very ill
- shows no signs of improvement after you give him acetaminophen
- has had a fever more than 72 hours
- was better, but the fever returned
- seems to have ear pain
- has difficulty or pain when urinating
- has a febrile seizure (seizure accompanied by fever)

Your doctor may prescribe various treatments to deal with a fever. He or she may recommend

- alternate ibuprofen with acetaminophen
- antibiotics for an infection causing fever, if it is easily identified
- hospitalization for further testing, fluid hydration and intravenous (IV) antibiotics

develops, antibiotics may also be given. In stubborn or severe cases, baby may be referred to a dermatologist.

Toys and Play This Sixth Week

Let Baby Enjoy Many Sounds

Lots of babies enjoy toys that play or make various sounds. You may be using a player to play CDs or cassettes of lullabies. Baby

Some toys that play music or sounds have timers that turn off automatically after a certain period.

enjoys other sounds, too, such as water sounds or the sound of waves. You may find cassette tapes and CDs of these sounds. Some toy manufacturers now make toys that play many different sounds, such as white noise, rain, ocean waves, wind chimes and the tick-tock of a clock.

The Reaching Game

Play this game with baby to encourage him to begin using his arms. When you hold a toy near him, he may arch his neck and crane his head to see it in his field of vision. Move it a little closer, and place it near his hands. Does he reach for it? If not, place one of his hands on the toy. See if he will hold it for a second or two. If he doesn't hold it, try again, but don't force him.

> Your kitchen sink may be just the right size and height for baby's bath. It's small enough to make him feel secure, and it's the right height so your back won't be strained!

Gentle Pulling Up Can Be Fun

While baby is lying on his back, grasp his hands and gently pull forward just a little. He will probably flex his neck and lift his head slightly. This encourages him to lift his head and to hold it steady. Make a game of it by singing some rhythmic song as you pull him forward. Be sure you don't pull him up too hard or too fast.

Week 7

Baby weighs 9-3/4 pounds and is 21-1/2 inches long this week.

Baby Care and Equipment

Diaper Rash

Nearly every baby experiences some form of diaper rash. Your baby may be encountering it already. Fortunately, diaper rash is not a serious problem. The best way to prevent it is to change baby's diapers as soon as she is wet to keep her skin dry. See the discussion about treating diaper rash on page 91.

The most common cause of diaper rash in babies older than 6 months is the ammonia, which forms when bacteria from feces reacts with baby's urine. Ammonia can be trapped in a diaper against baby's delicate skin. You'll be able to smell the ammonia.

Avoiding Burns

One of the worst feelings you can experience as a parent is to know you have hurt or allowed your child to be hurt accidentally, whether by sticking her with a diaper pin or tugging her hair too much when combing it. More serious accidents, such as burning or scalding, fortunately can be avoided in most cases if you think ahead. Here are important ways you can help protect your child from burns.

- Never carry baby and a hot beverage at the same time. If baby jerks or squirms, you might accidentally bump her with the mug and spill some of its contents on her.

- Never cook with baby in your arms. Reaching for back burners or frying foods exposes her to unnecessary risks.
- Place her crib well away from a radiator or heater.

Think ahead. With a little forethought and planning, you can reduce or eliminate some of the hazards that are common around every house. It's a smart idea to take some safety precautions well before you expect baby to start creeping and crawling. Start by covering electrical cords and putting appliance cords out of reach now.

Know Basic First Aid

Every parent should have five basic first-aid skills. Bear in mind that treatment can be somewhat different when an infant is involved. You should know how to

- **administer CPR**
- **give the Heimlich maneuver**
- **deal with poisoning**
- **control bleeding**
- **treat burns**

Contact your local hospital or the Red Cross for information on first-aid classes.

Diaper Bag Essentials

It's always best to be prepared when you take baby out, even if you're just running to the store for a bottle of milk. Take your diaper bag along; you'll probably need it if you leave it behind.

Stock up. Make sure the diaper bag is well stocked with clean diapers, baby wipes, a changing pad, extra clothes, a light blanket and a pacifier, if baby uses one. If you bottle-feed, include formula and bottles for longer outings. You don't have to worry about these if you breastfeed.

When Baby Is Restless

By this age, your baby is crying less and interacting more. However, she'll still have periods of fussiness. Because she's a little older, you might want to try some new tips to help calm her.

- Let her look around her environment to help calm her. Put her someplace safe where she can gaze about, such as near a window so she can see outside.

> It's normal for your baby to have flat feet at this time. It takes a few years for the arch to become prominent.

- While holding her, do vertical knee bends to provide a rhythmic motion. (If you do them correctly, they're good for you, too.)
- Try having an older sibling or your partner distract baby with songs or stories, or just by talking to her. Sometimes interacting with a different person can distract her.
- Massage her using the techniques already described and those listed below.
- Some devices offer distraction, such as a battery-operated vibrating infant seat or a crib-rocking device.

As you get to know your baby better, you'll discover what helps calm her. One baby may prefer a technique that another baby does not like!

Baby Massage

Legs. Place baby on her back on the floor or the bed. Put your right hand around baby's ankle and your left hand around her thigh. Slide your left hand down to her ankle as you gently squeeze her leg. Then move your right hand up to the thigh. Repeat. When you finish, press the bottom of baby's foot gently with your thumb. Trace a line from the heel to the toe.

Massage if baby's tummy is upset. If baby has an upset tummy, try the following massage technique. Gently stroke her tummy from top to bottom. Use the outer edges of one hand, then the other. Push her knees to her tummy, and hold for a count of 8. Massage her tummy in clockwise

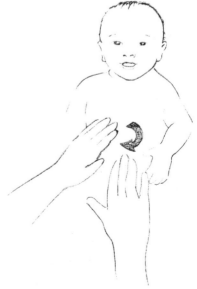

Gently massage baby's tummy from top to bottom using the outer edge of one hand, then the other.

circles, one hand following the other. Walk your fingers across her tummy from one side to the other. Repeat as needed.

Milestones This Seventh Week

Her Senses Are Developing
Your baby's senses are becoming more coordinated around this time. You may notice that she looks toward an interesting sound— she's coordinating sight and sound! She may begin to suck vigorously when she sees a bottle or your breast.

> **She prefers to watch moving objects.**

Baby's eyes can easily track a moving object now, beginning from side to side and progressing to up and down. Her focus is adjusting, too. She prefers to watch moving objects. She may be distracted when she's feeding if she watches what's going on around her.

She may let you know what she likes to look at, such as bright colors instead of drab ones. She also prefers three-dimensional objects to two-dimensional ones. She's becoming more sophisticated in what she likes to look at.

Baby loves brightly colored mobiles.

Baby Begins to Use Her Hands
She is noticing her hands. She may open and close them, bring them together, wave them around and move her fingers. She may hold a toy for a short time if you put it in her hand. She'll reach toward a toy held in front of her with both hands. She'll even bat at something hanging near her.

She Uses Her Mouth to Explore
You may notice that your baby is using her mouth to explore her environment each day. She'll put many things in her mouth, including hands (hers and yours), toys, a blanket and anything else she can get there. She doesn't want to eat the things she puts in

her mouth; it's her way of exploring. She's using her senses—touch, smell and taste—to get information about her world.

Her Strength Is Increasing
She can raise herself onto her forearms and holds her head more steadily. She can lift her chest off the surface she's lying on and turn her head from side to side. This gives baby a much better view of what's going on around her.

She May Need to Suck
Sucking is still very satisfying to her, especially now that she can find her mouth a little more easily. Some babies have an extremely strong desire to suck. Don't worry if your baby has this need. It may continue for a number of months yet.

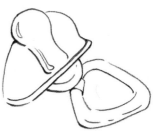

Thumb or pacifier? There is controversy about the thumb versus the pacifier for sucking. Some say a pacifier looks like the parent has "put a plug" in their baby. The thumb is better. Others say the pacifier has the advantage of being permanently removable after a certain age and it's better for baby's teeth when they come in. Whatever your preference, realize your baby may need something to suck on!

At 7 weeks old, baby needs something to suck on.

She Responds to Sounds
Baby may be more vocal; she listens to many sounds. She may quiet and stop sucking to listen closely to a sound. She may vocalize more in response to what she hears. She still prefers the human voice.

When She's Tired
When baby's tired or bored with interacting with you, she'll turn away from eye-to-eye contact. This is your clue to give her some quiet time.

Note: See also the box on page 90, *Milestones This Week.*

Feeding Your Baby

Feeding your baby is one of the most important things you do as a parent. With your newborn, you must decide whether to breastfeed or to bottle-feed her. See the discussion in Week 2 of breastfeeding and the discussion in Week 3 of bottle-feeding. As baby gets older, you will begin adding solid food to her diet.

Baby's Feeding Routine, 0—4 Months

In the first few months of your baby's life, she settles into a feeding schedule. She feeds about 6 to 8 times a day and takes in about 2 to 5 ounces at each feeding. If she's nursing, she spends about 5 to 10 minutes on each breast. As she gets older, she may drop a feeding but increase the amount she takes in at each feeding by about an ounce.

By the time your baby is 4 months old, she's taking in between 25 and 40 ounces a day of formula or breast milk. Around this time, she may be ready to start solid foods. Discuss with your pediatrician, before you make any changes, when and how to introduce solid foods to your baby. In this discussion, you will also cover the amounts of and kinds of solid foods to offer your baby.

What Is Solid Food?

You may be confused about solid foods. When baby starts solids, is he ready for hot dogs and bran cereal? Does it mean she'll be eating "grown-up" food?

When applied to baby's diet, the term "solids" or "solid foods" means any food that is not breast milk or formula. Even though you will introduce her to many different

Solids for Baby's First Year

Solid food for baby's first year is actually a progression from watered-down cereal to table food you eat. Even very thin cereal is considered a "solid food." Below is a guide to the kinds of foods baby will be eating at various times during her first year. Remember—baby will continue to receive most of her calories and nutrition from breast milk or formula until she is 1 year old.

- **4 to 5 months**—infant's rice cereal, very thin, made with breast milk or formula
- **4 to 6 months**—infant's rice cereal, thicker, made with breast milk or formula
- **5 to 6 months**—in addition to infant's rice cereal or barley cereal made with breast milk or formula, pureed foods, such as meat, fruit and vegetables
- **7 to 8 months**—in addition to oatmeal or infant's rice, barley or wheat cereal made with breast milk or formula, strained foods, such as meat, fruit and vegetables
- **9 to 10 months**—infant cereal and lumpy or mashed foods, such as meat, fruit and vegetables
- **10 to 11 months**—infant cereal and junior commercial baby foods
- **12 months**—bite-sized table ("people") food

types of solid food during this first year, they do not supply her with the nutrients and calories she needs. She will continue to get that from the breast milk or formula you give her. You offer her solid food to help her learn how to move food around in her mouth with her tongue and to learn how to swallow it. You also expose her to different food textures.

Is She Ready for Solid Food?

Some babies are ready to start solids before other babies of the same age. Before a baby can begin eating solids, she must be able to control her neck muscles, sit with support, show when she is full and indicate her wants by reaching or leaning toward something. She also needs to be able to move her tongue back and forth. Most babies can't do these things until they are between 4 and 6 months old.

Feeding Your Baby

The amount of food your baby eats changes during her first year. You will probably begin with two feedings each day of thin cereal made with breast milk or formula. Each feeding may be as small as 2 teaspoons or as large as 2 tablespoons. As she grows older, you will add more variety to her diet. Below is an overview of baby's first year of feeding.

Baby's Age	Amount, type of food	Number of feedings/day
Newborn to 1 month	2 to 5 ounces breast milk or formula	6-8
1 to 2 months	3 to 6 ounces breast milk or formula	5-7
2 to 3 months	4 to 7 ounces breast milk or formula	4-7
3 to 4 months	6 to 8 ounces breast milk or formula	4-6
4 to 6 months	6 to 8 ounces breast milk or formula	4-6
	very thin baby rice cereal: 1 to 3 tablespoons	2
6 to 8 months	6 to 8 ounces breast milk or formula	3-5
	baby rice or barley cereal: 2 to 4 tablespoons	2
	fruit: 2 to 3 tablespoons	2
	fruit juice: 3 ounces diluted with 3 ounces water	1
	vegetables: 2 to 3 tablespoons	2
8 to 12 months	6 to 8 ounces breast milk or formula	3-4
	baby rice, barley or wheat cereal: 2 to 4 tablespoons	2-3
	bread or crackers: ½ slice; 2 crackers	1
	fruit juice: 3 ounces diluted with 3 ounces water	1
	vegetables: 3 to 4 tablespoons	2-3
	meat, egg yolk or cooked dried beans: 3 to 4 tablespoons	2

Milestones This Seventh Week

Changes in Baby You May See Now

Physical Development

• stays awake for longer periods during the day

Senses and Reflexes

• visually tracks from outer corner of eye past midline of body

Mental Development

• is interested in sounds
• may glance at hand

Social Development

• responds with excitement to a person's presence

Every baby is an individual, and your baby may do some of these things more quickly or more slowly than another baby. If you are concerned about your baby's progress, discuss it with your healthcare provider. Also see page viii.

What's Happening This Seventh Week?

Establishing Bedtime Routines

About this time, your baby's physical development stabilizes somewhat, and she'll begin sleeping better. Now is a good time to introduce a bedtime routine or ritual. She'll learn it's time to settle down and go to sleep when you begin your routine each night.

Now is a good time to introduce a bedtime routine or ritual.

What is a routine? A routine can include bathing her, dressing her for sleep, feeding her, singing to her or saying her prayers. Place her in her crib while she's still awake. Offer her something to help her settle, such as a pacifier or her thumb. Keep the crib free of anything that isn't necessary. Don't give her a blanket or a stuffed toy in the crib. See the discussion of SIDS in Week 8.

Should I Give My Baby Water?

Often parents ask about giving baby water as she gets older. Your baby still doesn't need this extra fluid. Breast milk and formula contain enough water for her at this age. Too much water can dilute a baby's blood, which could cause sodium levels and electrolytes to fall, sometimes dangerously. In severe cases, overhydrating with water has caused seizures and coma in an infant.

Until baby begins solids, don't give her extra water. Be sure you mix formula exactly as directed. After she begins eating solids, 1 or 2 ounces of water each day is OK.

Baby's Sweat Glands

Your baby's sweat glands aren't very active this early in her life. That's why you may notice she doesn't sweat, even when it's hot! A baby doesn't usually begin perspiring until about 2 months old. You'll also note that the oil glands in her skin don't produce as much oil as an adult's skin.

Diaper Rash

What it is. Diaper rash is common for babies, but that doesn't make it any less distressing. When it occurs, skin in the diaper area is irritated and bright red. It often resembles a sunburn when it begins.

What to do. To treat baby's diaper rash, thoroughly clean the irritated area with mild soap and warm water when you change her. Rub as little as possible. Avoid baby wipes because they might contain alcohol. Then let her "air dry" for a while. Exposing her skin to air helps. Apply a soothing ointment, such as petroleum jelly or zinc oxide, to the area to protect skin from further irritation. Change her as soon as she is wet again.

> ## Diaper Rash or Yeast Infection?
>
> **If you think baby has a diaper rash but the redness appears in the skin creases and has lasted more than 3 days, with no improvement, it may be a yeast infection. Your pediatrician may prescribe an antifungal cream to treat the problem.**

Diaper options. The type of diaper you choose when baby has diaper rash may help her feel better. (The diapers discussed next are all disposable diapers.) Some diapers contain aloe to soothe and to protect baby's skin. Some contain baking soda to deal with the ammonia odor associated with diaper rash. Some diapers contain an antibacterial application. Others are superabsorbent to keep urine away from baby's skin. Another type has a hypoallergenic solution that protects baby's skin against irritants.

When to call the doctor. Diaper rash needs medical attention if your measures don't deal with the problem in a few days. Baby's doctor may prescribe a mild hydrocortisone cream. If the rash persists, your baby may be referred to a dermatologist. To help prevent diaper rash, change your baby's diapers frequently to prevent irritation.

Hernia

What it is. Some babies develop a hernia; it is most common in baby boys. The main symptom of a hernia is a bulging on either side of the groin. This may include pain or bloating of the abdomen.

What to do. There is nothing you can do to treat the problem. If you believe your baby has a hernia, contact your pediatrician. Surgery is usually recommended to correct it.

Toys and Play This Seventh Week

Continue with many of the games and play you've been engaging in with baby. She still enjoys many of the games you play together.

Talk, Talk, Talk!

Encourage your child's language development by talking to baby as often as possible. Describe what you're doing as you feed her, bathe her, change her or put her to bed. Show her different articles of clothing, and tell her what they are. Take her on a walk outside, and describe the flowers, plants and trees. Go to a park, and point out the play equipment there. You may feel silly as you carry on this one-sided conversation, but it actually helps baby in learning to speak later.

Week 8

Baby weighs 10-1/4 pounds and is 21-3/4 inches long this week.

Baby Care and Equipment

Baby Massage—Relaxation

This massage technique helps baby relax, and it can also help relieve any gas he may have. You might even feel the gas bubbles releasing under your fingers as you massage baby's chest and tummy.

Place baby on his back on the floor or on the bed. Use your fingertips to walk across his tummy lightly from right to left. Next, massage baby's chest by placing your hands in the center of his chest. Moving your hands in a heart-shaped motion, move hands out to the side at the same time, down the side of his chest. Move down the rib cage, then back to the starting position. Repeat 8 to 10 times.

Move your hands in a heart-shaped motion outward on baby's chest.

Are Plastic Baby Bottles Safe?

Recent news stories have suggested that clear plastic baby bottles might be unsafe because they contain the chemical substance BPA (bisphenol-A). It was implied that heating a baby bottle could cause BPA to leach into formula or breast milk.

The Federal Drug Administration (FDA) maintains these bottles are safe. They have found no problems with baby-bottle usage and no risk from other food containers that contain BPA.

If you want to make sure your bottles are OK to use, don't heat them in the microwave. Instead, heat formula or breast milk on the stove, then put it in a bottle. Using soft plastic liners made of opaque, colored plastic is also safe.

Facts about SIDS

In the United States, sudden infant death syndrome (SIDS) strikes about 3,000 babies a year. It most often occurs in children under 1 year of age. There are few warning signs, and its cause is unknown.

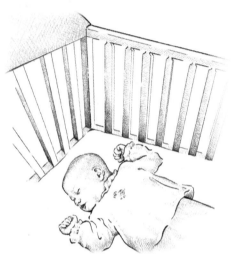

Sleep position is important. A few years ago, the American Academy of Pediatrics began advising parents to place a baby on his back or his side to sleep. This advisory was based on foreign studies that showed

Remember—"back" to sleep is best!

babies who slept on their stomachs were at higher risk of SIDS. Since this sleep position has been used, some researchers claim a 50% reduction in the rate of SIDS. Be aware that when a baby sleeps on his side or back consistently, his head may become flattened as a result. This isn't a serious problem, but discuss it with your pediatrician if you notice it.

Keep crib free of clutter. Other factors are believed to contribute to the occurrence of SIDS. Recently, parents have been advised to remove everything from baby's crib except a fitted crib sheet and baby himself. Keep baby's crib free of bumper pads, toys, blankets, sheepskin pads, pillows and comforters. Make sure his mattress is firm and flat—don't use a waterbed mattress! If baby needs added warmth, dress him in warm sleep clothes, such as a blanket sleeper. Researchers believe this practice could reduce the rate of SIDS by an additional 30%!

Other safety recommendations. Further recommendations to reduce the risk of SIDS include the following.

- Don't smoke around baby! We know that second-hand smoke contributes to the problem.
- Keep baby off of soft surfaces, such as couches, waterbeds,

> ## 2-Month Checkup
>
> **Make your baby's 2-month well-baby checkup appointment now. See page 97 for any immunizations he may receive at this next visit.**

bean-bag chairs, adult beds, quilts and comforters. Some of these surfaces may trap carbon dioxide and suffocate him.
- Breastfeed baby. We aren't sure why this protects him, but it appears breastfeeding offers added protection against SIDS.
- Don't keep your house or baby's room too warm. Keep your house at a temperature that is comfortable to you. Babies who become overheated are at higher risk of SIDS.
- If your baby sleeps with you, keep him near but not too close to reduce the possibility of suffocation.
- If you are concerned, discuss the situation with baby's doctor. With certain medical conditions, such as symptomatic gastroesophageal reflux, it may be better for baby to sleep on his tummy.

Alternative sleep position. If baby has a difficult time sleeping on his back, place him on his side, with his lower arm brought forward. This keeps him from rolling onto his stomach. You might also use a special cushion designed to keep baby on his side. Many stores sell these cushions.

If your baby sleeps on his side, he might develop a flattening of the side of his head. It's not a serious problem, but it's not attractive either. Place him on his other side if the problem occurs, or turn his crib around so he turns his head to the other side to see what's going on around him.

Milestones This Eighth Week

Baby's Memory Is Growing
You may not realize it, but your baby is storing memories already, which enables him to associate certain events with particular consequences. He begins to anticipate certain events when given a particular clue. For example, he may show excitement at the sight of a bottle because he associates it with being fed.

Well-Baby Checkups

During this first year of baby's life, you'll probably see your pediatrician a lot. It's not uncommon for a baby to have ear infections, colds, diarrhea and other ailments that require medical care. In addition to seeing baby's doctor for illnesses, you'll also visit the office for well-baby checkups.

According to the American Academy of Pediatrics (AAP), your pediatrician should see your baby about eight times during his first year. Checkups are done within 24 hours after birth in the hospital, a few days after discharge if you were in the hospital less than 24 hours, at 2 weeks, 4 weeks (1 month), 8 weeks (2 months), 16 weeks (4 months), 24 weeks (6 months), 36 weeks (9 months) and 52 weeks (1 year).

What Happens at Well-Baby Checkups?

When you take baby in for his well-baby checkups, he will receive his scheduled immunizations. (See the chart next page.) His weight, height and head circumference will be measured at each visit. His progress will be noted on a weight-and-height chart. Your baby's doctor will also check him out from head to toe. At each appointment, your pediatrician will check the following.

Head check. Your pediatrician will examine the fontanel to see how it is closing. He or she will measure baby's head and record it on his growth chart.

Eye check. Baby's eyes are examined to see how his pupils dilate. The doctor will look for any vision problems and check his vision and eye movement by moving a light in his visual field.

Mouth check. An examination of his mouth will reveal any problems, such as infections. Signs of teething will also be noted.

Nose check. Looking into his nostrils will reveal signs of infections. Doctor also examines nasal passages for signs of abnormal development that could interfere with breathing.

Ear check. Your pediatrician may do some things to test baby's hearing. He or she will also look for signs of ear infection. If there's any wax buildup, your doctor will note it, as well as fluid behind the eardrum.

Abdomen check. Feeling baby's abdominal area reveals any abnormal growths or enlarged organs. Your doctor may ask questions about your baby's feeding routine and any problems he may be experiencing. His bowel habits will also be discussed.

Chest check. Examining baby's heart and lungs is important. The doctor will evaluate the heart for abnormal sounds or rhythms. He or she will examine your baby's lungs and listen for signs of infection or breathing difficulties.

Legs, hips and feet check. The

doctor rotates baby's legs to check for a dislocated hip. Legs and feet are examined for proper growth and development. When your baby starts walking, your doctor will check for proper leg-and-feet alignment and for any walking difficulties.

Genital check. Your pediatrician will check baby's genitals to make sure there are no unusual symptoms or signs of infections. With a baby boy, the doctor will check that a circumcised penis has healed properly. If a boy is uncircumcised, the doctor will make sure the penis is being cleaned properly. He or she will also check the testicles.

Baby's development check. Your doctor will ask questions about your baby's development. These questions will cover physical, mental and emotional development. Your observations of baby's development are important in this assessment.

Diet and sleep check. Your pediatrician will ask you questions about how your baby is eating and sleeping. As baby gets older, his diet will change as you offer him solid foods. Sleep problems may appear then disappear throughout this first year.

Baby's Immunization Schedule

During the first five years of baby's life, he will receive various immunizations to protect him against many illnesses. Your pediatrician will give him these injections, or you may take your child to a community health center or local public-health clinic for them. It's important for your baby to receive these immunizations for his protection and for the protection of all the other children he'll be around.

Birth
- **Hepatitis B—first shot**
- **Vitamin K—only one shot**

2 months
- **DTaP: diphtheria, tetanus and pertussis—first shot**
- **Polio—first shot**
- **Hib: influenza, type b—first shot**
- **Hepatitis B—second shot**

4 months
- **DTaP: diphtheria, tetanus and pertussis—second shot**
- **Polio—second shot**
- **Hib: influenza, type b—second shot**

6 months
- **DTaP: diphtheria, tetanus and pertussis—third shot**
- **Polio—third shot**
- **Hib: influenza, type b—third shot**

12 months
- **Varicella: chicken pox—first shot**
- **MMR: measles, mumps, rubella—first shot**
- **Hib: influenza, type b—fourth shot**

15 months
- **Hepatitis B—third shot**
- **DTaP: diphtheria, tetanus and pertussis—fourth shot**

4 years
- **MMR: measles, mumps, rubella—second shot**
- **Polio—fourth shot**

5 years
- **DTaP: diphtheria, tetanus and pertussis—fifth shot**

Milestones This Eighth Week

Changes in Baby You May See Now

Physical Development

- head remains fairly erect when baby is in the sitting position, but it is still wobbly

Senses and Reflexes

- cycles arms and legs smoothly

Mental Development

- can discriminate among voices, people, tastes and size of objects
- picks out mother's voice from a group of others
- repeats actions for own sake

Social Development

- watches a person alertly and directly

Every baby is an individual, and your baby may do some of these things more quickly or more slowly than another baby. If you are concerned about your baby's progress, discuss it with your healthcare provider. Also see page viii.

He's Smiling More Now

By this week, he's smiling when you smile at him. He may even smile on his own! He's making many different noises now, such as gurgling, grunting and humming, to express his feelings. He may try to imitate your exaggerated facial expressions, and he'll probably enjoy looking at himself in the mirror.

His Physical Control Increases

Lifts his head somewhat. His physical abilities are increasing, too. He can lift his head up 45 degrees when he's hungry. When you hold him in a sitting position, he can keep his head up most of the time. His eyes can focus up to 10 feet away, and they will follow you when you move away from him. Bright colors are still favorites. He may turn his head and look toward a sound that interests him.

Increasing activity! His increased physical control spurs him to constant activity. When he's on his back, he may make bicycling motions with his legs. In a sitting position, he may circle his arms above his head. When he's on his tummy, he may rock back and forth with his arms and legs stretched out and his back arched.

He's Fascinated by His Hands

Now that he has discovered his hands, he may examine them closely. He'll bring them to his face and touch his nose, eyes and mouth. If he puts something in his mouth, such as a toy, he'll suck on it and his fingers! He experiences the double sensation in his fingers and his mouth. Sucking helps him realize that his fingers are a part of him and the toy isn't. He's beginning to distinguish between what is part of his body and what is separate.

Note: See also the box on page 98, *Milestones This Week.*

What's Happening This Eighth Week?

Traveling with Baby

Because baby is getting a little older, you may be planning to take him to meet his grandparents or other relatives. Our discussion here provides general advice to follow when getting ready to go. We cover travel by car and by plane in later weeks.

As we and almost every other parent we know has discovered, when you travel with baby, you're going to need a lot more stuff than you would normally. It might seem like a lot to cart around (and it is), but we know from experience that if you don't pack it, you'll undoubtedly need it!

Diaper-bag essentials. As you pack, think about what you'll need short-term (have at hand in your diaper bag) and long term (in the suitcase). For the diaper bag, consider the following:

- two changes of baby clothes, including extra socks
- plenty of disposable diapers, at least 8 or 10
- a few cloth diapers to use as bibs and burp cloths (they also can be used as diapers in an emergency)
- one resealable plastic bag containing a damp washcloth
- baby wipes
- something for baby to eat, already prepared, such as premixed formula
- a couple of large plastic bags for soiled things
- 4 or 5 medium-sized resealable bags
- 2 or 3 bottles
- toys for baby—include his favorites
- several pacifiers—more than a couple, in case you lose one or two
- an object that comforts baby, such as a blanket or stuffed toy
- a "mother's first-aid kit," which includes infant pain reliever, bulb syringe, diaper cream, decongestant or antihistamine, ear drops and any prescription medicines your baby uses

Suitcase essentials. In addition to the clothes you pack for baby, you may want to include other things in your suitcase that may make traveling a little easier for all of you. Select those items you believe you'll need from the list below:

A stuffed animal may comfort baby.

- more of the familiar toys baby likes to play with
- clothes for various climates—if you're going to a warm place, don't forget to pack a couple of sweaters, because air-conditioned buildings can be quite chilly
- a copy of baby's medical history and important telephone numbers for reference, if needed
- prescriptions to be filled, if baby will need any medications
- extra formula, bottles, nipples and liners, if you use them
- extra diapers

Malabsorption Syndrome

What it is. Some babies do not absorb enough nutrients from the food they eat. When a baby has malabsorption, he loses weight, displays physical weakness and has gas and diarrhea, often with foul-smelling bowel movements. The problem can arise from, or be associated with, infections, lactase deficiency or antibiotic treatment.

What to do. If you believe your baby may be experiencing this problem, observe his bowel movements. Make note of their amount and regularity. Indicate whether they are particularly foul smelling. Increase the number of times you feed him each day, and offer him more at each feeding.

Call the doctor. Call your doctor for advice. He or she may want to see the baby, especially if there is no obvious reason for the problem, such as baby has been taking antibiotics. Your physician may change baby's diet or prescribe vitamins. Further testing may also be necessary.

Diarrhea

What it is. When your baby gets diarrhea, it's not an illness. It's a symptom of a medical problem, usually one involving the gastrointestinal area. It's more common in older infants, although babies of almost any age can have diarrhea.

How to recognize it. If your baby has more than five loose, liquid or watery bowel movements in one day, and he is otherwise healthy, he has diarrhea. Loose stools may be accompanied by irritation or diaper rash around the anus. He may also be fussy or have cramplike pains in his lower abdomen. In some cases, he may run a fever.

What to do. When baby has diarrhea, the most important thing you can do is increase his fluid intake. Don't give him medications, unless your pediatrician tells you to do so. If baby is eating solids, decrease the amount you feed him.

When to call the doctor. Contact your pediatrician if you notice any of the following.

- Diarrhea lasts longer than 36 hours.
- There is blood in the stool.
- His temperature is higher than 102F (38.9C).
- He isn't feeding well or refuses to eat.
- He appears dehydrated—his mouth is dry or urination decreases.
- You see worms or other parasites in the stool.

Your doctor probably won't prescribe medication to treat the diarrhea if baby is less than a year old. Your pediatrician may recommend you stop feeding him his regular diet of formula or breast milk and solids. You may be advised to give him an electrolyte solution to replace those he has lost. In some cases, you will be advised on how often to feed baby and the amounts to give him.

Toys and Play This Eighth Week

Your baby continues to learn from toys that appeal to his developing senses. Bright colors, bold patterns, interesting textures and fun sounds will make him smile as they help him learn.

Baby may "ask" for quiet time. By this time, baby will begin sucking, wrinkling his face, staring vacantly, yawning, squirming or crying when he's tired of playing. Be aware of these various clues that he wants some quiet time.

> **Playing helps strengthen family bonds, while it helps your baby develop physically and mentally.**

Encourage His "Push-Ups"

Because his neck muscles are getting stronger, your baby may start doing "mini-push-ups," which raise his head and chest off the floor. Put him down on the floor several times a day to practice. Place an unbreakable mirror or a dangling mobile (be sure it's completely out of reach) a little off the floor in front of him, to encourage him to practice this activity. It strengthens his neck muscles.

Tell Him Stories

Storytelling may be one of your earliest interactions with baby. Make up stories about what you're doing with any activity. You might want to show him some simple pictures in a magazine or book, and make up a story about them. They don't have to make sense. It's fun to be silly together.

The Bell Game

Find a tiny bell to use with baby. Tinkle it on one side of his head, then move it slowly to the other side while ringing it. Bring it into his line of sight, and let him reach for it. This helps him develop eye-hand coordination. It also strengthens his ability to locate a sound while it's moving.

Act Like Baby's Mirror

Act like a mirror with baby. When you're interacting, such as changing his diaper or giving him a bath, imitate his facial expressions. When he smiles, you smile. When he grimaces, you grimace. Exaggerate your expressions. When he sees his face reflected in yours, it reinforces his self-awareness.

Weekly Milestones at a Glance

Week 9

Physical Development
- may sleep through the night
- can hold object for a few seconds
- body tone improves

Senses and Reflexes
- walking reflex disappears
- coordinates eye movements in a circle when watching light or an object

Mental Development
- sucks at sight of breast
- recognizes breast or bottle, and squirms in anticipation

Social Development
- smiles easily and spontaneously
- begins to enjoy taking a bath
- may laugh and chuckle

Week 10

Physical Development
- holds chest and head up for a short time while lying on stomach
- may move arms together or legs together at same time
- brings own body up compactly when picked up

Senses and Reflexes
- grasping reflex disappears
- may bring hands together
- follows slowly moving object with eyes and head, from one side of body to the other

Mental Development
- explores own face, eyes and mouth with hand
- stops sucking to listen

Social Development
- gurgles and coos in response to sounds
- crying decreases

Week 11

Physical Development
- leans on elbows while on stomach

Senses and Reflexes
- turns head and neck to find source of sound
- may hold and wave a toy

Mental Development
- begins to show memory

Social Development
- reacts differently to each parent's presence

Week 12

Physical Development
- holds head at 90-degree angle when on stomach
- facial expressions increase
- vocalization increases

Senses and Reflexes
- hands usually held open
- likes to gum objects
- may gaze at hands for 5 to 10 minutes

Mental Development
- distinguishes speech from other sounds

Social Development
- begins to recognize and to differentiate among family members

Week 9

Baby weighs 10-1/2 pounds and is 22 inches long this week.

Baby Care and Equipment

Front Carriers

A soft carrier that you wear on your chest can comfort and entertain baby. If she's fussy or needs calming, face her toward your chest. She'll feel secure, and this helps calm her. When she's alert and active, face her out so she can see the world. She'll enjoy seeing what you see.

Some carriers serve more than one purpose. Some can also be worn on the back. Others can be used as infant seats. These carriers can be used until baby weighs a little more than 20 pounds, although some models support higher weights. Check weight specifications when you are comparison shopping.

An added plus—because these carriers look so much like a backpack, men don't usually mind wearing them. Carrying baby is a great way for dad to interact with baby.

Should You Pierce Baby's Ears?

Many mothers want to have baby's ears pierced at an early age. Some doctors advise against the procedure, stating that during the first few months, baby's immune system is not fully developed. Others believe that if a sterile technique is used to pierce the ears and other precautions are followed, it's OK.

Caution. Some physicians advise against piercing the ears until at least two immunizations against diphtheria, whooping cough and tetanus have been given to your baby. This is usually done by the time your baby is 4 months old.

Take steps to prevent infection. Be sure the person who is piercing baby's ears has experience piercing the ears of very young children. Use 14k gold posts to avoid allergic reactions. Some babies develop an allergy to the nickel in sterling silver or stainless-steel posts. Keep the area very clean after piercing (follow the technician's instructions) to avoid infections. Strep or staph bacteria can get into an open wound, causing the earlobe to become red, swollen and sore. This type of infection is treated with antibiotics.

Choose earrings carefully. Once the ears are healed, your greatest concern will be the earrings themselves. It might be best to choose earrings that have a screw-on back so they have less chance of coming off. When baby starts playing with her ears, you don't want her to put an earring in her mouth and choke on it.

Radiators and Forced-Air Heat
Safety first. When placing baby's crib in her room or yours, keep it away from heaters or radiators, and out of the line of air flow from hot or cold air ducts. A baby who touches a hot radiator can get a bad burn.

Heated air affects baby. Her chances of getting a cold or other respiratory infection increase when she is exposed to heated air from air ducts. It dries out her nose and throat, increasing her chances of infection.

Car Essentials
When you travel with baby in the car, keep various items at hand— not for baby but for you, in case of a roadside emergency. Keep the following with you, if possible:

- cell phone or CB radio
- first-aid kit
- jumper cables
- flares or reflectors
- flashlight and batteries
- reflective clothing
- blankets and towels (a lightweight solar blanket is a good choice)

> **Always carry extra baby basics when you go out, like pacifiers and burp cloths.**

- water and basic foodstuffs
- fire extinguisher
- basic tool kit
- flat-tire aerosol repair kit

> **Holding, rocking and stroking baby can affect baby in two ways. It helps calm her when she's upset, and it makes her more alert when she's tired.**

You may never need these things, but having them available gives you an added sense of security.

Milestones This Ninth Week

A child's early experiences in life actually help her brain grow. That's why it's so important to interact with baby as often as possible. It takes effort on your part, but the payoff is a happier, healthier baby.

Patterns Become More Established
Baby is settling into sleeping and feeding patterns now. She is more alert and responsive at certain times during the day. She may be sleeping as long as 7 hours at night.

She's Attracted to Sounds
Your baby is becoming more attentive to various sounds, and she can locate a sound source with her eyes. She can pick out her mother's voice from a group conversation. She listens intently and watches your eyes and mouth when you speak to her. She may enjoy listening to some sounds and may stop feeding to listen more closely.

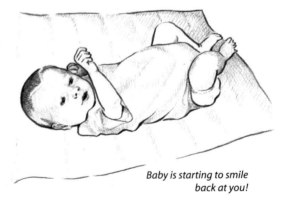
Baby is starting to smile back at you!

Even though baby cannot speak, she always is listening to the sounds around her. The more words she hears before she speaks, the larger her vocabulary will be when she does start to speak. She is now cooing and gurgling. She makes vowel sounds, such as "ah" and "oh," in response to what she sees and hears.

Milestones This Ninth Week

Changes in Baby You May See Now

Physical Development
- may sleep through the night
- can hold object for a few seconds
- body tone improves

Senses and Reflexes
- walking reflex disappears
- coordinates eye movements in a circle when watching light or an object

Mental Development
- sucks at sight of breast
- recognizes breast or bottle, and squirms in anticipation

Social Development
- smiles easily and spontaneously
- begins to enjoy taking a bath
- may laugh and chuckle
- quiets when held or when she sees faces or hears voices
- prefers to watch a person as compared to an object

Every baby is an individual, and your baby may do some of these things more quickly or more slowly than another baby. If you are concerned about your baby's progress, discuss it with your healthcare provider. Also see page viii.

She's Responding More Actively

Baby is more responsive, too. She smiles in reaction to someone smiling at her. She smiles for pleasure. There is more recognition in her eyes now. You'll notice how she anticipates a feeding and starts sucking when she sees the breast or a bottle.

She discovers new objects every day. She likes patterns that are more complex now, with curved lines and shapes. She will study the interior pattern as well as the outer edge. She enjoys looking at hanging objects; one safe object is a hanging green plant. Baby still enjoys the human face. She's especially interested in the area between the tip of the nose and the hairline.

Some Reflexes Begin to Fade

Baby's reflexive actions are beginning to fade now, as they are replaced by voluntary movement. Her arm and leg motions are becoming less jerky and more rhythmical. She may be making creeping movements on her tummy. You may find that she scoots forward in her crib until her head touches the end. She may even roll from her back to her side or accidentally push from her tummy to her back.

She may be making creeping movements on her tummy.

Dad's an Important Stimulant

Baby's father represents a different kind of stimulation for baby than mother does. Playing together is important for both dad and baby because it helps establish a good relationship between them. Sometimes a father must be encouraged to play and interact with baby. Often a man doesn't feel comfortable handling a small baby, but with patience and practice, he'll soon be a pro!

Note: See also the box on page 107, *Milestones This Week.*

What's Happening This Ninth Week?

Baby's Crying Can Mean Many Things

Why is baby crying? A baby is born with very little patience; this is essential to her survival. A human baby is one of the most helpless creatures born. Everything she needs to survive—food, shelter, warmth—must be provided for her. Crying is the only way she has to communicate. Often when she cries, she is telling you she needs something. You must take care of her needs. Sometimes, she's crying because she's bored or tired. At other times, you have no idea why she's crying.

Coping strategies. Most of the time you'll be able to discover what she needs when she cries. But sometimes, you'll be at a loss to know what she needs. When that happens, try some of the following coping strategies.

- Check for signs of an illness, such as a fever, warm, red ears or swollen gums. Call baby's doctor if there are signs of illness.
- Put baby in a front carrier, and hold her close to your body. If you speak to her softly and calmly, she may settle down.
- If you are breastfeeding, evaluate your diet. Avoid foods that could cause her problems, such as onions, garlic, broccoli and cauliflower.
- Massage baby, using the techniques we have described in previous weekly discussions.
- If you are bottlefeeding, you may want to discuss the possibility of allergies to formula with baby's doctor.

Baby's Sleep Schedule

By now, your baby gets most of her sleep at night and has a regular nap routine—probably several 1- to 1-1/2-hour naps a day. Typically, she'll have her first nap about 2 hours after she gets up in the morning. Her midday nap may occur shortly after lunch and her afternoon nap between 3 and 4 P.M.

When baby's sleep schedule becomes more regular, it makes things easier on you in some ways. You have an idea of when she'll need to nap so you can make plans to go out or take a nap of your own! It's harder in other ways, though, because when baby needs her sleep, she may get very fussy if she's not put down for her nap.

Conjunctivitis (Pinkeye)

What it is. Acute conjunctivitis, also called *pinkeye,* occurs for a variety of reasons. The causes are typically age-related. In a newborn, conjunctivitis can occur from infection during birth, most often from Chlamydia Trachomatis. In infants, recurrent conjunctivitis may be a sign of tear-duct obstruction. In older infants and children, the cause is usually a viral infection if a cold or a bacterial infection accompanies it. Not all irritation is caused by infection. Irritation may be allergy related or possibly caused by a foreign object.

Symptoms. Symptoms of conjunctivitis include redness and swelling of the eyelids and inflammation of the white part of the infant's eyes, giving it a bloodshot appearance. Both eyes are usually infected with bacterial, viral and allergic conjunctivitis. Mucus or matter may also be present; it can range from thick yellow-green, to thin and watery. Eyelids may stick together upon awakening and may need to be washed to get them open. Your baby may also experience sensitivity to bright light. If only one eye is affected and accompanied by pain, a foreign body may be involved.

Highly contagious! Conjunctivitis is highly contagious. Wash hands carefully to prevent spreading the infection to other family members. Don't use baby's towels, washcloths, blankets or pillows with other family members.

What to do. Wash the outside of the baby's eyelid with plain warm water and cotton balls. Clean the eyes by wiping from the inner part of the eye to the outside part to prevent spreading infection. Use a clean cotton ball for each eye.

When to call the doctor. Consult the doctor if your baby develops any of the following symptoms:

- a red, swollen eyelid with a lot of discharge
- a fever

> **Even young babies can wiggle and roll off the changing table, the bed or the sofa. Always keep one hand on the baby if you place her on a high surface!**

- starts acting ill
- the symptoms of an ear infection are present (see the discussion in Week 28)
- doesn't seem to improve after you begin using drops or ointment

Your doctor may treat your baby with antibiotic eye drops or ointment. Symptoms should start to clear up within the first few days, although redness may persist a little longer. Note: Within the first hour of birth, all newborns are treated with a silver nitrate solution or an antibiotic ointment to prevent conjunctivitis.

Hives

What it is. Hives is an allergic reaction that produces a splotchy, red, raised rash that is irregular in shape. The affected area also itches. Hives can appear anywhere on the body, or it may be localized in one specific area. It may also come and go over a period of several days.

In infants, viral infections are the most likely cause of hives. Hives may also occur as an allergic reaction to food, soaps or medications.

What to do. If your baby develops hives while taking a medication, don't give her any more doses until you check with your pediatrician. Keep a journal of possible causes to avoid future reactions. Dress baby in cool, loose-fitting clothing to minimize discomfort. Bathe your baby in lukewarm water to reduce itching.

When to call the doctor. Contact the doctor if your baby has any of the following problems.

- She develops hives while taking a medication.
- She experiences any difficulty breathing or swallowing.
- Her joints appear to be sore.
- Her symptoms last longer than 1 week.

Your pediatrician may recommend giving your baby an antihistamine, such as benadryl, to reduce allergic reaction. In severe cases, epinephrine may be used.

Toys and Play This Ninth Week

You don't have to buy a lot of toys for the baby to play with. Use many of the things you have at hand to engage her in play. Help her develop her grasp by wearing patterned scarves and ties while you're interacting with baby. Let her reach and grab for the patterned piece as you play together. Measuring spoons securely fastened on a ring make a good rattle. Pictures cut from magazines can be fun to look at.

Choose Easy-to-Hold Toys

Toys that are easy for baby to hold are good choices at this age, such as blocks made of wood or plastic. Balls of various sizes are also good choices— just be sure they aren't too small, to prevent choking. A small cloth doll can be held easily and may be comforting.

Encourage Her Muscle Development

Help baby's muscle development with a beach ball. Inflate it until it is almost full, then hold baby on her tummy on top of the ball. Hold her securely as you gently rock her from side to side, and back and forth. Sing or play music as you roll her around on the ball.

Begin very slowly, and gradually increase the speed as she gets used to it. You'll help her to develop her muscles as she uses her body to help maintain balance.

Week 10

How Big Is Your Baby This Tenth Week?

Baby weighs 11 pounds and is 22-1/2 inches long this week.

Baby Care and Equipment

Don't Feed Baby Solids to Help Him Sleep

Some people have been told that a baby needs solid food to help him sleep through the night. A friend or relative may mistakenly have given you this advice. Please ignore it.

According to the American Academy of Pediatrics, until your baby is at least 4 or 5 months old, he should not be given anything to eat except breast milk or formula. Solid food offers no nutritional advantage, and it does not help baby sleep longer. In fact, feeding your baby cereal or other solids before the fourth or fifth month could give him a tummy ache. That could defeat the purpose of helping him sleep through the night by keeping him awake. (See the discussion of readiness for solids in Week 17.)

Milestones This Tenth Week

Development in your baby usually progresses from his head to his feet. This means you will see your baby develop strength and skills in his head and arms before he develops them in his legs or feet. Development moves from the center of baby's body outward. He will be able to control his torso before he can control his hands or feet.

Milestones This Tenth Week

Changes in Baby You May See Now

Physical Development

• holds chest and head up for a short time while lying on stomach
• may move arms together or legs together at same time
• brings up own body compactly when picked up

Senses and Reflexes

• grasping reflex disappears
• may bring hands together
• follows slowly moving object with eyes and head, from one side of body to the other

Mental Development

• explores own face, eyes and mouth with hand
• stops sucking to listen

Social Development

• gurgles and coos in response to sounds
• crying decreases

Every baby is an individual, and your baby may do some of these things more quickly or more slowly than another baby. If you are concerned about your baby's progress, discuss it with your healthcare provider. Also see page viii.

Baby's head is less wobbly. By this time, baby's head is less wobbly because his neck muscles are developing. He can probably sit with your help, although he won't be sitting erect. When he's on his tummy, he can push up off his chest a little.

Arm movements are more controlled. You may notice his arm movements are more controlled. You may see him moving his arms and legs symmetrically while he's on his back. Or he may move them in a bicycling motion.

He may swing his arms and reach for objects that are hanging near him. He likes to feel different textures, and he may explore his face with his hands.

Language development is moving right along. Your baby may coo and gurgle while eating. He may babble when someone talks to him. When he coos or gurgles at you, and you respond in kind to him, you're playing a game. When you do this, you're also helping him discover sounds that eventually become language. You may hear him growl, squeal, screech, coo, gurgle and chortle. He can also

> **Development in your baby usually progresses from his head to his feet. This means you will see your baby develop strength and skills in his head and arms before he develops them in his legs or feet.**

All Around the Town— Choosing Baby's Stroller

A stroller is one of the most important pieces of equipment you will buy for your new baby. It makes taking baby outside the home a more enjoyable experience for everyone. You may use this piece of equipment for years–some strollers are designed to carry children up to 5 years old. If this is your first baby, you may want to choose a stroller that you can use with other children in the future.

You'll find many types of strollers on the market, so it's important to decide how, where and when you'll use the stroller and which features you need most before you begin shopping. Elements to consider include size, weight, portability and convenience of opening and closing, appearance and optional features. Cost is also a consideration; prices vary considerably, but some models start at well under $100.

Types of Strollers

Which type of stroller is best for your needs? The different types available include carriage, carriage/stroller combination, umbrella stroller, two-seat stroller, jogger stroller and stroller/car-seat combination.

Carriage stroller. This stroller has a flat surface, which is useful for a newborn. Use this type only as long as your baby is lying down. Once he begins sitting up, he could fall out of the carriage.

Carriage/stroller combination. This type does not have a flat surface for your baby to lie on. Its flattest position is one that reclines, which is OK for newborns. As baby gets older, adjust the handle to raise the back of the seat to convert the carriage into a stroller. This type of stroller is usually very comfortable for baby because it offers a well-padded seat and backrest.

Umbrella stroller. An umbrella stroller is lightweight and easy to fold, carry and pack in the car or carry onto a bus or plane. It's great if you take your baby with you a lot. However, an umbrella stroller is less comfortable for baby because designers sacrifice some of the padding to make it portable and convenient to fold. If baby will be in the stroller for long periods, this type may not be the best choice.

A stroller comes in handy for all kinds of activities.

Two-seat stroller. A two-seater is great if you have twins or two babies of different ages who can be transported together. Some of these strollers have special features that make it easier to push two in a stroller, including some that are described for jogger strollers, below.

A jogger stroller is great for heavy-duty use.

Jogger stroller. This stroller is built for heavy-duty use. Often it has a heavier frame, special shock absorbers and oversize or all-terrain tires that make it sturdy on any type of surface. Some jogger strollers have a unique design, with one tire in front and two in the rear, to make it more aerodynamic.

Combination stroller/car seat. The combination stroller/car seat connects the stroller to the baby's car seat after it is removed from the car. This is convenient if baby is sleeping or if you're moving from vehicle to vehicle (less stuff to take with you).

In addition, consider some other stroller features carefully. Removable padding that can be washed is a good choice, especially if you plan to keep the stroller for a long time or use it a great deal. (Accidents do happen!) A canopy is great if you take your baby outside a lot because you must be careful with baby's sun exposure for the first year. (See Week 48 for more about sun exposure.)

Check Safety Features Carefully
Be sure the stroller meets the Juvenile Products Manufacturers Association (JPMA) standards. To be certified by this organization, a stroller must meet the following specific safety guidelines.

• The stroller's seat or safety belt fastens securely to the stroller, is easy to fasten and unfasten by you, and is designed so it does not allow baby to slide out the bottom. The best design features a "T-strap" that comes between the baby's legs and fastens at the waist. *Always* use the safety strap when your baby is in the stroller.
• The stroller system (because it is foldable) locks securely when in use, and the brake is easy to set.

Some strollers have a brake on one wheel; others have brakes on two wheels. The two-wheeled brake system is the more secure of the two options. Always set the brake when you stop for any length of time.

> **Always use the safety strap when your baby is in the stroller.**

• If the stroller comes with a shopping basket or bag, it is located at the back of the stroller, preferably over the back wheels. Sometimes this feature is provided so you can carry a diaper bag, purse or packages. Never hang packages on the handles or place them on the top of the stroller (if it has a canopy)!

Nice-to-Have Features
Some strollers have additional features you might find useful.
• Safety mesh, to keep your baby from sliding out of the stroller.
• Height-adjustable handles, one-touch reclining and one-hand steering, to make moving and handling the stroller easier.
• Double tires on the front and rear wheels, to add durability and stability to the stroller.
• Canopies with plastic windows, to offer baby the opportunity to see what's going on around him.

A Word of Caution

Never leave your baby alone in a stroller–it's too easy for mishaps to occur. And when you're opening or closing the stroller, make sure baby is out of the way. His little fingers could be pinched in the process.

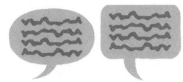

hear the emotional changes in your voice. He will even begin responding to his name.

Begins to recognize family members. By this time, your baby may be smiling at you (and everyone else he sees), but he is beginning to recognize family members. He may widen his eyes, smile and wiggle his body when someone familiar approaches.

Enjoys interacting with other people. Even if your baby seems content to stay in his crib, interact with him. He needs it, and it's good for him. Get him up and make him part of family activities going on around him. Put him in his infant seat, a carry sling or in his stroller, and keep him near as you work or relax. He enjoys interacting with other people.

Baby can see color. Your baby can see color, and it is becoming exciting to him. He likes vivid colors because pastels are harder for him to distinguish. Bright primary colors (red, green, blue, yellow) and bold patterns are interesting and give him a lot to look at.

What's Happening This Tenth Week?

A big accomplishment by this week—baby may be sleeping through the night. If he isn't, don't despair. He will soon. He can also hold his head up without support. His neck muscles grow stronger every day.

You may be concerned about how your baby is growing. The best indicator of how well he's doing is how much he grows. If his growth is progressing normally, he'll be gaining weight steadily, he will be growing in length and he will be starting to

> Signals that baby has had enough visiting for now include whimpering, looking away or closing his eyes.

imitate your behavior and gaining control of his muscles.

You'll also discover how much baby enjoys interacting with others. He'll like meeting new people. But beware of overstimulating baby; it's easy to do. Watch for signals from your baby that he wants to be left alone for a while—we all need that sometimes, even babies! Signals that baby has had enough visiting for now include whimpering, looking away or closing his eyes. Quiet time, either alone by himself or with you rocking him or speaking softly to him, can help calm him.

Smoking around Baby

Studies show that smoking around a baby has many harmful effects on him. Secondary smoke contains more than 200 poisonous substances, which your baby breathes in any time you or someone else lights a cigarette near him. Now is the time to think about quitting or asking others in the home to quit if they haven't already.

When your baby inhales secondary smoke, it increases his risk of developing many problems, including respiratory infections, middle-ear infections, asthma, breathing problems after being given general anesthesia, bronchitis and pneumonia. Secondhand smoke may also be a factor in SIDS (sudden infant death syndrome); see the discussion in Week 8. In addition, anyone smoking around the baby could accidentally burn him with a lit cigarette.

What to do. You can take several measures to protect your little one. If you or others can't quit smoking, be sure no one smokes around your baby–not anywhere in the house. Smoking should be done outside. Never smoke in an enclosed space, such as a car, when you have baby with you. Avoid smoke-filled areas when possible, such as restaurants or places in public areas where people may smoke. Make sure that no one smokes around baby when he's in child care.

When Baby Catches a Cold

What it is. The common cold is an upper-respiratory-tract infection (URI) caused by many viruses. A cold generally lasts a week or two but can occasionally persist longer. Colds are commonly spread through droplets in the air from others coughing or sneezing, or by person-to-person contact.

What to do. When your baby gets a cold, give him plenty of liquid to drink. Because it may be difficult for your baby to

What If I Have a Cold?

If you've got a cold or cough, it's no cause for alarm. Nursing baby or cuddling with him won't pass your cold on to him. Be sure to wash your hands often.

nurse or bottle-feed, encourage frequent feedings. Drain his nose with a bulb syringe as needed, especially before eating. By nature, babies are nose breathers and don't breathe through their mouths. If he can't breathe well, he can't eat well. Nonprescription saline nose drops can be used to thin nasal secretions, which makes it easier to suction mucus.

Use a cool-mist humidifier to keep air moist. Run the humidifier in the room where your baby spends most of his time. Don't let the mist spray directly over your infant or his crib. Bedding can become damp and chill your baby.

Babies younger than 6 months of age are rarely given over-the-counter (OTC) medications. Don't use them unless your doctor tells you to do so. Ask your doctor if it's OK to give your baby fever-reducing medication, such as baby acetaminophen or baby ibuprofen. Follow package instructions very carefully. Infants under 2 months of age should not be given medication unless specifically ordered by your pediatrician.

When to call the doctor. Contact the doctor if baby

- has difficulty breathing or is breathing rapidly
- flares his nostrils with each breath
- wheezes
- has bad color, such as pale, ashen, gray or bluish-tinted skin
- is not eating well
- cries uncontrollably
- is listless
- has a fever that rises above 101F/38.3C, or if fever persists
- tugs on his ears
- is not having wet diapers

If your baby has some of the above symptoms, your pediatrician may want to see him

Preventing Colds

You can do several things to help prevent your baby from getting lots of colds.

- **Wash your hands frequently and have others wash their hands before touching or holding baby.**
- **Avoid taking your infant out in crowded places where he might be exposed to people with colds.**
- **If possible, try to keep your older baby from putting his mouth on objects that have been handled by others.**

to rule out something more serious. Your baby may be treated with antibiotics, if a secondary infection has occurred, such as an ear infection. Antibiotics don't work on viruses, so don't ask your pediatrician to prescribe one. Unnecessary antibiotics may be more harmful to your baby than the cold itself.

Fluoride Supplementation

Fluoride helps the development of baby's healthy teeth. Discuss with your pediatrician your baby's need for a fluoride supplement. Most pediatricians begin the supplement when a baby is about 6 months old. Correct dosage is based on the amount of fluoride in your water supply and whether your baby is receiving any of that water.

Your use of powdered formula, made with local water, compared to ready-to-use formula or breast milk, may determine when your baby will start supplementation. Too much fluoride can result in discolored or mottled teeth, so follow your pediatrician's recommendation.

Toys and Play This Tenth Week

Looking Game

One simple game you can play with your baby is to sit him on your lap. Look into each other's eyes; your baby may look away. Then you glance away; when baby looks back and sees you aren't looking at him, he will make noise to draw your attention again. This is a fun game.

Reaching Game

This game involves holding a string of bright, colorful objects above baby's head. He will reach out and try to grab it. Hold the objects just a little out of his grasp, to encourage him to stretch and reach. You're also helping him develop eye-hand coordination with this game. *Caution:* Don't tie anything, such as this string of objects, onto his crib or leave it where baby could become tangled in it.

Be Aware of Toy Hazards

It's important to become more aware of potential toy hazards now that baby is getting a little older. Avoid toys that have small parts, such as eyes or noses that a baby might pull off a stuffed toy. Don't let your baby have toys that are too small or that have small pieces to them.

Week 11

Baby weighs 11-1/2 pounds and is 22-3/4 inches long this week.

Baby Care and Equipment

Ways to Relieve Baby's Gas
A baby often swallows air when she eats, so it's not unusual for her to have gas. Burping may take care of the problem, but when it doesn't, you may need to try something else.

Slanted baby bottle.

- Use a different burping position. Lay her face down on your lap, and pat her back. Or sit her on your lap and rub her back.
- Stop in the middle of her feeding and burp her. Burp her again when she finishes.
- Don't let her cry for long periods. When she cries, she gulps in air, which can cause gas.
- Keep her upright when you feed her, at least at a 30-degree angle. She swallows food more easily. She'll swallow less air.
- If bottle-feeding, be sure the nipple is the right size. Too much milk going through too fast or sucking too hard on a nipple with an opening that is too small can cause her to swallow air.
- Be modern—use an angled bottle or disposable plastic liners that collapse as baby sucks.

Rarely, gas may be caused by a digestive problem. If baby has diarrhea, vomits, cries inconsolably and suffers from bloating, call your doctor. Baby may have lactose intolerance, be allergic to her formula or have some other problem.

Feeding Tips–Travel

Bottle-feeding. Prepare before you get in the car with baby. If you feed her formula, refrigerate any prepared formula, if directions call for it. If you can't do that, premeasure water into a clean baby bottle. When baby's hungry, just add powdered formula to the water. Or buy premixed, ready-to-feed formula in cans or bottles. Pour canned formula into a bottle when she's hungry. Discard leftovers.

Breastfeeding. It's easy to feed your baby on the road if you breastfeed, as long as you can find a place to feed her where you feel comfortable. Feed baby when she's hungry. If you have to be away from her for a time, pump extra breast milk, then refrigerate or freeze it. Breast milk doesn't have to be refrigerated immediately. It will stay fresh up to 4 hours at temperatures as high as 77F (25C) and 24 hours at 60F (15.6C). You can refrigerate breast milk for up to 72 hours. It can be frozen for up to 6 months in a refrigerator freezer and up to 12 months in a deep freezer. Label all containers clearly with the date.

> When possible, bring water from home to mix with formula so it tastes the same.

You can combine fresh breast milk with frozen breast milk. Cool the expressed milk before adding the thawed breast milk. Use more thawed breast milk than fresh breast milk. Once milk is thawed, use immediately or store in the refrigerator up to 24 hours.

> By this time, your baby has probably settled into her sleeping pattern and eating pattern.

Help to Get Baby to Sleep

To help baby get a good night's rest, keep her comfort and safety in mind. Place baby on her back to go to sleep. When she's old enough to turn over, she can choose her own sleeping position. Room temperature should be about 70F (21.1C) for her comfort and yours. Keep her away from soft surfaces that can mold to her face and interfere with breathing. Use only approved mattress covers for her crib or bassinet. Avoid plastic bags or wrapping material that could come loose and suffocate her. Never leave baby alone on a sofa or bed. Even if she's not rolling over yet, she could wiggle and fall off.

If you have a family bed and share it with baby, avoid using soft materials. Don't use a feather-bed pillow. The mattress should be firm. Do not place quilts, pillows or comforters under the baby. If you share your bed with baby, don't use any substance, such as alcohol, that could interfere with your ability to wake up.

Baby Bouncers

When baby wants to jump and wiggle, consider buying a bouncer. A bouncer is an angled, wire-framed, fabric chair, with a harness that holds baby. Its semireclining seat is designed to allow her to see the world and to bounce her gently when it is put in motion. It can be used until she's about 25 pounds or until she can sit up on her own. *Caution:* When she can sit by herself, she's no longer safe in it.

Most bouncers are well padded and comfortable for baby to sit in. Sitting in a bouncer gives your baby the opportunity to see you and to see what's going on around her. At the same time, the rhythmic motion can soothe her, if you choose to "start her bouncing."

Many bouncers have removable, washable cushions and covers. Some have a toy bar across the front so baby can look at, and eventually play with, brightly colored toys.

Cautions for Using Bouncers

- **Never place the baby bouncer (with baby in it) on a chair, counter or other place where it could fall.**
- **Don't place a bouncer on a bed or upholstered furniture. If it falls over, baby could suffocate.**
- **Never try to move a bouncer when baby is in it. It's *not* a carrier.**
- **As baby gets larger, her weight and movement causes the bouncer to become very unstable.**
- ***Never* use a bouncer as a car seat for baby when she's riding in a car.**

Milestones This Eleventh Week

She Uses Her Senses to Explore

Baby now recognizes familiar sights and sounds. She uses all of her senses to explore her world. She's learning self-control. You'll be amused how she may stop crying and start smiling when you make silly noises or funny faces.

Understanding Her Cry

Your continuing experiences with her help you understand many things about your baby. By this time, you recognize her "crying language." You probably know now if she's hungry, in pain, tired, bored or wants attention when she cries. Her crying is decreasing because she's more involved in interacting with her environment.

Playing Together

You've also probably come to understand when is the best time to play with baby. Some days she wants to play more than others. If she's sleeping and eating a lot due to a growth spurt, she may be less interested in playtime. Other times, when she's learning a new task, she'll want to continue to play long after her usual limit. Be flexible. Let her help set the playtime.

When awake, baby may no longer want just to cuddle. She wants to play and to interact. She doesn't like being left alone for long. She has many facial expressions now, such as frowns, smiles and grimaces. She may stop nursing to smile at you, then return to sucking.

She's Getting Stronger

Her strength is increasing. By now, she may be able to sit up quite well if she's securely propped against something. Lying on her stomach, she can push up her chest using her elbows and forearms.

Baby's Hands Help Her Learn

She no longer holds her hands in fists. Her hands are now loosely clenched. Sometimes they are open. She has discovered her hands are more than mere fists—now they are fingers and a thumb. They interest her greatly.

The reflexive grasp she was born with is disappearing. Now she must learn to use her hands to hold onto something. Your baby will bring her hands together at the center of her body. She's beginning to coordinate the look/grasp/suck system. She's putting everything into her mouth. Be careful of what she puts in her mouth. Unclean objects may expose her to germs. Small objects could choke her. Other than that, don't worry too much.

She likes to touch or to handle just about anything. She's not content to just look any longer—she wants to touch, too! She'll study a plastic rattle placed in her hand, then wave it around. She likes to make noise.

Different textures interest her—a hard rattle, a soft doll, a fluffy stuffed toy. She'll repeat an action many times as she plays with something. Does the rattle always make noise when she shakes it? Does the foam toy always pop back into shape when she lets go of it? Through repetition, she learns much about her environment.

Baby Likes to Look at Patterns
The contrast of light and dark still pleases her, but she also likes bold, contrasting colors. Pastels don't excite her much. She pays attention to details, patterns and the play of light on an object. And when she drops something, she will stare in puzzlement at the place where it disappeared!

Note: See also the box below, *Milestones This Week*.

What's Happening This Eleventh Week?

Sleeping All Night?
Your baby should be sleeping all night now. However, pediatricians define "all night" as not waking up between midnight and 5 A.M. Most people don't consider this 5-hour period as an entire night, but if you've been sleep-deprived since baby's birth, even sleeping this amount of time is cause for celebration!

Milestones This Eleventh Week

Changes in Baby You May See Now

Physical Development
- stays awake for longer periods during the day

Senses and Reflexes
- turns head and neck to find source of sound
- may hold and wave a toy

Mental Development
- is interested in sounds
- may glance at hand

Social Development
- responds with excitement to a person's presence

Every baby is an individual, and your baby may do some of these things more quickly or more slowly than another baby. If you are concerned about your baby's progress, discuss it with your healthcare provider. Also see page viii.

Help establish this pattern by feeding baby more frequently during the day. If she naps longer than 3 hours, wake her up. Establish a bedtime routine, as we've previously discussed, which helps her know it's time to go to sleep. If you get up at night to feed her, keep lights low and interaction to a minimum. Change her, feed her and put her to bed with as little stimulation as possible.

Taking Baby on the Road

When traveling with baby, a family car trip is often the way to go. You can go on the spur of the moment and take along whatever you need. You can stop whenever you want. It's OK when baby fusses. You probably won't set any speed records. What used to take you 3-1/2 hours will now take at least 5, but the car is great for family travel.

Be prepared so the trip is enjoyable for everyone. Build in extra time for unplanned stops. Below are ideas for making your next trip a happy experience.

- Feed baby just before you leave, so you won't have to make a feeding stop too soon. Never take baby out of her car sear to nurse or to bottle-feed her while the car is moving.
- Leave just before naptime, if possible, or when she's awake but close to her naptime.
- Know baby's tolerance for being confined. This usually isn't a problem until she gets older. Many parents drive while baby is napping or sleeping.
- Be prepared to stop often. It's hard for her to be in a car seat for a long time. You'll need to stop often to give baby a break (you, too).
- Factor in extra time for everything. You need to feed and to change baby, sometimes not at the same stop. You may need to comfort baby if she's fussy. Some babies have a hard time sleeping in their car seat, so you may need to let her lie down for a while.
- Keep cassette tapes handy that she likes. Include funny songs. Even stories can entertain her. Don't play lullabies—they can lull the driver to sleep as easily as the baby!
- Have her favorite toys and comfort objects at hand.

- Pack all the supplies you'll need—disposable diapers, baby wipes, extra pacifiers, formula, bottles, nipples, burp cloths, clean clothes, blankets.
- Take your food with you—picnic whenever you can. It's often easier to picnic when and where you want than to go into a restaurant with a young child.
- Neck supports or a rolled, soft blanket provide baby with a comfortable sleeping position.

Think before you pack the car. Plan what you want to take with you. Pack the things last that you'll need soonest. That way, they're on top in the trunk and readily available. Keep essentials up front with you.

Carry a small cooler for snacks and formula or expressed breast milk. If baby wants warmed formula, put the correct amount of powdered formula in a bottle. Add warm water from an insulated bottle when it's time to feed her.

Keep as close to your routine as possible, such as the time you put her to bed. Put her down about the time you normally do, and follow your bedtime ritual. This helps her fall asleep, even when she's not in her own bed. If you travel to a different time zone, let her adjust gradually, just as you do.

Reserve a crib and bedding if you're staying at a hotel. If you're visiting relatives, ask them to borrow or to rent a crib. Bring baby's favorite blanket or toy to comfort her. Take along a crib monitor if you're staying at a suites-hotel (with separate bedrooms) or at someone's home.

You may have to adjust *your* routine somewhat. You may have to go to bed when baby does, or wait until she falls asleep before turning on the TV or radio softly. Often, you get up when she gets up.

> **Plan to make part of your trip when your baby is asleep.**

If baby is curious and crawling, consider bringing childproofing supplies with you. Most hotels and motels don't supply them. Family members and friends don't usually have these devices either. See the discussion in Week 20 on childproofing away from home.

Anal Fissure
What it is. An *anal fissure* is a small tear in or around the opening to the anus (rectum) that can occur at any time. You may notice a little

bit of blood in baby's stool or on her diaper. There may be a red rash around the rectum that itches and causes discomfort. Baby may cry with a bowel movement or be constipated.

What to do. Begin by increasing baby's fluid intake. Do *not* give her water if she is not eating solids. Instead, increase the amount of breast milk or formula you give her. If she is eating solids, give her foods that soften bowel movements. Ask your pediatrician for advice. If you give her vitamins or formula that contain iron, stop for a while. Discuss this with baby's doctor before making any changes.

When to call the doctor. Call your baby's doctor if you notice any of the following symptoms.

- You see blood on the diaper or in the stool.
- She's crying or fussing with bowel movements.
- She suffers from severe or prolonged constipation.

Baby's doctor will prescribe treatment for the problem. You may be advised to use a small rectal suppository or a lubricated, gloved little finger to dilate the rectum gently. You may need to give her medications to soften the stool. Sometimes mineral oil is used. The problem usually heals fairly quickly.

Gassiness

What it is. Problems with gassiness or flatulence can occur at any age. It is more common once baby starts eating solid foods, between 4 and 6 months. Symptoms include

- abdominal pain
- bloated or distended abdomen
- fussiness
- frequent passing of gas

What to do. If you are breastfeeding, note the foods you have eaten. Some of them could cause baby to be gassy. Avoid these foods in the future. If she's eating solids, keep track of the foods your baby is eating that might make her uncomfortable.

Lay her on her tummy on top of a hot-water bottle or a warm (not hot!) heating pad for a short time. Massage her tummy. See the discussion in Week 7 for tips on relieving gas. Burp her. If she's crying, try to soothe her. Crying causes her to swallow more air, which could cause more gas.

When to call the doctor. Most of the time you won't have to call your doctor about this problem. It usually goes away by itself. However, call the doctor if you notice any of the following symptoms:

- severe abdominal pain that is not relieved by passing gas
- baby is still uncomfortable after you try the above treatments
- she has a fever
- you notice blood in her stools

If baby's problem is severe, your pediatrician may prescribe medications to help eliminate gas in the intestines. Do *not* give her medication on your own, before consulting the doctor. If the problem becomes chronic or severe, your doctor may do further testing .

Toys and Play This Eleventh Week

Capture Baby's Attention
When you talk to baby, capture her attention before you begin. You'll hold her attention longer, and you're more likely to get a response. Keep using her name. She may not associate her name with herself yet, but if she hears it frequently, she'll eventually realize it is a special sound.

Use short sentences of four or five words when you talk with her. Choose one- or two-syllable words that can be drawn out when you speak them, such as "liiitttle prinncesss." When possible, show her what you mean. When you say, "Wave bye-bye to grandma," wave as you say it. It's easier for her to recall a word associated with a gesture.

At 11 weeks old, your baby may like a little "conversation" with you!

Ask her questions. She can't answer, but the change in the way a question sounds (raising the tone at the end of the question) exposes her to different language patterns.

Read to her. She'll love nursery rhymes and poems with a sing-song cadence. Sing, too; she'll love to hear familiar songs over and over again. She may wiggle with anticipation when you begin one of her favorites.

Finding Her Playmate

Your baby is fascinated by noise and movement. Entertain her by slowly moving around her while you talk so she can practice finding one of her favorite playmates—you. You may find baby cooing with pleasure when you play this game.

See if baby can focus on your voice from the direction of the sound. In a singsong voice, say, "Baby, baby, baby" while you stand in front of her. Then move behind her, and sing out again. Move to her side. Change the rhythm of the chant, or chant faster or slower. Chant loudly, then chant softly. Is she listening alertly? Does she follow your sound?

Bells on Her Wrists!

Use her fascination with sound to play a fun game. Tie a ribbon around her wrist that has one or two small bells attached. Lift her arm, and shake the bells gently. If she notices the sound, she may start moving her arm to hear it again. Then put bells on her other wrist, then her ankles. Be sure bells are securely attached to the ribbon. *Never* leave her alone wearing the ribbon.

Week 12

How Big Is Your Baby This Twelfth Week?

Baby weighs 12 pounds and is 23-1/4 inches long.

Baby Care and Equipment

Pets and Baby

You may have a pet that was your "baby" until your child was born. When you bring baby home from the hospital, it means a lifestyle change for your pet, too.

Your pet is sensitive to routine, so making changes slowly, before baby is born, may be easier on your pet. During your pregnancy, try the following.

- Decrease the time you spend with your pet—you'll have a lot less time after baby's birth.
- Change and adapt your pet's feeding, exercise or play schedule in the weeks before baby's birth.
- Make any changes in where your pet will be kept. If baby will be in your room and your pet has slept there, move your pet's sleeping site to another location so it will become familiar.
- Evaluate your dog's obedience training. He should respond to basic commands.

Authors' note: About this time in baby's life, you may stop referring to his age in weeks and begin to refer to it in months. For that reason, we will also provide a monthly reference for baby's age for each week that follows.

- Expose your pet to other children when possible. It can be a shock to an animal to be confronted with a small baby. A baby's crying and other reactions can startle or frighten an animal.
- Put out baby's things, such as the bassinet or crib and the changing table. Let your pet smell everything.
- Keep pets off baby furniture and out of baby's room.
- Give your pet an area that is all its own and off-limits to baby.

Introducing your dog to baby. After your baby is born, before you bring him home, have someone bring home a piece of baby's clothing. Let your dog sniff it. This enables your pet to become familiar with baby's smell.

When you bring baby home, go into the house alone to greet the pet. Put your dog on a leash before you bring your baby in, then sit in a chair with baby in your lap. Cover baby's head with your hand to show your pet you are protective of this new addition to the household. Don't put your baby on the floor. Don't hold baby over your dog's head—it might encourage your dog to jump up. Speak to your dog in a normal voice, and pat him for reassurance. If your dog displays any aggression, such as growling, flattening his ears or putting his tail down, remove baby immediately. If your dog seems OK with baby, let it sniff him.

Never leave baby unsupervised around your pet, even if everything seems all right. You don't want to create an unsafe situation in which baby could be harmed.

Don't let your dog lick your baby—it's not sanitary. A dog's mouth is filled with germs.

If your dog shows unacceptable behavior, say "No!" If he backs off on his own, praise him. If he doesn't, remove the dog from the room. To be on the safe side, keep your dog on a leash for the first few weeks around baby.

After 3 or 4 weeks, if all seems to be going well, you can begin to include your pet in your daily routine. Let him follow you around as you care for baby. Give your pet attention when baby is present, not when baby is asleep or in another room. In this way, your pet will accept baby's presence and not see it as a threat. If your dog walks well on a leash, take him with you when you take baby out in the stroller.

Never leave baby unsupervised around your pet, even if everything seems all right.

Introducing your cat to baby. Cats can be unpredictable. It's best to keep a cat away from baby when possible. Let the cat watch from a distance. If it shows any signs of aggression, such as biting, nipping, growling, raising its hair, spraying, flattening its ears or pointing its tail down, remove the cat from the area. If the cat slinks toward baby, it is a sign of aggression, so do not let it near the baby. Reward your cat for any positive actions, such as staying off furniture or away from baby.

Old or young pets. A puppy or kitten has a lot of energy. Handling a young pet can be a challenge. You may have to allow extra time to spend with it.

If your animal is fairly old, a change in routine could cause other problems. If your pet has enjoyed the run of the house, for example, it may take time to train it to stay out of certain areas. Your pet may also be jealous of the time and attention you give the baby. You may have to set aside some time alone with your older pet.

Dealing with Unwanted Advice from Others

Your mother may tell you you're starving your child. Your mother-in-law may advise you to let baby cry "for his own good—you'll spoil him if you pick him up all the time." If you're like most new parents, you may wonder if what other people tell you is true. You may doubt your own instincts.

Everyone means well. They're not saying you're a bad parent. They have baby's best interest at heart. Much of the advice they share with you was acceptable when they were parents. Today we know that some of that well-intentioned advice isn't best for baby.

If you are given unwanted counsel, don't get upset or angry. Follow your own plan for rearing your baby, and trust your instincts.

Thank your helpers for their advice. Use what you think is acceptable, and ignore the rest.

Does Classical Music Make Baby Smarter?

Recent studies have debunked the idea that a child who listens to classical music may grow up to be smarter and to do better in math, which researchers in one study reported some years ago. Researchers now believe there is no correlation between listening to classical music and brain development. However, the soothing sounds of classical music might help calm and settle a restless baby. Listening to classical music could be enjoyable for baby *and* you!

First-Aid Kit

Keep these items on hand to provide baby the best at-home care. Items on the list below can help you deal with almost any minor medical situation. Keep them together in a handy location.

- **thermometer–ear or rectal**
- **rubbing alcohol**
- **cotton balls and cotton swabs**
- **premoistened baby wipes**
- **diaper-rash cream**
- **baby medication to reduce pain and relieve fever (ask your pediatrician for suggestions)**
- **cool-mist humidifier (don't use a steam humidifier with a baby)**
- **dropper or oral syringe to measure accurately any liquid medication you must give baby (a kitchen teaspoon is *not* an accurate measurement)**
- **electrolyte solution, to use if baby has diarrhea (ask your pediatrician for suggestions)**
- **nasal syringe for clearing nasal congestion**

Milestones This Twelfth Week

Baby Can Lift His Head

Your baby's strength and body control continue to increase. He can lift his head easily now. When you hold him, he may push away and look over your shoulder. He turns his head when lying on his stomach.

His Vision Sharpens

By this time, baby's vision is becoming sharper. Now when you hold him, he can see details of your face, such as your eyebrows and lips. He's becoming familiar with your facial features and those of others in the family. He's beginning to distinguish among family members. You'll notice that his face lights up when he recognizes you. He's also better able to track objects and can follow them as they move through his field of vision. Move a brightly colored object in a circle in front of him. Watch his eyes track the movement!

> ## Infant Carrier Seat
>
> **When choosing an infant carrier seat for baby, make sure it has a wide, sturdy base to keep it from tipping over and causing a head injury.**

Baby Notices His Fingers

Your baby may spend a lot of time watching his hands. He enjoys watching his fingers move. He may grab one hand with the other or suck on his fist. He wants to touch anything he can reach. If he drops an object he's holding, he doesn't search for it.

Baby's Sleep Needs

Your baby sleeps about 15 hours a day—10 hours at night and two or three naps during the day. The time he awakens in the morning may depend on the time of his last feeding the night before. Some babies wake up at about the same time every morning, no matter when they last ate.

> ## Baby's Sleep Cycles
>
> **By this time, your baby's sleep cycles begin to resemble those of an adult. He passes through cycles of deep sleep and active sleep (REM). Both stages are critical to his physical and mental development. Human growth hormone is released when the child is in deep sleep. This sleep stage is required for physical growth. Active sleep is believed to be necessary for the development of learning and memory.**

Note: See also the box on the opposite page, *Milestones This Week.*

Milestones This Twelfth Week

Changes in Baby You May See Now

Physical Development
• holds head at 90-degree angle when on stomach
• facial expressions increase
• vocalization increases

Senses and Reflexes
• hands usually held open
• likes to gum objects
• may gaze at hands for 5 to 10 minutes

Mental Development
• distinguishes speech from among other sounds

Social Development
• begins to recognize and to differentiate between family members

Every baby is an individual, and your baby may do some of these things more quickly or more slowly than another baby. If you are concerned about your baby's progress, discuss it with your healthcare provider. Also see page viii.

What's Happening This Twelfth Week?

Baby's Soft Spots
Soft spots on your baby's head enable his head to grow. The soft spot at the back of the head should be closing about this time. The large one at the top of baby's head takes longer to close. He'll be about 18 months old before this spot hardens completely.

It's OK to touch these soft spots, just be gentle. If a soft spot sinks in or bulges, or becomes hard before it should, call your pediatrician. He or she may want to see baby.

Begin Thinking about Babyproofing Your Home
It won't be long before baby is moving around. Think now about babyproofing your home. In the following weeks, we go into detail about things to do to make your home safe for your baby. This discussion applies to what to do and how to do it.

Some people believe that nothing around the home should be moved or put away. In this way, baby learns what he can and cannot touch. Other people believe that anything baby might reach should be moved so you never have to say "No" to baby.

Consider taking the middle ground. You don't have to put away everything that baby might touch. That's no fun for you, and it's boring for baby. You may want to put away some of your valuable, breakable or dangerous items, or at least place them out of reach for a while.

Baby will explore as he becomes mobile, so put only what is safe for him within his reach. Sooner or later, your baby has to learn "No." Let him learn this lesson on expendable objects that won't hurt him. Everyone is happy: Baby expands his horizons without destroying your most prized possessions.

Bronchiolitis/RSV (Respiratory Syncytial Virus)

What it is. Bronchiolitis is a lung infection that occurs primarily in the winter and spring months. It is rare in children older than 2 years. It begins as a cold, with nasal discharge and mild fever. Gradually the baby develops increasing respiratory distress, with rapid breathing, coughing, irritability and possible wheezing. He may also have episodes of apnea. See the general discussion of apnea in Week 2.

What to do. Use a cool-mist humidifier in his room. See Week 13 for information on humidifiers. Give him lots of fluids. Keep baby quiet. Depending on baby's age, acetaminophen may be given to ease discomfort and to reduce fever. Keep baby away from others because the virus is easily spread by hand-to-nose or hand-to-eye contact.

When to call the doctor. Contact your pediatrician if baby's coughing increases, he wheezes, breathes more than 70 breaths a minute, or if the skin between and underneath the ribs is pulled taut with breathing. Notify the doctor if baby's skin becomes blue or gray, he is extremely irritable, he has apnea spells or is very listless.

In some cases, baby will be hospitalized and given mist therapy combined with oxygen. He may be given an IV if he cannot eat. X-rays may be taken to check for pneumonia. In severe cases, a ventilator may be used to assist and to control breathing. An antiviral agent may be given to your baby, but its use is controversial and expensive.

Clubfoot

What it is. Clubfoot, also called *talipes,* is a term that applies to any number of foot deformities. Most are present at birth (congenital), although one type of clubfoot may occur after infection with polio.

When present at birth, clubfoot is either an inherited condition or is caused by the positioning of the fetus in the uterus. It is more common in boys than girls. Symptoms of a clubfoot vary, depending on the part of the foot involved, and include

- heel and foot turn outward
- heel turns inward
- foot is extended
- arch is exaggerated
- foot points down, turns inward and curls under

What to do. Your pediatrician should recognize the disorder when the physical exam is done after birth. Medical treatment is necessary to correct the deformity. Your doctor may advise stretching exercises, massage, physical therapy, splints for day or night, or casts. A positive attitude on your part during physical therapy is very important.

The goal of treatment is to correct the problem. If left uncorrected, it prevents normal walking. The deformity is not painful, but it may be uncomfortable when treatment begins. Your doctor may recommend surgery if the noninvasive treatment methods described don't solve the problem.

Toys and Play This Twelfth Week

Your baby loves to reach for and swat at objects. He's beginning to grab at things. Introduce your baby to a gym toy if he's at this stage. Objects are firmly attached to a bar that hangs above baby's head. Your baby will enjoy looking at the colorful objects and may take a swipe at them. As his muscle control improves, these bright toys help him develop eye-hand coordination. He'll quickly lose interest in the objects if they are beyond his reach.

Push-ups
Help baby increase his upper-body strength by placing him on his stomach with his arms stretched in front. Shake a rattle above his head to encourage him to look up. Then shake the rattle below him so he looks down. Do this a few times so he moves up and down.

Baby's Kick Toy

Baby is using more than his hands as he becomes more active. He likes kick toys, too. Baby can activate some toys to make noise or to flash lights when he kicks them.

Make baby his own kick toy. Attach a rattle or bell to baby's ankle with self-adhesive cloth tape. When he kicks, he'll delight himself with the noise he makes! Don't leave baby alone with this toy.

Little Piggies Go to Market

It's time to introduce your baby to some of the fun interactive games you remember from your own childhood. Babies love "This Little Piggy Went to Market." Sit baby on your lap, or lay him on the floor. Say one line of verse as you gently wiggle each toe on his foot. As you say or sing the last verse, run your fingers up baby's body, tickling him lightly.

> This little piggy went to market.
> This little piggy stayed home.
> This little piggy had roast beef.
> This little piggy had none.
> And this little piggy cried, "Mama!"
> All the way home!

Hand-Puppet Playtime

Hand puppets are fun, creative toys. Your baby will enjoy exploring a puppet with his eyes and his hands. Puppet play with baby encourages his visual, verbal and motor development. You can buy simple hand puppets. Or you can make one by sewing two washcloths together on three sides. Add a simple face with a permanent marker. You're ready to play!

Weekly Milestones at a Glance

Week 13

Physical Development
• able to sit with support

Senses and Reflexes
• may bat at object with closed fist

Mental Development
• waits for expected reward, such as feeding

Social Development
• tries to attract attention when a parent or sibling is nearby
• may be attentive for up to 45 minutes

Week 14

Physical Development
• can focus eyes at different distances
• holds head steady and erect for short periods

Senses and Reflexes
• clasps fingers and hands in play

Mental Development
• smiles and vocalizes more to an actual face than to an image

Social Development
• attempts to soothe self
• may prefer a particular toy
• can be quieted with music

Week 15

Physical Development
• can turn head in all directions

Senses and Reflexes
• splashes and plays in bath

Mental Development
• has memory span of up to 7 seconds

Social Development
• interested in mirror image; may smile at it
• adjusts responses to different people

Week 16

Physical Development
• may roll over from back to stomach or stomach to back
• sits, with assistance and support

Senses and Reflexes
• pulls dangling object toward himself and brings it to his mouth
• stares at the place from where object dropped
• displays interest in smells

Mental Development
• initiates several tonal sounds

Social Development
• begins to recognize and to differentiate between family members

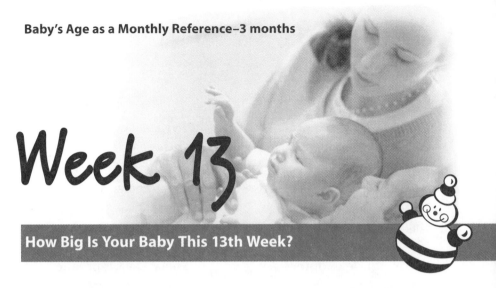

Week 13

How Big Is Your Baby This 13th Week?

Baby weighs 12-1/2 pounds and is 23-1/2 inches long this week.

Baby Care and Equipment

Humidifiers

When baby suffers from a cold or other respiratory problem, your pediatrician may recommend a humidifier to increase the moisture in the air. A humidifier is used most often when it is dry outside and when your home heating system is running, usually during the winter months. Choose from two types: A *cool-mist* humidifier forces cool mist into the air. A *warm-mist* humidifier heats water before sending the warm mist into the air.

Dry air dries out baby's nasal passages and causes dehydration. When the delicate layers of the mucous membranes dry out and become thicker, mucus stops functioning the way it should. This condition can weaken the respiratory-defense system. Moisture also helps to prevent mucus from crusting inside and outside the nose, and it relieves itchy skin and dry throats.

Clean humidifier regularly. To prevent mold and bacterial growth in the appliance, clean and thoroughly disinfect a humidifier on a regular basis. Use fresh water each time you fill the humidifier. Empty the humidifier when you aren't using it. Always check the

> ### Caution!
> Because a humidifier is an electrical device that also contains water, exercise extreme caution when using it to prevent electrical accidents.

When to Call the Doctor

You may be unsure when to call the doctor or when to seek medical treatment for your baby. Knowing what to watch out for may help you relax a little. Be alert to the symptoms listed below. If you notice any of these signs or symptoms, call your pediatrician immediately.

- **Skin looks blue around baby's mouth or on her body.**
- **Baby is struggling to breathe, *or* she breathes more than 50 breaths a minute.**
- **Skin or whites of her eyes look yellow.**
- **Soft spot on her head sinks or bulges.**
- **She is lethargic.**
- **She cries and is inconsolable, or her crying is high-pitched and frequent.**
- **Baby has fewer than six wet diapers a day.**
- **She is shaking and extremely irritable.**
- **She has a convulsion.**
- **She vomits forcefully (vomit travels several inches—*not* spitting up or dribbling) or repeatedly.**
- **She refuses two feedings in a row.**
- **She has a rash that causes her discomfort.**
- **Her temperature is higher than 100F (37.7C) or lower than 96F (35.5C).**
- **She has persistent diarrhea.**
- **There is blood in her urine or her stool.**
- **There is an unusual discharge from her eyes, navel or genitals.**
- **She has white patches in her mouth (it could be thrush, which isn't serious but can make her very uncomfortable).**

humidifier before you turn it on to be sure it contains enough water.

Don't leave a humidifier too close to baby's crib or bed when it is running. It might chill her. Run it *only* when necessary. When baby gets older and is more mobile, place the humidifier completely out of her reach on a high, stable surface.

If you notice bumps on baby's gums and the roof of her mouth and she seems OK, don't worry. The bumps are immature oil glands that should disappear very soon.

When Baby Gets Excited

Sometimes baby becomes overstimulated. When it's time to go to sleep, she has a hard time settling down. You can help her calm down so she can get the rest she needs. Offer a pacifier or her thumb. Hold your baby close, and rock her fairly quickly—about one rock per second. Or walk her around, but don't bounce.

As you get to know your baby better, you'll know what works for her. You may need to make some changes in these techniques as she gets older. What may work with her when she is very small may not work as she grows up.

What Babies Don't Like

Here is a list of things that most babies *don't* like. Keep them in mind as you interact with your little one.

Bitter or very sour tastes are unpleasant to your baby. If you give her anything bitter or sour, she'll probably scrunch her face and turn her head away from it.

Irregular movements and sounds can distress baby. A baby prefers regularity in sound and motion. Unusual patterns can upset her.

Sudden changes around her may unsettle your baby. Let her know what you're going to do before you do it.

Don't overstimulate baby if you can avoid it. She reacts to stress in many of the ways you do.

Abrupt volume changes can disturb your baby. She likes gradual change, so keep this in mind as you deal with her. Avoid sudden changes from soft to very loud sounds.

Milestones This 13th Week

Tonic Neck Reflex Disappears

The tonic neck reflex, which kept baby's head turned to one side most of the time, has just about disappeared by now. Baby can turn her head to either side, which makes it easier for her to turn toward a sound.

Her Visual World

Baby may be able to follow a moving object with her eyes. She can follow something as it moves vertically or in a circular pattern. She can also see things as far away as 15 to 20 feet. Her view of the world is vastly different from yours. Get down on the floor to see what she sees: chair and table legs and whatever was left under the coffee table! You'll understand her better when you look at the world from her perspective occasionally.

Milestones This 13th Week

Changes in Baby You May See Now

Physical Development
• sits with support

Senses and Reflexes
• may bat at object with closed fist

Mental Development
• waits for expected reward, such as feeding

Social Development
• tries to attract attention when a parent or sibling is nearby
• may be attentive for up to 45 minutes

Every baby is an individual, and your baby may do some of these things more quickly or more slowly than another baby. If you are concerned about your baby's progress, discuss it with your healthcare provider. Also see page viii.

She Sits when Supported
She sits up when supported at her hips and enjoys sitting in a semi-upright position. This position is best for learning and play.

She Uses Her Hands
Her hands are now open most of the time. She holds and shakes a rattle. She may grab at your hair, your jewelry or your clothes. She may swipe at a toy with her closed fist.

When She Vocalizes
It's a thrill to hear your baby laugh and chuckle, which she may be doing now. She is also vocalizing more—cooing, squealing, whimpering and gurgling. Because you talk to her, she is beginning to understand a message is made up of syllables. Soon she will start making vowel sounds, such as "ooh" and "aah."

Note: See also the box on this page, *Milestones This Week*.

What's Happening This 13th Week?

If Baby Has Difficulty Getting to Sleep
Baby sleeps about 10 hours at night, although she may wake for short periods in that time. If your baby has trouble going to sleep when you put her down, she may not have been awake

long enough during the day. Don't leave her in her crib too long when she wakes up from a nap. She needs to associate being in her crib with sleeping. Avoid overstimulation of your baby, especially just before bedtime. These situations could contribute to baby's sleep problems.

> During the first 4 months of her life, baby's skull grows faster than at any other time during her lifetime. Your baby's doctor measures her head at well-baby checkups to see that her brain is developing normally. During the first month, baby's head may have grown as much as 1 inch. For the remainder of her first year, average head growth is about ½ inch per month.

Acid Reflux

What it is. Acid reflux, also called *gastroesophageal reflux*, occurs when baby's stomach contents bubble up into the esophagus. This can irritate baby's throat and cause her to pull away from the bottle or breast while she's feeding. She may refuse to feed for a bit but then want to feed again immediately.

Acid reflux can occur at any age; everyone experiences it at some time. Only the frequency and persistence of the problem make it abnormal. Acid reflux is usually a mild problem that improves by about 1 year of age. Symptoms baby may have acid reflux include
- spitting up
- vomiting (can be forceful)
- weight loss
- gagging or choking at the end of a feeding
- respiratory problems
- irritability
- hiccups
- coughing
- apnea

What to do. For a mild case, burp baby and hold her upright for about 30 minutes after she eats to address the problem. Give small, frequent feedings. Burp baby more frequently than before. Change the position of her infant seat or the head of her crib to be more upright. Sometimes adding rice cereal to formula can help, but *do not do this* unless your pediatrician says it's OK. If the problem is severe, discuss it with your pediatrician. He or she may want to treat baby with medication.

When to call the doctor. Contact baby's doctor if she vomits excessively, loses weight or has respiratory problems. If you see blood in the vomit or she has apnea spells, contact your pediatrician. Medications may be prescribed to decrease the amount of acid in the stomach contents or to promote gastric emptying.

If the problem is serious, nasogastric feedings (putting a tube through the nose into the stomach) may be necessary for a baby who has severe reflux. Acid reflux could result in her failure to thrive. Surgery may be needed if there are severe complications, such as recurring aspiration pneumonia, apnea or severe irritation or inflammation of the esophagus or if medication doesn't work.

> Don't be surprised when baby shows you a new trick: She can blow bubbles with her saliva! If she hasn't already taught herself how, she soon will.

Chapped Skin

What it is. Chapped skin is common, especially during the winter. Baby's skin appears dry and flaky and often slightly reddened. It may itch. To ease baby's discomfort, try the following measures.

- Bathe baby less frequently.
- Use warm, not hot, water in her baths.
- Use soap sparingly.
- Pat skin dry, rather than rubbing it.
- Apply lubricants to dry skin before chapped areas become inflamed.
- Use a cool-mist humidifier in rooms with very dry air.
- If you live in a very dry climate, add a humidifier to your heating system or put humidifiers in various rooms of the house.

What to do. For minor discomfort, use nonprescription skin lubricants, such as petroleum jelly, mineral oil or alcohol-free, fragrance-free lotions. For serious discomfort, you doctor may prescribe topical cortisone creams or lotions.

When to call the doctor. Contact the doctor if your baby has severely chapped skin and home care doesn't relieve symptoms in 1 week. If her chapped skin becomes inflamed, call your pediatrician.

More Than One Baby!

Having one baby is a wonderful experience—having two or more is incredible! You'll need more of everything—equipment, assistance, time and patience. You'll probably get less sleep, but your rewards will be great as your babies grow.

Adjustments ahead! If you are the lucky parents of multiples, you will make many adjustments as a family. It's in everyone's best interest, including your babies', to ask for help. Don't try to do everything yourself, or you'll be overwhelmed and exhausted. Take good care of yourself and your partner so you can both tend to babies' needs. The following ideas can lighten your load.

- Keep diapers and supplies close at hand, around the house. It saves energy and provides you more time with your babies.
- Take care of yourself. Get out of the house when you can. Ask others to help. They'll love the opportunity to interact with your babies. Eat well, and rest when babies rest. Keep your energy and strength levels up.
- Hire at least one mother's helper for part of each day. A teenager may be a good choice to help around the house. If you can't leave a helper alone with the babies, he or she can tend and entertain them while you relax or do things you've put off.
- Don't do anything you don't have to. Let some chores go for a while, if they can be ignored.
- Alternate tasks with your babies. For example, bathe one baby one day and the other the next day. As long as faces, hands and diaper areas are clean, babies don't need a bath every day.

- Be as efficient as you can. Plan ahead. If you bottlefeed, make up bottles 24 hours in advance and store in the refrigerator. Don't change babies' clothes if they're not dirty.

The equipment equation. You'll need more equipment with multiples, but you don't need two of everything. You will need a crib for each baby, although a drawer or basket will work while a baby is small. You must have an approved car seat for each baby. Individual infant seats and highchairs are necessary, as are diapers and clothes for each baby. One stroller with a seat for each baby is a good investment.

With some equipment, one item is enough. You probably need only one swing, playpen, rocking chair, diaper bag, changing table and infant tub. Use these items in turn.

Feeding. One of the greatest challenges for parents of multiples is deciding how to feed them. Some mothers want to breastfeed exclusively. (It's an added bonus for multiples because they are usually smaller than single-birth babies, and breast milk is extremely beneficial for them.) Some moms say bottle-feeding is the only way to go. Others combine the two to breastfeed *and* bottle-feed their babies. Breastfeeding, even for one or two feedings a day, gives your babies the protection that breast milk provides.

Breastfeeding multiples is a challenge. Experiment with positions to find what works best. Some mothers nurse both babies at the same time. You can purchase cushions designed to help you hold and nurse two babies at once.

Switch babies from one breast to the other at different feedings, so each baby gets visual stimulation on both sides. It also helps prevent problems for you, such as engorgement in one breast if one baby isn't feeding as well as the other. By switching breasts, overall demand for milk remains about the same for each breast, so breasts tend to remain equal in size.

Supplementing with formula enables others to help you feed the babies. Breastfeed one while someone else bottle-feeds the other. Or nurse each one for a time, then let another person finish the feeding with formula.

Get them on the same schedule. Work toward getting both babies on the same feeding and sleeping schedules. One baby may be more interested in feeding than the other, but try to feed them at the same time when possible. It helps if babies sleep on the same schedule. You'll gain precious free time in the process.

Spending time with the babies. You may not have as much time to spend playing and interacting with your babies as you'd like. Set aside time alone with each baby. Giving your exclusive attention to baby is an important part of the bonding process. Choose a time when she's quiet and alert. Play with her and interact as we've described in previous discussions. Talk with each baby and get to know their different personalities.

Fighting favoritism? You may be shocked to find yourself feeling closer to one baby than another. One baby's temperament may be more

Put twins on the same schedule.

easy-going. Maybe you prefer the sex of one baby to another's. Some parents harbor a little resentment toward the second, unplanned-for baby.

The first step to overcoming such feelings is to admit you have them. They are not abnormal, so be kind to yourself. Admit you have the feelings, and go from there. If one baby is more demanding than another, focus on her positive traits. Give each of your babies time and attention. As you get to know them both, the feeling will pass.

No two babies are alike. Accept each as an individual and treat them fairly. Soon you will feel loving affection for each baby.

Find moral support. Contact groups in your area for parents of multiples. Talking about your stresses and distresses with others who have been there can be a great help. These organizations are usually listed in the telephone book. Also see the Resources section, page 492, for a list of national organizations.

> **Tip: When you want to go out when babies are older, and you wonder if a sitter can handle more than one baby, hire a sitter for each baby!**

Toys and Play This 13th Week

A baby likes to explore textures. Touching different objects gives her much pleasure. It helps her learn what the

> **Ask relatives and family members to kiss baby's hands, not her face. The skin on her face is very sensitive and easily irritated.**

world is like. Offer a variety of safe things to touch and feel, such as soft cloth, sheepskin, a shiny leaf (from a nonpoisonous plant, of course!), a smooth plastic spoon. Stay alert when you give her various objects. She'll probably try to put everything in her mouth!

Reach for the Rattle

Help baby develop her eye-hand coordination with a brightly colored rattle or toy. Hold it at different distances in front of her. Encourage baby to reach for it. Be sure you give it to her often, or she may become frustrated.

Pat-a-Cake

Finger-play games stimulate your baby to hold, stare at and clench her hands. One time-honored game that encourages this development is "Pat-a-Cake."

Clasp one of baby's hands in each of yours. As you sing, clap baby's hands together in time to the song.

> *Pat-a-cake, pat-a-cake*
> *Baker's man.*
> *Bake me a cake*
> *As fast as you can.*
> *Pat it, and roll it*
> *And mark it with "B."*
> *Put it in the oven*
> *For baby and me!*

Object in Motion

Baby's eyes can now move in a circular pattern. Above her head, hold a shiny object tied securely on a string. Move it slowly in a circle as baby watches. Then hold it at her eye level. Move it around her head. She will follow it with her eyes. She may learn to anticipate it as it moves behind her head, then back into view. She is beginning to grasp the concept of motion.

Week 14

How Big Is Your Baby This 14th Week?

Baby weighs 12-3/4 pounds and is 23-3/4 inches long this week.

Baby Care and Equipment

Does Baby Need a Social Security Number?

Your baby needs a social security number, although most parents don't think of it right away. You need one to claim him as a dependent on your income tax and to make your child eligible for benefits he may be entitled to in the future. You'll need a social security number to open baby's bank account, buy him a savings bond or apply for some government services. However, getting a social security number is voluntary—you won't get one unless you ask.

The government has made it easy for you. No need to fill out special forms to apply for a number! Direct your hospital representative or doctor to have your state's vital-statistics office share information from baby's birth certificate with the Social Security Administration. This information is confidential. After the information is forwarded to the Social Security Administration, a card with baby's number on it will be mailed to you.

Questions?

If you have questions or concerns about the application process, call the Social Security Administration at 800-772-1213. On the Internet, contact them at *www.irs.gov*

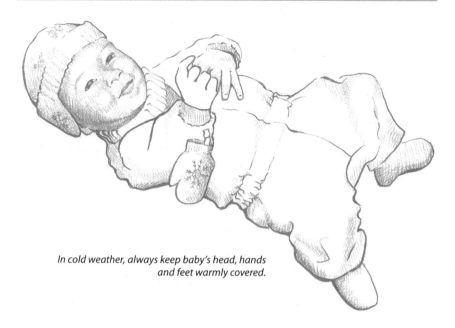

*In cold weather, always keep baby's head, hands
and feet warmly covered.*

If you apply for a number when baby is born, you save yourself
time and effort. You won't have to visit the Social Security office in
person, fill out forms or submit a birth certificate.

Follow Your Instincts when Dressing Baby

Has someone older than you told you your baby is cold, even
though you dressed him in one more layer than you have on? Don't
be disturbed. The older generation tended to overdress babies and
overheat their homes when their children were little.

It isn't healthy to keep baby too warm. Fortunately, it's easy to
dress him properly for the weather. Dress baby depending on what
you're comfortable wearing. One more layer than you are wearing if
it's cold, the same number of layers if it's warm. In cold weather, keep
baby's hands, feet and head covered to preserve body heat.

Don't overheat your home—72F (22.2C) is fine when baby is
sleeping. According to some research, overheating a room may be
linked with SIDS.

A Few More Minutes with Your Doctor

In this first year, you'll see your baby's doctor at least five times for
well-baby checkups—and probably more. You may find your office-
visit time limited by your doctor's busy schedule. You may feel there
is never enough time to discuss all of your concerns.

You can get the most from your next doctor's appointment. In Week 15, we discuss specific ways to get the most out of a well-baby checkup. Below are some ideas for every office visit:

> ## Routine Is Important
>
> **Provide your baby with a predictable routine. A routine helps him anticipate events that occur regularly in his life. This in turn helps him develop skills of attention and memory.**

- At the time you make your appointment, ask if it's possible to schedule a longer visit with your doctor. It may mean coming into the office early or late in the day, but if it's important to you, it's worth it.
- Prepare before you go. Think about your concerns, and write them down. You'll save time, and you'll be able to cover the topics you want. Limit your questions to these topics.
- Before you leave, be sure you understand the answers to your questions. Ask for clarification if you don't understand something.
- If some of your questions can be answered by a nurse practitioner or someone else in the office, ask to speak with him or her. Get to know everyone on the office staff. They are available to answer your questions, too.
- Don't bring other children with you when you go to the appointment.

Milestones This 14th Week

Baby Tracks Objects with His Eyes
Your baby follows objects with his eyes easily now. Earlier in infancy, he had trouble fixing both eyes on an image. Now he can lock his gaze onto an object moving several feet away from him. He watches people moving around him, and he gazes across the room. He sees in full color, and prefers red and blue.

His Strength Improves

> **It's time to put away baby's infant mobiles.**

His arm and leg movements are more controlled. He holds his head up when sitting. His grasping ability is much better, and he makes greater efforts to use it. It's time to store the infant mobiles and bring out toys he can grab and hold. A crib gym encourages him to reach for and to hold an object.

Drooling

You may notice your baby begins drooling around this time. Some babies drool so much they are constantly wet around their neck

> **Baby should sleep about 10 hours a night, nap about 4-1/2 hours and be awake for interaction and play time about 9 hours each day.**

and face. Some people attribute drooling to teething, but this isn't always the case. Some babies cut their first tooth this early, but most don't start teething until they're at least 6 months old. If your baby drools profusely, put a bib on him. Read the discussion below on the rash that can develop with excessive drooling.

When Baby's Tired

By now, you can probably tell when baby's getting tired. Obvious signs are yawning, rubbing his face and eyes, avoiding interaction with others, crying or fussiness. A very tired baby will regress in behavior to earlier kinds of reflexes and actions. He may suck his thumb, roll his head, cry or act unhappy and be hard to soothe. When you become aware of what these actions mean, you can remove him from a stimulating environment and let him rest or go to sleep.

Note: See also the box below, *Milestones This Week*.

Milestones This 14th Week

Changes in Baby You May See Now

Physical Development
• focuses eyes at different distances
• holds head steady and erect for short periods

Senses and Reflexes
• clasps fingers and hands in play

Mental Development
• smiles and vocalizes more to an actual face than to an image

Social Development
• attempts to soothe self
• may prefer a particular toy
• can be quieted with music

Every baby is an individual, and your baby may do some of these things more quickly or more slowly than another baby. If you are concerned about your baby's progress, discuss it with your healthcare provider. Also see page viii.

What's Happening This 14th Week?

Rashes from Drooling

What it is. Some babies drool a lot beginning about this time. Their neck and face area get wet and stay that way. Constant dampness and the irritation of wet skin against clothing can cause a rash.

> You may be tempted to start baby on solid foods because you've heard solids help him sleep better. They don't—just the opposite! If started too early, solids may cause gas and keep baby awake.

What to do. If your baby gets a rash like this, protect his face with petroleum jelly. Dry his face and apply the jelly. Dusting a little cornstarch on his neck can help protect that area. If the rash becomes severe or seems to cause baby major discomfort, call your pediatrician for advice.

Constipation

What it is. A constipated baby has difficulty passing bowel movements, has infrequent bowel movements or sluggish bowel action. It occurs more often in older infants, when baby begins eating solids or with other dietary changes.

> If your baby is breastfeeding and goes a few days between bowel movements, this is not considered constipation.

The main symptom of the problem is baby's difficulty passing dry, hard stools. This may be accompanied by abdominal pain, which decreases after a large bowel movement. Baby may go several days between bowel movements. You may notice stool is streaked with blood.

What to do. If your younger baby seems constipated, use a rectal thermometer lubricated with petroleum jelly to stimulate the passage of stools. Gently place the thermometer in the rectum, then remove it.

If your baby is older and eating solids, offer fluid and diluted juice. Apple juice often has a laxative effect. Increase the fiber content of baby's diet. Most cases of constipation go away in time if they are caused by a change in diet.

When to call the doctor. Contact your pediatrician if the above measures don't work. Call the office if baby's constipation is accompanied by severe abdominal pain or vomiting. Do not use medication to relieve constipation without consulting the doctor first.

Air Travel with Baby

Air travel is one of the best ways to make a long journey with a baby. With a little planning and preparation, the trip can be enjoyable for everyone.

Plan ahead. These tips can help make your trip more enjoyable. Keep your trip short when possible. Book a nonstop flight. The faster the trip, the better.

- Allow extra time for everything. Time your arrival at the airport at least 30 minutes earlier than when you travel alone. You may need the extra time for checking baby's car seat, for changing diapers or feeding him.
- When you make your reservation, get your seat assignments so the whole family can sit together.
- Check baggage at the curb.
- When possible, schedule your trip for baby's naptime or bedtime. With luck, he'll sleep through at least part of the trip.
- If you can travel during quieter times of the day, such as late night, you may find an empty seat next to you, and you can spread out a little.
- Dress baby comfortably, in layers. Bring an extra blanket or two because planes tend to be chilly.
- Change baby just before you board the plane. If your trip is short, you may not have to change him again until after you land.
- If you have an umbrella stroller, take it with you. It's easy to stow in the plane, and it's helpful when you have to walk long distances in the airport. If you can't take it on board, you can check it at the gate as you board the plane. You'll get it back at the gate at your destination.

> When traveling with baby by air, be prepared for any situation. Don't assume the airline will provide anything to make your trip easier or more comfortable.

- If your baby is less than 3 months old, use a front carrier and keep your hands free. A backpack carrier is a good choice with an older baby.
- Most airlines offer preboarding if you have a small child. Use it! You'll have more time and room to get settled in your seats and to stow all your gear.
- Although most airlines let a baby fly free and sit in an adult's lap until age 2, consider buying him a ticket and securing him in the plane's seat in his car seat. See the discussion on page 156.
- Offer baby a pacifier or a feeding during take off and landing. This helps equalize pressure in his ears. See the discussion below.
- Carry extra of everything you normally have in your diaper bag. If you're delayed anywhere, you'll have the supplies you need.

Where to sit? When you make airline reservations, state clearly you are traveling with a baby. You might request the seat behind the bulkhead, which provides more legroom. Bulkhead seats do have drawbacks. Armrests are fixed in place, so you can't raise them to increase your space if no one else sits in your row. You also lose under-seat storage.

Your Carry-on Bag

Most airlines limit passengers to two pieces of carry-on luggage. If you carry a purse, your other piece of luggage has to carry everything you'll need for baby during your trip. Include

- disposable diapers and baby wipes
- diaper-rash ointment
- a small changing pad for your lap or other surface
- a few pacifiers
- at least two changes of baby clothes
- formula, bottles and nipples

- baby food (if baby's eating it)
- burp cloths
- a favorite comfort toy
- a blanket
- at least 6 resealable plastic bags
- a frozen washcloth in a plastic bag, if your baby is teething

A window seat is a good choice because no one has to climb over you and baby to get in and out. If you have a seat for baby, place yourself between your baby and another passenger.

Advice about ears. Taking off or landing in a plane can make your ears feel stuffy and may cause discomfort. The change in pressure affects the Eustachian tube, which closes temporarily. Fluids in the ear build up. You may lose some hearing temporarily. Chew gum, swallow often or suck on hard candy.

Your baby experiences the same feelings in his ears. Help him clear his ears to relieve his discomfort. Feed him or offer him a pacifier to suck on during takeoff and landing. If baby is asleep when you're preparing to land, wake him up and try to feed him.

Mom's Travel Tip

Some moms carry a couple of diaper bags. They put their wallet, tickets and a few necessary things for themselves in a pocket of one bag. They pack their empty purse in their luggage to use when they get to their destination.

Can a baby fly with a cold? It's usually OK for a baby to fly if he has a cold, but air-pressure changes in the cabin can cause fluid buildup, and his risk of developing an ear infection increases. If baby is congested, ask your pediatrician if you should give him a decongestant the night before your trip. With an ear infection, baby should receive antibiotics at least 48 hours in advance of the trip. This should keep symptoms from getting worse during the flight. Acetaminophen for children can relieve discomfort. Ask your doctor about it.

Discuss your plans to fly with your pediatrician, if your baby has a cold or an ear infection.

Keep baby (and you) hydrated. The cabin air in a plane is dry. Offer baby fluids to prevent dehydration. You should drink extra fluids, too. Use saline nose drops or nasal spray to help with the lack of humidity. Spray a little into each of baby's nostrils about once an hour. Or let baby breathe through a damp washcloth held close to his nose. *Note:* Never place the washcloth *over* baby's nostrils.

(more)

Changing baby on the plane.
Most airplane bathrooms don't have
a changing table for baby, and even
when they do exist, they're small.
You won't have many options about
where you change diapers. You may
have to do it on an empty seat or
on your lap. If your baby is quite
small, you might get by with using
the closed lid of the toilet seat.

Carry plastic bags with you.
Airlines require you to use plastic
bags for disposable diapers. If you use
cloth diapers, put any soiled diapers
in a plastic bag until you can rinse
them out after you land.

**Getting baby to sleep during
the flight.** Some parents plan a trip
so baby naps during the flight. Others
want to travel after baby wakes up, so
he'll be rested. Don't change baby's
schedule to try to fit your flight time.
Try to make baby comfortable during
the flight so he can relax and sleep.
If he doesn't sleep, be prepared to
entertain him.

Feeding baby during the trip.
If you bottle-feed, bring enough
formula for an entire day. Using
powdered formula and boiled and
cooled water you've packed avoids
spoilage. Mix a bottle as you need
it. With an older baby, take prepared
baby food in addition to formula.
Some airlines provide baby food.
Request it at least 24 hours in
advance.

Using baby's car seat. The
Federal Aviation Administration (FAA)
strongly recommends a baby be
placed in a car seat, then strapped
into an airplane seat when flying.
It's impossible for an adult to hold
onto an unrestrained child in severe
turbulence or during an accident.

If you choose to have your baby
ride in his car seat for the flight, you'll
be required to pay for his seat. Ask
the airline about discount prices for
infants; some offer half-price seats for
children less than 2 years old if they are
placed in a child-restraint system. The
safety seat must be an approved car
seat and marked with the tag "certified
for use in an aircraft." When you book
the tickets for you and your baby, ask
for adjoining seats in a row that is not
an exit row. Some airlines require the
car seat be placed in a window seat.

Mom's Travel Tip

**If you can't afford to buy an
extra ticket, ask your travel
agent or the airline
reservation clerk which flights
are likely to have empty seats.
You might be able to book
this type of flight and use
an empty seat for free.
Unfortunately, you can't count
on a seat to be available unless
you purchase a ticket for it.**

When things don't go smoothly.
Some trips won't go according to plan.
Flights are canceled or rerouted, or
long delays occur. Do what you can to
deal with the situation, then ask the
airline for help. You are entitled to food
vouchers if you are delayed beyond a
certain length of time. Ask if the airline
has a family area where you can take
baby and rest a little yourself. You may
be entitled to hotel accommodations if
your delay is very long.

Your doctor may suggest an enema or a mild laxative for baby. If constipation becomes chronic or serious, testing may be ordered to determine the cause.

Measles

What it is. Measles, also called *rubeola,* is a highly contagious virus that can occur at any age. Symptoms of measles include

- cough
- runny nose
- fever
- fussiness
- a rash of small red bumps that begins on the face and spreads downward to baby's trunk, arms and legs

The rash is more severe at the beginning of the breakout, then becomes less intense as it spreads.

A vaccination to prevent measles was developed years ago in the United States, so cases of measles don't occur often. However, measles must be considered if baby has not been vaccinated and he develops these symptoms.

What to do. Isolate baby during the early stages of the disease. Give plenty of fluids and acetaminophen for fever and discomfort. Keep baby's skin clean. Give warm, tepid baths to reduce the itching. Call your pediatrician. He or she probably will want to see baby to confirm the diagnosis. Prevent measles by vaccinating your baby!

> **Your baby's hair may be changing in color and texture. His baby hair is being replaced with new hair. This process continues for the next few weeks.**

When to call the doctor. Once measles has been confirmed, call baby's doctor if baby develops a high fever, becomes extremely irritable or if the rash becomes infected.

Toys and Play This 14th Week

Your baby probably needs practice grasping different objects with his hands. Offer toys that make noise, such as rattles. When he's lying on his stomach on the floor, place several toys within his reach. Let him choose the ones he wants to reach for and to hold.

Family Pictures

Make a display of family photos for baby to look at. He likes to gaze
at people's faces, or pictures of them, especially people he knows.
Put enlarged photos on the wall or on a table where he can see
them. Point to and name the people in the pictures as he looks at
them. He may reach for the photos. Let him touch them. It helps him
recognize those around him.

Shake that Rattle!

Help baby develop his visual acuity and
motor skills at the same time: Give him a toy
that is easy to hold and makes noise. Out of
his line of vision, shake his hand gently so

> **Offer toys that feel
> good to his gums,
> such as rubber or
> plastic teething rings.**

the toy makes noise. Does he lift the toy into his line of vision to
see what's making the sound? If he doesn't, raise his arm, and shake
the toy again. Tell him what's happening. Do this with both of his
hands.

Horsie Ride

If you're like most parents, you'll soon become your baby's "horsie"
and will be for quite a long time. These games help your baby bond
with you and improve his ability for social relationships. He also
develops muscle coordination and balance.

While reciting the nursery rhyme "Banbury Cross," cross one
knee over the other and place baby on your free foot. Holding baby's
hands firmly, gently swing your foot up and down, bouncing him
while singing

Ride a cockhorse to Banbury Cross
To see a fine lady upon her white horse.
With rings on her fingers and bells on her toes
She shall hear music wherever she goes.

Week 15

How Big Is Your Baby This 15th Week?

Baby weighs 13 pounds and is 24 inches long this week.

Baby Care and Equipment

Does Baby Need Vitamin D?

Years ago, parents were advised to put a baby outside in the sunshine because the baby got vitamin D from the sun's ultraviolet rays. Dr. Benjamin Spock's famous baby book even included a sunbathing schedule for baby.

Today, we advise you to protect your baby from the harmful rays of the sun. Don't worry about your baby getting enough vitamin D. She gets it from breast milk or enriched formula.

As a rule, keep your baby out of the sun. Sunscreens and sunblocks can protect her delicate skin, but nothing protects better than no exposure at all. (Do not use sunscreens and sunblocks on babies younger than 6 months of age.) See the discussion in Week 20.

Medication Guidelines

Be very careful when giving your baby any type of medicine. Medicine must be the correct type and given exactly as prescribed. Follow these guidelines when giving medications to your baby.

- When you give your baby liquid medication, use a measuring spoon, a plastic medicine spoon or an oral syringe. Don't use tableware—these utensils aren't accurate.

- Be sure the measurement unit on the device you use is the same unit of measurement you need.
- Give baby the correct amount of medicine—don't confuse tablespoon (T. or tbsp.) with teaspoon (t. or tsp.).
- Store medication for each family member on a separate shelf in a safe place, out of a child's reach.
- Don't keep medicine in a bathroom cabinet. Steam and moisture can affect its potency.
- Tape a note on each prescription stating the dosage schedule.

> **If you use a spoon out of your silverware drawer to give baby medication, the dose may be incorrect. If your "teaspoon" is off by even 1ml (0.0338 fluid ounce), you could be giving her 20% more or less of the medication than she needs! Use proper measuring devices when giving your baby medicine— every time.**

- Be sure you have the correct medication. Double-check the label.
- Never guess at the amount of medicine to give. Double-check the dosage amount.
- Don't make conversions. If directions call for 2 teaspoons, don't try to convert it to ounces.
- If your baby is prescribed more than one medication, be sure they are OK to take together. Consult your physician or pharmacist.
- Don't keep old medications; get rid of them.
- Use clean droppers and spoons. Rinse them between use, then air dry. When you have finished giving a medication, wash these utensils in warm, soapy water. Store in an airtight plastic container or sealed plastic bag. Don't wash them in the dishwasher. The openings are too small to be cleaned properly. Soap residue might not be washed out.
- Don't give medicine to anyone other than the person it was prescribed for.

Well-Baby Checkups

Follow the suggestions in Week 14, and add these specific points to your list to ensure a good doctor visit.

Medication syringe.

- Ask the doctor to describe the procedures he or she performs on your baby, the reasons for them and what the results may indicate. This approach gives you a way to ask questions during the procedure. You may forget questions if you wait until the end of the appointment.

- If tests are performed, ask about the results. When will they be available? Do you have to call the office for them? When would other tests be indicated? When would further treatment be indicated?
- Ask questions about nonmedical issues, such as emotional development, discipline, learning and socialization of your baby.
- Request printed material that might be useful. Doctors' offices offer pamphlets, booklets and other handouts. These can reinforce information your doctor may have told you, especially when you've discussed many topics with your physician at one appointment.
- Ask if a nurse, nurse practitioner or physician's assistant can help you with questions and problems. These professionals often are more readily available to help you than the doctor.
- See if your pediatrician has a recommended-reading list. He or she may have suggestions for a book that will help you with a particular situation.

Helping Baby Relax

When a baby feels relaxed, she falls asleep more quickly. These suggestions help set the mood for baby.

- *A warm bath.* Some babies like to be in the water. Others like the sound of running water and the steam that hot water produces. Try bathing your baby when she's fussy. If that doesn't work, put her in a safe place in the bathroom while you take a shower.
- *Noise.* White noise is often helpful for calming baby. Run the clothes dryer or the vacuum cleaner. Be careful with very loud sounds. They could distress baby.
- *Music.* Try different types of music with your baby. Some babies like lullabies. Others prefer classical music. Some are calmed by music with a strong beat.
- *Motion.* Riding in a car, walking, bouncing, rocking–they can all work
- *Her own bed.* Put your baby to bed at the first signs of fatigue. She may relax more easily.

Infant Carrier Seats

Lots of parents use their baby's car seat as an infant carrier seat. It's convenient, and it saves money because you don't have to buy a second piece of baby-transport equipment. Other parents use an infant carrier seat—a different piece of equipment—in the house or on errands, and leave the infant car seat in the car. It's easier than hooking and unhooking the baby's car seat every time they get into or leave the car.

If you choose to use an infant carrier seat, be aware of certain safety issues. The three greatest safety concerns are

- a baby becoming entangled in restraining straps
- a carrier seat falling over on a soft surface, resulting in suffocation
- an unrestrained baby falling out of a carrier

The Consumer Product Safety Commission (CPSC) has made recommendations for parents to follow to ensure baby's safety in infant carriers. By following them, you will help prevent injury to your baby.

- Make sure the carrier you select has a wide, sturdy base.
- Never leave baby alone in an infant seat when it is not placed on the floor. In fact, you should never be farther away than arm's reach when baby is in an infant carrier.
- Place an infant carrier only on a hard surface. Keep it off upholstered furniture and beds.
- Use safety straps and belts when baby is in the carrier.
- Keep an eye on your baby when she's in her infant carrier. Keep her away from pets and out of drafts. Place her in areas where she can't be hurt.
- Be careful when carrying baby in an infant seat—avoid bumping the carrier into walls and other objects.
- Never use an infant seat as a car seat!

When you put your baby in an infant carrier, maintain your vigilance. You may believe she's out of harm's way just because she is strapped into a carrier. However, it's your care that keeps her safe.

Milestones This 15th Week

When Baby Is Happy

Your baby is learning something new all the time. When she's excited about something, she may jerk her arms and legs crazily to demonstrate her joy. She's not in total control of her body yet, so her actions appear spastic and jerky. When baby is unhappy, soothe her by holding and talking to her. Sometimes your presence is all she needs to calm down. This is a sign of her increasing trust in you.

Her Legs and Feet Strengthen

Baby loves to kick her legs and feet now! You may notice her hold up her legs, flex her feet and make bicycling motions in the air. She may be able to touch her knees with her

> In the next few weeks, she may become attached to something soft or cuddly as a security object.

hands. She delights in splashing in the bathtub. These practices help develop the strength she needs in the coming months to support her weight.

Evidence she's preparing to begin the rudiments of creeping and crawling can be seen in her "swimming" motions. She may lie on her tummy, hold her head up, and kick and move her legs and arms at the same time.

She May Partially Roll Over

A big accomplishment around this time is baby's ability to roll herself over partially. She may roll from back to front, or front to back. She'll probably master rolling in one direction in the next few weeks. Then she'll concentrate on rolling the other way. At this time, she probably can't make it all the way over, but she'll soon accomplish that feat.

Baby Pleasures

Your baby may enjoy being rocked and bounced. Receptors in her brain make this activity pleasurable. Whirl her securely in your arms. She may enjoy her swing now more than ever because of its back-and-

> Babies love to look at faces, especially other babies'. Don't be surprised if your baby stares at another baby, then reaches out to push and poke her.

forth motion. She likes to look at bright colors and is less interested in black and white. She recognizes family members and may become more attached to individuals, especially her mother.

Milestones This 15th Week

Changes in Baby You May See Now

Physical Development
• turns head in all directions

Senses and Reflexes
• splashes and plays in bath

Mental Development
• has memory span of up to 7 seconds

Social Development
• interested in mirror image; may smile at it
• adjusts responses to different people

Every baby is an individual, and your baby may do some of these things more quickly or more slowly than another baby. If you are concerned about your baby's progress, discuss it with your healthcare provider. Also see page viii.

She Makes an Assortment of Noises

Your baby may spend a lot of time making noises. You may hear her pant, grunt, groan, coo, babble and shriek. She listens to herself talk. You may hear her making "ba, da, ga, pa" sounds. These sounds let her express her wants and needs with less crying. She vocalizes more to an actual person than to a picture of a person. She loves to laugh and to play with people.

Note: See also the box above, *Milestones This Week*.

What's Happening This 15th Week?

Sitting Pretty

By this time, your baby may be sitting very well when she's propped up. To help her practice, sit cross-legged on the floor. Place her in your lap facing outward. Your stomach and legs provide support for her back. She'll enjoy being close to you while she increases strength in the muscles she'll use to sit up on her own.

Eyes Changing Color

Your baby's eyes may have changed color by this time, if they are going to. Blue eyes may start to darken. If they're still blue by age 6 months, they'll remain that color. Babies of color are usually born with brown or dark-colored eyes. If eyes are light brown, they may darken gradually.

Make Her Car-Seat Experience More Interesting

Your baby is still facing the rear when she's riding in her car seat and will continue to until she turns 1. But it bores her. She'll be happier if you add some interesting things for her to look at and to do while she's in the car.

Dangle a toy at a safe distance in front of her car seat. This encourages her to reach forward and bring her hands together. An activity bar on the car seat can engage her, too. As she gets older, rattles, other toys and books will keep her entertained.

For your peace of mind, a mirror that attaches to the rear window can provide you with a view of her while you're driving. You can check on her quickly without stopping the car.

Cat-Scratch Disease and Cat-Scratch Fever

What it is. *Cat-scratch disease* is an infection transmitted by the bite or scratch from a cat. An abscess forms at the site, followed by swelling in the lymph nodes within 2 weeks. The lymph nodes may feel hard or soft, and are usually tender. Fatigue and fever may be present. Cat-scratch disease is benign and goes away without special treatment.

Cat-scratch fever is also believed to be transmitted by cats. A few days after a minor scratch, a pustule develops at the site. Fever, a general feeling of ill health and headache are seen with this problem.

What to do. The best way to avoid the problem is to keep baby away from cats. If she does get scratched, clean the area thoroughly with soap and water. Apply a topical antibiotic to the scratch to deal with any infection. You can give acetaminophen for fever and discomfort, if baby's doctor OKs it.

When to call the doctor. Contact the doctor if your baby develops a high fever or experiences severe pain or extreme irritability. If lymph nodes get larger or if there is redness of skin above and around the lymph nodes, contact your pediatrician. Lymph nodes can be found under the arms, on the sides of the neck and in the groin.

In severe cases, lymph nodes may be aspirated to relieve the pain. Antibiotics may also be given.

Kidney Problems

What they are. The most common problem you may see is a kidney infection (pyelonephritis). In general, kidney problems also can include problems such as kidney stones, polycystic kidneys (kidneys have small cysts or collections of fluid) or kidney injury. These are significant medical problems and require a doctor's care. Fortunately, they are unusual in newborns and young infants.

Symptoms of a kidney infection include

- blood in urine
- decrease or very low amount of urine
- bruising of the body
- seizures
- irritability
- itching
- nausea
- vomiting
- lethargy or stupor

When to call the doctor. You can do nothing for kidney problems at home. If you think your baby has a kidney problem, contact your pediatrician. Kidney abnormalities can indicate other problems. Treatment is determined by the underlying cause.

Pyloric Stenosis

What it is. The pyloric muscle pushes the food from baby's stomach into her small intestine. Pyloric stenosis occurs when baby's pyloric muscle begins to swell and grow. If the muscle increases in size, food will be vomited because it cannot pass into the intestine to be digested. This vomit is different from spit-up because the entire contents of baby's stomach are emptied in one intense motion.

What to do. Tests usually determine the cause of the problem. It is fairly common and occurs more often in boys. The condition is easy to correct with minor surgery. If left uncorrected, a baby can become malnourished and dehydrated, and may even suffer developmental delay.

Toys and Play This 15th Week

It's tempting to buy your little baby all sorts of toys to delight her, but play it safe. Choose age-appropriate toys. Don't buy her a toy if the box suggests it is best for babies "12 to 18 months." She won't enjoy it for some time.

Don't provide toys with small, detachable parts, long strings or sharp edges. Check toys periodically to be sure they're still safe for play and haven't developed wear-and-tear spots.

Here Comes the Bumblebee!

A surprise tickle game is lots of fun for baby. Babies usually love "Here Comes the Bumblebee!" Lift one hand high above baby. While slowly spiraling your hand downward toward baby, sing

> *Here comes the bumblebee, the bumblebee, the bumblebee.*
> *Here comes the bumblebee, and he's going to get* (baby's name)*!*

When you sing baby's name, tickle her lightly in the ribs or tummy. As she gets older, this game demonstrates her memory skill and her ability to anticipate events. She'll start giggling and wiggling when she knows the bumblebee is going to "get" her.

Week 16

How Big Is Your Baby This 16th Week?

Baby weighs 13-1/4 pounds and is 24-1/4 inches long this week.

Baby Care and Equipment

Watch Out for Stray Threads

As you dress or bathe your baby, you may notice occasionally that his toe or finger is swollen. Did he get an insect sting? Did he pick up a splinter? Many scenarios may run through your mind, but you might overlook the obvious. Check the area very closely. A thread or hair may have wound around the finger or toe and cut off the circulation. It's as if baby is wearing a tourniquet.

A baby is at greatest risk of this during his first year because he cannot respond to the problem. He can't tell you his finger hurts. He has to wait until you notice it. You may not see what's causing the problem right away. Sometimes the thread or hair is so fine, even a physician has difficulty spotting the cause.

Play it safe and check your baby's toes, fingers and penis (cases have been reported) for swelling when dressing or changing him. If you notice swelling, examine the area for a strand of hair or thread wrapped tightly around the swollen spot. Clip the hair or thread with small manicure scissors to release the pressure.

If you can't clip the hair or thread, see your pediatrician. Contact your doctor whenever you notice *any* unusual swelling anywhere on your baby's body.

Prevent Choking

Your baby continues to put objects in his mouth. He's exploring and learning about his environment when he does. Unfortunately, a baby doesn't have any idea about what's safe for him. It's up to you to be vigilant about these objects.

When you find him putting things in his mouth that aren't safe, such as a button, a small toy or one of your earrings, substitute a safe toy. Know how to perform CPR and the Heimlich maneuver, in case of an emergency. See Emergency Situations, page 479, for further information.

Front and Back Baby-Carrier Safety Tips

A carrier you wear on your front or back is a convenient way to carry baby with you. It keeps him safe and happy while freeing your hands for various tasks. It gives baby a different view of the world and may increase his learning experience. Use carriers safely, as indicated below.

- Read the directions, and follow them exactly as to weight limits.
- Position baby in the carrier correctly to avoid falls and other hazards.
- Never bend over while carrying baby; he could fall out.
- Don't use a front carrier while drinking a hot beverage or working over the stove.
- Don't use any type of carrier while riding a bike.
- *Never* leave baby alone in a carrier; it could tip over.
- If you have a second-hand carrier, contact the Consumer Product Safety Commission to check for recalls. See the Resources section, page 492.

> **Make your baby's 4-month well-baby checkup now. See page 97 for any immunizations he may receive at this next visit.**

What Is Baby Eating?

Baby's nutrition still comes from formula or breast milk. He's drinking 25 to 40 ounces a day. He may be ready to start on solids soon. See the discussion in Week 17.

If you believe your baby is ready to begin solids, discuss it with your pediatrician before you do anything! He or she will help you determine whether your baby is ready to take this important step. Your baby's doctor will also recommend the type of cereal to offer (probably iron-fortified), when to offer it and how to introduce it to baby.

Back Sleeping and Baby's Development

As we discussed in Week 8, back sleeping is the safest position for baby in the crib because it decreases the risk of sudden infant death syndrome (SIDS) by 50%. However, back sleeping may delay some development milestones slightly. Studies show babies who slept on their backs rolled over, sat up, crawled and pulled themselves to a standing position 2 to 4 weeks later than babies who slept on their tummies.

Is this anything to be concerned about? Most doctors say no, because the delay was not significant. Keep putting baby down to sleep on his back. It's worth it.

Milestones This 16th Week

Eye-Hand Coordination

Baby's eye-hand coordination is improving. When he sees an object, he moves his hand toward it. His fingers open to its approximate size. Both of his hands grasp the object to manipulate it, and he often grasps with either hand. He can manipulate an object more easily. Whatever he finally gets his hands on eventually ends up in baby's mouth.

He is more deliberate in reaching for an object, too. He'll grab at a woman's necklace or a man's mustache. He likes to explore his body with his hands.

Why Is My Baby Crying?

When baby cries, run through this checklist, and ask yourself the following questions. Your answers may lead you to a solution that will help your baby stop crying.

- Is my baby thirsty?
- Is he hungry?
- Does he need to be changed?
- Is he too hot?
- Is he too cold?
- Is he wrapped in his blanket and is his circulation cut off?
- Is he sick? What's his temperature?
- Is he bored?
- Is he tired?

Baby's Emotions

Your baby enjoys the stimulating interaction he shares with you and other family members. He's beginning to express an array of emotions, including joy, unhappiness, contentment, displeasure. His crying diminishes as he uses newfound emotions to express his feelings. When he's tired, he lets you know by yawning, rubbing his eyes or face, refusing to play or by becoming restless and cranky.

Ways Baby Interacts

Your baby's temperament and interests determine how much he will focus on an activity. His personality is developing and is determined partly by his daily routine. You are learning how active he is, how he responds to activities, how patient or impatient he is and his frustration level.

Baby may be responsive to interaction for as long as an hour at a time. He will often let you know he wants to play by vocalizing to you. If your baby is left alone for long periods, he may become drowsy or fussy because he isn't stimulated.

His smiles now indicate true recognition. When he smiles at you it's because he knows you. While he'll smile at different faces, he still prefers yours.

> **His smiles now indicate true recognition.**

He "Talks" Now

You may be surprised to hear your baby putting together a series of syllables when he "talks" to you. These are the basic sounds of language development. Keep talking with him when you are together and he will continue to develop his language skills.

He's Getting Stronger

When baby lies on his stomach, he can support his head and chest with one arm. He may roll over easily now from his tummy to his back.

His Focus Sharpens

Your baby focuses at different distances, but he prefers to look at what is close by—within 3 feet. In a few weeks, he'll be able to focus on near or distant objects as well as you do. His eye movement is less jerky.

Note: See also the box on page 172, *Milestones This Week*.

Milestones This 16th Week

Changes in Baby You May See Now

Physical Development
- may roll over from back to stomach or stomach to back
- sits, with assistance and support

Senses and Reflexes
- pulls dangling object toward himself and brings it to his mouth
- stares at the place from where object dropped
- displays interest in smells

Mental Development
- initiates several tonal sounds

Social Development
- plays alone for longer periods
- vocalizes to initiate socializing
- laughs when tickled

Every baby is an individual, and your baby may do some of these things more quickly or more slowly than another baby. If you are concerned about your baby's progress, discuss it with your healthcare provider. Also see page viii.

What's Happening This 16th Week?

A Bedtime Routine

Your baby is definitely growing up. He's more of an individual and is more independent. Now may be a good time to think about easing him away from some dependencies, such as rocking him to sleep every night.

Instead of waiting until your baby falls asleep in your arms, put him to bed when he's still awake. A bedtime routine helps him understand it's time to go to bed, and that bed is for sleeping. See the discussion in Week 7. If you haven't established a bedtime routine, begin one now. You and your baby will benefit from it.

View a bedtime routine as a parent-child interaction that is special to you. This lets baby know his bedtime is different from other times of the day, such as playtime, feeding time and naptime. His bedtime also becomes a reliable occurrence. It signals to him that the day is over.

Each family develops different rituals for bedtime—a bath, stories, rocking, prayers, soft lullabies. Try different things, and keep what works best. Using the routine every time you put baby to bed, even when you're away from home, offers him security that this day is over and a new one begins tomorrow.

Common Misconceptions about Babies

Parents may have preconceived notions about babies—often they are wrong! A recent survey of more than 800 parents revealed many had misconceptions about a baby's emotional development. Below are some common misconceptions that were cited.

- *Misconception:* The greater the number of caregivers a child has before age 3, the better he will be able to cope with change. **Fact:** Too many changes actually can make him reluctant to form new relationships.
- *Misconception:* Young children do not get depressed. **Fact:** Studies indicate that babies can show signs of depression as early as 6 months of age. When these symptoms appear, every effort is made to work with the entire family to treat the problem.
- *Misconception:* The more stimulation the baby receives, the more he'll learn. **Fact:** We know that too much stimulation can irritate a baby and interfere with learning.

Read and Sing to Baby

Reading. Reading to your baby enhances his language skills and promotes his emotional development. When you read to your baby, he feels loved. He feels special because you're holding him on your lap, interacting only with him. Later, he'll associate those wonderful feelings with reading!

When you read to him, read slowly. Change your voice for different characters. Pause often to watch his reactions. You may discover he loves rhythm—most babies do. Share the rhythmic nursery rhymes of Mother Goose with your baby. You'll undoubtedly enjoy this time together as much as he does.

Singing. Baby enjoys hearing songs and music, too. Sing to him, even if you can't carry a tune. Play songs on cassettes and CDs that are written especially for young children. Lullabies are good choices for soothing baby. Play classical music, jazz and pop tunes, but don't play the music too loudly. Expose him to everything in your musical library!

Bowed Legs

What it is. Your baby may have legs that bend outward in the lower part of the limb. It can occur from infancy through 2 years of age.

> **Your baby's knees and elbows may "crack" often. As his muscles become stronger, this disappears.**

Legs bow when the baby stands, and the space between the knees is greater than 2 inches. Toddlers are usually bow-legged, after they begin to walk, until their lower-back and leg muscles are well developed.

What to do. Don't be concerned about bowed legs at this early age. Don't worry unless baby has bowed legs beyond age 2 to 3 years.

Your pediatrician will monitor baby until he begins to walk. If baby has persistent bowing after age 2, if bowing is increasing, not decreasing, or if only one leg is bowed, you may be referred to an orthopedist for further evaluation. Applying a brace may be appropriate. In rare cases, surgery corrects the problem.

Wandering Eye (Lazy Eye)

What it is. A baby with a wandering eye or a lazy eye, also called *strabismus,* can't focus both eyes on an object at the same time. Wandering eye is common in the first 3 months of life because babies' eye muscles are not fully developed. Baby's eyes look crossed or appear to be wandering. By 4 months, baby usually can fix both eyes on an object.

What to do. Play vision games with baby to develop his eye muscles. Help him track a moving object. Move a bright, colorful object slowly from side to side, and up and down. Read the Toys and Play sections of each week in this book, and try the vision games we mention.

When to call the doctor. If you notice your baby has difficulty tracking objects after 4 months of age, tell your pediatrician, who will assess the situation. Treatment ranges from glasses, an eye patch, eye exercises or medication, to surgery, in extreme cases.

Ichthyosis

What it is. Ichthyosis is a skin disease. Skin is dry and scaly, and looks like fish scales. Some forms of ichthyosis are inherited; others are not. Ichthyosis may be present at birth, or it may not appear until later. Symptoms include

- scales on the skin of varying thickness
- scales may be yellow or dark in color
- skin thickens on palms of hands and soles of feet

What to do. If your baby has ichthyosis, your physician will probably advise you to apply lotion or ointment to soften and soothe his skin. Use soap sparingly. Baths may have to be limited. If medication is necessary, your physician will prescribe it.

Toys and Play This 16th Week

Think about replacing some of baby's toys in the next few weeks. If your baby has a mobile or other toys fastened to his crib, remove them when he can push up on his hands and knees. Because he puts everything in his mouth, and will for quite a while, these toys can be dangerous if he gets hold of them. Mobiles and other toys are often made with string or cord, and may have small parts.

Versatile toys are the best toys. When selecting toys for baby, choose those that serve more than one purpose. It may be less expensive to buy these toys in the long run, and they may keep baby entertained for a much longer time. For example, some toys can be used as a rattle and as a stackable toy.

Make life interesting! Your baby will enjoy looking at interesting things every day. To help him develop coordination, place him on the floor on his tummy. Place an array of brightly colored toys in front of him, near his hands. He'll reach out to touch each one as he enjoys looking at them.

> **Choose toys that serve more than one purpose.**

Soapy Bubbles

Because your baby's eyesight is so good now, you might entertain him with soap bubbles. Buy some soap bubbles or make your own mixture out of a little dish soap and water. Blow bubbles away from baby using a straw or bubble wand; soap from a bubble can sting his eyes. He'll enjoy watching the bubbles drift slowly around the room. The exercise also helps him practice tracking a moving object.

Roll, Baby, Roll

Help baby develop upper-body strength. Lay him on the floor and gently roll him from side to side or from stomach to back. Using a large beach ball, hold baby firmly with both of your hands as you rock him slowly on his tummy on the ball.

    Help baby learn to roll. If baby doesn't turn over on his own yet, play a game to help him along. Lay baby on his back on the floor. Place a bright toy to one side. If he turns toward it, give him a gentle push to help him go all the way over. He'll enjoy this game, and it will help him develop the coordination to roll over on his own.

Yarn Play

To encourage finger dexterity, let baby play with short lengths of yarn. Braid several thin strands to make one thicker strand that is easy for baby to grasp. While you're interacting with baby, let him play with the yarn strand. Watch him closely; never leave him alone with the yarn pieces. Take away the yarn when you have finished playing this game.

Weekly Milestones at a Glance

Week 17

Physical Development
- may make swimming motions, resulting in movement around his crib

Senses and Reflexes
- may be ready to start solid food
- can distinguish between smells
- may hold object between index and second fingers

Mental Development
- has responsive periods of 1 hour or more
- is interested in making new sounds

Social Development
- laughs when playing
- may cry if playing is disrupted
- may interrupt feedings with play

Week 18

Physical Development
- balances head steadily in different positions
- brings feet to mouth; may suck on toes

Senses and Reflexes
- grasp is steadier
- plays with rattle, if placed in his hands

Mental Development
- can squeal, grunt and make a "raspberry" sound

Social Development
- smiles and vocalizes to gain attention and to make social contact

Week 19

Physical Development
- lifts both arms and feet while lying on her stomach

Senses and Reflexes
- raises hand near object
- will grasp onto an object
- brings object to mouth

Mental Development
- utters vowel sounds and a few consonants

Social Development
- likes to play at mealtime

Week 20

Physical Development
- may move by rocking, twisting or rolling

Senses and Reflexes
- aims well when reaching
- may be able to hold bottle with both hands

Mental Development
- wants to touch, hold, turn, shake and mouth objects
- deliberately imitates sounds and movements

Social Development
- imitates facial expressions
- waves arms to be picked up

Week 17

How Big Is Your Baby This 17th Week?

Baby weighs 13-1/2 pounds and is 24-1/2 inches long this week.

Milestones This 17th Week

How Baby Develops
Babies usually develop "from head to toe." As she grows, your baby gains strength and muscle control from her head down to her toes. She can control her head quite well at 17 weeks of age. When she's on her tummy, she can hold her head at a 90-degree angle. She turns her head in all directions. A big accomplishment is her developing ability to raise her head when she's lying on her back. She can look at her toes. She can move her head far back to see what is above her.

Safety Do's and Don'ts
- Never leave baby alone in the car or the house.
- Stay near baby when she's eating.
- Stay with your baby when she is in the bathtub—no exceptions!
- Keep crib side rails up when baby is in bed.
- Pick up baby by grasping her chest; don't pull her up by the arms.
- Attend baby when she's on the changing table, bed or sofa.
- Never use a plastic bag as a cover for the changing table, bed or sofa.
- Keep a watchful eye for small objects she could choke on.

Sitting Skills Improve

Your baby enjoys sitting up. Her back still needs support, such as pillows or an infant seat, but she is easily propped in a sitting position. She can sit for longer periods. Her neck is stronger now, and she holds her head erect. She is getting strong enough to lift her head and almost pull herself up to a sitting position when you hold her hands.

In the next few weeks, her strength will increase to the point she'll be able to sit in your lap with very little help from you. She once molded her body to yours when you cuddled. Now she sits a little straighter and farther away from you. She's becoming more independent.

Exercise Her Legs

When you lift baby to a standing position, her legs straighten as her feet press against the hard surface. She likes to stand briefly. This exercise is good for her.

Baby's Socialization

Baby is socializing more each day. She likes to listen to speech and music. This is a special time: Her brain can respond to every sound produced in every language of the world! She makes many noises, entertaining herself and others. She may cough at will (there's nothing wrong with her) and loves to mimic the expressions and movements of others. When you tickle her, she laughs out loud. This response is a sign of social development.

The Beginning of Speech

She repeats sounds many times. These sounds will become words in the months to come. When she "talks," her speech may have the inflections and intonations of actual speech. You may hear some of her speech ending in a high note, as if she were asking a question.

Her Behavior

Your baby is beginning to react to your tone of voice and to your expressions. She senses when her behavior is unacceptable. She may demand attention by fussing and may cry when her play is disrupted.

Note: See also the box on page 183, *Milestones This Week.*

Is Baby Ready for Solid Food?

Every baby is different. Some babies may be ready to start eating solids before other babies of the same age. Discuss your baby's diet with your pediatrician before you make any changes.

Before baby can eat solids. If your baby is ready for solids, most or all of the following conditions should apply to her. Baby . . .

- controls her neck
- sits up with support
- has doubled her birth weight
- shows when she is full (turns her head or refuses to open her mouth)
- shows interest in food when you eat
- mimics you when you eat, such as opening her mouth when you open yours to take a bite
- indicates her wants by reaching or leaning toward something
- seems hungry for more food

Besides controlling her head and neck muscles, she also must be able to move her tongue back and forth. These two skills help her avoid choking. Most babies do not achieve these skills until they are between 4 and 6 months old. Before that age, your baby's tongue-thrust reflex is still very strong. This reflex helps baby draw a nipple into her mouth but it pushes out solid food. The reflex begins to diminish around 4 months. Then baby will be better able to take food from a spoon and swallow it.

Don't introduce solids too soon. Solid food will not make baby sleep through the night, so don't feed her solids because you want her to sleep longer. If you begin feeding her solids before she's ready,

> To prevent accidents and choking problems, never leave baby alone while she eats.

you may actually create problems. A baby's digestive system isn't ready for solid food when she's very young. She'll be about 9 months old before she develops certain digestive enzymes, which help her get the most nutritive value from the foods she eats.

What to feed baby. Most pediatricians recommend baby start on rice or oat cereal made for babies. Dry cereals have more iron than jarred baby cereal. Mix the dry cereal with breast milk or formula. Make cereal very thin, then thicken it as baby gets used to it.

If you breastfeed baby, you might feed her mashed bananas as a first solid food. Bananas are sweet, like breast milk, and aren't likely to cause food allergies. If you bottle-feed baby, she is used to blander-tasting formula, so mix formula with dry cereal.

Continue feeding baby breast milk or formula. At this time, cereal is only a small portion of her diet—2 or 3 teaspoons to begin with. Discuss with your pediatrician the amount of formula or breast milk and the amount of solids to feed baby.

For now, you'll only use a baby spoon. Baby has to learn to keep food in her mouth—it isn't automatic.

What about fat in the diet?
Some parents believe that by reducing fat in baby's diet they will keep baby from gaining too much weight. This is a misconception where infants are concerned. Fat and protein are crucial for tissue growth and brain development in the first 2 years of life. Your baby needs fat in her diet. When she is eating well, and you begin to add more variety to her diet, do *not* reduce the amount of fat your baby consumes.

How to begin feeding solids to baby. You might begin by using your finger as baby's first spoon. Wash your hands well, then dip your finger into prepared cereal. When she opens her mouth to eat, place a few drops on her lips. Let her suck on your finger. Next, place some cereal on the tip of baby's tongue. When she swallows this bit of cereal, place some in the middle

of her tongue. If she make faces, it's only her reaction to this new experience.

Watch her closely to see how your baby responds to eating solids. She may open her mouth wide for more. If the food comes back out, it doesn't mean she doesn't like it. She may need to learn to keep her mouth closed to keep the food inside.

If baby rejects the food, her tongue-thrust reflex is still strong. Let her practice. If she still has trouble, you may need to wait 1 or 2 weeks before trying again.

Gradually increase amounts. As baby becomes more adept at eating cereal, gradually increase the amount she consumes. In a few weeks, she may eat as much as 1/4 cup for a meal. Feed her solids once a day. Within a month or so, they'll become a regular part of her meals.

Offer one new food at a time. Once you begin feeding solids, offer baby only one new item at a time. Over time she will become familiar with many different tastes. If she has an allergic reaction to any of the foods she eats, it's also easier to identify the problem food.

Feeding position and equipment. Make sure baby is in a sitting position when you feed her
(more)

A food grinder.

solids. Place her in your lap or her infant seat. As she gets older and sits more confidently, place her in a highchair. Use a baby spoon or some other small spoon. Her mouth isn't very large, so she won't eat comfortably from a larger spoon.

Be patient! Your baby will take time to settle into an eating routine. She may eat a couple of tablespoons one day, then not eat well for the next day or two. She may like one food one day, and refuse it the next. Remain calm and reassuring as you begin this new adventure. Never force her to eat something she doesn't like. Wait awhile, then try again.

Be careful of your own reactions, too. If you don't like a particular food, baby may sense it and refuse to eat it.

Will baby stop drinking formula or breast milk? As your baby begins solids, she'll be exposed to new tastes. As solids become part of her daily diet, she may want to nurse less or drink less formula. During the first year,

breast milk and formula should be the *main source* of her nutrition. Encourage her to keep nursing or taking formula. These are the most complete sources of the nutrition, vitamins, minerals and other important substances your baby needs.

A word of caution. You may have heard someone, such as your mother or mother-in-law, say that putting cereal in a baby's bottle is a good way to start solids. Don't do it! Eating solids is a new learning experience for your baby. She needs to practice the techniques for eating solid foods.

Milestones This 17th Week

Changes in Baby You May See Now

Physical Development
• may make swimming motions, resulting in moving around in her crib

Senses and Reflexes
• may be ready to start solid food
• distinguishes among smells
• may hold object between index and second fingers

Mental Development
• has responsive periods of 1 hour or more
• interested in making new sounds

Social Development
• laughs when playing
• may cry if playing is disrupted
• may interrupt feedings with play

Every baby is an individual, and your baby may do some of these things more quickly or more slowly than another baby. If you are concerned about your baby's progress, discuss it with your healthcare provider. Also see page viii.

What's Happening This 17th Week?

Teething May Begin Soon
If your baby pulls at her jaw or ear, drools or acts fussy for no reason, teething may begin soon. Because symptoms are often the same, it may be difficult to decide whether she has an earache or is teething. If in doubt, rub her gums. If she's teething, she'll probably yell because her gums will be tender and sore.

Should We Discipline Baby?
A lot depends on your child, but as a rule of thumb, it's too early to start discipline yet. She is not mentally developed enough to understand the consequences of her actions. For example, if she drops food from her highchair, you may want her to stop so you don't have to keep cleaning up the mess. To baby, it's a new game, and she enjoys it very much. Repetition is still very important in baby's life. It'll be quite awhile before she'll begin to understand what she is doing or why she should not do it.

Motor Skills
Baby is probably warming up for the crawling she will be doing in the coming months. When she's lying on her tummy, she

lifts her head, arches her back and kicks her legs. She may also make swimming motions with her arms. The kicking and bouncing strengthen her leg muscles. The arm motions help develop those muscles, too.

She'll probably begin with a little creeping. This moves in quick succession to crawling, pulling up, cruising, then walking. Don't be concerned if she skips one step entirely or seems stuck on another. She's making progress at her own pace—she'll be moving soon enough.

When Baby's Activities Affect Her Sleep

This is a time of great change and accomplishment for your baby. As she begins to move more, her activities may affect her sleep. She may move around her crib and get herself into situations she can't get out of, such as jamming her head against the rails. When she begins standing, she may find herself up, with no way to get down. She'll need your help when this happens, especially during the night.

When she begins to crawl and walk, her muscles might be sore from her exertions. She may not be able to sleep because of the soreness or because she's excited about her accomplishments. On the other hand, she may sleep more soundly because she's so exhausted.

The key is to be tuned in to what's happening in baby's life that could affect her in ways you might never imagine. Be patient and offer help if she needs it.

Celiac Disease

What it is. Celiac disease is an allergic condition caused by gluten, a protein found in many grains and cereals. Gluten prevents the small intestine from absorbing some nutrients. The problem can occur any time from infancy through early childhood. It usually occurs when baby begins eating foods with gluten. Symptoms include

- weight loss or slow weight gain after adding cereal to her diet
- loss of appetite
- diarrhea
- foul-smelling stools
- frequent gas
- swollen abdomen
- abdominal pain

• mouth ulcers
• baby's skin is pale in color
• tendency to bleed easily
• failure to thrive, in some cases

What to do. If you suspect your baby may have celiac disease, monitor her diet carefully. Note any changes you see as you introduce or withhold foods.

When to call the doctor. If your baby has many of the symptoms described above, and there is a family history of the problem (most forms are inherited), call your pediatrician. If symptoms don't decrease within 3 weeks of changing baby's diet, your pediatrician will probably want to see her. It's also serious if your baby doesn't regain lost weight, or she fails to grow and to develop as expected. Call if a fever develops. Your doctor may prescribe oral cortisone drugs to reduce baby's inflammatory response during a severe attack.

Shaken Baby Syndrome

What it is. Shaken baby syndrome can cause serious physical and mental harm to a baby. People who would never think of hitting a baby might give her a "good shake" to quiet her or to discipline her. They do not realize how dangerous it is. One out of four babies subjected to shaking dies from injuries related to shaking.

The problem usually occurs when a baby cries persistently. Out of frustration, the parent or caregiver shakes baby in an attempt to make her stop crying. Most occurrences of shaken baby syndrome last less than 20 seconds. In that short time, a baby may be shaken up to 50 times, which can seriously harm or kill her.

Shaken baby syndrome is particularly serious in young babies because their neurological systems are still developing. There may be few outward signs, but symptoms a baby has been shaken violently include

• brain damage
• seizures
• blindness
• problems with speech
• bruising
• change in behavior after being cared for by someone else
• any signs of abuse

What to do. The best advice we can give you about shaken baby syndrome is never shake a child or baby for *any* reason. Make sure anyone who cares for your baby knows that one shake can seriously harm or kill a child.

Prepare for times when baby can't be comforted with a strategy to deal with your own frustration. All babies cry, some more than others. If you don't think you can deal with a crying situation, ask family members or friends for help. Don't let your emotions get out of control.

Caution: It's OK to play with baby, just don't play too roughly. Be careful when you toss her into the air, swing her or spin her around. Even bouncing may be done with too much vigor.

When to call the doctor. If you believe your baby has been shaken, contact your pediatrician immediately. He or she will treat specific problems.

Toys and Play This 17th Week

Your baby delights in discovering her actions can make something happen. She enjoys shaking toys that make a sound. Offer toys that reinforce the cause-and-effect relationship. Because she can sit up well when propped, she may be interested in toys that she can play with more easily in a sitting position. When she's in her infant seat or highchair, attach an activity bar to it. She'll enjoy playing with the different and colorful toys on the activity bar.

Share Reading Time
Continue to read to your little baby and enjoy the intimacy it creates between you. The words you read aloud help baby develop language skills. Because she sees color quite well now, she'll enjoy a book with brightly colored illustrations or pictures. She sees small objects easily, too, so choose a book with lots of things to look at.

Give Precrawling Help
Help your baby to feel what it's like to crawl. When she makes pushing or swimming motions on her tummy, press your hands firmly against the soles of her feet. She may inch forward as she pushes. If she doesn't move, stop and try again later.

Week 18

How Big Is Your Baby This 18th Week?

Baby weighs 14 pounds and is 24-3/4 inches long this week.

Baby Care and Equipment

Transition to Solids
Once your baby begins eating solids on a regular basis, he may be less interested in breast milk or

> **Even at 1 year old, baby gets about half of his caloric needs from breast milk or formula.**

formula. However, breast milk or formula continues to be the primary source of protein and calories for his first year. Even at 1 year old, baby gets about half of his caloric needs from breast milk or formula.

Before baby began eating solids, he was drinking 35 to 40 ounces each day. In the next few months, his interest in food will increase and his interest in nursing or bottle-feeding will decrease. However, he should still drink a little more than 20 ounces of breast milk or formula at age 1.

The Scoop on Baby's First Cereals
When baby is ready for his first cereals, you'll have a lot of products to choose from. Keep these points in mind as you begin feeding cereal to baby:

> **The ability to taste salt develops around this age.**

- Begin with rice cereal. It causes the fewest food-allergy problems.
- Buy iron-fortified cereal.

- Buy single-ingredient cereal, such as rice, barley or oatmeal. As baby gets used to eating different foods, and has no allergic reactions, you can add foods to his cereal or choose cereals that include other foods.
- Begin with a thin mixture—mix 1 teaspoon of cereal with 4 teaspoons of breast milk or formula.
- Make only a small amount because leftovers go to waste.
- If your baby has problems eating the cereal, call your pediatrician before offering the cereal again.
- After baby learns how to move food to the back of his throat and swallow it, you can make the cereal thicker.
- Offer baby cereal once a day, at breakfast or dinner.
- As he becomes more adept at eating, offer him two "meals" a day, one at breakfast and one at dinner.
- If baby refuses to eat the cereal, don't push it. Wait a few days before trying again.
- Feed your baby only one new food a week. In the beginning, this will be one new cereal each week. As he gets older, you can add different types of baby food, such as fruits and vegetables. Discuss your particular strategy with your pediatrician.

> **If baby refuses to eat the cereal you offer him, don't despair. Try again in a few days.**

Protect Baby from the Sun

The best advice your pediatrician will give you about exposing baby to the sun is "Don't, when possible." Keep baby out of the sun whenever you can. The worst times of exposure for a baby are between 10:00 A.M. and 3:00 P.M. in spring and summer months. At other times of the year, avoid the sun between 11:00 A.M. and 2:00 P.M. If you live in a very hot, bright climate, such as the Southwest, just about any time of the day during the summer can be hazardous. (Even if the sky is overcast, baby can be exposed to harmful UV rays. Take these same precautions on cloudy days.)

Keep your baby under an umbrella or completely dressed to avoid sun exposure. Use sunhats and sunglasses on your baby, too. Don't use sunscreen or sunblock on baby until he's at least 6 months old. When you can use sunscreen or sunblock, always choose an SPF (sun-protection factor) of at least 15. Apply lotion to every part of his exposed skin; do not let it go into his eyes. He'll probably put his fingers in his mouth, so avoid putting lotion on his hands when

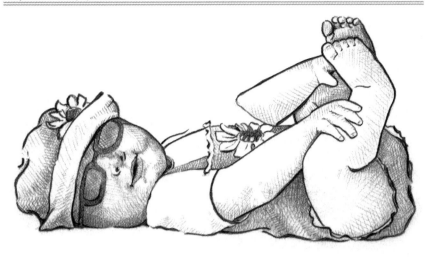

Keep baby well covered and preferably out of the direct sun altogether.

possible. Reapply lotion every 2 hours, and always reapply if he's been in the water.

Some sunscreens have stronger ingredients than others. You may find your baby gets a rash from one product. Try another. Try products made especially for children, which may not contain some of the more irritating ingredients.

Use sunscreen and sunblock year-round. Sun damage can occur at any time of the year. The damage is cumulative—it builds up as time passes. Avoiding sun damage now may decrease your child's risk of developing skin cancer later in life.

> **Infant car seats must be installed properly to reduce the risk of injury in an accident.**

Car Seats Save Lives

All 50 states have laws requiring infants and young children to be restrained in car seats or safety-restraint systems when riding in a vehicle, yet many parents don't take this necessary precaution. More than half of the children killed in car accidents in 1996 (the latest statistics available) were not in safety restraints.

If you don't use a car seat, you cannot protect your baby. In addition, infant car seats must be installed properly to reduce the risk of injury in an accident. One study showed that 85% of parents who use car seats installed them incorrectly!

Install car seats correctly. Check your baby's car seat periodically to be sure you've installed it correctly. It's easy to make a mistake when you move a car seat from one vehicle to another. Take time to double-check the installation every time you use the car seat. Also keep in mind these tips:

- If baby is under 20 pounds and less than 1 year old, use a rear-facing car seat.
- Harness straps should be secure. You should be able to place only one finger between the car-seat straps and your baby.
- Secure the car seat in the middle of the back seat–it's the safest position.
- Don't place a car-seat in a front seat that has an air bag.
- Don't use a car seat if it has been in an accident; it might have structural damage.

Milestones This 18th Week

Baby Anticipates Some Outcomes, but Not Others
Your baby is learning to anticipate the outcomes of certain actions. He demonstrates this skill when he reaches for his bottle to satisfy hunger, or shakes his rattle to make noise. He looks for an object when it drops. Hidden objects still mystify him, however. Baby knows where his hands are when they disappear, but he can't find a hidden object yet, even when he watches you hide it.

Rotate Toys
Baby can play alone with toys for up to 15 minutes. Think about rotating his toys every so often. Put some away when you take out others. He doesn't need too many toys—a few at a time are the most enjoyable. If you put some away for a while, it'll be like having new toys when you bring them out again.

Baby's Eyesight Improves
Your baby's eyesight is sharp. He sees things at various distances and follows moving objects easily. His depth perception is improving. He may look where you look. He likes the colors blue, green and orange. He will watch your face closely and may imitate your expressions. If he can't imitate them exactly, he's making the effort!

> ## Vocalizations
> He continues to practice talking, while listening to everything around him. He may make sounds to draw your attention to him if you're talking or interacting with someone else.

Eating Solid Food

Feeding baby solid food may be a challenge at times. He may want to play between bites. Maybe he'll let the food ooze out of his mouth after it goes in. He may even blow the food out of his mouth! These actions are baby's way of exploring his environment. Food is new to him. He's trying different ways to learn about it.

Rolling Over and Sitting Up

Your baby may roll over from front to back fairly easily now. He starts by pushing himself onto his side with his arms, then drawing up his top leg. Its weight helps pull him over the rest of the way onto his back. The more difficult back-to-front roll occurs a few weeks later.

Because baby can roll over now and reach for objects, be extra careful of his safety! Pick up every small object you see on the floor. If you don't, baby may get it and put it in his mouth.

Now that baby is sitting up more comfortably, it's fun to take him out in the stroller. Baby gets to see things he doesn't usually see at home.

Note: See also the box on this page, *Milestones This Week.*

Milestones This 18th Week

Changes in Baby You May See Now

Physical Development
• balances head steadily in different positions
• brings feet to mouth; may suck on toes

Senses and Reflexes
• grasp is steadier
• plays with rattle placed in his hand

Mental Development
• squeals, grunts and makes a "raspberry" sound in effort to communicate

Social Development
• smiles and vocalizes to gain attention and to make social contact

Every baby is an individual, and your baby may do some of these things more quickly or more slowly than another baby. If you are concerned about your baby's progress, discuss it with your healthcare provider. Also see page viii.

What's Happening This 18th Week?

Can Baby Learn a Foreign Language?

If you want your baby to learn a foreign language, it's never too early to begin. Researchers say that children learn languages most easily between birth and age 10. You could expose your child to many different languages at this special time; the ability is not limited to just one language!

Uno, Due, Tre...
Eins, Zwei, Drei...
Un, Deux, Trois...
Uno, Dos, Tres...

A baby can learn additional languages as easily as he can learn his native language. If a baby's parents each speak a different language, he can learn both languages if they are spoken to him. If grandparents have a different native tongue and speak to baby in that language, he will be multilingual. It's a matter of exposure.

Trust Builds Baby's Self-Esteem

We all know how helpless a baby is when he is born. He depends on you for everything. By responding to his needs and caring for him, you let him know he can count on you. He learns to trust you.

Your baby's trust represents a crucial point in his development. Trust in others is a major building block of self-esteem. If a child cannot trust his environment, he will be hesitant to try things in the future. By meeting your baby's needs, you contribute to his well-being now and in the future.

Convulsion

What it is. A convulsion occurs when a baby has an episode that includes strong involuntary muscle contractions and relaxations. Sometimes it is called a *seizure*. Convulsions can occur at any age and be caused by a number of things, including meningitis, epilepsy, tetanus, blood poisoning and other types of poisoning. When triggered by rapid rise in body temperature, it is called a *febrile convulsion*. This is the most common type of convulsion babies experience.

An infection accompanied by fever often precedes a febrile convulsion. Occasionally a convulsion is the first sign of fever. Up to 5% of all children between 6 months and 3 years old experience a febrile convulsion. Boys are more susceptible than girls to these types of seizures. Symptoms a baby has had a convulsion include
  • loss of consciousness or baby is unresponsive

- jerking or irregular movements of the limbs or face that lasts up to 3 minutes
- irritability after baby regains consciousness
- baby very quiet or "lifeless," or sleeps for several hours

What to do. During a convulsion, lay the baby on the floor or in a safe area. Move any dangerous objects out of his way. Take immediate measures to reduce a fever when he has one, especially if baby has had a febrile convulsion in the past.

When to call the doctor. Call your doctor immediately if your baby has a seizure with a fever. He or she will treat the underlying cause. Despite its frightening appearance, a convulsion caused by fever in a baby is rarely serious.

Hair Loss

Hair loss is not a medical problem. It's a natural part of baby's growth. When baby's hair falls out, it will be replaced by hair that is more permanent.

Infant hair usually grows slowly. When the new hair does appear, it may be different from the hair your baby had when he was born. It can differ in texture, color and thickness.

Hair loss in certain spots on your infant's head may indicate he is lying in the same position too much. Friction on baby's scalp causes his hair to fall out. The hair will grow back once baby begins to move around.

Toys and Play This 18th Week

Continue to offer your baby the noise-making toys he has been enjoying during the past few weeks. If you want to add to his toy box, choose brightly colored balls he can roll around and watch. He likes to play with toys with handles or loops that are easy to grasp, too. Be sure loops are small enough that he won't get entangled in them. He may like playing with your plastic measuring cups or measuring spoons best of all.

> **Keep playing tickle games with baby—he loves them. They stimulate his senses and help him learn to anticipate your words and corresponding actions.**

Mirror, Mirror on the Crib

If baby doesn't already have a mirror with which to gaze at himself, now's the time to get one. Choose a mirror *made for babies* out of unbreakable material. The mirror should be about 6 inches across and not distorted, so baby can see himself clearly. Attach the mirror to the outside of his crib, so he can see it through the bars. Or put it near his changing table, so he can look into it when you change him. You may find he spends quite a long time (for him) studying the "other baby." If you have a full-length mirror in the hall or a bedroom, let him gaze into that. He'll delight in seeing you in the mirror *and* sitting next to him!

Telling and Reading Him Stories

Stories continue to be important. Read aloud from books or make up stories as you go along. If you tell baby a story, it can be as simple as describing what you plan to do next. For example, "First we'll take a bath. Then we'll eat lunch," or "We're going to take our nap, then go to the store," can be considered stories for your baby.

If you read your baby a story from a book, point out pictures and describe them as you turn the pages. If you have a book about trucks, point out the trucks and identify each one for him. He may not understand what you're saying, but you're helping him understand that trucks fall into a category—a certain kind of object with lots of possible variations.

So Tall!

To increase baby's strength and help him practice his balance, play this game: Place baby on his back. Gently grasping his forearms, slowly pull him into a sitting position. He'll use his muscles to help you pull him up. Then gently pull him into a standing position so he can practice balancing on his feet while being supported by you.

It's easy to make this exercise a game. Recite in a singsong voice what you're doing. "We're helping baby to sit up, sit up, sit up." When you pull him to a standing position, recite in a singsong voice, "We're helping baby to stand up, stand up, stand up." When he's standing, sing "Baby's standing, he's standing, he's standing *so tall!*"

Week 19

How Big Is Your Baby This 19th Week?

Baby weighs 14-1/4 pounds and is 25 inches long this week.

Baby Care and Equipment

Should You Wait to Introduce Solids?

There are advantages to starting baby on solid food at between 4 and 6 months, so don't postpone it beyond 6 months of age. She needs experience eating different foods to become proficient. At this age, she also learns to appreciate the tastes and texture of food.

By the time your baby is 9 months old, she may have difficulty accepting solids if she hasn't experienced them already. Some children gag and have trouble swallowing if they are not offered food until they are older. When this happens, it is hard to overcome the problem.

Your baby will enjoy the new foods once she's used to them. She'll be more satisfied after eating, too, because solids fill her up more than only formula or breast milk.

Feeding Tips for Baby

Helping baby learn to eat solid food is fun and frustrating. It's exciting to see her growing and beginning to eat food. Soon she may be part of the family during mealtimes. It may also be frustrating to feed her because this new activity takes time to master. Keep your cool when you feed her, and keep in

> **Wait to introduce a new food if baby has a cold or isn't feeling well. Her appetite is probably affected, and she may not want to eat much of any food.**

mind the following suggestions.

- When she is able to sit up well, put her in a highchair at mealtimes. It's more convenient for you and more fun for her.
- When you warm her food, make sure it isn't too hot. Stir the food well and taste it before you feed her. Her mouth is sensitive, and food that is too hot can easily burn her tongue.
- Don't add flavoring to baby's food, such as salt, sugar, pepper or anything else. Avoid honey above all! See the discussion in Week 29.
- Use a small spoon to feed baby. She has a small mouth, and a regular-sized spoon is too big. Baby could get too much food at one time, and the big spoon is harder to get in and out of her mouth.
- Don't put food in her bottle. The bottle is for liquids only, such as formula or breast milk.
- Keep trying! Baby needs time and a lot of practice to learn all she needs to know to eat solids. She may reject food one day, then eat hungrily the next. It'll be awhile before she settles into eating solid foods.

Baby spoon.

Superabsorbent Diapers

This type of diaper keeps baby's bottom drier because of special liners. Some contain aloe to protect her skin. Their stretchy sides and gathered leg openings help stop leaking when baby's on the move, crawling or walking. You may want to consider these diapers as baby grows.

These "premium diapers" cost a little more, but they can be worth the price. You don't have to use them at every diaper change, but they can make baby more comfortable during the night. It's no fun to wake up in soaked pajamas and a sodden diaper.

Milestones This 19th Week

When Baby Is Active

Baby is a lot more active now. She reaches out and grabs things on her own. Be careful of her attempts to grab your hair, jewelry, glasses or scarf—she's playing a game. She's also practicing leg and arm movements, getting ready to creep and crawl.

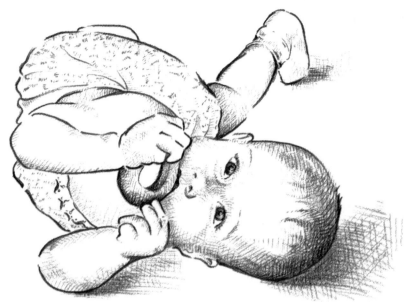

She'll put anything into her mouth that she can grab.

Because she is so active, it may be time to put her infant carrier seat away—she is just too mobile to be left in it safely. Use the infant seat for feedings, if she can't sit well in a highchair, but never leave her alone in an infant carrier seat! A bouncer or play chair may be a good substitute for the infant carrier seat now.

She May Need to Suck More

You may be surprised if your baby displays a need to suck more now—at a time when baby sucks less on the breast or bottle because she is eating solid food. She may be frustrated by her attempts at locomotion and be trying to soothe herself. She may need a pacifier to satisfy her desire to suck. She may suck on her hands and her feet.

Exploring with Her Mouth

She still puts everything she grasps into her mouth to learn more about it. She explores its texture and shape thoroughly with her lips and tongue. She'll put anything into her mouth that she can grab, such as daddy's tie or mommy's necklace. Keep a close eye on her when she puts things in her mouth.

> **Don't attach rattles, pacifiers or other toys to baby's crib or stroller with string, ribbon or elastic. Baby could get tangled in them.**

Quiet Periods

Your baby may have quiet periods during the day. She may spend an hour or more playing by herself. She may play longer with you. She still enjoys looking at your face and may focus on your eyes, if you return her gaze. In addition to your face, she'll now study your body and your clothes!

If she wants to skip a nap, encourage her to rest in her crib. Even if she doesn't fall asleep, the quiet time is good for her.

Putting Sounds Together

Putting together consonants and vowels happens more often now. She may double some consonants, such as "da" into "da-da." Respond positively to her efforts and she may repeat "da-da" more often. She has no idea what it means at this point, but she will make the connection soon.

Name Objects and Actions for Baby

When you interact with baby, label or name various objects by pointing them out specifically. When reading to baby, point to the child's eyes, nose and mouth in the book. Then point out baby's own eyes, nose and mouth. Label the actions found in the books, too. Point out that the child in the book is jumping, running or swimming, for example.

When She Discovers Her Genitals

You may notice baby has discovered her genitals. Don't be alarmed. She's exploring this part of her body just as she explores her hands and feet. Because the area is usually covered, she may be more interested in exploring it when she's undressed or in the bathtub. This type of exploration is normal. Don't convey it as unacceptable. When baby touches her genitals, use the correct names for her body parts.

Note: See also the box on page 199, *Milestones This Week.*

What's Happening This 19th Week?

How Much Is Baby Sleeping Now?

At this age, your baby needs only two naps a day. She sleeps longer during the night—up to 12 hours! She probably naps in midmorning and again soon after lunch.

Milestones This 19th Week

Changes in Baby You May See Now

Physical Development
• lifts both arms and feet while lying on stomach

Senses and Reflexes
• raises hand near object
• grasps an object
• brings object to mouth

Mental Development
• utters vowel sounds and a few consonants

Social Development
• likes to play at mealtime
• adjusts responses to different people

Every baby is an individual, and your baby may do some of these things more quickly or more slowly than another baby. If you are concerned about your baby's progress, discuss it with your healthcare provider. Also see page viii.

Limit baby's naps to no longer than a couple of hours. She should be up at least 4 hours between waking from her afternoon nap and going to sleep at bedtime. If she sleeps a lot in the afternoon, she may have trouble falling asleep at night.

She'll want to sleep more during certain periods than others. If she is going through a growth spurt, the extra sleep helps her catch up with the changes her body is going through.

Does Baby Still Wake Up at Night?

Some parents find baby still wakes up at night, as often as three or four times during her longest sleep period. All babies wake up at night. However, many babies do not fuss or cry when they waken. They soothe themselves and fall back to sleep.

Babies who cry out during the night, waking their parents, are the ones parents usually are most concerned about. They are often described as "problem sleepers." Experts believe these babies don't have a problem *sleeping;* they have a problem *soothing themselves back to sleep.*

Parents of these babies are advised to give baby a chance to fall asleep on her own. By taking her out of bed and feeding her every time she wakes, you encourage baby to wake up. She learns to expect to be taken care of in the middle of the night.

As difficult as it may be for you, if baby wakes up regularly at night, give her a chance to fall asleep on her own. Wait 5 minutes before you go to her. Gradually lengthen the time each night until she learns to soothe herself. *Caution:* If baby has been sleeping through the night regularly (or has not been waking you, at least) and uncharacteristically wakens during the night and fusses, tend to her. She may be having a problem that she needs you to take care of.

Impetigo

What it is. Impetigo is an inflammatory bacterial infection that affects the skin, most often around the mouth and nose. It is highly contagious. Children are especially susceptible to it. Symptoms include

- a red rash, with lots of small blisters
- some blisters contain pus
- yellow crusts form when pus-filled blisters break
- blisters aren't painful but may itch
- a low-grade fever
- child is contagious until after all lesions are healed

Call your doctor. If you think your baby might have impetigo, call your doctor. Impetigo is highly contagious, so your pediatrician will probably prescribe treatment. Call the doctor if baby has a fever or the sores spread or don't begin to heal in 3 days, even with treatment. Your doctor may prescribe treatment as follows.

1. Gently scrub lesions with disposable gauze and antibacterial soap. Break pustules, gently remove crusts and clean lesions. If crusts are hard to remove, soak them in warm, soapy water; then scrub gently.
2. Cover cleaned sores with gauze and tape.
3. Your doctor may prescribe oral antibiotics or an antibiotic ointment.

In addition, you will probably be advised to follow the measures below:

- Keep baby's fingernails short.
- If there is an outbreak of impetigo in your family, have everyone wash with antibacterial soap.
- Use separate towels for each family member.
- Wash bed and bath linens in hot water daily.

Coughing

What it is. Coughing can occur at any time. Baby may have a dry, hacking cough or a wet one that produces mucus. A cough often accompanies a cold or viral infection.

What to do. If baby coughs more than just occasionally, use a cool-mist humidifier to help relieve the dryness often associated with coughing. Put the humidifier in her room when she's sleeping. Direct the mist so it doesn't hit her directly or dampen her bedding. Keep the humidifier out of her reach. Also see the discussion of humidifiers in Week 13.

If you don't have a humidifier, take baby with you into the bathroom. Close the door, and turn on the hot water in the shower. Let it run. Expose baby to the steamy room for at least 10 minutes.

Some coughs, such as those associated with croup (see Week 23), respond better to cold air for about 10 minutes. In winter, some pediatricians recommend bundling baby warmly and taking her for a short walk outside when she has a croup-related cough. If she's warm enough, a jaunt at night is OK if it's not bitterly cold outside.

In addition to using a humidifier, you might increase the amount of fluids you offer baby to help thin secretions. Decrease her activity level because activity can make her cough more.

When to call the doctor. It's important to call her pediatrician if she experiences any of the following symptoms:

- difficulty breathing
- shortness of breath
- fever
- irritability
- marked decrease in appetite
- difficulty eating
- wheezing
- coughing persists

> **Caution:**
> **Don't give baby cough-suppressing medication without your doctor's recommendation.**

If coughing is caused by a bacterial infection, the doctor may prescribe an antibiotic. If it's caused by a viral infection, you can only treat the symptoms. If a cough is severe or persistent, X-rays may be taken to rule out pneumonia. In very severe cases, a baby may need to be hospitalized for oxygen therapy and fluids by IV to treat dehydration.

Toys and Play This 19th Week

Tickle Me!
Tickle games are lots of fun. This tickle game involves identifying different parts of baby's body. Begin by softly touching parts of her body, according to the rhyme. Trace circles on her tummy soothingly at the end.

> *Where are baby's fingers?*
> *Where are baby's toes?*
> *Where, oh where, oh where . . .*
> *Is my baby's nose?*

You can change the parts of her body that you identify in the song—point out ears, chin, forehead, hands, feet, tummy. The words don't have to rhyme. Name whatever comes to mind. Repeat a few times, if baby is enjoying this tickle game.

Imitate Her Sounds
To encourage your baby's efforts at talking, imitate the sounds she makes when she babbles. Hold her facing you in your lap. Let her babble. Wait until she pauses, then repeat one groups of syllables, such as "da-da-da." She'll probably listen closely. She may try to repeat the sound, or she may babble something else. Smile and hug her when she tries to repeat your sounds. Continue the game even when she doesn't always repeat sounds. You are helping her learn through imitation, one important way she'll master language.

Week 20

How Big Is Your Baby This 20th Week?

Baby weighs 14-3/4 pounds and is 25-1/4 inches long this week.

Baby Care and Equipment

Feeding Your Baby

Your baby is making progress in learning to eat solids. By the 20th week, he probably eats two meals each day of cereal made with breast milk or formula. He may be taking in as much as 2 tablespoons at each feeding. He is still drinking lots of breast milk or formula—it's his main source of nutrition. Four to six servings a day, 6 to 8 ounces at each serving, is normal.

    New items for your diaper bag. Now that solids are a part of baby's daily diet, consider making adjustments in or additions to what you pack when you go out. These tips may make your life a little easier.

- Before you leave the house, put a premeasured amount of dry cereal in a plastic bowl with a lid. When you want to feed baby, add breast milk or formula.
- Even simpler, if you bottle-feed, add the correct amount of dry formula to the dry cereal. Then simply add water when you want to mix it up.
- Keep an extra baby spoon and bib in your diaper bag.
- Put a premeasured amount of dry cereal in a zipping plastic bag. Or buy dry cereal in premeasured packets.
- Always pack more dry cereal in your bag than you believe you might need. Baby may be hungrier than you thought he

would be, or you might get stuck someplace with a hungry baby. With extra food along, you're always prepared!

Mealtime for baby. Some parents are concerned about when baby should be fed. Does he need one large meal and one small meal? Should meals be the same size? Is it better to feed him at one time of day instead of another?

It doesn't make a difference nutritionally. However, you might want to offer new foods in the morning. If he has any problem with the food, tummy upset should wear off before he goes to bed that night. Your baby is probably the hungriest in the morning and in a good mood, so offering him a new food then might work best for you.

If breastfeeding. If you breastfeed baby, offer solid food toward the day's end. Your milk supply is probably at its lowest then, and baby may be keener to eat. Offer solids between breastfeedings. Solid foods may interfere with the absorption of some nutrients in breast milk.

If bottle-feeding. If you bottle-feed, you might give him his larger feeding of cereal in the middle of the day. It helps him get through the day. You don't have to feed him solids at dinnertime if you feed him in the morning and at lunch. At night, he can join you in his highchair. Give him a cracker to play with (he probably won't eat it) while you eat.

When he begins eating a more varied diet, you may decide to feed him his main meal at night. Offer solids when he seems the hungriest. In this early exposure to solids, allow lots of time to feed baby. He'll want to play with his food, smear it, drop it and examine it closely to learn more about it.

Do You Have a "High-Maintenance" Baby?

Now that you've grown to know your baby so well, you may realize he's more difficult than your sister's baby or a friend's baby. A high-maintenance baby displays some, if not all, of the following characteristics.

- He startles easily and acts jumpy or cries at various sounds.
- He's extremely sensitive and is uncomfortable with bright lights, lots of activity, some clothes.
- He protests about everything, from bathing to sleeping.
- He is restless and refuses to take a nap.
- He may be upset by new people, places or experiences.

- He may rarely smile; instead, he cries, whimpers, wails or screams.

Within a few weeks of birth, most babies show some sign of their temperament. A parent may be frustrated when he or she realizes baby is not going to be "easy." Recognize that most of baby's traits are in place at birth. High-maintenance babies have many of their characteristics before birth. Don't feel guilty if he's fussy or difficult. There's nothing wrong with you or your baby—it's just the way he is.

Learn what upsets your baby. You can't change your baby's temperament, but you can clue in to what may upset him. Try to avoid those situations. Respond to his needs in any way you can. This will take experimentation and work on your part, but it pays off in the end.

Look for patterns in his mood swings. This may help you discover what sets off his fussiness. If he's hungry when he gets up from his nap, feed him then. Establish a routine; it helps him know what to expect and when to expect it.

Reduce stimulation, especially if he's sensitive. By stimulation, we mean lights, noise, color, activity. Set up a routine to calm him before bedtime, such as a bath, then rocking or cuddling. If he's sensitive to the clothing he wears, dress him in natural fabrics. Keep him comfortably layered.

Be consistent. Set up a routine baby can depend on. Be consistent in your dealings and interactions with baby. Respond to him in the same way, as far as possible, when he fusses. Keep your cool; don't get overwhelmed and frustrated. Baby may sense your feelings, which could agitate him more.

Ask for help when you need it. Get a sitter when you need to get out, or ask family members to sit for you. Encourage your partner to take care of baby, to bond with him and to provide you with some free time for yourself.

Stay focused on the positive. As baby gets older and becomes more mobile, you may see a change. Take comfort in the fact that you have done your best for him.

Protect against Sunburn

In the discussion of sun protection for baby in Week 18, we advise you not to apply sunblock to a baby's skin until he is at least 6 months old. Keep baby in the shade when you go outdoors. It's better to keep infants out of the direct sunlight entirely when there is a risk of sunburn. Cover your baby with light, loose clothing that covers his skin completely. In addition, be sure he wears a sunhat and baby sunglasses if baby must be in the sun for any length of time.

Milestones This 20th Week

How Much Does He Weigh?
In the next few weeks, baby will probably have doubled his birth weight. His weight gain will slow, and he may gain at half the rate he did during the first 6 months. He may go through growth spurts and gain weight at irregular intervals.

Baby's Hearing
Hearing tests. Hearing is a very important part of baby's life. Even if his hearing was tested at birth, you might have it checked again now, if you are concerned. If testing reveals a moderate hearing loss, helpful steps can be taken now to deal with it.

Listening to storytelling. When you read baby stories, you are doing more than just interacting together. Reading exposes him to speech sounds and intonation. Listening to words helps him put together the sounds he babbles into actual speech. He is developing a type of rhythmic dialogue that he will soon use in his "conversations."

Baby loves hearing people's voices. He can pick out each of several different voices of people talking around him. If he hears his name, he may turn his head toward the speaker. He can distinguish among tones of voice, such as displeasure, approval and acceptance. He frowns or cries when he hears an angry voice.

Baby likes music; he may swing his body when he hears a tune. He may also hum to himself. He loves it when you sing and clap.

> Don't push baby too hard in your efforts to help him learn. Your love and nurturing are the secrets to his development, not toys, gadgets or programs.

Using His Hands
He continues to use his hands. He "reaches" with his eyes first; his eyes direct his hands. He can grab an object fairly easily. He reaches for a toy with one hand, and his hands adjust to an object's shape.

Milestones This 20th Week

Changes in Baby You May See Now

Physical Development
• may move by rocking, twisting or rolling

Senses and Reflexes
• aims well when reaching
• may be able to hold bottle with both hands

Mental Development
• wants to touch, hold, turn, shake and mouth objects
• deliberately imitates sounds and movements

Social Development
• imitates facial expressions
• waves arms to be picked up

Every baby is an individual, and your baby may do some of these things more quickly or more slowly than another baby. If you are concerned about your baby's progress, discuss it with your healthcare provider. Also see page viii.

He may transfer objects from hand to hand or grasp one object with both hands. He wants to touch everything near him. He still likes to put things in his mouth. He may chew on objects, too.

His Personality
Baby begins to demonstrate other emotions and reveals more of his personality about now. Your baby may be quiet and contemplative, or active and babbling. He may be physical and concentrate his energies on constantly moving. Or he may focus on one task, excluding most others. He may be "easy" or "high-maintenance." Whatever his personality, it is unique to him.

Note: See also the box above, *Milestones This Week*.

What's Happening This 20th Week?

Baby's Body Language
Your baby is beginning to express himself. His body language tells you a lot about what he's feeling. When he's fearful or afraid of something, he may express his fear by raising his eyebrows or furrowing his brow, pursing his lips and then opening his eyes wide. He may draw back from you or tense his body. He may express anger or frustration by lowering his eyebrows, staring and pressing his lips together.

Babyproofing Your Home

It's time to start thinking about babyproofing your home. Baby may be crawling soon, so you'll need to make changes for his safety. Take care of these safety precautions in the weeks to come, before baby becomes even more mobile.

- ❑ Buy and install electrical outlet covers. Little hands love to poke things into open sockets.
- ❑ Put appliance cords up so they can't be pulled down by an exploring baby.
- ❑ Push heavy appliances to the back of your kitchen counters.
- ❑ Store knives, glasses and other kitchen hazards, such as toothpicks and twist ties, where your child can't reach them.
- ❑ Keep matches and lighters out of reach.
- ❑ Put away tablecloths. A baby can easily pull a tablecloth, and everything on it, onto himself.
- ❑ Keep refrigerator magnets high and out of baby's reach. He can choke on them if he grabs one or if one falls off.
- ❑ If you have radiators for heating, place guards around them so baby can't touch.
- ❑ Store collections of small items, such as coins, shells, rocks, in a safe place.
- ❑ Move furniture away from any window baby could fall out of.
- ❑ Clear bedside tables and end tables of small items baby could choke on.
- ❑ Keep sewing supplies out of reach.
- ❑ Store office supplies in a cabinet out of baby's reach.
- ❑ Keep jewelry, hairpins and other small objects in a safe place.

- ❑ Put corner guards on tables.
- ❑ Unplug appliances in the bathroom, such as hair dryers and electric toothbrushes.
- ❑ Buy a toilet lock for every toilet.
- ❑ Be sure safety razors and razor blades are safely put away.
- ❑ Check floors and baseboards for loose nails and splinters.
- ❑ Be sure curtain and blind cords are out of baby's reach.
- ❑ Plan where to put gates and other barriers, such as at stairs and in doorways without doors.

Check out areas that baby uses from the floor—crawling around at baby's level may reveal hazards you can't see when you're standing. Baby's curiosity leads him to explore things you didn't even know were there! Also see the box on page 209 about protecting baby from common poisons in the home.

Cover electrical outlets, put bumpers on furniture, and wrap up loose cords before baby starts to crawl.

Childproofing When You're Away from Home

Your family may travel a lot, or you may spend extended periods of time with relatives or friends.

Keep Baby Safe from Poison

These suggestions will help you make your home poison-safe for baby when he becomes mobile.

- Keep telephone numbers of the poison control center and local hospital near the phone.
- Store household products, such as cleaners, bleach and other toxic substances that could harm baby, in a locked cabinet.
- Install latches on cabinet doors and drawers.
- Lock up all alcoholic beverages.
- Check out your garage. Store products you keep there, such as gasoline, kerosene, turpentine, weed killer, plant food, charcoal-lighter fluid, batteries and insecticides, in locked containers.
- Keep toiletries, perfumes, aftershave and cosmetics out of reach.
- Lock medicines and vitamins in a cabinet.
- Use door-handle safety covers to keep some rooms off-limits.
- Pick up and dispose of any cigarette or cigar butts smokers might leave in your yard.
- Choose plants carefully—some are highly toxic if a baby eats them.
- Keep a bottle of syrup of ipecac in your refrigerator, in case of accidental poisoning. Some pharmacies supply a bottle free to parents of small children. (Be aware that syrup of ipecac isn't appropriate for every kind of poisoning situation—read label directions.)

You must childproof your baby's environment wherever you are.

At your own home, you are aware of various hazards to baby. Someone else's home may have dangers you might not think to check for. Childproof using the suggestions below when you're away with a baby or small child.

❑ If you borrow or rent a crib, be sure it meets safety standards: Crib slats no farther apart than 2-3/8 inches, a snug-fitting mattress, no high posts, no decorative cutouts.

❑ When possible, push crib and other furniture away from windows baby could fall from.

❑ Remove from tables small items baby could choke on, such as candies or nuts.

❑ If anyone smokes, empty ashtrays often.

❑ Take steps to protect baby from hazards such as a fireplace, wood-burning stove, pool.

Travel Safety Tips

Pack these safety devices along when you travel. They help childproof wherever you stay away from home. Take along plenty of

- outlet plugs
- corner guards
- portable locks for cabinets and toilets

When baby is bored, he may show it with glassy or glazed eyes that don't blink much, and a display of sleepiness or dullness. He may hold his body still. If he is disgusted or repulsed by something, he may wrinkle his nose, purse his lips and lower his eyebrows to show his displeasure.

It's easy to see when he's happy and satisfied. Smiling and laughing out loud are typical indicators of happiness. He may wrinkle the corners of his eyes while he relaxes his eyebrows. When baby becomes engaged in an activity, he usually indicates his involvement by opening his mouth and raising his eyebrows. He may also relax his shoulders and open his hands.

Sometimes baby becomes upset when he is startled or surprised. It's not unusual for him to cry at such times. If he is not unduly startled, you may see him furrow his brow, drop his jaw and raise his eyebrows. He may form his hands into fists.

As he grows older, there will be more situations when baby is unhappy or sad. When he feels this way, he may turn down the corner of his lips, his lower lip may tremble and he may open his mouth. He may raise his eyebrows and make circles in the air with his arms.

How Babies Express Pain

You may have wondered how your baby will let you know when he's in pain. You'll be on the front line—the first to recognize it—so trust your intuition about whether your baby is in pain.

Unfortunately, no single sign or symptom indicates an infant is in pain. Different babies express pain in different ways. The following indicate a baby might be in pain:

- crying for long periods
- cannot be comforted or consoled
- pulling away if you touch a part of his body
- swelling, redness or misshapen appearance of part of body
- after a long bout of crying, baby becomes very still and may even stop crying
- pulling, rubbing or scratching part of the body
- changes in sleeping patterns
- changes in eating
- changes in the way he moves or how much he moves
- changes in other aspects of his usual behavior

If your baby displays any of these signs, or if you believe your baby is in pain for any reason, contact your pediatrician. He or she will advise you.

Intestinal Blockage

What it is. Intestinal blockage may be a complete blockage or partial blockage of the intestinal tract. Symptoms include
- abdominal pain and swelling
- nausea
- vomiting
- weakness
- decrease in or absence of bowel sounds
- diarrhea (with a partial obstruction)
- no stools (with a complete obstruction)

When to call the doctor. There is no helpful treatment to try at home. When an obstruction occurs, it usually becomes an emergency fairly quickly. Call the doctor if you notice a change in baby's bowel pattern accompanied by abdominal pain and vomiting. Hospitalization is necessary to diagnose the problem by X-ray. Surgery is done to remove the obstruction. Also see the discussion of Intussusception in Week 34.

Allergy

What it is. An allergy is defined as an acquired sensitivity to some substance that doesn't usually cause a reaction. When we speak of "allergies" in this weekly discussion, we include hay fever (allergic rhinitis), contact dermatitis, atopic dermatitis or any other dermatitis. *Dermatitis* is any inflammation of the skin accompanied by itching, redness and skin lesions. Some of these are covered in other weeks, so you may want to check the index for further references.

An allergy may occur at any time in life. Symptoms include
- itching
- dry skin
- difficulty breathing
- runny nose
- watering or tearing of eyes
- rash
- red skin
- congestion
- shortness of breath
- sneezing

What to do. If you believe your baby suffers from an allergy (and you've ruled out a cold or other illness), try to identify the cause. Is soap or lotion causing it? Is it a food, a plant or something in the air? If you think you know what it is, keep baby away from it. If it's hay fever, consult your pediatrician for treatment options.

When to call the doctor. Call your pediatrician if baby has symptoms of an allergy. Any time she has breathing difficulties, she needs immediate attention. Call about a rash that doesn't improve or one that gets worse. Skin tests can identify the cause in some cases. Medications, such as benadryl, or lotions may be suggested, but don't use them without asking your pediatrician first.

Toys and Play This 20th Week

Just about any safe object you have around the house can be used as a toy. Be sure baby can't damage the object or be hurt by it. Most plastic kitchen spoons are fun to wave around and shake. They're virtually indestructible, too. Rubber spatulas and stirring spoons are large enough to make handling them easy for baby. Plastic measuring cups and spoons on a ring are good for little fingers to manipulate. Even a pan lid and a large spoon can entertain him for a while.

Encourage Baby to Move
Now is a good time to begin encouraging baby to practice his crawling skills. Place him on the floor with a few toys he likes just out of reach. Let him choose which toys to play with, then encourage him to move forward to get one. In addition to stimulating him to move, putting out several toys at one time gives him the opportunity to begin making simple choices.

Baby, Do What I Do
Encourage baby to imitate you to stimulate his visual sense. With baby facing you, open your eyes wide. Stick out your tongue. Wiggle your nose. Puff your cheeks. Have fun with this! Baby may try to imitate you. When he does, imitate him back. Games like this delight baby. He can play this game with his siblings, too. Everyone enjoys the interaction.

Follow the Toy!
This game helps baby develop the muscles he needs to roll over, even if he doesn't roll over completely on his own quite yet.

Lay baby on his back, and get his attention with a toy. Move the toy slowly above him in an arc, so he turns his head and shoulders to keep it in view. He should also have to arch his back and neck to see the toy. His effort to keep the toy in sight may help him complete a rollover. If he's close but not quite there, a gentle push on his bottom may help.

Weekly Milestones at a Glance

Week 21

Physical Development
- alert at least half of her waking hours

Senses and Reflexes
- can grasp large ring

Mental Development
- looks around in new situations
- holds one block, looks at second; drops first to take second

Social Development
- will protest and resist someone who tries to take toy away

Week 22

Physical Development
- when lying on his back, he may move by kicking against a flat surface
- turns and twists in all directions

Senses and Reflexes
- sits supported for up to 30 minutes

Mental Development
- can discriminate self from others in mirror
- leans over to look for fallen object
- can recognize object from only seeing part of it

Social Development
- interest in breastfeeding lags
- vocalizes pleasure and displeasure
- smiles at self in mirror
- may prefer a particular toy
- can be quieted with music

Week 23

Physical Development
- sits with little support; may slump forward on hands for balance
- reaches with one arm

Senses and Reflexes
- may bend herself almost into sitting position when rolling from back to side
- turns head freely

Mental Development
- will gaze at object for a long time
- can utter several additional consonant sounds

Social Development
- giggles and laughs
- coos, hums and stops crying when she hears music

Week 24

Physical Development
- while lying on back, grabs and holds foot in play

Senses and Reflexes
- may manipulate objects

Mental Development
- shows different emotions, such as happiness, unhappiness, even a temper
- may have abrupt mood changes

Social Development
- coos and gurgles with pleasure
- turns when own name is heard

Week 25

Physical Development
- tries to move by propelling herself on stomach with legs and steering with arms
- rotates wrist to turn and to manipulate objects

Senses and Reflexes
- likes to play with food
- begins to pass object from hand to hand

Mental Development
- enjoys looking at objects upside down
- likes a change in perspective

Social Development
- may cry when parent leaves the room

Week 21

How Big Is Your Baby This 21st Week?

Baby weighs 15 pounds and is 25-1/4 inches long this week.

Baby Care and Equipment

Baby Highchairs

Once baby is eating solids, it's time to think about a highchair—one of the most-used baby products you'll buy. You can feed baby in the highchair. She can sit in her highchair while the family eats. Use it as an activity center when you're busy preparing a meal. When your baby is in her highchair, you know she's off the floor and out of harm's way.

Some highchairs can be adapted according to baby's age and developmental abilities. Some can be made into a youth chair. Other types attach to the table; they save space, are portable and less expensive than a regular highchair. See the discussion in Week 44.

Choosing a highchair. A highchair is appropriate for baby for 2 to 3 years. Choose a sturdy model that you can live with for a long time. Some styles serve only one purpose—holding baby so she can eat. Others have a variety of uses.

A wooden highchair looks appealing, but has drawbacks. The seat may be too deep and the footrest too low for a small baby. A wooden tray is harder to keep clean than plastic or metal. A wooden chair may not fold, so storing and transporting it can be difficult.

A basic metal-framed or plastic-framed model is a fairly inexpensive way to solve baby's feeding needs. These are usually lightweight, collapsible and portable.

Highchair features. Consider these before you buy a highchair.

- a wide base helps prevent it from tipping
- well-padded seat is covered with sturdy plastic
- no sharp edges
- easy to clean
- tray is easy to attach and to remove—at best, with one hand
- restraint system securely fastens baby across hips and between legs; straps are adjustable
- wheels lock to keep chair from rolling while baby's in it
- adjusts so baby will be able to use it for a long time
- folds up compactly for storage between uses or for easy transport when eating away from home

Use a Drop Cloth

A drop cloth may be a good investment. Put a large, heavy-duty piece of plastic under baby's highchair to keep your floor neat and make cleanup easier. As baby learns to eat, she experiments with food. She's sloppy, and a lot of what she "eats" ends up on the floor.

Foods to Avoid with Baby

Do not feed babies under 1 year of age the foods listed below. Our list explains why each could be harmful to your baby. Although baby is not eating anything like this yet, it's a good idea to be aware of what not to give her this first year. Avoid the following foods.

- *Any food that is a choking hazard,* such as cut-up hot dogs, peanut butter, grapes, popcorn, nuts and hard candy.
- *Cow's milk,* because the proteins are too hard for baby to digest.
- *Spinach, beets, carrots and turnips prepared at home.* Each contains large amounts of nitrates and could cause anemia. Prepared baby food is OK because manufacturers remove harmful substances.
- *Egg whites,* because the protein is too hard to digest. They may also cause allergic reactions. It's OK to feed baby egg yolks.

Milestones This 21st Week

Your Baby's Vision

Your baby's world is becoming more 3-dimensional. Both eyes are working together, and her depth perception is improving. She may study her hands or feet with fascination; she sees them differently now. Her color perception has improved, too. She can distinguish among several shades of one color. She still prefers primary colors.

To evaluate baby's vision, hold a toy some distance in front of her. Move it closer. See where she begins to notice it. Watch her hands—are they beginning to reach for it? Don't move the toy. Let her focus on it. Her eyes direct her hands more now. Keep your face out of the way so she doesn't focus on you. Let her practice looking and reaching without interrupting her.

Her eye-hand coordination is also improving. She can reach out and grab objects easily. She can also find her toes, grab them and put them in her mouth. Baby delights in this new trick.

Baby Shows Emotions

Baby's emotions are fairly evident—she shows disgust, fear, anger, happiness and boredom. She expresses emotions with facial expressions and sounds. Her moods may change quickly. She gives you behavioral cues, such as holding up her hands when she wants to be picked up. She squirms, looks at the floor and fusses when she wants to be put down. She stares blankly when she's bored and is cranky when she's tired.

Your baby smiles easily, but she may no longer smile at everyone she sees. She may be more sociable with strangers if she has a chance to watch and to study them first. She needs to size them up before she makes an overture.

She Likes Listening to the Human Voice

She listens intently to many sounds, but a person's voice interests her most. She picks out your voice from others' easily. She likes rhythm, especially verses and songs. Her "passive vocabulary" is increasing, which means she understands the meaning of more words. Soon she may look at an object when you name it.

Food—Not Just for Eating!

Eating is more enjoyable for baby now because she can manipulate a few foods. She likes to feed herself a cracker or small piece of bread. She wants to taste food, but she also wants to play with it, squeeze it, smell it, crumble it, mash it and smear it. She is still messy as she experiments with food.

More Active!

Baby likes to change her body position and to move. When you grasp her arms, she helps pull herself to a sitting position by lifting her head and flexing her elbows. She may be able to lift her arms and her legs when she's on her tummy. Soon she may be able to get one leg up under her when she's lying on her tummy. If she's very active, she may slowly propel herself across an area by kicking with both legs. Prop her with pillows so she can sit up and watch the world, but never leave her alone when she's propped up.

Note: See also the box below, *Milestones This Week.*

Milestones This 21st Week

Changes in Baby You May See Now

Physical Development
• alert at least half of her waking hours

Senses and Reflexes
• grasps large ring

Mental Development
• looks around in new situations
• holds one block, looks at a second; drops first to take second

Social Development
• protests and resists someone who tries to take away toy

Every baby is an individual, and your baby may do some of these things more quickly or more slowly than another baby. If you are concerned about your baby's progress, discuss it with your healthcare provider. Also see page viii.

What's Happening This 21st Week?

Private Time for Baby

Even at this age, baby may need quiet time by herself. If she seems irritable or fussy, turns her head away, cries or closes her eyes, she may be signaling she wants to be by herself.

If you notice baby acting this way, put her down on the floor on a blanket or in her playpen. Don't put her in her crib—that's for naps and bedtime. She may enjoy playing with a toy or she may be content just to sit and look around her.

Right before a nap may be a good time for baby to be by herself. The time she spends alone can serve as a transitional time between wakefulness and going to sleep. After a nap may be a good time to let baby play quietly by herself. This enables her to nurture her self-play skills. She needs to learn that she can entertain herself, so let her practice.

> **If baby is playing by herself and seems content, let her continue. You are encouraging her independence.**

Ready to Drink from a Cup?

Your baby may show an interest in drinking from a cup about now. Help her hold a cup and see how she responds. If she seems interested and willing to drink from it, use it as a supplement

Spillproof cups may come in handy now.

to bottle-feeding or breastfeeding. Don't use it as a replacement.

You can buy spillproof cups made especially for a baby. Usually they have two handles for baby to grip and a cover with a spout. Even better, the cup may have a weighted bottom. These sturdy cups help keep baby from spilling liquid on herself.

Let baby sit in her highchair or infant seat for her first sips. Show her how to drink from one of her cups. Then help her drink from hers. After she gets the hang of it, let her experiment. Put a few sips of water in the cup while she's learning. It's not as messy or as wasteful as using juice, breast milk or formula. A small amount is also easier for her to handle.

Baby may master drinking from a cup quickly if she has your help. Don't be frustrated if it takes her awhile to catch on. Some babies need months to master drinking from a cup. If she doesn't seem interested or ready, wait for a time, then try again. Some babies are not ready to drink from a cup until they're 8 or 9 months old.

Drinking from a cup represents an important transition for baby. Smile and praise her when she practices.

> **Give baby 2 to 4 ounces of vitamin C-fortified juice a day, diluted with equal amounts of water.**

Itching

What it is. Itching is a symptom of a problem, not an illness. You'll notice baby rubbing or scratching her skin. Itching can occur for different reasons, including as a reaction to a drug, food, lotion or soap, from a fungal infection or from an insect bite.

What to do. If your baby appears to have a problem with itching, look for the cause. Has she been exposed to something that could cause the irritation? Has she eaten or taken anything unusual or not normally part of her diet? Have you started using a new lotion or detergent? Often you can find the source of the problem. Eliminating it stops the itching.

When to call the doctor. Call the doctor if baby's skin is yellow (jaundiced), or if baby has difficulty breathing. Call if the itching doesn't improve in 24 hours or if she has scratched enough to cause the skin to bleed or get infected. Call if she develops a fever.

Ointments containing zinc oxide or Benadryl might be prescribed. It may be necessary to put socks or mittens on baby's hands to prevent her from scratching herself.

Thrush

What it is. Thrush is a common yeast infection of the mouth, also called candida albicans. It isn't serious, although the initial appearance may startle you. It often looks like curdled milk in baby's mouth or on her lips. Thrush occurs most often in newborns and infants. It may be passed from mother to baby as baby passes through the birth canal, if the delivering mother has a yeast infection.

The most common symptom is white patches or "plaques" in the mouth. They may be found on gums, tongue, cheeks, lips or the soft palate. Patches appear white or cream-colored and may be raised. They are not usually painful. Baby's mouth may be dry. Thrush has been seen as early as a few hours following birth.

What to do. If you are nursing and believe you have a yeast infection on your breasts, take care of the infection. Signs of a breast yeast infection include dry, itchy nipples that are also painful. If you don't tend to the problem, you can pass it to the baby.

If your are bottle-feeding, sterilize nipples and bottles by boiling them. If these items are not sterilized, baby can become reinfected. Antibiotics can also trigger the infection. However, if your baby is taking antibiotics, don't stop giving them to her without consulting your doctor.

When to call the doctor. Call the baby's doctor if she is feeding poorly, is dehydrated or loses weight. If she develops a fever or has signs of a secondary bacterial infection, with redness or bleeding, contact your pediatrician.

Your doctor may prescribe an oral antifungal medication. Keep up her fluid intake. If you have the infection on your nipples, you will need to be treated while baby is being treated.

Toys and Play This 21st Week

Splashy fun. Bath toys may be some of baby's favorites, and she may love playing in the tub. Inexpensive plastic toys that float are fun to play with in the tub. Let her watch you pour water out of a plastic cup when she's bathing. She may want to try it, too.

Attraction to music and objects. Because babies like music, you might want to give her a musical toy. She might enjoy a music toy that she can start herself by pulling a handle or pushing a button. A floor gym that she can lie under is fun if it has lots of things she can grab, pull or swing at.

Emphasize colors now. Baby likes the colors red and blue. Find a poster with these two colors dominant in the

Entertain baby with plastic bath toys that float in the tub.

picture, and put it up in her room for her to look at. Try putting it on the ceiling over her crib. She'll enjoy looking at it when she's having quiet time or when she wakes up.

Enjoying the Outdoors

Take her outside to see outdoor colors. Sit with her on the porch or in the yard, or go to the park, and tell her what she sees. Let her examine trees with leaves and plants close up. Let her touch them, but don't let her put them in her mouth.

Shake It Up, Baby!

Play a game with baby and her rattle. Shake the rattle as you sing-song this verse:

> *Shake it up, shake it up,*
> *Shake it up, baby.*
> *Do it like, do it like*
> *Do it like this, baby!*

Hand her the rattle and sing the verse to her again. If she doesn't shake the rattle, help her along.

You can continue the game by engaging in other activities as you sing to her, such as brushing her hair, washing her face, tying her shoes. Sing about anything baby does!

Week 22

How Big Is Your Baby This 22nd Week?

Baby weighs 15-1/4 pounds and is 25-1/2 inches long this week.

Baby Care and Equipment

From Breast to Bottle

You may decide about this time to wean baby from breastfeeding and start him on formula. It's best to ease a breastfed baby into formula when you make the switch. Don't do it all at once, or baby may not cooperate.

> Once baby starts eating solids on a daily basis, he'll cut down on the amount of formula or breast milk he drinks. For now he should still get most of his calories from formula or breast milk.

Many breastfed babies don't like the taste of formula. To make the change, give him a bottle that contains only one-fourth formula. Express your breast milk, then mix one part formula to three parts breast milk. He will slowly become accustomed to the different taste. Every few days, replace a little more of the breast milk with formula.

If he refuses the bottle when you change the ratio of formula to breast milk, go back to the ratio he accepted before. Offer that for a few days, then add a little more formula while cutting back on the breast milk. Keep it less than the amount he refused. Some breastfed babies take weeks to accept straight formula.

If your baby has difficulty drinking from a bottle, or refuses to drink from one, you may have to try something else. It's not too early for him to begin drinking from a cup (see Week 21). This might be the solution if you can't get him to take his formula mix from the bottle.

Is Baby Enthusiastic about Solids?

Many babies like solids and eat solid food with gusto from the time they are first introduced to cereal. Other babies don't like the taste or texture of solid food and refuse it.

> By the time he reaches his first birthday, your baby will probably be eating three meals a day and only nursing or taking a bottle at bedtime.

If your baby doesn't want to eat solids, don't tussle over it with him. It may be a good idea to make the decision now that you will never fight with your child about food—at any age! Fighting about food can lead to eating problems later.

If baby refuses solid food, continue offering a spoonful of cereal at each meal. Your purpose in offering him solids is to introduce him to taste and texture. If he won't eat, call your pediatrician for advice. He or she may suggest you wait a couple of weeks, then try again.

Milestones This 22nd Week

Imposing Restrictions

As baby begins moving more, you will have to impose certain restrictions. You may need to block access to some areas and remove him from potentially harmful situations. Don't be surprised when he resists your efforts. It's normal. He isn't defying you or acting naughty. He's just reacting in the only way he knows.

When he resists, don't make too many other demands of him. He needs stability and regularity in his life to feel secure. Be flexible when the situation calls for it. Realize your baby's actions are normal. Don't expect more than he is capable of giving.

He Likes to Play to Learn

Baby engages in play that makes noise. He loves toys that shake and rattle. He's learning that some toys make noise and others don't. He doesn't realize it's the toy making the noise, not his hand. He compares sounds when he bangs two objects together or drops them on the floor.

When he drops the same toy over and over again, he's testing his world. He's trying to see if the toy falls the same way and makes the same noise each time it drops. Although this can be frustrating to you, it's fascinating to him.

May Be Wary of Strangers

In a short time, baby may become wary of strangers. This is called *stranger anxiety*. You may be surprised when he suddenly hesitates to go to someone he doesn't know. He may study a stranger when he or she comes close. He may react by crying loudly when left alone with a baby-sitter he doesn't know. It's natural. Explain to those people baby sees only once in awhile that it's just a phase.

Creeping Soon

Your child may be moving around more now. He wants to investigate things. He will begin creeping soon so he can get where he wants to go. When he creeps, he moves on his tummy while he pushes against the floor. He doesn't crawl on his hands and knees, and won't for a while. He may go backward instead of forward. He may scoot or roll as well as creep. It may amaze you when you see how he gets to where he wants to go when he really wants to get there!

Note: See also the box below, *Milestones This Week*.

Milestones This 22nd Week

Changes in Baby You May See Now

Physical Development

- baby may move by kicking against a flat surface when lying on his back
- turns and twists in all directions

Senses and Reflexes

- sits supported for up to 30 minutes

Mental Development

- discriminates self from others in mirror
- leans over to look for fallen object
- recognizes object from only seeing part of it

Social Development

- interest in breastfeeding may lag
- vocalizes pleasure and displeasure
- smiles at self in mirror

Every baby is an individual, and your baby may do some of these things more quickly or more slowly than another baby. If you are concerned about your baby's progress, discuss it with your healthcare provider. Also see page viii.

What's Happening This 22nd Week?

Teething Symptoms
Teething signs can appear weeks or even months before you see baby's first tooth. As baby's tooth moves through gum tissue and bone, symptoms may appear and disappear.

When he starts teething, your baby may refuse to eat solids. Eating puts pressure on his gums, which increases his discomfort. He may want more formula or may want to nurse more. But this also puts pressure on his gums, so he may not want to continue after he begins. If you find baby pulls away from the breast or bottle after his initial sucking effort, it may be that he feels some discomfort in his mouth.

Solitude for Baby
Continue to allow baby quiet time by himself. It's OK to leave him safely on the floor or in his playpen while you attend to tasks. Don't feel guilty when you leave baby alone; it's an important part of his development.

When he's alone, baby processes various pieces of information. He observes his surroundings at his own pace. He also gets needed rest.

Being by himself gives baby a chance to practice skills such as soothing himself. He may learn to fall asleep on his own without you being there to comfort him with cuddling or rocking.

Anemia
What it is. Anemia is the condition in which the number of red cells in the blood decreases. Sometimes it is referred to as *low iron*. It is not a disease in itself but a symptom of various diseases and can occur at any time. Symptoms include

- fatigue
- feeling of ill health
- change in his sleeping habits; he sleeps too much
- pale skin

What to do. You can do some things before you contact your physician. Be sure the baby's vitamins contain iron. If you are bottle-feeding your baby, use formula that contains iron. Call your doctor's

How to Give Your Baby Medication

Medications can be given to your baby by mouth, as an injection, as a suppository or directly, as with eye, ear or nose drops. To give a baby or young child any medication, you may want help! One way to give medication is to wrap your baby gently in a blanket, with his arms at his sides. This keeps him from batting at your hand with his. Also see the discussion on page 425.

You can buy "medication syringes" at the drug or grocery store. They are easier to use and more effective than a spoon. The syringes enable you to measure accurately how much medication to give. They may be easier for you to control. Do not use a spoon from your kitchen tableware set to measure medicine! It is an inaccurate way to measure—you might give your baby a lot more or a lot less medicine than was prescribed.

Some medications can be given in food, juices or formula. A good resource for help is the nurse at your pediatrician's office. Grandma may also have some good advice that will help.

Caution: Don't give your baby any medications unless directed to do so by your doctor. This includes over-the-counter medications. What may be all right for you or an older child may not be OK for a baby.

office for dietary supplement suggestions.

When to call the doctor. If the above measures don't help, contact your baby's doctor. Be alert for any signs of bleeding, such as blood in bowel movements or on the diaper, or blood in urine. Call the office immediately if you think your baby is bleeding. If your baby develops new symptoms, call the office for advice.

Anemia has different causes, so each cause may be treated in a different way. The most common treatment is vitamins and iron supplementation. Your doctor will prescribe different treatments if they are necessary.

Toys and Play This 22nd Week

Prism on the Wall

It's not too early to introduce some "science" to baby. Buy a prism at a toy store. Hang it in a window, or hold it in the light when you interact with baby. Show him the beautiful rainbows it makes on the wall. You'll enjoy his reactions when he sees the patterns glitter and sparkle on his hands or on your face. If possible, hang the prism in a window in baby's room where he can watch it when he wants to.

Play the Trumpet
A fun interaction between parent and child is playing the trumpet on baby's tummy. After his bath or when you're dressing him, put your lips against his bare tummy and blow! The sound comes out like a bad trumpet player trying to blow a horn. Baby will laugh and giggle. It tickles, and it's a funny sound. It'll delight you, too.

This Is the Way the Lady Rides
You can play a bouncing game now that baby is older. Seat him on your knees, with your legs together and feet flat on floor. Hold his arms or hands firmly so he won't fall off. Support his upper back, head and neck. Very gently bounce the baby while singing

> *This is the way the lady rides, lady rides, lady rides.*
> *This is the way the lady rides, so early in the morning.*

With the next verse, bounce the baby a little harder while singing

> *This is the way the gentleman rides, gentleman rides,*
>   *gentleman rides.*
> *This is the way the gentleman rides, so early in the morning.*

With the last verse, bounce baby a little more vigorously while singing

> *This is the way the farmer rides, farmer rides, farmer rides.*
> *This is the way the farmer rides, so early in the morning.*

At the last "farmer rides," while firmly grasping and supporting baby, straighten both of your legs or open your knees so he dips a little.

Week 23

How Big Is Your Baby This 23rd Week?

Baby weighs 15-1/4 pounds and is 25-3/4 inches long this week.

Baby Care and Equipment

Framed Baby Carriers

Now that baby is older and heavier, you may be considering a different kind of carrier than a front carrier to carry her in. A good choice is a framed carrier, similar to the type of backpack hikers and campers use. These carriers have a sturdy metal frame that hold baby in a cloth seat. They offer greater back support for you. They adjust to fit most adults.

Most framed carriers are designed for use with babies older than 6 months. Baby needs to be able to hold her head and body steady. When she's on your back, you can't see her. You need to be confident she is able to sit well so you won't worry about her slipping. Many framed backpack carriers have a kickstand to hold the carrier steady while you load and unload baby.

Use a framed carrier for baby until she is between 40 and 45 pounds. There are different weight maximums depending on the carrier. This type of carrier can often be used with baby until she is 3 or 4 years old.

Caution: Be careful when you carry your baby in a backpack carrier. Even though you've strapped her in, never bend forward when carrying her. If her straps have come loose, she can fall out and could be hurt.

Furniture Hazards

You've probably taken many steps already to prevent baby from hurting herself around the house. In previous weekly discussions, we've pointed out precautions to take at home and on the road. Baby isn't moving too much yet, but when she does, she'll be vulnerable to dangers posed by the furniture and equipment in your home. Help protect baby by being aware of these hazards and taking steps to minimize them.

You may need to keep baby from going into certain areas of the house. Safety gates block areas, but avoid accordion gates with diamond-shape openings. Many have openings large enough for baby to stick her head into; she could get stuck.

When baby starts pulling herself up, she'll practice on anything handy. Be alert to situations in which she can tip furniture onto herself when pulling up. Bookcases and cabinets may be dangerous for this reason. Block access to them, or bolt them to the wall. Bedroom dressers can be hazardous, especially when children start opening drawers to use as a ladder to climb up. Bolt these to the wall, too.

Put your TV high enough to be out of reach, or fasten it to the wall securely. If you own a recliner, be careful using it when baby's in the room. Her head, legs or arms can become trapped when it's closing. Do not leave the recliner open when you're not using it, and keep a close eye on baby when you recline in one.

Your exercise equipment can pose hazards. Be careful with it. Exercise machines can pinch or catch fingers. Free weights can roll onto little hands and feet. If you use a jump rope, baby could get tangled in it.

Laundry Detergents and Skin Rashes

When baby gets a rash, many parents wonder if their laundry detergent is the cause. Detergents are not often the cause of skin irritations, however.

If your baby has normal skin, you can use your regular detergent. You don't need to buy hypoallergenic soap to wash her clothes. To protect a newborn's skin, rinse her clothes twice for the first few months.

Fabric-softener sheets used in the dryer occasionally cause itchy, red patches on baby's skin. Some of the softener chemical remains on clothes. A liquid fabric softener added to the *wash cycle* leaves less residue, which may mean less chance of irritation.

If your baby does have sensitive skin, take steps to protect it. Choose a gentle, fragrance-free soap or detergent to wash her clothes. These contain fewer additives, so she may be less likely to have a reaction to them. Rinse clothes twice to be sure you rinse out all soap residue. Dry items in the dryer without fabric sheets.

> # Watch for Food Allergy
>
> **After introducing a new food to your baby, call the doctor if any of the following symptoms occur within 24 to 48 hours:**
> - **wheezing**   • **skin rash**
> - **diarrhea**   • **vomiting**

Taking in Less Formula or Breast Milk
As baby begins to take in more nutrition from solid foods, she may begin to cut back on her intake of formula or breast milk. This is normal. If she is breastfed, she may do this on her own. If she is bottle-fed, she may need some help.

Ask your pediatrician for advice on how much formula or breast milk baby should be drinking. Although you want her to eat solid foods, you don't want her to give up her other important nutrition sources. Neither do you want her to take in too many calories. It's best to work this out with help from baby's doctor.

Milestones This 23rd Week

Social Interactions
Your baby is becoming a social butterfly. She smiles and laughs, and expresses her feelings better. She doesn't wait for you or other family members to initiate social interaction. She may smile and coo at you to let you know she wants to play or snuggle. When you reach to pick her up, she may hold out her arms. She is attached to you but willing to relate to others, too. However, her anxiety around strangers may be more evident now.

She Studies Faces
Your face is very interesting to baby; she studies it from every angle. She wants to touch your face all the time. She sticks her fingers in your eyes and nose. She grabs onto an ear and hair, and doesn't release it. She's doing this to learn more about you and herself. She's beginning to realize you are a separate person from her. She can pull your hair, and it doesn't hurt. When she pulls her own hair, it does!

Development May Be Erratic
You may notice your baby focuses temporarily on a particular area of development at a time. If she does, she may ignore other things. She may concentrate on trying to move and won't vocalize as much as she did. She may become frustrated when she can't do something. You may hear her whine or see her get angry.

Exploration Continues
She's more coordinated now. She's curious about exploring her environment and goes about it seriously. She reaches, grabs, holds and tugs at various objects. She may need to practice letting go— she doesn't quite have the hang of it yet. You may notice she transfers an item from one hand to the other. This helps her practice releasing her grip.

Understanding of Speech Increases
Her understanding of speech is growing. She responds to you in different ways. When you say hello to her, she pays attention to the sound of your voice. When you repeat yourself, she may coo and gurgle. She may imitate some of the sounds you make.

She's Getting Stronger
Her arm and trunk muscles are getting stronger. When she's on her tummy, she can hold herself up on her arms for longer periods. She may twist her entire torso to look over her shoulder. She can sit erect

Milestones This 23rd Week
Changes in Baby You May See Now

Physical Development
- sits with little support; may slump forward on hands for balance
- reaches with one arm

Mental Development
- gazes at object for a long time
- utters several additional consonant sounds

Senses and Reflexes
- bends herself almost into sitting position when rolling from back to side
- turns head freely

Social Development
- giggles and laughs
- coos, hums and stops crying when she hears music

Every baby is an individual, and your baby may do some of these things more quickly or more slowly than another baby. If you are concerned about your baby's progress, discuss it with your healthcare provider. Also see page viii.

briefly, using her hands for support and balance. Note: See also the box on page 231, *Milestones This Week.*

What's Happening This 23rd Week?

Teaching Babies to Fall Asleep on Their Own

Many parents want baby to learn to fall asleep on her own. You may still be rocking your baby to sleep, or keeping her up if she's fussy, then putting her down after she goes to sleep. It's OK to put up with an occasional sleepless night, but you don't want baby crying every night when you put her down. You may be growing tired of having to make an extra effort to get baby to sleep.

Richard Ferber, M.D., directs a well-regarded sleep-disorder clinic for children. He believes many poor sleep habits are learned, and they can be unlearned. He developed a method to use with babies older than 6 months to help them with this. You may have heard the term *Ferberize;* it refers to the program Dr. Ferber originated.

Implementing Dr. Ferber's plan will take effort on your part, but you may decide it's worth it. Baby learns to soothe herself independently, and this may offer you some respite. Below is a description of each step of the plan.

1. Put baby down in her crib while she's still awake. Tell her it's time to go to sleep. Leave the room. If she doesn't start crying, you don't need to do anything. If she cries, let her cry for 5 minutes before going back into her room.
2. Don't turn on the lights in her room. Keep physical contact to a minimum. Speak softly to her again. Tell her she's a big girl, and she can go to sleep on her own. Leave the room again.
3. If she continues to cry, this time wait for 10 minutes before entering her room. Speak to her again. Don't stay too long; leave within a minute or two.
4. If crying continues, wait 15 minutes between each visit to her room, until she falls asleep.
5. On the second night, start with 10 minutes of crying before you first enter her room.
6. Gradually increase the length of time from there. If it's too difficult to let baby cry for 5 minutes the first night, wait 2 or 3 minutes before going in. Do what is comfortable for you.

The results. Parents have reported that after only a few nights of using this system, baby fell asleep on her own.

Setbacks. When baby is sick, she's often sleepless. While she is sick, you may have to get up with her in the middle of the night. This might cause a setback in the progress you have made in helping her learn to fall asleep on her own, but it is a necessary setback. Once she feels better, begin the process again if you need to. Because she was successful in learning to fall asleep on her own before, she can be successful again.

Encouraging Baby's Motor Development

No need to buy anything fancy to help baby develop her motor skills. The best thing you can do is give her the opportunity to explore and to practice newfound skills.

Of course there will be times you need to restrict baby for her safety, but try not to do it unnecessarily. Provide a babyproofed area where she can practice some of the skills she's developing that help her move around. In addition to giving baby the space she needs, get down on the floor with her. Play games that encourage rolling or crawling. Roll a ball back and forth with your baby. Play "baby tag." Maybe you won't go far but baby will love the idea of being chased. You'll help her practice the motor skills she'll be using in the upcoming months while having a lot of fun.

Croup

What it is. Croup, also called *laryngo-tracheo-bronchitis,* can occur at any age. It is a viral or bacterial infection or inflammation of the vocal cords (larynx) and the surrounding tissues. Croup may be caused by allergies also. When a baby gets croup it can be a little scary for parents because the cough is unusual. Attacks happen most often at night. Symptoms include

- a "barking" cough that sounds like a seal
- difficulty breathing
- hoarse or raspy voice

What to do. You might like to set up a cool-mist humidifier in baby's room. See the discussion of humidifiers in Week 13. You might consider adding a humidifier to your home heating and air-conditioning system. This can help avoid the problem entirely and may decrease her symptoms if she has croup.

When to call the doctor. Call the doctor if your baby is having trouble breathing or swallowing. You may be directed to go to the emergency room. If her respiratory rate (number of breaths in a minute) is above 60 or if her fingernails turn blue, contact your pediatrician or go to the nearest emergency-medicine facility.

Don't panic if baby has croup. Your anxiety may add to the problem by scaring her. Take her into the bathroom and run hot water (creating steam). Exposure to cold night air (go for a walk) may help. Keep her in a semi-upright position. Don't lay her flat or sit her directly upright. Symptoms of mild croup should improve in less than 1 hour. If they don't, call the doctor.

Medications are given if the cause is believed to be bacterial. Most of the time antibiotics are not helpful. Steroids may be given to improve breathing. Frequent, smaller feedings with liquids may help in some situations.

Nasal Congestion

What it is. A baby with nasal congestion has trouble breathing freely through her nose. It may occur with a cold, an upper-respiratory infection or with allergies. Symptoms include

> Whenever you are worried about your baby's health, call your pediatrician's office. Talk to the nurse or physician's assistant about baby's specific symptoms. He or she will determine if the doctor needs to see baby. You may be reassured that baby is OK. If you can do anything at home to keep baby comfortable, you'll be given suggestions.

- discharge (thick or watery) from either or both nostrils
- difficulty breathing
- fever (sometimes)
- agitation or fussiness
- snorting or sniffling sounds
- difficulty sleeping or feeding
- baby may rub or scratch her nose
- other symptoms of a cold, such as cough or sore throat, may be present

What to do. Use a cool-mist humidifier to help keep secretions flowing and draining. Gently clean her nose with a soft tissue or cloth. Use a bulb syringe to clear nasal passages for easier breathing. You can also use mild soap and warm water to wash mucus from her nostril area. Don't give her any medications, including over-the-counter medicine, without consulting your doctor.

When to call the doctor. Call the doctor if baby has a respiratory rate of 60 breaths per minute or more, difficulty breathing, shortness of breath, appears blue or has a dark color around her mouth or nose. If the discharge from her nose is bloody, yellow or green, or if she runs a persistent temperature, contact your pediatrician.

In addition to using a humidifier, you may be advised to use nose drops, antibiotics and decongestants. However, use these only under the direction of your doctor.

> **Doctor Tip**
>
> **If baby feels ill during the day, call your doctor's office. Don't wait until later, in hopes she'll get better. It usually is wiser to deal with the problem during the day, when doctor's appointments can be made or prescriptions can be called in to the pharmacy easily.**

Toys and Play This 23rd Week

Play Ball!

Now's a good time to introduce your baby to playing with balls. She can sit up well and she's becoming more mobile, so playing with a ball is fun. It gives her practice tracking a moving object with her eyes. This type of play also helps her develop coordination.

Choose a brightly patterned ball. One that makes noise is even more fun! Roll it against the wall so it comes rolling back. Watch her watch it. Slowly bounce it up and down. These two activities help her exercise her visual skills. And you both have fun playing together.

See if she reaches for the ball. When she does, give it to her so she can feel its texture and weight. She won't be able to throw it, but show her how to roll it. She'll enjoy your interaction.

Water Play

Your baby continues to enjoy the novelty of playing with water. Let her play in the bathtub, the sink, outdoors in a baby pool or anywhere you won't mind making a big mess.

Gather together different-sized plastic cups. Plastic or aluminum measuring cups are great because they are different sizes. Pour a little water into one cup. Let her watch you pour the water from one cup to another. Or pour the water onto the grass or into a pail. While you play together, use words such as *pour* and *splash* to describe what baby sees. She may want to put her hand in the water as you pour it from one container into another. Let her feel the water, if she wants to. Be prepared to get wet yourself!

Week 24

How Big Is Your Baby This 24th Week?

Baby weighs 15-1/2 pounds and is 26 inches long this week.

Baby Care and Equipment

Baby Jumpers

A baby jumper is a swinglike device suspended from a doorframe. Baby sits in the jumper and jumps, bounces and wiggles as much as he wants. Viewing the world from an upright position in the jumper can be a thrill for him at this age.

Baby stays safe because the jumper doesn't move, as a walker does. (See the discussion of walkers in Week 38.) He can rock, spin, bounce and jump while sitting in a jumper. He can develop strength and coordination, and have fun doing it.

Some jumpers are basic models that hold baby in an upright sitting/standing position. Some have padded seats. Some seats are adjustable to various positions. Other bouncers come equipped with trays to hold baby's toys.

A baby can usually use a jumper between 4 and 12 months of age. It can be used until baby gets too heavy for it or is too mobile to be restrained in this way. Follow manufacturer's weight-limit guidelines. Until he starts walking, your baby might have a great time observing the world from his jumper.

Caution: Be sure the jumper is secured in a safe place, away from stairs, opening doors and any other hazards to baby.

Bathtub Seats

Your baby is probably ready for the big bathtub now. Bathe him in only a few inches of water. Once your baby can sit up unsupported, try putting him in a bathtub seat when you bathe him in a big tub. You don't have to hold him up any more, so he can splash and play in the tub with greater freedom. Follow the manufacturer's guidelines for weight and age for the particular seat you choose.

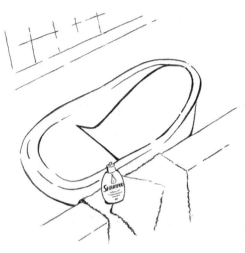

Use a bathtub seat once your baby can sit unsupported.

Suction cups on the bathtub seat should stick properly to the tub for safety. If you have a used bath seat, be sure the suction cups are in good condition and clean, or they might not stick. Before placing the seat in the tub, clean the tub surface thoroughly. Cups won't stick to a vinyl bath mat, nonslip decals or a film of soap scum.

> **Never** assume baby is safe in a bathtub seat. Keep an eye on him while he's in the bathtub, and remain at his side until he's finished with his bath.

Have at hand all the bath products you will need *before* you put baby in the tub. A seat does not guarantee protection—never leave baby alone in it while he's in the tub! If you have to leave the room, take baby with you.

When the bath is over, lift baby from the bathtub seat. Don't lift the seat with him in it. It's too easy for him to fall out.

Is Baby Getting Enough Nourishment?

Babies this age need about 800 calories a day—from a combination of formula or breast milk *and* solid foods. Baby is probably getting enough nourishment. As long as he takes in formula or breast milk, and eats the various solid foods he can manage, he'll get enough calories.

The best indications he is eating enough are his growth and well being. If he's growing and putting on weight, and he is energetic, then he's getting enough nourishment.

Remember, feeding him solids at this time *isn't* for the nutrition he receives from the solid food. It's more to socialize him and to introduce him to the taste and texture of "grown-up" food.

His Developing Taste Buds

Your baby has hundreds of more taste buds for sweets than you do. That's one reason he loves sweet-tasting foods, such as applesauce or mashed bananas.

Don't offer foods sweetened with sugar or any other sweetener. He doesn't need them. The fruits and vegetables he eats that taste sweet naturally will satisfy him for a long time.

Milestones This 24th Week

Baby's Expanding Memory

Your baby's memory continues to grow. He recognizes names, basic words and sounds he is familiar with. He looks at what you point at and may point at things when you name them. Touching objects helps him learn about their texture—he wants to touch everything! He remembers daily rituals, so establishing routines may boost baby's memory. A nice daily ritual is to greet him with the same phrase every morning.

> **Establishing routines may boost baby's memory.**

His Moods Change

You may notice baby has abrupt mood changes. He may get mad when something doesn't suit him. But he may forget his anger just as quickly when distracted by a toy. In a few weeks, this tendency tapers off as baby begins to gain some control over his feelings. Don't expect too much, though—the process of learning to control his emotions continues for years.

His Interest in Sounds

Baby's babbling may be taking on a definite shape. He may combine certain consonants with vowel sounds. If you repeat his sounds, he may listen intently. He is learning to vary the pitch and volume of his "speech" and may be using sounds more deliberately now to get your attention.

He Likes to Play

Playing is so important to your baby. He plays by himself for longer periods, in part because he sits better. He can now grasp an object purposefully with one hand and manipulate it. He still enjoys dropping things. He seems to make decisions when he chooses which toys to play with. Soon he may attempt to stack one block on top of another, if he watches someone else do it first.

> **Games are important "work" to baby. Games that involve movement and action enhance your baby's body awareness and improve his motor skills.**

He's Stronger Now

Your baby's strength is increasing in lots of ways. He may be able to sit alone. (If he still slumps forward or to the side a bit, he's not ready for sitting alone yet.) His arms are strong, and he may be exercising his leg muscles. He may develop the urge to stand but probably can't do so without your help. If he's rolling over confidently, he may use the technique to move around the room. Occasionally you'll have to help him when he rolls himself into someplace he can't get out of.

If baby slumps forward or to the side, she isn't ready for sitting alone yet.

Note: See also the box on page 240, *Milestones This Week.*

What's Happening This 24th Week?

> **Make an appointment for your baby's 6-month well-baby checkup now. Check page 97 for immunizations he may receive at this visit.**

Establishing Trust

Bonding with your baby helps establish his trust in you. It gives him a sense of security and faith in others. It also gives him security in himself.

You have bonded with baby by responding to his basic needs—feeding, changing and caring for him.

Milestones This 24th Week

Changes in Baby You May See Now

Physical Development
• grabs and holds foot in play while lying on back

Senses and Reflexes
• may manipulate objects

Mental Development
• shows different emotions, such as happiness, unhappiness, even a temper
• may have abrupt mood changes

Social Development
• coos and gurgles with pleasure
• turns when own name is heard

Every baby is an individual, and your baby may do some of these things more quickly or more slowly than another baby. If you are concerned about your baby's progress, discuss it with your healthcare provider. Also see page viii.

You have done it in other ways, too, such as by talking, singing and playing with your baby. The introduction of rituals increases his feeling of safety.

You may not realize the impact your daily interaction has on baby. But you are shaping his view of his world and those in it.

Reading Together

Reading with baby is a wonderful way to combine learning with closeness. You expose baby to language's rhythms and tones. You also create a bond between you as the two of you share this experience.

When you read to baby, you open a new world to him. Introducing him to books may shape his future reading habits. He may

Colorful pictures attract baby's attention.

become a lifelong reader because of the interactions you share now.

> By this time, baby has his own predictable sleep pattern. He probably goes to sleep, wakes up and takes a couple of naps around the same times each day.

To instill in your child a love of reading, choose books and stories that are age-appropriate. Think about the books you liked as a child. Many are still available in libraries and bookstores. It may be especially meaningful for you to read a story you loved as a child to your own child.

If you are unsure what books might be appropriate for your baby, visit your local library. The children's librarian can direct you. Borrowing books from your local library is a great way to expose baby to all kinds of stories. Choose books that are fun to read. With young babies, colorful pictures are often the key. Singsong verses are also good because baby likes hearing the rhythm of the language.

When you read a story to baby, your voice conveys a great deal. Read with pleasure in your voice. Be enthusiastic! Change voices for different characters. Make it enthralling for baby to listen. He will sense your enjoyment and pay closer attention to you.

Keep in mind that baby can get tired from this activity, just as any other. Watch for clues that he's had enough. When he's tired, stop reading. Continue another day.

Bronchitis

What it is. Bronchitis is an upper-respiratory-tract infection (URI) that can occur at any age. If your baby has bronchitis, you may feel a "rumbling" with each breath when you place your hand on his chest. Other symptoms include

- cough that may produce phlegm
- fever
- difficulty breathing
- wheezing
- symptoms of a cold

What to do. Use a cool-mist humidifier to help relieve congestion. See Week 13 for a discussion of humidifiers. Run the shower to create steam in the bathroom. Don't expose baby to secondhand smoke or other airborne irritants.

When to call the doctor. Bronchitis is more complicated than a cold and may require antibiotics or other medications. Call your baby's doctor if you suspect your baby has bronchitis. Call if baby is coughing up yellow or colored sputum, his fever increases, if phlegm contains blood, if he experiences shortness of breath or if he vomits.

To treat bronchitis, the doctor may prescribe antibiotics or decongestants. Other medications, such as acetaminophen, may be given. Give these only as directed by your doctor. Follow your doctor's instructions on ways to make baby more comfortable. If baby doesn't improve on antibiotics or other treatments, your doctor will want to know.

Vomiting

What it is. Vomiting is usually a symptom, not an illness. It's a sign that something might be making baby feel ill. Vomiting usually results from stomach or intestinal upset. It can also be a symptom of problems including appendicitis, pneumonia, strep throat or meningitis. It may occur after ingestion of a medication or chemical.

Vomiting is different from "spitting up." That usually occurs after a feeding, and baby spits up only a little of the total amount he has taken in. See the discussion in Week 2. When your baby vomits, he expels the contents of his stomach. Other symptoms that may accompany vomiting include fever, listlessness, poor feeding, coughing, constipation, diarrhea or dehydration.

What to do. When baby vomits, try to identify the cause. Is he getting a cold or the flu? Don't force him to eat, but offer liquids to avoid dehydration.

When to call the doctor. If your baby vomits repeatedly or if vomiting lasts more than a few hours, contact your physician. If your baby is under 6 months old, it's important to contact your doctor.

Your doctor may advise you to stop feeding your baby solids and offer only liquids. Your doctor may prescribe medication, depending on the cause of the vomiting.

Toys and Play This 24th Week

Tickle games are still favorites. Continue playing these games with your baby. You might want to buy a feather and use it to tickle him, too. He will enjoy the game, and you'll be providing him the opportunity to examine a new object (the feather). Don't pick up feathers from outdoors because they harbor mites and germs.

Make Baby's Own Storybook

Now that you're reading together more, make a soft storybook for baby. Buy pieces of different-colored felt at a craft store or fabric store. Cut some pieces into squares to use as "pages." Cut familiar shapes out of different colors. Mark on them with black permanent markers to add details. Use nontoxic glue to attach pieces to the pages, or sew them on. Punch a couple of holes on the left side of each page, and tie together with yarn. Baby has a book all his own!

Where Is My Toy?

Start teaching your baby to search for things, but make it a game. Seat him on the floor. Using a toy he likes, hide it partway under a blanket that is close to him. Leave enough of the toy visible so he knows what it is. Ask him to find the toy. Help him lift the blanket to find it, if he needs help. When he finds the toy, act surprised and happy. Continue the game by concealing the toy, then slowly pulling the blanket to reveal it. Once he catches on to the game, hide the toy under the blanket completely.

Week 25

How Big Is Your Baby This 25th Week?

Baby weighs 15-3/4 pounds and is 26-1/4 inches long this week.

Baby Care and Equipment

What Is Baby Eating?

Your baby is eating larger amounts of cereal now. Previously you've given her only formula or breast milk and cereal. Baby takes three to five servings of formula or breast milk a day; each serving is probably 6 to 8 ounces. She's also eating two servings of cereal a day; each serving is probably 2 to 4 tablespoons by now. Because her appetite is increasing, it may be time to add more variety to her diet.

If your baby has tried all the different varieties of baby cereal and seems ready for more food, you can add a few new choices. Call your pediatrician before you feed baby more than just cereal. He or she may have particular suggestions or advice for your baby.

Begin with strained fruit and vegetables. You might also offer your baby fruit juice in a cup. Finger foods, such as toast and plain crackers, are also good to try. Suggested foods to offer baby at this time, and the amounts of each, are listed below.

- bread or toast, unbuttered—1/2 slice
- crackers—2
- fruit—2 to 3 tablespoons per serving, 2 servings a day
- fruit juice (diluted with equal amount of water)—3 ounces, 1 serving a day from a cup
- vegetables—2 to 3 tablespoons per serving, 2 servings a day

Adding fruits and vegetables to baby's diet. After eating baby cereal, baby may have to get used to eating fruits and vegetables.

> **Let baby hold a cracker or small piece of toast while you feed her. It may keep her from grabbing the spoon when you feed her—at least with one hand!**

Even strained baby food can have a strong taste after such bland fare. Buy strained fruits and vegetables first. They are a little easier for baby to swallow and to digest. She doesn't have to chew the strained variety.

Offer baby only one new strained fruit or vegetable each week. You can see if she has any problems with the food, such as an allergic reaction or trouble digesting it. Give her 1 to 2 tablespoons of either a fruit or vegetable at two meals when you first offer it. The goal is to work up to feeding 2 to 3 tablespoons at each meal.

If baby doesn't like the food you offer, wait a couple of days before trying again. Let her eat what she was eating before you introduced the new food.

Juice choices. When selecting juice for baby, buy vitamin C-fortified apple, pear or grape juice. Avoid orange juice or grapefruit juice for now. They're too acidic for her. Dilute any juice with water that you give baby. Add as much water to the juice as the amount of juice. If you want to give baby 4 ounces of fluid, mix 2 ounces of juice with 2 ounces of water. Offer her the juice in a cup.

Are fruits better than vegetables? Vegetables are more nutritious than fruits. However, offering vegetables before you offer fruits may not entice your baby to eat them. Fruit tastes better, so baby may accept them more readily in the beginning.

Remember, at this point in baby's life, you aren't trying to meet all her nutritional needs with solids. That's one reason you continue giving her formula or breast milk. The goal at this point is to teach baby to swallow foods with different textures. You will probably have more success at this by feeding her fruits rather than vegetables.

> **Your baby is eating solids pretty well by now. To encourage her to try new foods, start offering a new food to her before you nurse or give her a bottle.**

When you introduce vegetables, try the sweeter ones first. Carrots and sweet potatoes are good choices. She may not like them as well as the fruit, but keep trying. If you keep offering them, she'll learn to like vegetables.

Milestones This 25th Week

What Baby Sees
Although baby's eyesight is fairly well developed by now, she will continue to perfect her visual abilities for a long time. Her vision is about 20/50. Things she sees are only mildly fuzzy. She can see details fairly well, such as patterns on fabrics or details on a face. She sees colors and can distinguish among them quite well.

She's More Physically Developed
She probably likes rolling from her tummy to her back, and from her back to her tummy. She may propel herself around the room in this manner. She isn't crawling yet, but she may raise herself into a crawling position and rock back and forth. She can sit well alone but may need help getting into the sitting position. She has a different view of the world when she's sitting up!

> **By this time, baby is sleeping close to 11 hours at night, and her naps total about 3-1/2 hours. She's awake and active about 9-1/2 hours each day.**

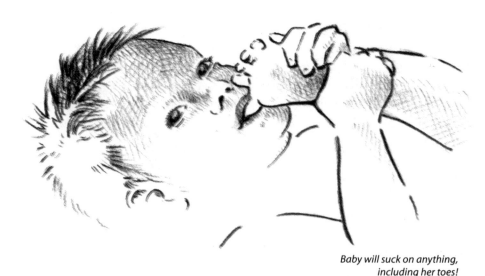

Baby will suck on anything, including her toes!

Baby Uses Her Hands
Baby's using her hands to feed herself. She can clap. She manipulates objects more easily as she passes them from hand to hand. She grabs anything within reach, including her body parts

and your body parts. She sucks on your fingers and hands to learn about them. She sucks on her toes, too! Don't worry; it's not unsanitary. Her toes are about as clean as her hands because she's not getting them dirty by walking on her feet.

> **Sucking on her toes isn't unsanitary for baby right now. Her toes are about as clean as her hands because she's not getting them dirty by walking on her feet.**

Baby Wants Her Own Way

Her glances, facial expressions and gestures invite you to play with her. She becomes absorbed in studying an object. She may protest loudly—or get angry—when you take away something from her, such as a toy.

Teething May Begin Soon

Teething symptoms may appear. She may play with her ears or suck her lower lip. Some babies suffer more than others while teething. Teething can cause a low-grade fever and a change in bowel movements. If baby displays these and other symptoms, check with your pediatrician to rule out anything more serious.

Note: See also the box below, *Milestones This Week.*

Milestones This 25th Week

Changes in Baby You May See Now

Physical Development
- tries to move by propelling herself on stomach with legs and steering with arms
- rotates wrist to turn and to manipulate objects

Senses and Reflexes
- likes to play with food
- passes object from hand to hand

Mental Development
- enjoys looking at objects upside down
- likes a change in perspective

Social Development
- may cry when parent leaves the room

Every baby is an individual, and your baby may do some of these things more quickly or more slowly than another baby. If you are concerned about your baby's progress, discuss it with your healthcare provider. Also see page viii.

What's Happening This 25th Week?

Let Baby Make Mistakes

Your baby is attempting many new skills. She's moving around a lot, working on her gross (large) motor skills (arms and legs). She's also developing her fine motor skills (use of her hands). You see evidence of this when she tries to hold a spoon. Give her a helping hand to get started, then back off a little. Let her make mistakes. She learns from them.

She may get a few more bruises from falls, but letting her make mistakes also lets her experiment. While watching over her as carefully as always, provide her freedom in which to explore her environment independently. Praise her when she does something correctly, like putting the spoon in her mouth.

Your Baby Is an Individual

Don't expect your baby to be like any other baby, even if you have multiples. No two babies are alike. Different personality types will approach the same situation differently. If you try to push her to do something, and it just isn't in her personality to do it that soon or in that way, more harm than good could result. Let her be. Try again another day.

Baby's Learning Capacity

It may seem impossible, but by the time your baby reaches this age, her brain has reached 50% of its weight at maturity! She is developing at an incredible rate. Marvel at what she's accomplished by this time. She's grown from a newborn, unable to do much at all, to an active baby who rolls over, probably sits up, plays actively and tries to feed herself.

Your baby is also learning at an incredible rate. She is prepared to learn certain skills at certain ages. Her *visual development* begins at birth and continues for many years. Even before birth, her *understanding of speech and syntax* was developing. This will also continue for years to come. Her *emotional attachments* and *social attachments* develop the most during her first 18 months. Her *motor development* begins at birth and develops in stages for years.

As we mentioned in Week 18, now is the time to expose her to a foreign language. She's like a sponge—she soaks up the experience. She's also ready to learn other new skills and accomplish new tasks, so allow her the freedom to experiment *safely* within her environment.

Allergic Reaction to Medications

What it is. An allergic reaction to a medication, also called *drug allergy* or *drug hypersensitivity,* can occur any time following administration of a drug. Symptoms that your baby is experiencing an allergic reaction include

- itching
- red or flushed skin
- rash
- hives
- restlessness or anxiety
- fever
- lethargy or hyperactivity
- anaphylaxis—severe difficulty in breathing (only in rare instances)

Nausea and vomiting following a medication dosage is not usually due to a medication allergy. However, if you observe this reaction, contact your doctor. He or she may want to consider switching your baby to a medication used to treat the same problem that is different from the one causing the reaction.

When to call the doctor. If your baby experiences a mild reaction, with itching, she may not need treatment. But it can be helpful to identify the cause. Severe reactions, including anaphylaxis, are serious and require medical help. Call the doctor if you think your baby is having a reaction to a medication.

Your doctor may treat the problem with medication, including antihistamines or cortisone. Some adults wear a bracelet identifying their medical allergy in case of an accident. However, this isn't usually done with a baby.

Moles

What they are. Moles, also called *pigmented nevi,* are flat or raised areas on the skin. Babies can have moles. Some moles have hairs growing out of them. Moles range in color from dark or black to blue, yellow, red or brown. Moles vary greatly in size, from a small skin tag the size of a grain of wheat to one that is a few centimeters in diameter.

What to do. Most moles do not require treatment. Stay alert for any changes in the mole, such as a change in size, color or shape. Show your baby's doctor any mole you find at one of your regular visits.

When to call the doctor. Contact the doctor if the mole bleeds, gets darker (changes color), grows larger or changes shape in any way. A biopsy of the mole is taken, or the mole may be removed by surgery.

Toys and Play This 25th Week

Peek-a-Boo, I See You!

It's fun to play the peek-a-boo game with baby. She'll giggle with pleasure as you hide your face behind your hands, then reappear. This game helps her learn about her environment. It teaches her that you can go away and come back—an important concept for her to learn.

Baby loves to play peek-a-boo!

Upside Down Is Fun

Baby enjoys looking at her world from a different perspective, such as upside down. To give her practice in looking at things from a different angle, turn a toy upside down in front of her. See if she turns it right-side up. If she doesn't, show her how. Repeat a few times.

Listen to the Sounds

It's good for your baby to hear a wide variety of pleasant sounds. Introduce her to the sounds all around her. Give her some tissue paper, and let her crumple it. (Watch her so she doesn't eat the paper.) If you have fall leaves on the ground, take her outside to hear you scuff through them. If she has a toy piano or xylophone, tap the keys or bars. Help her make some of the sounds so she begins to realize she can create sounds herself.

Weekly Milestones at a Glance

Week 26

Physical Development
- may be able to sit alone
- stands with support

Senses and Reflexes
- holds own bottle
- may hold cup handle
- displays some interest in feeding self with fingers
- has strong taste preferences

Mental Development
- may compare two objects

Social Development
- may be disturbed by strangers

Week 27

Physical Development
- balances head well
- may begin teething

Senses and Reflexes
- likes to explore body with mouth and hands
- may like to suck on toes

Mental Development
- plays vigorously with noisemaking toys, such as a bell or rattle

Social Development
- may chew fingers and suck thumb
- recognizes family members

Week 28

Physical Development
- turns over easily

Senses and Reflexes
- sips from two-handled cup with assistance

Mental Development
- can concentrate attention
- shows greater interest in details

Social Development
- shows humor and teases
- pats at mirror image

Week 29

Physical Development
- may use rolling over to move around room
- may raise and lower buttocks, while lying on back, to move about

Senses and Reflexes
- grasps, manipulates, mouths and bangs on objects

Mental Development
- likes to say "ma, mu, da, di"
- may associate picture of baby with herself and make appropriate sounds

Social Development
- wants to be included in social interaction

Week 30

Physical Development
- pushes up on hands and knees; rocks back and forth

Senses and Reflexes
- holds two objects at same time, one in each hand
- uses fingers to grasp objects

Mental Development
- understands that objects don't disappear when hidden
- imitates sounds and series of sounds

Social Development
- is learning meaning of "no" by tone of voice used

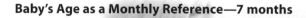

Week 26

How Big Is Your Baby This 26th Week?

Baby weighs 16 pounds and is 26-1/2 inches long this week.

Baby Care and Equipment

> It's not unusual for a baby to have doubled his birth weight by this time.

Baby Wants to Feed Himself

Your baby may enjoy feeding himself foods he can hold in his hand easily. He may thwart your efforts to feed him because he wants to do it himself. Unfortunately, he doesn't have the coordination. He can't guide the spoon to his mouth on a consistent basis, so it's too soon to let him feed himself with a baby utensil. Keep giving him finger foods to help him develop the skills he needs so he can feed himself in the not-too-distant future.

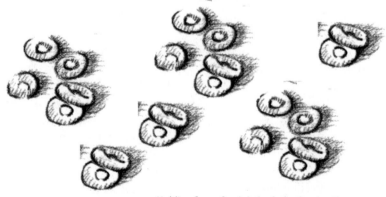

Holding finger foods helps baby develop the dexterity he will need to hold a spoon later.

Tips for Feeding Baby

- Take out only enough jarred baby food for one feeding. Don't feed baby out of the jar. Store remaining jarred baby food in the refrigerator to prevent bacterial growth.

- Buy small jars of baby food when you're traveling. If you can't refrigerate leftovers, throw them away. Or buy dried baby food and mix up the amount needed for one meal.

- Give baby his juice in a cup to help him learn to drink from a cup. He enjoys the taste of juice and may be more willing to drink juice, rather than formula or breast milk, from a cup.

- Buy a spillproof infant cup, which you may use for months to come. This cup holds 6 to 10 ounces. Some have handles. The top is secure, so when baby drops it, it stays sealed. Cups with a self-sealing valve stay sealed even when the cup is turned upside down.

- Keep a baby spoon handy. A baby spoon with a rubber or heavy plastic coating over the bowl area is easier and more comfortable for a teething baby to eat from.

He May Be Bored with His Bottle

About this age, a baby may become bored with the bottle. If he drinks well from a cup, he may be ready to give up a few bottles a day, but don't push it. Even at 6 months, a baby needs to suck and may not be ready for weaning. Total weaning from the bottle can wait another 6 months.

Milestones This 26th Week

Baby's Depth Perception

Because his pictorial depth perception has improved, baby distinguishes relationships among objects better. When he looks across his bedroom and sees a toy lying in front of his dresser, for example, he realizes the toy partially blocks his view of the dresser. The toy is in front, and the dresser is in back. This insight expands his understanding of his environment.

Holds a Bottle

Baby's ability to grasp objects is more developed. He can hold his own bottle. He may use his fingers to pick up something. He passes items from hand to hand and lifts, shakes, pushes, pulls, squeezes and tosses things close to him.

> **Your baby has reached half a year! He may be in a cheerful mood most of the time, when he's not frustrated with trying to become mobile. He's a lot of fun!**

Baby Vocalizes More Sounds

Vocalization is an important part of baby's activities. He indicates pleasure with many different sounds. He may try to imitate sounds you make to him. He may string together sounds and repeat them, such as "ma-ma" or "da-da," but he doesn't know they have meaning. It won't be long before he knows who "mama" is. Watch baby when you use his name in conversation. Does he respond to it? If he does, he knows his name!

> **Don't be tempted to compare your baby to others. Your baby is an individual and will do things according to his own schedule. Enjoy each of his accomplishments.**

He Chews and Bites Objects

In addition to putting everything from play keyrings to favorite toys in his mouth, baby may chew or bite them—yet another way baby learns more about his world. Just be sure that these objects are safe for him to chew on.

Milestones This 26th Week

Changes in Baby You May See Now

Physical Development

- may be able to sit alone
- stands with support

Senses and Reflexes

- holds own bottle
- may hold cup handle
- displays some interest in feeding self with fingers
- has strong taste preferences

Mental Development

- may compare two objects

Social Development

- may be disturbed by strangers

Every baby is an individual, and your baby may do some of these things more quickly or more slowly than another baby. If you are concerned about your baby's progress, discuss it with your healthcare provider. Also see page viii.

His Ability to Sit

His strength is increasing, so he can sit briefly without support.
When he starts to tip over, he may place one hand on the floor
to keep himself erect for a short time. He may grab at an object
with one hand, while supporting himself with the other. This action
displays how his strength and balance have developed. He couldn't
have done this a few weeks ago.

Note: See also the box on page 254, *Milestones This Week.*

What's Happening This 26th Week?

Baby's Fear of Strangers or Fear of Separation

You may have noticed your baby is less willing to approach strangers
lately. In some situations, he may be afraid to part from you. To help
baby through this difficult time, be alert to conditions that intensify
his fears.

- Baby may respond differently to others when he's tired or
  hungry. When you have to leave him, try to do so after he's
  been fed and is rested.
- Illness can be stressful to baby. He may not want to be apart
  from you when he's not feeling well. If possible, stay home
  when he's sick.
- A change in routine, such as taking a trip, can upset baby.
  Stick to his schedule, when possible. Put him down for his
  nap and feed him just as if you were at home to help him
  feel more secure.
- If you've been away from baby for a while, spend time
  alone with him on your return. He may cling more, or he
  may ignore you. Extra time together helps ease his fear of
  separation.
- Leaving him with a new sitter or at a new infant-care center
  can make him feel unsettled. He needs time to accept this
  new situation, whether it's a new person or a new place, so
  be patient.

The way your baby expresses his fears is tied to his personality
and experience with previous separations. If your baby tends to be
clingy and needs security, these situations may cause him greater
stress. If he's more independent, he may display less fear, but he
will still be unhappy about separations. It's a natural part of his
development.

Baby Starts to Creep

If your baby is starting to creep, he's progressing in a normal pattern. Many babies creep before they crawl. When he creeps, your baby uses his arms to pull himself

> **When baby can sit up in his crib, remove all objects that hang above or near his crib, such as mobiles.**

forward while keeping his legs flat on the floor. A baby often creeps first because he has better control of his arms than his legs. When he starts to crawl, he will use his legs a lot more.

When Baby Stands

When your baby is helped to stand, suddenly the whole world is at his feet—literally! Of course, he can't stand alone yet, but he may be able to stand with your help. Standing enables him to see more of his surroundings.

When you lift baby to a standing position and hold him there, he may support his own weight. He may even bounce up and down as he flexes his legs. This is an exciting moment for baby, and he may become very vocal and animated at his accomplishment.

Bruises and Contusions

What they are. Bruises result from an injury to tissue but skin is not broken (as it is with a cut). Now that baby is more active, you may notice he bruises more. Symptoms of bruising include

- discoloration of the skin—may appear red, blue, purple or any shade in between
- pain, at times
- tenderness
- swelling

What to do. When baby gets a bruise, apply ice, a cold cloth or an ice pack in the first 24 hours. (*Note:* Be careful when putting ice on baby's skin. Wrap the ice or ice pack in a towel. Never lay it directly on the skin.) After 24 hours, apply heat, such as a warm, damp towel. This may help with discomfort if the bruise is painful.

Keep an eye on bruises. Note any changes in size and color. Find out the cause of the bruise if you can. You may be able to prevent the accident from happening again.

When to call the doctor.
Contact the doctor if bruises occur
for no apparent reason. Tell your
doctor if you suspect abuse. A
bruise becomes serious if baby
bleeds from somewhere on the
body, such as from the mouth, if it seems to take a long time to go
away, if baby has a fever that increases or if pain is severe or doesn't
go away.

> Be careful when putting ice on baby's skin. Wrap the ice or ice pack in a towel. Never lay it directly on the skin.

Tapeworm

What it is. A tapeworm is a parasite that can live in a person's
intestines. A person can get a tapeworm from eating raw or
undercooked meat that contains the tapeworm larvae. The condition
is not contagious. To avoid the problem, avoid eating or serving raw
or undercooked meat. Symptoms of a tapeworm include

- diarrhea
- tenderness of the upper abdomen
- failure to thrive
- weight loss
- listlessness
- poor feeding
- irritability
- worms or eggs in the stool

Call the doctor. Call the doctor if you notice diarrhea or blood in
the stools. Antiparasitic medication may be prescribed.

Toys and Play This 26th Week

A Little Roughhousing Is OK

Baby may start to enjoy roughhousing with you now. He may yelp
with pleasure as you roll around on the floor together. Be careful
when you roughhouse. He's still a baby and can be hurt more easily
than you might imagine.

Baby may also enjoy being swooped up into the air in your arms.
If he giggles and laughs while you swing him, it's fun. However,
some babies don't like being swung into the air. If he protests, stop
immediately. It's *never* a good idea to throw a baby into the air

and then catch him in your arms because you may drop him or the jolting might injure his neck or spine.

More Peek-a-Boo

Many of the games you play with baby right now promote eye development and intellectual development. When you play peek-a-boo, you teach baby that you're still there, even if he can't see you. When you play hide-the-toy-under-a-blanket, you reinforce his understanding of *object permanence* (an object is permanent, even if you can't see it for a while). Perhaps most important, baby will love playing these games with you!

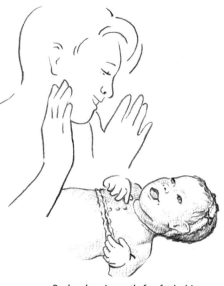

Peek-a-boo is gentle fun for babies.

Mist Him with Water

When baby is in the tub—or outside on a warm day—spray his arms and legs with a water mister. Tell him how soft the spray feels. Let him see how the water falls lightly through the sunlight if you are outdoors. Mist water above his head, and let it drift down on him. Help him spray water with the mister. He'll enjoy the differences in the way water feels as mist and as a body of water in the bathtub.

> **When baby can sit up on his own, it's time to lower the mattress in his crib. Lowering the mattress helps prevent him from falling out of the crib. Lower it to the level that you feel will keep him safe.**

Week 27

How Big Is Your Baby This 27th Week?

Baby weighs 16-1/4 pounds and is 26-1/2 inches long this week.

Baby Care and Equipment

Helping Baby Learn to Eat

It's best for baby to get calories from many different foods; however, it's not absolutely necessary yet. Offer solids to encourage baby to learn to enjoy eating. Offer new foods fairly often, and urge her to try them, but don't battle over it. She doesn't need to eat everything you offer. Her tiny stomach fills up quickly. She still gets most of her nutrition from breast milk or formula, so relax—let meal times be enjoyable times for her and you. When she loses interest in her food or gets fussy, she has finished eating for the time being.

> When you feed baby, take her mood into account. If she's happy when it's time to eat, feed her solid foods first, then give her a bottle or breastfeed her. If she's fussy, give her a bottle or breastfeed first to help her settle down, then feed her the solids.

Outdoor Stroller/Backpacks

If you and your family love to be outdoors, a stroller/backpack carrier may be a smart investment. This equipment goes quickly from stroller mode to backpack mode. The stroller is perfect for outings around a park or forest area that's paved or firmly packed. When you want to "pack" your little one closer to you, the stroller converts to a carrier for your back.

> Is baby starting to teethe? See our suggestions for helping baby cope with teething that appear in Week 34.

Coping with Colds— Treatment Ideas

Colds are common, but it's no fun seeing your baby suffer with one. (See the discussion of colds and prevention in Week 10.) The symptoms your baby suffers may include a slight fever, sneezing, a runny nose, decreased appetite and coughing. Her glands may be slightly swollen and her eyes may get red. The good news: You can help your baby cope with the discomfort colds cause. Simple actions you take may make baby feel better.

When baby gets a cold, her lips and nose chap if her nose is runny. A bit of petroleum jelly or lip protector dabbed on the nose and around the lips helps ease dryness and protects the area.

Saline nose drops can help thin mucus congestion in the nose and remove it, when used with a bulb syringe. A nasal bulb syringe removes mucus from the nose. It is a necessity for a little one who cannot yet blow her nose. Use the syringe after the saline drops. First squeeze the bulb, then gently insert it into the nostril. Release to suck out mucus. Clearing baby's nostrils makes it easier for her to breastfeed or bottle-feed when she has a cold.

If you use tissues to wipe baby's runny nose, be sure they are soft and thick. Choose one with aloe to help prevent further irritation.

A humidifier can bring relief because dry air irritates breathing passages. See the discussion of humidifiers in Week 13. A cool-mist humidifier helps baby breathe more easily because it puts moisture in the air.

The box on this page offers a quick checklist of products that are helpful to use when your baby has a cold.

Provide Plenty of Fluids
There is no cure for the common cold. While antibiotics work for bacterial infections, they do not work for colds, which are caused by viruses. Your best bet is to make your child as comfortable as possible, watching for improvement. It's important to provide baby with plenty to drink— offer extra fluids.

First-Aid Kit for Baby's Cold

These products may help your baby feel more comfortable when she has a cold.

- **Petroleum jelly or lip protector**
- **Saline nose drops**
- **Nasal bulb syringe for infants**
- **Tissues, preferably with aloe**
- **Humidifier, especially the cool-mist type**

Let Baby Rest

Along with providing more fluids, do your baby a favor by giving her plenty of opportunity to rest quietly while she's under the weather.

When baby is ill, you may have to change your plans. Taking baby out shopping or visiting friends when she doesn't feel at her best might not be fun for either of you.

> **It is OK to call your doctor's office and talk to the nurse about your baby's symptoms. It is helpful to be ready to answer questions such as, "Baby's temperature," "measures already tried" or "changes in symptoms." Ask what warning signs might be important.**

Dressing Baby when She Has a Cold

Pay attention to the way you dress baby when she has a cold. If it's very cold when you go out with baby, don't expose her to the elements for more than about 15 minutes. Cover her face with a light blanket or with a cover on her infant carrier.

Consider what you are wearing first. When you dress baby when she has a cold, consider what you're wearing first. Add one extra layer to baby's outfit to keep her warm but not hot. When you go outside, dress her in clothing appropriate to the season.

Dressing for cool or cold weather. In cool or cold weather, remember that body heat escapes through the head, so always put a hat on her, even if it's not extremely cold. Keep fingers and toes covered, too; she loses heat quickly from her hands and feet. A blanket wrapped around your dressed baby helps keep hands and feet warm. A pair of socks worn under a snowsuit with feet should also do the trick. If you need to take off your sweater or coat when you've gone indoors, take off baby's also.

> ## Is It a Cold or the Flu?
> **Compare symptoms in the box on page 378.**

Dressing for warm weather. If the temperature is very hot, dress baby in the same number of layers you are in. Be careful with air-conditioning—a light blanket can help protect her from a chill. In warm weather, be especially careful to protect baby's skin against sun exposure and sunburn.

> ## Making Baby More Comfortable
> **These ideas may also improve baby's mood when she has a cold and feels fussy.**
> - **Use a humidifier in her room at night.**
> - **It may help her breathe more easily if you rub a little mentholated jelly under baby's nose.**
> - **Elevate the head of baby's bed slightly.**
> - **Keep bottle in a more upright position when feeding baby.**
> - **Don't overdress her.**
> - **A bath before bed may help open nasal passages and also relax baby.**

Milestones This 27th Week

Time for a Highchair?

Your baby is making progress in her ability to control her body. By this time, she can sit unsupported, freeing her hands for other activities. Because she can sit up so well, now may be the time to introduce her to a highchair, if you haven't been using one designed for infants. She'll enjoy being part of the family and interacting at the table.

Baby Uses Hands More

With hands free when she's sitting, you may notice baby uses her hands more to play with toys. She may reach for an object, grab it, examine it, put it in her mouth, then drop it to move on to the next exciting item. She may be playing quite vigorously with toys now. She'll shake her rattle or plastic keys and listen to the noises she makes. She enjoys splashing with her toys in the bathtub.

Mastering Her Environment

Your little one is beginning to understand that to some extent she can affect her environment. You may see her use a tool to get something she wants. For example, she may pull her blanket closer to get a toy on it that is beyond her reach.

Look out below! She experiments by deliberately dropping objects. The objects might be toys, food or anything else! She drops as many things as she can find in rapid succession. You may be amused by the way she focuses on what happens when she drops an object. Dumping toys or items out of a box or pan is also great fun. Filling and emptying a container helps your baby learn the concepts *full* and *empty*. As simple as these activities are, they represent big achievements for baby.

Activity books are fun now. Baby's urge to explore may make it difficult for her to sit still for very long. Her attention span may not be very long, so your baby may not be ready for a long period of quiet listening at story time. If you introduce her to an activity book for very young children, however, she may be fascinated by what

Milestones This 27th Week

Changes in Baby You May See Now

Physical Development
- balances head well
- may begin teething

Senses and Reflexes
- likes to explore body with mouth and hands
- may like to suck on toes

Mental Development
- plays vigorously with noisemaking toys, such as a bells or rattles

Social Development
- may chew fingers and suck thumb
- recognizes family members

Every baby is an individual, and your baby may do some of these things more quickly or more slowly than another baby. If you are concerned about your baby's progress, discuss it with your healthcare provider. Also see page viii.

you and she can do together to explore the book's contents. If she wants to touch a book, pull it, chew on it or just hold it, that's OK! She's examining the book in her own way. She'll be interested in quiet listening again a little later.

Going Places

Your baby may be propelling herself across the floor in some manner. Some babies scoot backward; others move by rolling on their sides. Soon she'll be crawling, although it may not be by the right hand/left knee propulsion you expect. Some babies leapfrog (both hands followed by both knees) or crabwalk sideways (not on knees but on feet).

You may notice baby's legs are getting stronger, too. She may help more when you hold her in a standing position. Soon the strength in her legs will be even more fully developed, and she'll be pulling herself to a standing position.

Baby Notices Changes

Changes you make in baby's environment may surprise her or make her uneasy. For example, if you rearrange furniture in a room, she will notice. Her depth perception is fairly accurate, and she is

Sturdy books are best for baby right now.

able to distinguish objects near and far, so she can easily see such changes.

> Be prepared for baby to consider you a stranger if you make a dramatic change in your appearance, such as cutting your hair or shaving off your beard. She may regard you cautiously until she hears your voice and recognizes you!

Playtime and Tiredness

Tumbling on the floor, having fun with mom or dad or a sibling, is great entertainment for your baby. Playing in this way helps socialize her, too. Just be careful about active play near bedtime. Some babies become overexcited, then have a hard time settling down for sleep.

Baby may be exhausted after a hard day of play and activities. She may sleep well, or you may notice that she gets overtired and is unable to relax. This could lead to sleep problems. If she wakes in the middle of the night, let baby settle herself back to sleep when possible. Let her learn to comfort herself.

Note: See also the box on page 263, *Milestones This Week*.

What's Happening This 27th Week?

Baby's Eyesight Improves

By this time, your baby has close to 20/20 vision. She can differentiate among subtle color shadings. Bright toys, mobiles and other detailed objects entertain her.

Hearing Problems

Parents usually recognize or question hearing problems before healthcare providers do because parents spend so much time interacting with their infant. Notify your pediatrician as soon as you suspect a hearing problem because treatment is more successful for baby if established early. The first 6 months of baby's life are critical to her language development.

A baby may be at risk for hearing problems if she

- was born prematurely
- had oxygen deprivation at birth
- has severe ear infections
- has birth defects of the head, neck or spine, cleft palate or ear deformities
- had bacterial meningitis
- has a family history of hearing loss

Making Bye-Bye Easier

When your baby shows separation anxiety, doing certain predictable things may make parting a little easier on both of you.

- **Give baby time to check out anyone new, such as a baby-sitter. Ask people to approach quietly and to wait a bit before they interact with her.**

- **Consider providing a special toy or object for her to cuddle and hold when you leave. It can comfort her when you're not there.**

- **Develop a "parting" ritual. Routines and rituals give baby a sense of security— she may not be happy when you leave, but knowing what's happening is helpful to her.**

- **When it's time to leave, leave quickly—a quick hug and a kiss, and soothing words, then depart. Waiting for baby to stop crying or calm down might take forever. She's more easily distracted from crying if you're not there.**

Waving bye-bye can be a reassuring parting ritual for baby.

Observe your baby's development and her interactions with you. Notify your pediatrician if you have concerns regarding your baby's hearing. New technology uses electrodes and ear probes to detect hearing problems quickly. Newborns in many hospitals and birthing centers are tested for hearing problems within a few days of birth. She may have a hearing problem if she *doesn't*

- blink or startle at loud sounds
- turn toward a voice when spoken to
- look for the source of a sound
- recognize her name
- listen to simple songs or stories

Chickenpox

What it is. Chickenpox (varicella) is not common in infants; it's common in school-age children. However, your baby may be exposed if she's around other children. Chickenpox is highly contagious and usually appears 13 to 17 days after exposure.

Symptoms include a slight fever, fatigue and loss of appetite, which occur in the first 24 hours and may last 3 or 4 days. Your baby may also get a runny nose and cough. A rash generally begins on the trunk and face, and consists of small red blisters that can cover ears, eyelids, nose, mouth, throat and genitals. After 1 or 2 days, the first crop of blisters becomes crusty and begins to dry. New spots generally continue to appear for 4 or 5 days. The rash is extremely itchy.

What to do. There is no cure for chickenpox, so concentrate on keeping baby comfortable. Dress her in loose-fitting clothing. A cool bath every 3 to 4 hours helps soothe itching; you may add baking soda to bath water for further relief. Apply witch hazel, calamine lotion or hydrocortisone cream to reduce itching. Keep baby's fingernails short and clean; apply mittens to prevent scratching.

Caution: Do not give your baby aspirin—it increases the chance of Reye's syndrome. (See the discussion in Week 37.)

When to call the doctor. Call the doctor if your baby

- acts very ill
- has difficulty breathing
- has a prolonged high fever (lasts longer than 4 days)
- has difficulty eating or drinking
- has increased redness or tenderness around blisters, or if blisters drain pus

Prevention. You can take precautions against chickenpox. Have your baby vaccinated between 12 and 15 months of age. Keep baby away from children you know have chickenpox.

Toys and Play This 27th Week

Baby loves toys that make noise—rattles, bells, squeaky toys. She is interested in tracking the sounds she hears. When you hear various sounds in your environment, turn her toward the source of the sound and identify it. A cat's meow, birdsong, a car's revving engine, a jet flying overhead—all are sources of fun sounds. After you identify the sound, imitate it and name it again. She'll start to learn where different sounds come from.

Pick-up Game

Give your baby practice picking up objects that are different shapes and sizes to help her increase her dexterity. Place floating toys of various shapes and sizes in the tub, or give her different types of food to play with in her highchair. *Caution:* She'll probably put everything in her mouth—don't offer small pieces of food that she could choke on.

Listen to That! Look at That!

Toys to choose now include those that invite baby to react, such as rattles or squeaky toys. She probably loves looking in the mirror, so do some activities, such as combing her hair, while she watches herself.

Splish-Splash in the Bath

Bathtub play is especially thrilling for baby now. Let her pour water (with your help) from plastic cup to plastic cup. Or, using a small colander, pour water into it and let the water pour out the bottom.

Week 28

How Big Is Your Baby This 28th Week?

Baby weighs 16-1/2 pounds and is 26-3/4 inches long this week.

Baby Care and Equipment

The Ear-Check Monitor

When your baby rubs his ear and acts cranky, is he teething or does he have an ear infection? These days you can check for yourself, before you rush him to the doctor. Also see the discussion of ear infections on page 272. One of the newest devices on the market for parents of babies is the *ear-check monitor* or *home otoscope*. This useful device:

- helps determine if baby has an ear infection
- monitors symptoms
- monitors progress after treatment
- lets you examine ears, nose and throat, as well as eyes and teeth

Using sonar technology, the monitor measures the presence of fluid in the middle ear. It interprets the results in easy-to-understand language. If your baby suffers from frequent ear infections, you might want to keep this device in your medicine cabinet. This device can be used with the help of your doctor's office. It is not meant to replace your healthcare provider for diagnosis or treatment.

When Baby Refuses Food

Don't be surprised or frustrated when baby spits out a new food you offer. All babies do this at one time or another. The food's newness causes baby to spit it out. It doesn't taste bad or smell bad. If baby spits out the food more than a few times, wait a while before offering it again. Baby may need time to get used to it.

> **When you add new green vegetables to baby's food choices, add them slowly. Offer one at a time, every couple of weeks.**

Playpens and Portacribs

Playpens lost popularity among parents a few years ago. Times have changed—playpens are acceptable again. Playpens give a parent a bit of free time to do something, such as shower or get dressed, while keeping baby in a safe place.

Many of these devices serve two purposes—as a playpen and a portable crib. Safety issues have been raised about this equipment. The greatest risks to baby are suffocation or strangulation. If a mesh drop side is left down, it may create a pocket that can suffocate a baby. If the drop side is not locked properly, it may collapse and strangle baby. If mesh is too wide, baby could get his head caught in it and strangle.

To ensure safety when choosing a playpen or portacrib, consider the following.

- Mesh models have top rails that lock automatically.
- Mesh-netting openings are less than ¼-inch wide.
- Slats in a wooden model are no wider than 2-3/8 inches apart (the same standard as for baby's crib).

Feeding Solids—A Suggested Schedule

You're adding new foods regularly to baby's diet while continuing to breast- or bottle-feed. You could feed him solids at three meals now, so he doesn't get too much food at one feeding. Below is a suggested feeding schedule for baby.

Food	Which mealtimes?	How much?
cereal	breakfast and lunch	at least 2 tablespoons
fruit	breakfast and dinner	1 to 2 tablespoons
vegetables	lunch and dinner	1 to 2 tablespoons
meat	lunch *or* dinner	1 tablespoon

If you have questions about a certain playpen or portacrib you are considering, contact the U.S. Consumer Product Safety Commission. See the Resources section for contact information.

Milestones This 28th Week

Curiosity versus Fears

Your baby is full of curiousity. His curiosity struggles with his fear. Curiosity motivates him to leave your side to explore, but he returns often for reassurance. Each trip away from you may last a little longer. He may be desolate if you disappear while he's gone. If you're busy in different parts of the house, let him know where you are every few minutes. It makes him feel secure.

Baby Uses His Hands and Arms

Baby uses his hands to imitate actions. He may clap when you clap or imitate you when you wipe the counter. He enjoys feeding himself finger foods and likes to drink from a cup. He's becoming more independent in his actions.

Always use a baby-safe mirror around your baby.

He matches the feel of an object to its appearance when he examines it. He is learning how to release something voluntarily in a specific place. Soon he will begin creeping forward or backward by pulling himself along with his arms. He may not be using his legs, but he will as they get stronger.

Baby in the Mirror

If you show him his image in a mirror, he will reach out to pat it and smile at himself. He may touch a part of his clothing while he watches the baby in the mirror. He doesn't realize he's looking at himself, but soon he will make this discovery.

Note: See also the box on page 271, *Milestones This Week*.

Milestones This 28th Week

Changes in Baby You May See Now

Physical Development
• turns over easily

Senses and Reflexes
• sips from two-handled cup with assistance

Mental Development
• can concentrate attention
• shows greater interest in details

Social Development
• shows humor and teases
• pats at mirror image

Every baby is an individual, and your baby may do some of these things more quickly or more slowly than another baby. If you are concerned about your baby's progress, discuss it with your healthcare provider. Also see page viii.

What's Happening This 28th Week?

When Baby Wants Only Mom (or Dad)
Stranger anxiety is natural with baby; most parents learn to expect it. However, it can be unsettling when baby wants only mom and rejects dad. (It can happen the other way around, too.) Preferring one parent over the other is normal. A baby may turn to one parent for comfort and turn to the other for play and interaction.

If baby rejects you, it's best to back off a bit. Evaluate the situation. Determine what he needs right now, then approach him quietly. Speak gently. Cuddle him, if he wants it. If he still wants only the other parent, don't take it personally. Your baby isn't rejecting you. He is showing that he gets something different from his other parent. Allow him the freedom to express his preferences. This phase passes soon.

Signs Baby May Have a Vision Problem
What to look for. How can you determine if baby has problems seeing? Signs of a possible vision problem include

- pupils that don't focus
- a white pupil
- a fluttering eye
- when you offer him an object, he gropes for it
- he doesn't seem to notice you
- he tilts his head at an unusual angle to see an object

- one eye strays
- eyes move abnormally
- he doesn't seem to see what's happening around him

What to do. If you notice any of these signs, contact baby's doctor. Your pediatrician can conduct tests to determine if baby needs corrective lenses or some other treatment. Today we are fortunate to have options for improving eyesight.

Ear Infection

What it is. Ear infections vary considerably and are most common in infants and young children. Know about the different types so you'll be aware of the signs and symptoms of each one.

A *middle-ear infection* occurs inside the ear, where nerves and small bones are located, past the eardrum. An *inner-ear infection,* also called *otitis interna,* is the same as a *middle-ear infection.* An *outer-ear infection* occurs on the outside of the ear canal, away from the eardrum. It is also called *otitis externa* or *swimmer's ear.*

Ear infections often occur with a cold or the flu. Symptoms of middle-ear infections and outer-ear infections are similar, except baby usually has a higher fever and more pain (is "sicker") with a middle-ear infection. Symptoms include

- ear pain
- pulling or rubbing the ear
- touching or pulling baby's ear causes him pain
- fever
- discharge or liquid coming out of the ear (pus)
- decrease or loss of hearing
- flu-like symptoms
- increase in fussiness
- difficulty feeding

What to do. If you believe your baby has an ear infection, give him ibuprofen or acetaminophen, as directed by your doctor, for pain or fever. Clean only the outer ear. Use warm water, mild soap and cotton balls. Do not attempt to clean inside the ear canal, which could make the infection worse. Use ear drops and other medications, including over-the-counter medications, *only* under the direction of your baby's doctor.

Call the doctor. Call the doctor if you believe your baby has an ear infection. Take care of it as soon as possible. When you call, your doctor will want to know about these serious signs, if they are present:

- high fever (102F, 38.9C)
- worsening of other symptoms
- swelling of the ear
- muscles of baby's face twitch or jump

Your physician may suggest a variety of treatments, such as ear drops containing both antibiotics and pain medications, oral antibiotics or decongestants. If the problem recurs often, your pediatrician may recommend further measures, such as tubes that are placed in the ears with a minor surgical procedure.

Medication Poisoning

What it is. This type of poisoning results most often from a mistake by the person giving the medication—the wrong medication or the wrong amount is given. Fortunately, medication poisoning happens rarely. Medications and drugs are not given to babies often. Medication poisoning can also happen as baby becomes more mobile. A curious baby may consume a medication if he gets his hands on it.

Symptoms of medication poisoning depend on the medication. Symptoms to be aware of include

- listlessness
- hyperactivity
- nausea
- vomiting
- diarrhea
- difficulty breathing
- unexplained bleeding or bruising
- rash
- hives
- fever

What to do. Get medical help immediately! **This is an emergency.** Keep the telephone numbers for the nearest poison-control center and your physician's office by the phone at all times. If you are too distraught to call either of them, call 9-1-1.

When to call the doctor. Call the doctor immediately if you believe your baby has been given the wrong medication or the wrong amount of a medication. Call if it appears your baby has had a reaction to a drug. See the discussion in Week 25 on allergies to medications.

Treatment includes care in an emergency facility. The doctor will ask which medication and how much of it was given to or taken by baby. Bring any bottles or containers with you so the emergency medical staff will know the substance, the dosage and any other information they need to help them make decisions.

Toys and Play This 28th Week

Choosing Books to Read Together
Choose books your baby will be interested in. Books with pictures of other babies, animals, a ball or doll, a blanket and crib, or baby in the bathtub are fun to read together. Choose sturdy books made of cardboard, plastic or cloth that he can handle.

Roll Over, Baby!
If you have a bolster or large ball, help baby develop his leg muscles. Place a toy just out of baby's reach. While holding him, drape baby over the bolster or ball. Encourage him to reach for the toy. You may be surprised to see how he uses his feet for pushing and rolling himself forward to get the toy!

Find the Sound
A squeaky toy helps baby learn to use sound to locate what he can't see. Show him the squeaky toy, and squeeze it to show him how it sounds. Squeeze it, then hide it under his blanket or a cloth. Squeeze it again. Ask him where the noise came from. If he doesn't find the toy, help him. Repeat the game, and praise him when he finds the toy.

> **Periodically check baby's toys for damage and loose parts. Throw away damaged toys.**

Learning to Take Turns
Baby doesn't play with others yet, but he will soon. Now may be a good time to teach him about taking turns. Give him the end of a piece of cloth, such as a scarf. Hold the other end. Gently pull on your end, then release it. Does baby take a turn pulling on his end? If he doesn't, put your hand over his and gently show him how to pull.

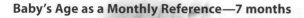

Week 29

How Big Is Your Baby This 29th Week?

Baby weighs 16-3/4 pounds and is 27 inches long this week.

Baby Care and Equipment

Fruits and Vegetables Baby Might Like

Applesauce and pears are both great baby foods, and parents often choose these first when introducing solids to baby. Applesauce has a great texture, and it's low in citric acid. Pears are easily digested and a good source of potassium.

You may not have considered giving baby unseasoned servings of the vegetables you eat yourself. Next time, try them with baby. Sweet potatoes and winter squash are often favorites with baby because of their taste, texture and color. Both contain beta-carotene. Thoroughly mash the cooked food. Don't add butter, sugar, salt or anything else to the vegetable. It's better for baby to try a food without anything extra added.

A ripe avocado is also great. Feed her a little right out of the shell. Avocados contain lots

Foods to Avoid in Baby's First Year

Avoid feeding baby the following foods for her first year. They are the most common allergy-causing foods.

- nuts and nut products, including peanut butter
- egg whites
- citrus fruits
- some citrus juices
- strawberries
- shellfish
- chocolate

275

Honey Caution!

Do *not* give your baby honey or foods made with honey during her first 2 years. Although honey is a natural substance, botulism poisoning is a potential risk for baby. Baby's digestive system is not ready to handle the botulism spores sometimes found in honey. See the discussion of botulism on page 279.

of vitamins and minerals—A, B6, E, folic acid, niacin, magnesium, potassium and phosphorous. The texture of an avocado is unique, and the flavor is mild.

Never give baby a lot of any new food. Give her a few tastes, then wait to see if she shows a physical reaction to it. The box on page 230 lists food reactions to watch for.

As baby eats more fruits and vegetables at each meal, offer her vegetables before fruit, which is sweeter. It's better for baby to be a little hungry when you feed her vegetables. She likes sweet tastes, so even if she's eaten a little food already, she doesn't have to be encouraged to eat fruit.

Giving Baby Sweets

Sweets contain calories with little nutritional value. It may be hard to exclude all sweets from your baby's diet, even though it is a good idea to limit them. Even if you don't offer your baby any sweets, someone else might, such as grandma or a sibling. If you deny your child all sweets, she could develop eating problems concerning sweets later.

A little sweet food may be acceptable as an occasional treat. All baby really needs is a taste. Offering sweets isn't a problem if you offer them infrequently and in small amounts. *Note:* During her first year, however, don't give baby ice cream. She can't digest the milk protein it contains.

Tips for Offering New Foods

As you begin to expand her diet, she may not take to a new food immediately. When that happens, combine a small portion of the new food with one she's been eating. For example, introduce

About Iron

By 7 months, baby needs a more balanced diet. She has nearly depleted the iron supplies she received from her mother before birth. Now she must get the mineral from other sources. If baby drinks iron-fortified formula, she's getting the iron she needs. If she's breastfeeding, she may need extra iron. Check with your pediatrician before you make any changes, such as giving her vitamins with iron.

green beans to baby with her sweet potatoes. If she normally eats 3 teaspoons of sweet potatoes, put 2 teaspoons of sweet potatoes in a bowl and add 1 teaspoon of green beans. The next day, add a little more of the green beans to a little less of the sweet potatoes. Keep doing this until she's eating only the green beans.

In this way, baby gets used to a new taste gradually. You also will find it easier to spot allergic reactions if they occur.

Milestones This 29th Week

She Needs to Explore
Your baby is probably busy now. She wants to move, open, pound on, chew, touch or empty everything she comes across. Keep baby's environment safe, and let her explore. Limit her time in a playpen so she has plenty of opportunity to investigate her world.

Sounds and Rhythms
Baby's interest in sounds and rhythms are paying off: She is beginning to pick up words. She may increasingly repeat the sounds of words you speak. She's also becoming aware of the differences among sounds. She is interested in hearing many different sounds. She has an easier time now finding a sound's source.

Stranger Anxiety
Stranger anxiety may be lessening now—or it may be getting worse! A baby this age has a strong attachment to family members. She may be wary of someone she doesn't recognize. Let her warm up to unfamiliar persons at her own speed. Don't force an interaction. As she recognizes more people, she will feel less threatened by an occasional strange face.

> **Separation anxiety is a good sign of a baby's healthy development.**

Baby's Accomplishments
Baby is becoming more coordinated. She reaches for and grasps a toy with her fingers, instead of her palm. She may point at what she wants. If you point to an object, she can probably find it and touch it.

Being able to sit on her own and shift position at will allows her greater freedom. She reaches toys and other objects more easily now. Turning her entire upper body to reach for something gives her access to objects she couldn't reach a short time ago.

Your baby may be trying to stand more often. You can't teach her to stand, but you can help her in her efforts. She'll make mistakes—and she'll learn from them. Soon she'll find her own way to a standing position. Once she stands, she'll spend several weeks practicing this new skill.

Sleeping through the Night
She is probably sleeping through the night consistently. Cuddling, rocking, reading or singing to her before she goes to bed helps her relax. If she cries excessively when you put her down at night, be firm. Soothe her, then leave her room after a short time. You show her in this way that bedtime is for going to sleep.

Note: See also the box below, *Milestones This Week*.

What's Happening This 29th Week?

Creeping Means Independence
Baby may be getting around more easily now. She may be moving forward on her arms while her tummy and legs drag on the floor. She may scoot backward on her bottom or sideways. Once she begins moving, she's no longer helpless. She can get

Milestones This 29th Week
Changes in Baby You May See Now

Physical Development
- may use rolling over to move around room
- may raise and lower buttocks, while lying on back, to move about

Senses and Reflexes
- grasps, manipulates, mouths and bangs on objects

Mental Development
- likes to say "ma, mu, da, di"
- may associate picture of baby with herself and make appropriate sounds

Social Development
- wants to be included in social interactions

Every baby is an individual, and your baby may do some of these things more quickly or more slowly than another baby. If you are concerned about your baby's progress, discuss it with your healthcare provider. Also see page viii.

things she wants on her own now. She's becoming more independent.

This baby boy is starting to creep, using his arms mainly.

She's Starting to Recognize Words

Researchers who have studied infant speech development believe a baby begins to recognize words at 7 to 7-1/2 months of age. In this research, babies of various ages listened to a couple of words for a short time, then heard paragraphs that included these words. Babies at 7-1/2 months old listened longer when they heard the familiar words. Younger babies didn't. The study also demonstrated babies at 7-1/2 months could tell the difference between like-sounding words, such as "cat" and "hat."

Botulism

What it is. Botulism is a severe form of food poisoning. The toxins that cause botulism are found in the soil and improperly canned meats and vegetables. In newborns and infants, exposure to botulism most often comes from raw honey and other uncooked foods. Symptoms include

- vomiting
- nausea
- dizziness
- weakness
- weak cry
- diarrhea
- abdominal pain
- dry mouth
- lethargy
- constipation (in infants)
- problems sucking, swallowing or eating

What to do. If you believe your baby has botulism, identify others who may also be sick. Determine if they ate the same foods or were exposed in some other way.

Call the doctor. Call the doctor immediately or go to the emergency room if you believe your baby has botulism. Your baby's doctor or an emergency-medicine physician will decide on baby's treatment. Baby may be given botulism antitoxin, which is given by injection. Bed rest and fluids may be prescribed. Baby may also be admitted to the hospital for IV therapy.

Vitamin and Mineral Supplementation

Some babies need additional vitamins or minerals in their diet. Your pediatrician may advise you to give your baby vitamins. *Note:* This is your doctor's decision. Do *not* give your baby supplements without discussing it with your pediatrician first.

If you bottle-feed, many formulas already contain the substances baby needs. Ask your doctor about this at a well-baby checkup.

If you breastfeed, baby may need a supplement. Your doctor will advise you. Most doctors suggest you continue taking prenatal vitamins. Don't take extra vitamins, minerals or herbs unless your doctor tells you to do so. If you have specific concerns or questions on this subject, check with your baby's doctor.

Notarized Medical Permission Slip

Are you going to be going out of town with your partner and leaving baby with others for a short time? If you leave baby in someone else's care, even for a day or two, be sure you leave a *notarized* medical permission slip with baby's caregiver. With this form, a caregiver can get medical treatment for baby if it is needed. No one expects to have to use such a form. But by thinking ahead, you protect baby in case she needs to be treated by your pediatrician or in an emergency facility.

You also may want to give one of these forms to the person who cares for baby regularly, if you and your partner work far from where baby is cared for. It could be important in an emergency.

Toys and Play This 29th Week

Keep the Music Playing!

Baby loves music, so let her enjoy it! Record and play different kinds of music for her. Let her listen to marches, rock-and-roll, lullabies, symphonies, children's songs and anything else you think she might enjoy. Play soft tunes before naptime, an upbeat march before you go out for a walk, or children's songs while she's playing. Expose her to many types of music.

Benefits of Playtime

Play peek-a-boo, hide-and-seek, copy-cat and other games with baby. Playing together helps her realize the pleasures of sharing a game. Your interaction will help her in the future when she begins playing with other children. She will begin to understand how to evaluate another person's mood. She will learn to sense when someone is interested in playing with her.

> When you choose toys for baby, be sure they aren't made of brittle plastic and don't have sharp edges. Avoid toys that have parts that could pinch or nip baby's fingers.

Water Play as a Teaching Tool

Baby is ready for more fun pastimes in the tub, and you can use her enjoyment to teach a few concepts along the way, such as movement and change. This week, find a plastic squeeze bottle or a plastic container. Fill it with water and a little baby shampoo that won't sting baby's eyes.

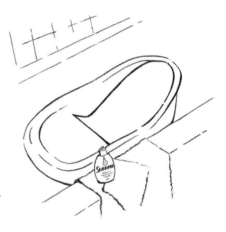

When baby's in the tub, tip over the bottle. Let her see how the water moves inside it. Describe how the water sloshes. Let her see you shake the container, then together look at the bubbles created inside.

If the bottle has a squeeze tip, pour some of the bubbles into and over her hands. Show her how to squeeze out some of the water from the bottle; then let her do it herself.

Week 30

How Big Is Your Baby This 30th Week?

Baby weighs 17 pounds and is 27-1/4 inches long this week.

Baby Care and Equipment

Forbidden Foods

As baby becomes more proficient at eating, you'll consider adding different foods to his diet. Once he is able to eat puréed food, you may mistakenly believe he can eat anything—he can't! Be especially cautious with the foods listed below until your baby has a full set of teeth and you feel certain he won't choke on food.

> You might not consider hard chunks of uncooked vegetables dangerous to your baby—but they are. Don't offer your baby such foods, or any others that present choking hazards, until he has a full set of teeth.

- *Raw foods that snap into small, hard pieces.* These include celery, carrots, green peppers, hard apples, hard pears, jicama.
- *Hot dogs, sausages or bratwurst.* Slicing this type of meat doesn't make it safer. If you want to offer your baby these foods, remove all the skin from the meat. Cut each piece into lengthwise quarters, then slice each quarter into 1/4-inch segments.
- *Chunks of meat.*
- *Peanut butter of any sort.* See the discussion in Week 37.
- *Fruit with seeds and pits.* Core, then remove pits and seeds. Mash the fruit before feeding to baby.

- *Fruit that has thick skin,* such as plums. Skin, remove pits and seeds, then mash fruit before feeding baby.
- *Seeds, even small ones,* such as sunflower seeds.
- *Olives, cherries or grapes,* unless they have been cut into very small pieces.
- *Any food that is smooth and round* that baby could easily choke on.
- *Chicken or chicken bones.*
- *Anything that might have bones in it,* such as fish.

> **Quick Tip!**
> **Teach your baby to open his mouth and say "aaah." If you find baby has something in his mouth that you want to see or remove, you can do it quickly when he says "aaah."**

Time to Check the Stroller

Your baby's stroller may have seen a lot of use by this time. Check it regularly to be sure there are no loose or broken parts. Be sure safety features work properly, such as brakes. Has anything come loose that baby could pull off and put in his mouth? Examine wheels, straps and other parts to ensure each is in proper working condition. Check for sharp edges that could poke or scratch your baby. Clean the stroller if it needs it. Wash the parts that are washable, and wipe off others.

Time to check the stroller.

Milestones This 30th Week

Your baby is becoming quite accomplished! At 7 months, he may be able to stand with support, transfer an object from hand to hand, push up on his hands and knees, roll around to get where he wants to go and sip from a cup with a little help.

Standing and Sitting

Your baby probably sits well without support for a fairly long time. He may be able to get into a sitting position on his own. As the leg muscles that he uses to crawl strengthen, he uses them to try to stand. But he needs more than just strong muscles for this. To stand up by himself, he needs coordination, balance and strength, in addition to some ability to plan ahead.

Attracting Your Attention

He knows he can attract your attention by "talking" to you or crying. He's also learning the meaning of "No" by the tone of your voice and your reaction. He may react to you by looking startled, crying or changing his facial expressions when you tell him "No." His curiosity may make him reluctant to stop what he's doing, however!

Helping Him Overcome Fear of Strangers

Fear of strangers can be lessened somewhat if you communicate trust in someone who is a stranger to baby. Even if he allows himself to be held by someone he doesn't know, he doesn't want you to be far away. He probably won't make eye contact with people he doesn't know.

Sense of Permanence

His sense of object permanence is increasing; for example, if he drops something, he will search the floor for it. If you hide a favorite toy under his blanket, he is beginning to understand it is still there even if he can't see it.

Avoid These Houseplants for Now

Certain common houseplants could poison baby if he eats the leaves or other parts of the plant. Check your house; remove these plants or keep them out of baby's reach when he starts exploring the house or yard. If baby ingests any part of the following plants, call your local poison control center:

- **caladium**
- **dieffenbachia**
- **hyacinth bulbs**
- **narcissus bulbs**
- **castor-bean seeds**
- **elephant's ear**
- **Jerusalem berries**
- **poinsettia leaves**
- **daffodil bulbs**
- **holly berries**
- **mistletoe berries**
- **rosary pea seeds**
- **some varieties of philodendron**

His Language Development

It's amazing to note that by this time, your baby has stopped making sounds he does not hear on a daily basis—he doesn't practice what he doesn't hear. The syllables he does make imitate the language he hears around him every day. If your baby is exposed to more than one language, you may hear him practicing sounds of the various languages he is exposed to regularly.

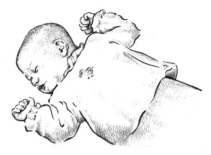

Baby's napping may have dwindled to one daily nap.

His Dexterity Improves

Holding two objects at the same time—one in each hand—is an accomplishment for baby. He holds objects between his fingers and his thumb. He also uses both hands for one task. He may study his hands as they manipulate a toy or other object.

Sleep Needs

Baby's napping may have dwindled to one daily nap. If he's very active, he may sleep more, or he may sleep longer during periods when he is "practicing" a new task. *Note:* See also the box below, *Milestones This Week.*

Milestones This 30th Week

Changes in Baby You May See Now

Physical Development
- pushes up on hands and knees; rocks back and forth

Senses and Reflexes
- holds two objects at same time, one in each hand
- uses fingers to grasp objects

Mental Development
- understands that objects don't disappear when hidden
- imitates sounds and series of sounds

Social Development
- is learning meaning of "No" by tone of voice used

Every baby is an individual, and your baby may do some of these things more quickly or more slowly than another baby. If you are concerned about your baby's progress, discuss it with your healthcare provider. Also see page viii.

What's Happening This 30th Week?

When Baby Spends More Time Playing with His Food

Your baby may spend more time playing with and smearing his food than he does eating it. You may want him to stop this business and attend to the task of eating. Playing with his food has a purpose, however; it makes baby aware of foods' different textures. Let the experiments continue. You don't have to let him become destructive, but a little testing won't do any harm. He'll find his mouth when he gets hungry.

Amebic Dysentery

What it is. Amebic dysentery, also called *amebiasis* or *entamebiasis*, is a parasitic infection of the large bowel or colon. It is spread when food is contaminated with human feces. It occurs most commonly when food handlers don't wash their hands after using the bathroom. Flies and insects can also contaminate foods. Some raw fruits and vegetables fertilized with human feces or washed in polluted water may be contaminated.

The problem can occur at any age. Symptoms include

- diarrhea
- nausea
- fever
- gas
- cramping and pain in the abdomen
- blood or mucus in the stool
- abdominal bloating
- vomiting
- foul-smelling stools
- irritability

What to do. Wash hands thoroughly after using the bathroom to avoid the problem. Wash raw fruits and vegetables well before preparing or serving. Cover food to keep flies and other insects off of it. Clean kitchen counters with soap and water, bleach or some disinfecting agent. Take care in preparing and storing food.

Call the doctor. Call the doctor if your baby has symptoms of amebic dysentery. It becomes more serious if baby experiences an increase in diarrhea, blood in his stools or pain increases.

Antibiotics may be prescribed. Rest and fluid replacement are also good measures. If your baby gets amebic dysentery, use extra care in the future with food preparation and storage. Practice good hand washing. When you can't wash your hands with soap and water, consider using the antibacterial gel hand cleaners that do not require water for rinsing.

Influenza

What it is. Nearly every winter an influenza or flu breakout seems to occur somewhere. Influenza is an acute, contagious respiratory infection that usually lasts from 2 to 7 days. Flu can occur at any age, but it is unusual in infants. Symptoms of an influenza attack include

- fever
- sore throat
- listlessness
- vomiting
- chills
- aches and pains
- cough
- runny nose
- disinterest in eating
- diarrhea
- headache

What to do. If the flu strikes your family, use a cool-mist humidifier in baby's room. See the discussion in Week 13 of humidifiers. Increase baby's fluid intake. Do *not* give your baby medication unless instructed to do so by baby's doctor. Be sure everyone practices hand washing to help prevent the spread of germs.

When to call the doctor. Call the doctor if your baby develops neck pain or neck stiffness, has diarrhea for more than 36 hours or his fever increases in spite of treatment. Contact your physician *immediately* if blood comes from his mouth, new symptoms appear, such as ear discharge or pain, or he has difficulty breathing. For minor symptoms, ibuprofen or acetaminophen, decongestants and cough medications may be suggested. If baby has additional problems or if symptoms become more serious, your pediatrician may recommend hospitalization.

Fecal Impaction

What it is. When a baby suffers from fecal impaction, he cannot pass a large amount of stool. His intestines are overloaded. Fecal impaction is a form of constipation and can be very uncomfortable. It can occur at any age. Symptoms include

- no bowel movements
- hard mass in the lower left abdomen

- abdominal discomfort
- irritability
- poor feeding

What to do. If you believe your baby is suffering from fecal impaction, increase the amount of fluid you offer him to avoid dehydration. Contact your pediatrician. You may be advised to bring baby into the office for treatment advice.

Toys and Play This 30th Week

Kitchen Exploration
Your kitchen may be one of your baby's favorite play areas, with fascinating drawers and cupboards to explore. He may want to empty them! You've probably babyproofed your home and locked the kitchen cabinets. If your kitchen is big enough, you might leave one lower cabinet unlocked, and put unbreakable kitchen things in it. Let him play with measuring spoons, measuring cups, plastic containers, an old pan and some wooden spoons when you're in the kitchen with him.

Which Toy?
To help baby learn to release one toy to get another, play this game. When baby is sitting on the floor and holding a toy in each hand, put another toy in front of him. Call his attention to the third toy. Ask, "Which toy do you want?" He will probably reach for the

Your kitchen may be one of your baby's favorite play areas.

third toy with the other toy still in his hands. Show him how to put down the toy so he can take the other one. He will soon learn how to drop one toy to pick up the other.

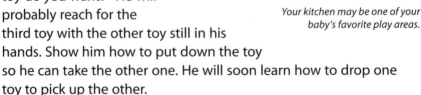

Clap, Clap, Clap

Baby learns by imitation. This game teaches him how to imitate gestures. As you sing a song, clap his hands together lightly in time to the rhythm. After a few times, clap your hands as he watches you. Or put his hands on yours as you clap. Next, ask him to clap as you sing. Learning to clap on his own can take time, so be patient. He'll soon get the hang of it.

Weekly Milestones at a Glance

Week 31

Physical Development
- may crawl (with tummy off floor) rather than creep

Senses and Reflexes
- may bang objects together
- transfers objects from hand to hand
- feeds herself cracker or small pieces of food
- tastes everything

Mental Development
- vocalizes several sounds in one breath
- begins to learn implication of own actions

Social Development
- resists doing something undesirable
- is attached to parents
- may be wary of strangers

Week 32

Physical Development
- crawls forward or backward

Senses and Reflexes
- claps and waves hands
- can hold and manipulate one object while watching another

Mental Development
- may say "mama" or "dada" as names
- enjoys games, such as "so big" or "catch me"
- looks for dropped object

Social Development
- shouts for attention
- pats, smiles and tries to kiss image in mirror

Week 33

Physical Development
- stands with hands free if leaning against object

Senses and Reflexes
- distinguishes smells
- follows a quickly moving object with eyes

Mental Development
- begins establishing differences between one and more than one
- combines known bits of behavior into new acts

Social Development
- pushes away undesirable objects
- imitates people and behaviors, out of sight and earshot

Week 34

Physical Development
- uses furniture to pull himself to standing position

Senses and Reflexes
- points with finger

Mental Development
- can recall past events
- can solve simple problems, such as getting an object by pulling it

Social Development
- may try to use parents to get things
- mimics other people's mouth and jaw movements

Week 31

How Big Is Your Baby This 31st Week?

Baby weighs 17-1/2 pounds and is 27-1/2 inches long this week.

Baby Care and Equipment

Sore Gums?

Your baby may be cutting new teeth soon. That could interfere with her sleep. She may start waking up again during the night. The cause—sore gums. Offer a pacifier when she's cutting teeth. Sucking on the pacifier may help soothe her sore gums.

In addition to sleeplessness, baby may run a low-grade fever and experience mild diarrhea. Experts believe the fever may be caused by gum inflammation. Swallowing excess saliva may contribute to the diarrhea. Ask your pediatrician about giving baby acetaminophen or ibuprofen to help relieve gum soreness and any fever.

More Safety Guidelines

You've already started babyproofing your home for your increasingly mobile baby, as described in previous weeks. By now, baby has a safe environment to play in. These additional safety guidelines can help protect your baby even more. Use all that apply to your home situation.

- Use a mat in the tub every time you bathe baby.
- Turn down your water heater so the water temperature is no higher than 120F (48.8C). Water temperatures set at 160F (71C)

can cause third-degree burns in *one second!* A temperature of 120F (48.8C) provides you 2 to 3 seconds to respond before the water causes burns.

- Dress your baby in fire-resistant nightwear. Check labels to be sure clothing meets safety standards.
- Store your iron in a safe place, out of baby's reach. It's heavy and can cause injury if baby pulls it down on herself.
- Keep all plastic bags out of baby's reach.
- Use a harness or belt to secure baby in her stroller or highchair.
- Don't give baby balloons as toys; she might choke on them.
- Begin teaching baby *now* not to touch matches, safety pins, ashtrays, cigarettes or cigars, the garbage, dog or cat food, or an animal's water bowl.

Feeding Tips for Solids

Baby may be eating solids fairly well by 8 months of age. She is becoming more adept at eating different foods. Keep these tips in mind when feeding baby.

- When you open a jar of baby food, take out only what you need for that meal. Refrigerate the rest for up to 2 days.
- If baby has any food left in her bowl, throw it out when she's finished.
- Don't add sweeteners to baby's food, especially honey.
- When you warm her food, check it before you serve it. Stir and taste before serving to identify and prevent food "hot spots" that could burn baby's mouth.
- Offer fruit juice in a cup. If you put it in a bottle, it may stay in contact with her teeth for a longer period. This could cause cavities.
- Even if you've already fed her, make baby part of the family table at mealtimes. She'll like to be exposed to social interactions during meals.

Milestones This 31st Week

Her Grasp Improves

Baby has learned to use her thumb to help her pick up and hold objects—she can grasp objects between her thumb and fingers. This accomplishment helps develop a "pincer grasp." Now baby can hold an object longer and examine it closely. She can pass it smoothly from hand to hand. She may shake a toy or bang it on the floor. You may see her grasp an object firmly in each hand and bang them together.

In the next several weeks her pincer grasp will become refined enough to enable baby to pick up very small objects, such as crumbs and bits of lint. Be alert for small items she could pick up and put in her mouth.

She has much greater control over her "reach, grasp and release" ability. This frees her to concentrate on the item she holds rather than on her ability to hold it. She doesn't have to think about what her hands are doing.

She's Interested in People
People-watching is still baby's favorite activity. She likes to watch you closely and to imitate you. She may try to imitate sounds you make. She likes to make series of sounds and may utter many sounds in one breath.

She May Be Developing Her Own Patterns
Eating and sleeping patterns are different for different babies. One

Milestones This 31st Week
Changes in Baby You May See Now

Physical Development
- may crawl (with tummy off floor) rather than creep

Senses and Reflexes
- may bang objects together
- transfers objects from hand to hand
- feeds herself crackers or small pieces of food
- tastes everything

Mental Development
- vocalizes several sounds in one breath
- begins to learn implication of own actions

Social Development
- resists doing something undesirable
- is attached to parents
- may still be wary of strangers

Every baby is an individual, and your baby may do some of these things more quickly or more slowly than another baby. If you are concerned about your baby's progress, discuss it with your healthcare provider. Also see page viii.

baby may sleep well. Another may wake several times throughout the night. A baby may refuse to feed herself or reject your efforts to feed her. If she's teething, she may have no interest in eating.

She's Active

She's been working hard on her crawling techniques. She may be fairly adept at getting around now. She may follow you around the house. Be cautious when opening and closing doors and cabinets around her. Babies love to put little fingers in the crack of an open door.

> Her new mobility may cause baby to see the world as an unstable place. She is learning to separate from you; sometimes this upsets her. Be understanding when she gets upset.

When she feels stable standing up, she may lean against some form of support, freeing her hands for other things. Once up, she may be unable to get down, which can frustrate her greatly. It will probably be awhile before she can get back down on the floor on her own (without falling over). She'll need your help until she masters this task.

Is There Sibling Rivalry?

If you have other children, you may see evidence of sibling rivalry. The novelty of having a new baby brother or sister has worn off by now. It's natural. Help the older sibling adjust: Devote special time to him or her and focus on that child's activities.

Note: See also the box on page 293, *Milestones This Week*.

What's Happening This 31st Week?

How Baby Responds when You Return

Baby may still be upset and anxious when you part. Some experts believe that the way your baby reacts when you are reunited is a better indication of her attachment to you than her reaction when you leave. If she's happy when you return, she is reconnecting with you in a healthy way.

However, if she's angry with you for 10 minutes or longer when you return, or she ignores you for more than 10 minutes, take note. You may need to spend more time together to establish a healthy bond.

> At this time, baby prefers reaching for objects that are about 8 inches away.

Babies Can Experience Stress

Just like an adult, a baby can experience stress. When your baby is under stress, it may change her sleep habits. She may sleep shorter or longer periods. She may sleep more deeply or sleep very lightly. Baby's sleep system responds to her environment.

> ### Baby and Stress
>
> **What things are stressful to your baby? Any of the following can contribute to an increase in her stress levels:**
> - **change in her routine**
> - **separation anxiety**
> - **teething**
> - **developmental advances**

If your baby is not sleeping well, consider whether she may suffer from stress. See the box on this page for examples of commonly stressful situations. Eliminating or alleviating a stressful situation for baby could mean peaceful sleep for the entire family.

Before Baby Starts to Crawl

You may notice baby rocks in place on her hands and knees these days. This is normal. She may spend a few weeks rocking back and forth while she tries to figure out how to move forward.

Babies at this age often have well-developed arms, but their legs are not as strong. When she starts to move, she may push herself backward rather than forward for a while.

Encourage her to move forward by placing one of her favorite toys a few feet in front of her. If she wants to reach it, she may crawl forward in an effort to get it. Or sit in front of her, and call her name. Your excitement at her achievement makes her want to try harder.

Your baby may spend a few weeks rocking on her hands and knees before she actually crawls.

Food Allergy

What it is. Although a food allergy can occur at any time, the chance of your baby having one is relatively low—only about 6%. It occurs most frequently in infants when they are introduced to solid foods or when they first drink cow's milk.

It's important to know the signs and symptoms of a food allergy. As you add new foods to your baby's diet, make note of what you offer. If baby has a reaction, you'll have a better idea of what may be causing it.

Different allergies may cause different symptoms. Symptoms of a food allergy include

- bloating and gassiness
- congested nose or runny nose, with a thin, clear discharge
- itchy nose
- itchy skin
- sandpaper-like red rash on the face
- watery, itchy eyes
- upset stomach
- diarrhea or mucus in the stools
- red rash around the anus
- vomiting
- fussiness

> **Foods that cause allergies most often are egg whites, cow's milk and some citrus fruits and juices.**

What to do. Follow your pediatrician's instructions for adding new foods to your baby's diet. Start one new food at a time. Keep a food diary. Note any reactions that occur after baby eats a particular food. If baby has a skin rash, bathe her with a mild, nondrying soap. Use a lubricating cream to decrease redness or itching. Avoid frequent bathing.

If your baby displays symptoms of a food allergy, eliminate foods you can identify that might be causing the problem. Wait until baby is at least 1 year old before you offer citrus juice.

When to call the doctor. Tell your baby's doctor if you or your partner have a food allergy. It might affect the types of food you feed your baby. Call the doctor if any reaction is severe. **Call immediately if your baby develops breathing difficulties!** Contact your pediatrician if the rash looks infected or if a treatment is not working. If it has been difficult to identify the food causing the problems, your doctor may decide to have allergy testing done.

If you are breastfeeding, nurse your baby for at least 6 months if your family has a history of food allergies. Breastfeeding for 6 months helps some babies avoid developing allergies. Many children eventually outgrow food allergies.

Be aware: If your baby is allergic to eggs, make your pediatrician and any other doctor who treats her aware of this. Certain vaccines are egg-based. You will need to take precautions with these vaccines.

Earwax Blockage

What it is. Wax is made by the ear to protect the canal that leads from the eardrum to outside the ear. Everyone has earwax, including babies. Too much earwax can cause a blockage. Symptoms include

- the earwax itself
- ear pain
- pulling, rubbing or tugging on the ear
- decrease in hearing

What to do. Clean *only* the outside of the ear. It may be tempting to clean the ear canal with a cotton swab, but don't do it. It's dangerous, and unnecessary, to put anything in your baby's ear. You could make things worse. Sometimes ear drops are used to soften wax. Soft-rubber ear bulbs can be used with warm water for irrigation also. However, do this only when your baby's doctor directs you to do so.

When to call the doctor. Usually earwax takes care of itself. Just let it move out of baby's ear. Clean it up when it reaches the outside of the ear. Call the doctor if you notice your baby has symptoms of earwax blockage or has a fever or ear pain.

Treatments include ear drops or irrigation of the ear canal and ibuprofen or acetaminophen for fever or pain. Your doctor will advise you on what to do. Don't do these things unless your doctor tells you to, however.

Folliculitis

What it is. Folliculitis is a contagious bacterial or fungal infection of the hair follicles. It can affect any part of the body but most often affects the arms, legs and face, at any age. Symptoms include

- few or many pimples or pustules on the skin, surrounded by red rings
- pustules may contain white or yellow fluid
- pustules may be blood-tinged
- pimple may be adjacent to hair follicle or have a hair growing through it

Symptoms of fungal folliculitis include

- patches or flat areas, with clearly defined borders
- white blisters in the patches or flat areas
- blisters often appear in clusters

What to do. If you believe your baby has either type of folliculitis, keep her skin clean and dry. Don't scratch or pinch pustules. If necessary, cover baby's hands with mittens so she can't scratch herself.

When to call the doctor. Call the doctor if baby develops a fever. If pustules spread after treatment or if they come back after treatment, contact your pediatrician. Treatment includes warm-water soaks, antibiotic gels or antibiotics. The doctor may prescribe antifungal drugs to treat fungal folliculitis.

Toys and Play This 31st Week

Bang the Lids!

Help baby develop coordination in her hands and arms. Gently tap together two pot lids or two spoons. Let baby watch while you entertain her. Then give her the objects. Move her hands together while she's holding them to show her how to tap them. She'll be delighted when she makes the same noises!

Dump-and-Fill Fun

Dumping things out of a container is fun for baby. Let baby play with a plastic bucket or other container filled with smaller toys that fit inside. Fill it up, then let her dump out the objects. Refill the container for baby as long as she remains interested.

Bye-Bye Game

Separation anxiety, and the way baby displays it, can be difficult for everyone. Help her realize you always return by playing this game. Even when you leave for a short time, such as going out of the room to get the laundry, say "Bye-bye!" Tell her you'll be right back. Return in a few minutes. She quickly learns you haven't gone for good. Gradually lengthen the time you are gone, but while you're playing this game, don't be out of sight for too long.

Week 32

How Big Is Your Baby This 32nd Week?

Baby weighs 18 pounds and is 27-1/2 inches long this week.

Baby Care and Equipment

Preventing E. Coli *Exposure*
E. coli is a bacteria that is present in the alimentary canal (the digestive tube from the mouth to the anus) of humans and other animals. *E. coli* can be responsible for infections, such as urinary-tract or gastrointestinal (G.I.) infections.

Exposure. Baby may be exposed through the foods you feed him and your own habits, among other ways. If you take your baby into a swimming pool that a lot of kids use, you also risk exposure. Some kids urinate in the pool. Others swim with dirty diapers. When they do, microorganisms can wash into the water. Chlorine may not kill all these organisms, so if baby drinks the water, he can be exposed.

Prevention. Take the following steps to protect baby from *E. coli* when you prepare and serve foods.

- Wash hands, utensils and other items that touch raw meat or raw poultry.
- Cook beef until it is well done or at least 160F (71C) internally.
- Cook chicken until the internal temperature reaches 180F (82C).
- Beverages should be pasteurized, if necessary (such as dairy products and some juices).

- Never place cooked meat on a plate that was used for raw meat unless the plate was thoroughly washed with soap and water.
- Wash all fruits and vegetables before serving them raw. Manure on the peel could cause contamination.

Swimming protection. To protect your baby when you go swimming, take the following measures.

- Don't let a child with diarrhea swim in your pool. Even if his diapers are clean, germs on his skin can taint the water.
- Check your baby frequently when he's in the pool. Change his dirty diaper immediately. Diapers made for swimming help somewhat, but they're not perfect.
- Don't let a child who is not toilet trained in the pool without a diaper.
- Change diapers in the changing room, not at poolside, to keep the area free of germs.
- Clean his bottom well with diaper wipes or soap and water after a bowel movement, before he goes back into the pool.

When Baby Refuses Food
At around 8 months, your baby may begin refusing jarred baby food because he wants to feed himself. His developing pincer grasp, (see Week 31), enables him to pick up some foods with his thumb and forefinger. He enjoys this accomplishment.

> **Safety Reminder**
>
> **Before you close car doors, make it a habit to check that baby's hands are out of the way.**

Baby is still eating solids during this time to help him learn to swallow different textures and to experiment with eating, not for nutritional value. He can't use utensils yet—he's just not coordinated enough. Eating food with his fingers is easier and a lot more fun!

Foods for self-feeding. If baby decides he doesn't want you to feed him or he wants to eat what he can put in his mouth, consider offering some of the following foods. He can feed himself, and they're not too messy. Foods that are easy for him to eat include

- very small bits of meat, such as ground meat (thoroughly cooked!)

- pieces of well-cooked macaroni or spaghetti
- bite-size chunks of soft foods, such as cooked, mashed yams or mashed bananas

Watch for choking hazards. Be sure the foods you feed your baby are not choking hazards. Baby may not realize yet exactly how much he can put in his mouth safely. It's easy for him to put too much into his mouth and choke or gag himself.

Milestones This 32nd Week

Baby Has Accomplished Much Already
By 8 months, baby can sit without support when his legs are stretched in front of him. His neck, hip and back muscles are getting stronger and more coordinated. As he begins crawling, his activity level increases dramatically. He no longer has to "sit there." He can go to whatever attracts his attention. He'll move quickly from one toy or one activity to another.

Practices knee bends. You may see baby practicing knee bends while he holds onto something for support. This will soon progress to squatting to pick up an object with one hand while he supports himself with the other.

Baby's Independence Can also Mean Dependence
Your baby will love being able to get around on his own. He is increasingly independent and will have longer play periods alone. But as he moves away from you physically, he may feel the need emotionally for your love and security even more. Having you in sight is still very important to your baby.

> When baby starts to crawl, his hands do most of the work pulling him forward.

Sleep Problems May Arise
You may notice your baby is having trouble sleeping at night. He may be waking up to practice standing and crawling in his crib. When he wakes up and needs soothing, however, offer reassurance. Then tell him it's time to go to sleep. This phase won't last too long.

Help Baby Learn to Sit Safely
Because baby is practicing standing, you may be able to show him how to sit down again safely. Make it a game so it's fun. Show him

Milestones This 32nd Week

Changes in Baby You May See Now

Physical Development
• crawls forward or backward

Senses and Reflexes
• claps and waves hands
• holds and manipulates one object while watching another

Mental Development
• may say "mama" or "dada" as names
• enjoys games, such as "so big" or "catch me"
• looks for dropped object

Social Development
• shouts for attention
• pats, smiles and tries to kiss image in mirror

Every baby is an individual, and your baby may do some of these things more quickly or more slowly than another baby. If you are concerned about your baby's progress, discuss it with your healthcare provider. Also see page viii.

how to bend forward from the waist as he begins to sit down. This way, he'll land on his fanny, not his back or front.

Uses Both Hands
Baby still uses either hand indiscriminately. Sometimes he'll use his right hand to pick up something, then he'll use his left hand. He isn't making the right-hand or left-hand distinction yet.

Sounds Are Important
Baby still responds mainly to a speaker's tone of voice. He doesn't fully understand the meaning of the words. But he's learning! He can pick out his name when he hears it used in a conversation. He will turn toward the person who said it. When you speak to your baby, watch him closely. Is he watching *you* closely? Often by this age, baby will study the movements of your mouth and jaw. If you repeat a string of syllables he vocalizes, he may try to imitate your mouth and jaw movements. Note: See also the box above, *Milestones This Week.*

What's Happening This 32nd Week?

Disorders Affecting Sleep
Does your baby sleep during the day and stay awake at night? Sometimes a biological problem can disrupt baby's sleep. The most

common disorders are listed below.

Asthma. This breathing disorder inflames small airways in the lungs, causing coughing and wheezing. It is often diagnosed before baby is 3 years old. If baby wakes up

> It's OK to offer baby cereals that contain wheat at around 8 months.

coughing, especially in the early-morning hours, asthma may be the problem. Coughing during the day when he's excited or running around could indicate baby has asthma. Medication, which will reduce sleep interruptions, is one way to treat asthma. Also see the discussion of asthma in Week 44.

Reflux. When the muscular valve between the esophagus (throat) and stomach doesn't work properly, stomach contents back up into the esophagus. This occurs more frequently when baby is lying down. It usually disappears by the time baby is 1 year old. Medication may relieve discomfort. Occasionally surgery is necessary to correct the problem.

Obstructive sleep apnea. Enlarged tonsils or adenoids block the upper airway during sleep, causing loud snoring. Surgery may be suggested to remove the tonsils or adenoids.

Crawling Takes Practice
It takes a lot of practice to master crawling. Baby must keep his head up and his chest off the floor. He must coordinate moving his arms and legs. Some babies learn to crawl as early as 7 months, others as late as 10 months old. Give your baby lots of opportunities to practice crawling!

> Baby has no awareness of danger to himself yet. Remain diligent about keeping him safe.

Stay Relaxed at Mealtime
Researchers believe that staying relaxed at mealtime is an important skill for *parents* to learn. Getting uptight at mealtimes could lead to feeding problems for baby.

A baby often gets rambunctious when he's eating. Stay cool, calm and collected when he does. Within reason, follow baby's wishes. If he wants to help out with holding the spoon, let him give it a try. If he wants to eat with his fingers, that's probably OK, too. He will experiment with his food to learn about it for some time.

So Curious!
All human babies and baby animals go through a stage of heightened curiosity. Your baby may be experiencing this now.

Human babies have few instincts to rely on. They depend on learned knowledge. When baby explores, touches, examines and experiments, he's storing the knowledge for future use. Baby has no awareness that his activities can sometimes harm him. That's why it's so important to provide baby a safe environment in which to explore.

Baby Eczema

What it is. Eczema is a skin disorder, also called *atopic dermatitis*. The problem can occur any time in early childhood and affects about 10% of all children. Sixty percent of cases occur during a baby's first year. Most cases are not severe. The problem tends to subside as baby gets older.

The problem at this age often occurs when baby's delicate skin comes in contact with the floor once he's crawling. It may also be triggered by a food-related allergy. Dry, scaly red patches first appear on the face. The rash then moves down to the trunk and limbs. It does not usually affect the diaper area. Symptoms include

- itchy skin
- flaking or peeling of skin
- small blisters that leak a little fluid (in some cases)
- infection

What to do. If your baby gets eczema, give fewer baths. When you do bathe him, pat him dry rather than rub him dry. Lubricate skin after every bath with a mild baby lotion. Reapply lotion to baby's skin 2 or 3 times a day. Ask your pediatrician which kind to use. Dress baby in loose-fitting clothing that lets his skin breathe. Keep layers light to help avoid perspiration, which may cause additional irritation. Avoid feeding baby foods to which he is allergic.

When to call the doctor. Call the doctor if you believe your baby has eczema. It's important to call if blisters appear to be infected or get worse.

Medications to treat eczema are used only under a doctor's direction. They may include ointments containing steroids (cortisone) or coal tar, antihistamines (for itching) or antibiotics, in case of an infection. If problems persist, you may be referred to a pediatric allergist or dermatologist.

Lice

What it is. Parents never want to believe *their* child could get lice, but it can happen. Head lice has nothing to do with cleanliness or hygiene. Lice thrive in crowded environments. Exposure may occur in day-care and child-care situations. Also called *crabs, head lice* or *body lice*, this infestation is caused by a small parasite that lives on the body, most often where there is hair. Symptoms include

- itching and scratching
- redness of scalp
- eggs (nits) in the hair
- hives

What to do. Check for head lice by examining the scalp on the back of the head at the hairline or around the ears. Use a magnifying glass. Tiny, gray, oval-shaped specks, called *nits,* may be visible that are firmly attached to the hair. If you can't see nits, you may see evidence of intense scratching.

If your child gets lice, wash all sheets, towels and clothing in hot water that contains a disinfectant. Dry everything on the hot cycle in the dryer. Also wash scarves and hats. Dry clean items that can't be washed. Soak combs and brushes in very hot water (more than 130F; 54.4C) for at least 10 minutes. Don't share towels, combs, brushes or other hair-care items.

When to call the doctor. Call the doctor if you believe your baby has lice or if someone in your household has lice. Don't use over-the-counter medicated shampoos without your pediatrician's recommendation.

If your baby's doctor advises using an over-the-counter medicated shampoo to deal with the problem, keep these shampoos out of baby's eyes. After shampooing, comb the hair thoroughly while it is wet to remove the nits. Sometimes application of a medicated shampoo must be repeated, but only as recommended by your physician.

If your pediatrician recommends an over-the-counter medication that doesn't work, you may have to use a prescription shampoo. Ask for one that *doesn't* contain lindane. Overuse of lindane has been linked to harmful side effects in children.

Toys and Play This 32nd Week

Drop-the-Spoon Can Be a Game
When baby drops his spoon from his highchair, make a game of picking it up. Reach down and pick it up, then say something silly such as, "Baby dropped the spoon. We have to pick it up!" (He'll drop it again quite quickly, no doubt.) This game reinforces to baby that an object continues to exist even when he can't see it.

Sooo Big!
Look at baby and ask, "How big is baby?" Stretch your arms far apart and say, "Sooo big!" Your baby will enjoy watching you do this. He may not be able to show you how big he is yet, but he soon will.

Make a Tunnel
To help baby satisfy his desire to crawl, make a fun tunnel for him. In addition to encouraging him to crawl, it gives him the chance to see the difference between "inside" and "outside."

Find a sturdy box larger than your child. Remove the flaps or fold them inside at both ends. Place baby on the floor near one end of the "tunnel." Then sit down at the other end. Encourage baby to come to you through the tunnel. If he doesn't quite get the hang of it, crawl into the box yourself and guide him to the other end.

After he's mastered the art of going through the tunnel, enter it from one end while he is also inside. Tell him you're "inside." When you crawl out, tell him you're "outside" the tunnel.

Week 33

How Big Is Your Baby This 33rd Week?

Baby weighs 18-1/4 pounds and is 27-3/4 inches long this week.

Baby Care and Equipment

Making Your Own Baby Food

Lots of parents want to make their own baby food. You can too and maintain baby's health by keeping in mind these important points:

- Use only fresh foods.
- Good choices to start with include sweet potatoes, peas and squash.
- Thoroughly cook the foods.
- Purée the cooked foods so they are very mushy.
- Don't add salt, sugar, spices or anything extra to the food.
- Make only a little at a time, so you don't have to store it.
- If you make more than you need, store leftovers in a sealed container in the refrigerator.
- Keep leftovers no longer than 2 days.

Toxic Mold

Water damage to your home that is ignored can lead to growth of a mold that could cause an infant to develop bleeding lungs, also called *pulmonary hemorrhage*. The problem is attributed to a toxic mold that grows on wet wood and paper products.

When the black mold dries, its spores can get into the air. If an infant inhales them, they can affect her rapidly growing lung cells.

This is especially true if baby is under 6 months of age.

Dry out wet areas as soon as possible. Throw out any items that were water-soaked if they do not dry within 24 hours. Clean walls and anything made of wood with water and bleach—one part bleach to four parts water. Take care of leaks so water damage doesn't recur.

Grain-Based Finger Foods

If baby wants to feed herself, offer her some grain-based foods. These foods become mushy in her mouth, so they are easy for her to chew and swallow. Baby crackers, well-cooked pasta (not al dente), bread and oat-circle cereal pieces are good choices. These foods offer nutrients— B vitamins and iron—that are also found in infant cereals. Getting baby to eat these foods helps you, too. You'll be able to eliminate one or two servings of cereal each day from her meal plan.

Now is a good time to offer baby oat-circle cereal pieces.

Milestones This 33rd Week

She Has a Strong Sense of Self

Your baby is developing—and expressing—likes and dislikes. She may turn away from a toy she isn't interested in or cry for one she wants but doesn't have. Baby enjoys playing alone for longer periods, and she also enjoys interacting with other people.

You may be surprised at your baby's range of emotions. She can express the emotions of anger and frustration. But they may disappear as quickly as they appeared.

She may still be somewhat anxious about separation from you. This may appear as bashfulness, nervousness, whining, crying and turning away from unfamiliar people. She wants to stay close.

Is She Standing Alone?

When baby can stand fairly steadily, you may notice she begins trying to pull herself up on anything handy. Some very active babies may try to *cruise* a little—move sideways while holding on to something solid.

Help her if she gets stuck standing up. It will happen frequently as she tries to master this new task. When she needs help, release her hands from what they're holding, and gently lower her to the ground.

She Sees Relationships between Objects

You may notice your baby is beginning to apply what she already knows to new situations. She is learning that there can be a relationship between objects. She'll place a lid on her drinking cup or put a used paper towel in the trash can. She may place her toy gently on the table. These actions demonstrate her awareness that some things fit together.

Hand Control Increases

You may notice your baby holding an object in one hand and banging it with something in her other hand. She may bang two objects together in front of her. These accomplishments are possible due to increasing hand control. She's using her thumb, first *and* second fingers to grasp larger objects.

Fun Sounds

Your baby is becoming more sophisticated in her appreciation of sounds. She can probably identify various household sounds and outdoor sounds by now. She will imitate rhythmic banging sounds. She likes banging things together for the sounds they produce.

She may display a sense of rhythm. When you turn on music (no matter what kind), your baby may bounce while she's standing holding on to something. Or you may see her sitting on the floor and bouncing on her bottom. She may move in time when you sing or play a song.

> Baby can crawl to the top of the stairs easily. But once there, she doesn't know how to crawl down. Until you can teach her how to do it safely (it may take months to accomplish), put a gate or other barrier across the stairs.

Milestones This 33rd Week

Changes in Baby You May See Now

Physical Development
- stands with hands free if leaning against object

Senses and Reflexes
- distinguishes among smells
- follows with eyes to what someone points to

Mental Development
- begins establishing differences between *one* and *more than one*
- combines known bits of behavior into new acts

Social Development
- pushes away undesirable objects
- imitates people and behaviors, out of sight and earshot

Every baby is an individual, and your baby may do some of these things more quickly or more slowly than another baby. If you are concerned about your baby's progress, discuss it with your healthcare provider. Also see page viii.

Baby May Be Less Interested in Breastfeeding

It's not unusual for baby to lose interest in breastfeeding now. But she still wants the closeness with you. Encourage her to crawl into your lap whenever she needs a little comforting. You'll both enjoy it. Note: See also the box above, *Milestones This Week.*

What's Happening This 33rd Week?

Respond Quickly to Baby

Two or 3 minutes is a long time for a baby! When you expect her to be patient about something, 3 minutes is about as long as you can reasonably expect her to wait. When baby's needs are not met quickly, she may cry harder. Any lessons she's learned about patience are forgotten quickly. On the other hand, she learns her needs will be met if you respond quickly, and this encourages her to trust you. It also encourages her to wait a little longer next time.

Can You Avoid Stereotyping?

Most parents want their children to grow up without stereotyping. Do boys always play with trucks? Do girls always play with dolls? Some experts believe certain basic differences between boys and girls cannot be eliminated. Others believe that although differences do exist, parents can do some things to embrace those differences.

Offer your child many different toys. Give your baby options when it comes to toys. Let girls play with trucks and cars. Let boys have a doll or stuffed animal. Offer all sorts of toys. But don't be surprised if your child favors gender-specific toys anyway. Girls do like dolls, and boys do like trucks!

Set an example. During the early years, your child will get most of her ideas about gender roles from observing you and your family. It's a good idea for parents to share chores and responsibilities. In that way, your child will learn that dads and moms do lots of different things.

Don't overprotect girls. Give girls the same experiences as boys. Encourage them when they get frustrated. Push them a little more when they need it.

Cuddle boys more. Comfort your son by holding him. Researchers believe that touch is powerful and can even lower stress-hormone levels. Boys need this benefit as much as girls!

Set Good Examples

You can help your child develop social skills. Set a good example, and provide her with an opportunity to practice social skills. Your baby needs to learn that everyone is important. It can be a challenge for parents to find a balance among the three goals of teaching a child others are important, meeting her needs and encouraging her self-esteem.

What works. Teach baby to be considerate of others. Don't give her everything she wants when she wants it. Don't let her win all the time (but she shouldn't always lose, either). Teach her to take turns and to follow the rules. Guide her in ways that teach her by demonstration to be considerate of others.

Although many parents find getting the balance right is a bit difficult at first, you'll be doing baby a favor by making the effort. When she goes to day care or preschool, she'll have learned valuable social skills for interacting with others.

Eye Injury or Contusion

What it is. When baby becomes more mobile, she falls occasionally and may hurt herself slightly. Sometimes she may hurt herself more seriously. Few things are as alarming as an eye injury. Injury is usually caused by trauma to the eye. Symptoms include

- swelling
- discoloration around the eye or in the white part of the eye—red, blue, purple or any shade of these colors
- tenderness or pain
- may be accompanied by a cut or laceration

What to do. If your baby has an eye injury, gently apply cool compresses to the area. After 24 hours, you can use a warm (not hot) compress.

When to call the doctor. Call the doctor if there is a cut or laceration near the eye, if swelling continues or increases or if baby is in pain. Most injuries to the eye are emergencies.

The doctor may prescribe eye drops or ointments. Sometimes a patch is recommended to protect the eye from bright lights.

Splinter

What it is. A baby can get a splinter fairly easily, especially after she starts crawling. Symptoms include

- splinter is visible
- pain in the area of the splinter
- redness or swelling in the area
- bleeding, occasionally

What to do. If your baby has a splinter of glass or metal, don't try to remove it unless it is tiny and hardly punctures the skin. If it is deep, a splinter like this must be removed by a medical professional.

When you notice baby has a splinter, wash the area with soap and water. Apply pressure about 1/4 inch from the puncture site to help dislodge the splinter so you can grasp it. If the splinter doesn't budge, carefully break the skin with a sterilized needle (see box).

Removing a splinter. You may remove the splinter if it seems easy to do so. Grasp the splinter with a pair of sterilized tweezers. Pull gently and

> ### How to Sterilize a Needle
>
> **Sterilize a needle by carefully heating the tip on a burner (stove) or by cleaning it with rubbing alcohol.**

slowly to remove it. Follow the angle at which the splinter appears to have entered the skin. It can be difficult to get a baby to hold still long enough to allow you to remove it. You may want to try this when she's asleep, or have someone else hold her.

After the splinter is out, wash the area with soap and water, then keep it clean and dry. Apply a triple antibiotic ointment to the area to avoid infection. Cover it with a bandage.

If a little inflammation or redness occurs, a bit of the material may have been left behind. Contact your physician.

When to call the doctor. If you can't remove a splinter, call the doctor, especially if it is large or deep in the skin. Call the doctor if red streaks become visible, if the area appears to be getting infected, or if yellow or green pus comes from the area of the splinter. These are signs of infection. Your pediatrician will treat the problem with antibiotics.

Toys and Play This 33rd Week

"Baby, Baby Dumpling"
While your baby's lying on her back, pretend to cook her and eat her up. Make the following gestures while you sing this nursery rhyme:

> *Baby, baby dumpling*
> *Cook her in a pan* (tickle her legs)
> *Sugar her* (lightly tap her tummy)
> *Flour her* (stroke her tummy lengthwise, then use the back of
>   your hand the other way)
> *And eat her when you can!* (make munching noises as you
>   "nibble" her tummy)

Teach Baby to Anticipate Actions
This simple game helps teach baby to anticipate your actions. Hold her firmly on your lap. Bounce her gently while you sing a simple song she knows. At some point in the song, lower her between your knees a little as you open them. Look at her and laugh. Sing the song again, lowering her between your knees at the same point in the song each time.

Soon she'll begin to anticipate your lowering her at that point in the song. You'll see her anticipation as she smiles or laughs when you get near the part of the song where you open your knees. Or she may tense her muscles in readiness for the slight dip.

Week 34

How Big Is Your Baby This 34th Week?

Baby weighs 18-1/2 pounds and is 27-3/4 inches long this week.

Baby Care and Equipment

Facts on Plastics and Vinyls

You may have seen newspaper headlines recently stating, "Chemical elements in vinyl toys cause liver damage in rats," or "Plastic toys linked to cancer agent." Should you worry and throw out all of your baby's pacifiers, teething rings, bottle nipples and plastic or vinyl toys?

A number of agencies have done research on the hazards of various substances like these. The culprit they found was the chemical *diisononyl phthalate,* better known as *DINP* or just *phthalate.* This chemical often is used to soften hard plastic into PVC (polyvinyl chloride). Despite the findings, the U.S. Consumer Product Safety Commission (CPSC) reports few, if any, children are at risk. According to the commission, a child can't ingest enough DINP to be harmed from contact with products made from phthalate. The commission does suggest that, as a precaution, parents not keep any single item too long, especially if baby has chewed on it a lot.

The CPSC hasn't banned phthalate. The commission did ask companies to stop using the chemical voluntarily in soft rattles, teethers and toys for babies younger than 3 years old. Most manufacturers complied with the request. By the middle of 1999, nearly all such products were DINP-free. Some companies have chosen to label their products as "phthalate free." Check product labels before you buy. If you have older plastic or vinyl toys that you used with previous babies, or if someone else gave you these items, you may want to toss them, just to be safe.

> **Don't rush to wean baby from his bottle. It won't hurt him to continue with it, even into his second year. If you don't make an issue of it and his emotional needs are being met, he'll stop bottle-feeding on his own.**

Reptile Warning

If you have a reptile as a pet, take note. The Centers for Disease Control advises keeping children younger than 5 away from all pet reptiles. These animals can be a source of life-threatening salmonella infections. Symptoms of a salmonella infection include fever, vomiting, bloody diarrhea and abdominal pain.

Bottle-feeding may continue into baby's second year.

A child can become infected from handling the animal or by handling objects contaminated with the reptile's feces. Cases have been reported in infants who never touched reptiles personally. Researchers believe they were infected when they were held by others who did handle reptiles. It may be best to give away your reptile to a good home without children.

Milestones This 34th Week

His Intellectual Capacity Grows

Baby understands the model of a human face now. He studies everyone's faces to compare them. Baby also notices objects and may point at what he wants. He pays greater attention to details.

These days, baby is even exploring the concept of *cause and effect*. He is beginning to understand that when he repeats an action in the same way, it almost always has same effect. When he drops a spoon, it always falls to the floor. A toy that offers more than one possible activity, such as an activity ball that he can put things into and also roll on the floor, helps baby realize that when he makes a different movement, he sees a different effect in his toy.

Baby's Eating Plan at 8 Months

At 8 months of age, your baby may be eating lots of different foods. He is still taking in 24 to 32 ounces of formula or breast milk each day. However, he's probably started tasting (and eating) other new foods as well. His daily diet now may consist of

- ½ cup each of cheese, plain yogurt or plain cottage cheese
- 2 or 3 servings of 2 to 4 tablespoons of iron-fortified baby cereal
- 2 or 3 servings of ½ slice of bread or 2 crackers
- 2 servings of 3 to 4 tablespoons of fruit
- 2 ounces of fruit juice from a cup—dilute it with water before serving
- 2 or 3 servings of 3 to 4 tablespoons of vegetables
- 2 servings of 3 to 4 tablespoons of protein, including chicken, beef, pork, cooked dry beans or egg yolks

If you offer baby meat products, they should be strained or finely minced. Feed him only one new meat a week. When you offer eggs, just offer the yolks. Some babies are sensitive to egg whites until after they are 1 year old.

His Muscular Development

Muscular development is finally reaching baby's legs and feet. He may kick vigorously when he's on his back. He may propel himself across the floor on his back by squirming and kicking. Baby may also move himself around by creeping on his tummy, using his arms to pull himself along. It won't be long till he's crawling, if he isn't already.

He may throw things. Throwing develops as a controlled motion of his hand and arm. He likes to throw things to see what happens! Because of increased muscle control, he may be able to fit small objects through a hole in a larger object. He may build a tower of two blocks, or gather items for sorting and building.

He may also stand up and lean against an object, keeping his hands free. Now he has greater freedom to get into mischief! He may also divide his weight between his arms and legs when he plants his hands on an unmovable object for support.

Keep Talking and Reading

Continue talking to your baby. Use short, simple sentences. When appropriate, use exaggerated hand motions. Talk about the present, and repeatedly use the names of people and things. Avoid saying "it" and "them" because baby has a short memory and can't think in the abstract yet. He's listening and trying to understand you. He's learning to connect words with people, objects and events.

> **Baby will have many false starts before he learns to crawl. When he stumbles, don't make a big deal out of it, and he won't either.**

He enjoys having you read aloud to him from simple books. When selecting books to read, choose those with clear, colorful illustrations or pictures. If pages are uncluttered and simple, he can focus his attention more easily. About three objects is enough for one page.

When you read aloud to him, point to the pictures, and read slowly. Use your finger (and his, too) to trace shapes. Tell him about the animals, people or objects. Sing, exaggerate and use sound effects to add interest, emotion and emphasis to whatever you're reading.

Baby's Safety

Have you noticed your baby has an urge to climb? You will! It's instinctual. Once he's up, however, getting down can lead to

---

Milestones This 34th Week

Changes in Baby You May See Now

Physical Development
- uses furniture to pull himself to standing position

Senses and Reflexes
- points with finger

Mental Development
- can recall past events
- can solve simple problems, such as getting an object by pulling it

Social Development
- may try to use parents to get things
- mimics other people's mouth and jaw movements

Every baby is an individual, and your baby may do some of these things more quickly or more slowly than another baby. If you are concerned about your baby's progress, discuss it with your healthcare provider. Also see page viii.

Baby's Teeth

At 7 months old, your baby may begin teething, although symptoms of teething may appear even earlier. At 8 months, your baby may have his first two new teeth, soon followed at 9 months with two more. These and the teeth that follow soon after are only temporary or "baby teeth," but they are still important. Take good care of them from the time they first appear.

Teething

With teething, baby's first teeth start moving up through bone and gum to make their appearance in the mouth. Teething starts weeks or months before baby's first teeth actually appear. Drooling, chewing on anything available, fussiness, wakefulness and swollen gums are typical signs teething has begun. Not all babies have a problem with teething, but some do. Baby teeth often come in twos—you will probably see the two bottom-center teeth emerge first. These are followed by the upper-middle teeth. Some doctors believe the first teeth may cause the most distress because your baby has never experienced teething before. After the first teeth appear, teething may not be much of a problem.

Teething symptoms. When he starts teething, your baby may refuse to eat solids. Eating puts pressure on his gums, which increases his discomfort. He may want more formula or may want to nurse more. But this also puts pressure on his gums, so he may not

want to continue after he begins. If you find baby pulls away from the breast or bottle after his initial sucking effort, it may be that he feels some discomfort in his mouth.

The Difference between Teething and Illness

Your biggest challenge may be discerning between teething and illness. Even if your baby has common teething symptoms, if he *also* has a high fever and vomiting, teething is probably not the problem. Don't ignore these symptoms—discuss them with your physician if they last more than 24 hours.

What helps baby when he is teething. If you're fairly certain baby is teething, you can help him cope with the discomfort he feels. Cold sensations seem to offer limited relief. Let baby chew on something cold, such as a chilled plastic teething ring or a cold washcloth. Don't offer frozen foods, such as a piece of frozen banana. Small pieces could lead to choking.

A baby spoon with a rubber or heavy plastic coating over the bowl area is easier and more comfortable for a teething baby to eat from.

Massage baby's gums.
Massage baby's gums with a clean finger (yours) covered with gauze. Rub on gum-numbing medication; it can be purchased over the counter. Don't overuse it! Cold drinks or chilled food may also help. Let him chew on other foods that are fairly hard, such as zwieback.

Pain medication, such as acetaminophen or ibuprofen, can be

> **If your baby is teething, give him teething biscuits. They can help make his sore gums feel better.**

used to help baby sleep at night, if teething pain keeps him awake. Ask your doctor what the correct dose is and how long it can be used. *Caution*: Don't rub liquor, such as brandy, on baby's gums to help relieve pain.

Importance of Baby Teeth
In addition to helping baby chew his food, baby teeth enable him to speak clearly (when he learns to talk).

Temporary or baby teeth reserve jaw space for his permanent teeth when they come in, usually around 5 or 6 years old.

Baby teeth allow the jawbones and other facial bones to grow properly.

Begin early taking care of baby teeth. You'll both be glad you did.

> **Baby's teeth do more than chew food.**

How to Take Care of Baby Teeth
By 9 months of age, your baby has probably cut a tooth or two. (See the chart opposite.) Take care of them!

Clean the teeth regularly.
Clean baby's first teeth with a cloth or use a small, soft baby toothbrush. It isn't necessary to use toothpaste yet. Once your baby has more than four teeth, brush them at least once a day. When you brush his teeth, gently massage each tooth with a soft-bristled infant toothbrush. Massage in circles.

Keep massaging baby's gums.
If you've followed our suggestions, you've been massaging his gums with a soft cloth or gauze for quite a while in preparation for teething. Keep massaging baby's gums (where there aren't any teeth) with the gauze. It helps toughen the gums where new teeth will soon come in.

Let him try brushing his teeth.
You might want to let baby hold the toothbrush. Help him by holding your hand over his. (You don't want him to stick it in his eye!) He may just want to play with it or suck on it. That's OK. It's the exposure to brushing that's important at this point, so he will be more inclined to learn to brush his own teeth later on.

Baby Teeth

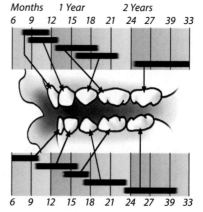

Baby's teeth will emerge slowly over the next 2 years, in roughly this order.

calamity. He'll find all sorts of places to climb. Most of them probably are less than safe: It won't be long before he'll be able to push a stool to the sink. He'll be able to climb high enough to reach the medicine cabinet. Or he may open drawers and use them

> Babies who can soothe themselves may not be born that way. When baby wakes up during the first few months, he'll cry out. If you have comforted him when he cries as a very young baby, by the time he's 8 or 9 months old, he'll feel secure enough to go back to sleep on his own.

to climb. Look around and take measures now to protect baby, such as turning furniture so it can't be used as a ladder. You may need to remove objects that invite baby to climb where he shouldn't. Note: See also the box on page 317, *Milestones This Week*.

What's Happening This 34th Week?

He Experiments with Standing and Balancing
When baby starts crawling, his perspective of his world changes. He sees everyone around him walking, so he wants to walk, too. Because his arm muscles are stronger, he will use them to pull himself up to stand. He'll use whatever's handy—even you! Once he's up, he'll hold on to anything at hand.

After he's practiced standing for a period of time, usually days or weeks, he'll begin to experiment with letting go. He'll put his arms out for balance and may stand for a few seconds before sitting down again.

Fever
What it is. When baby gets a fever, he has a temperature of at least 100.4F (36.3C) rectally. Fever is a *symptom* of illness and is frequently associated with other medical symptoms.

Getting an accurate temperature with a newborn or an infant can be challenging. Methods that work best include an ear thermometer, a rectal thermometer or an axillary thermometer (a rectal thermometer placed under baby's armpit). For information on different types of thermometers and how to take a baby's temperature using each one, see Week 4.

If your baby feels warm, if his skin and mucous membranes are dry, if he shows signs of not feeling well or has the symptoms of a cold or flu, you'll probably need to take his temperature. If you call the pediatrician's office to make an appointment, they often want to know first if your baby has a fever. It's a good idea to take his temperature *before* you call.

What to do. If your baby has a temperature, cool him by sponging him with a damp cloth or by giving him a cool bath. Increase his fluid intake. Don't dress him too warmly or pile blankets on top of him. Look for symptoms to help identify a possible cause of the fever.

When to call the doctor. Call the doctor if your baby has a rectal temperature above 100.4F (36.3C). Contact the office if your baby is irritable, won't nurse or take a bottle, and is getting dehydrated. Call if he's having problems breathing. If your baby is a newborn and running a fever, it's important to contact your pediatrician immediately.

Treatment depends on the cause of the fever. Acetaminophen or ibuprofen may be recommended. Medication to deal with the cause of the problem, such as an antibiotic for an infection, may be prescribed.

Intussusception
What it is. Intussusception occurs when the bowel folds into itself, causing a blockage or obstruction of the bowels. It most often involves the large intestine. The problem occurs most often in babies and children between 2 months of age and 5 years of age. It is twice as common in baby boys than in baby girls. Symptoms include

- sudden, acute abdominal pain
- drawing knees up to the chest
- screaming
- vomiting
- lethargy
- passage of red, jellylike stools (stools mixed with blood and mucus)
- tender, distended abdomen
- palpable, sausage-shaped mass in upper-right quadrant of abdomen

Baby appears normal and comfortable between episodes of pain.

Call the doctor immediately. Your quick response to these symptoms is crucial. If you believe your baby has intussusception, call your pediatrican immediately! **This is an emergency.**

Identified early, this problem can sometimes be relieved without surgery. A barium enema or a water-soluble contrast may be done to try to push the inverted bowel into its original position. If this doesn't work, surgery may be necessary.

Your doctor will probably recommend restricting fluids. When you get to the hospital, IV therapy, nasogastric decompression and antibiotic therapy will begin before surgery is performed.

Scabies

What it is. Scabies is a highly contagious skin disease caused by a mite. It is passed from one person to another when bed sheets, towels or clothing are shared. Symptoms of scabies usually appear on the hands, wrists, genitals, chest, inner thigh and between fingers, and include

- intense itching
- small blisters
- scaling or flakiness of skin
- slightly discolored lines on skin, up to several inches long in some cases

What to do. Keep baby from scratching or rubbing the infected area. At home, thoroughly wash hands before and after touching anyone who is infected. Wash all bedding, towels and clothing in hot water with bleach added to the wash cycle. Don't share towels, bedding or clothing.

Call the doctor. Call the doctor if you believe your baby has scabies. Contact your pediatrician if the blisters become infected or you see any redness or swelling in the area of the blisters. Baby's doctor may prescribe medication.

Toys and Play This 34th Week

Stand and Reach!

This game helps baby recognize that he can get objects by standing and reaching for them. Place a favorite toy on the seat of a sturdy chair. With words and movements, encourage your baby to pull himself up by holding onto the chair. If this is difficult or he doesn't understand, help him to his feet. Then lean him against the chair so he can reach the toy. When he gets the toy, applaud and praise him. Then place him back on the floor and start over again.

Using One Object to Get Another

Help baby understand he can use one object to get another. Tie a string around a favorite toy. Place the toy beyond his reach. Leave the end of the string in front of him. Show him how he can get the toy by pulling the string. Praise him when he does it on his own. (This may take practice.)

Caution: Never leave the string on the toy or let baby play this game by himself. Remove the string from the toy and put the string away before you leave the room.

Weekly Milestones at a Glance

Week 35

Physical Development

- if held in standing position, puts one foot in front of the other

Senses and Reflexes

- can rake a small object with fingers, then pick it up with fist

Mental Development

- understands simple instructions
- shakes head "No"
- examines objects as external, 3-dimensional realities

Social Development

- doesn't like to be confined

Week 36

Physical Development

- can stand up if she's holding on to something
- sits well in a chair

Senses and Reflexes

- approaches large objects with both hands
- can pick up and manipulate two objects, one in each hand

Mental Development

- may remember game that was played the previous day
- responds to his name

Social Development

- wants to play near parent
- imitates play
- objects when something is taken away from him
- feeds himself some foods

Week 37

Physical Development

- crawls with one hand holding something
- can turn around when crawling

Senses and Reflexes

- bangs objects together at center of body

Mental Development

- uncovers a toy that she saw hidden

Social Development

- deliberately chooses a toy for play
- imitates some sounds, such as cough, hisses
- manipulates and drinks from cup

Week 38

Physical Development

- can take a few steps if supported; walks with adult holding his hands

Senses and Reflexes

- reaches for small objects with finger and thumb

Mental Development

- grows bored with repetition
- is aware of vertical space

Social Development

- begins to evaluate people's moods

Week 39

Physical Development

- climbs
- crawls up stairs

Senses and Reflexes

- clasps hands

Mental Development

- can follow simple instructions
- is becoming afraid of heights

Social Development

- may learn to protect herself and possessions
- performs for audiences; repeats act if applauded

Week 35

How Big Is Your Baby This 35th Week?

Baby weighs 19 pounds and is 28 inches long this week.

Baby Care and Equipment

Seasonal Safety

Christmas or Chanukah is a time of wonder and excitement, especially this first holiday season you share with your baby. As you prepare your house for the celebration, be aware decorations and other trappings of the holidays could present hazards for baby. Practice precautions to protect your little one.

Keep candles to a minimum. Candles are beautiful at holiday time, but they can be dangerous, too. If you just can't do without the soft glow candles produce, use electric candles or light bulbs instead. Keep all of these attractive nuisances out of baby's reach. That includes keeping

Keep holiday candles out of baby's reach—or save them for another year.

candles off of tables with tablecloths or runners that baby might pull. If you must use candles, place them well out of baby's reach.

Christmas-tree tips. Never leave a crawling or toddling baby alone with the Christmas tree. If you have breakable glass ornaments on your tree, place them well out of her reach. Keep cords for tree lights well out of reach also.

Anchor the tree firmly so it can't tip over. Don't place the tree near radiators or the fireplace. Keep wrapped presents out of baby's reach. Don't put them under the tree until you are ready to open them. Otherwise baby may open them long before Santa arrives!

At holiday time or any time, keep baby away from electrical outlets!

Don't let the tree dry out—it becomes a fire hazard. Before putting them on the tree, check lights to be sure cords are not frayed or broken (also check this for other decorations around the house). Babies have been known to chew on or bite strings of lights, so keep her away from them.

Watch baby at parties. When you visit someone else's home, remember they may not be aware of what could harm your baby. Be vigilant when you attend holiday parties and family celebrations with your little one. Be alert for

- open sockets
- fireplaces
- small breakables within her easy reach
- nuts and candies placed on lower tables
- food she could choke on
- alcoholic beverages left within her reach
- ashtrays with cigarettes, cigars or pipe ashes
- decorations she could get at, including candles
- tablecloths she might pull, tipping drinks, or even lit candles
- the tree and presents, which will probably attract her attention

> **Always turn off holiday lights before you go to bed or leave the house.**

Evaluate ornaments and decorations. Some ornaments contain pieces baby could choke on. Keep these out of her reach, or use them another year. Pick up tree needles, tinsel and anything else off the floor so baby can't put it in her mouth and possibly choke on it. Keep an eye open for anything that might harm baby.

- *Holiday plants,* such as *mistletoe berries, amaryllis* and *holly,* are poisonous if eaten. *Poinsettias* can cause stomach upset if they're ingested. Don't let her touch any of these.
- *Artificial snow* can be poisonous if it's ingested. *Fire salts,* which produce colored flames, are also poisonous if swallowed.
- *Ribbons* used to decorate packages can cause harm if baby becomes entangled in them. Plastic wrap can be a suffocation hazard.

Some parents don't want to put all the decorations and presents up or out of baby's reach. They have devised various ingenious ways to protect baby and their decorations. One clever solution to the problem is to put up the tree, decorate it and put the presents underneath—all inside baby's playpen!

Other holidays. Other holidays may present hazardous situations too. At *Easter,* keep baby away from egg whites (from hard-cooked eggs). She shouldn't eat them until she's 1 year old. Eggshells may also be hazardous. Do not let baby eat chocolate. The *Fourth of July* may be dangerous if you live in an area that allows fireworks. Keep your little one away from anything that could burn her, such as sparklers, or damage her hearing, such as percussive fireworks.

When Baby Eats Food Off the Floor

Does your baby drop food all over the floor, then go back and eat it? As diligent as you may be about cleaning, it's easy to overlook something occasionally. When baby crawls on the floor, she's sure to find whatever you missed!

Most parents worry that the oat-circle cereal pieces or the cooked macaroni they didn't see could harm baby when she finds and eats it much later. Don't panic. The germs on your floors aren't usually the ones that make baby sick. The exception is a household with pets that are not housetrained. Food eaten off a floor contaminated with pet urine or feces could cause a problem.

Dropped pacifier. If baby drops her pacifier on the floor, you don't have to sterilize it in most cases. Do rinse it off to remove dirt.

Milestones This 35th Week

She Understands More Words Now

Your baby understands more of what is being said to her now. Keep talking to her, telling her stories and having conversations with her. Between 8 and 12 months old, baby comprehends common words including *juice, cookie, ball, baby, shoe, bottle, no, bedtime, mommy, daddy* and *bye-bye*. She follows simple instructions, too. She'll wave bye-bye when asked. If you ask her to "Come here," she'll probably come to you.

She continues to create dialog and babbles quite a lot. She may expect you to answer! You may notice she imitates various noises for her toys, like "rrrr" for a car.

Baby Is Getting Stronger

Baby is able to sit quite easily now. She can sit and pivot to get a toy. This is due to the increased strength in her trunk muscles.

She crawls on hands and knees, too. She can lift her chest and tummy off the floor and hold them parallel to the floor. If she's not moving along on all fours yet, she will be soon!

She's Interested in Little Things

Your baby is supremely interested in small objects. She uses her fingers to rake a piece of cracker off the floor, then pick it up with her fist. Occasionally you may notice her chasing a speck of dust on the floor.

She visually compares large and small objects. This skill enables her to adjust her grasp to fit the size of an item.

It's amusing to see her attempt to lift an illustration off the page of a book. She sees the object clearly. However, she doesn't yet understand the difference between two and three dimensions.

Exploring Objects

She continues to learn by exploring objects. She learns that an object remains the same (at least, most do) every time she plays with it. That's why she explores the size, texture, shape,

> Keep all small items out of baby's reach, even seemingly harmless ones. You might not believe dry beans or peas could cause injury. But they can if pushed into baby's ears or up her nose. They could swell and cause a great deal of discomfort.

Milestones This 35th Week

Changes in Baby You May See Now

Physical Development
• puts one foot in front of the other if held in standing position

Senses and Reflexes
• rakes a small object with fingers, then picks it up with fist

Mental Development
• understands simple instructions
• shakes head "No"
• examines objects as external, 3-dimensional realities

Social Development
• doesn't like to be confined

Every baby is an individual, and your baby may do some of these things more quickly or more slowly than another baby. If you are concerned about your baby's progress, discuss it with your healthcare provider. Also see page viii.

hardness, taste, smell and sound of something over and over. It reinforces the lesson for her.

Is It Time to Wean Baby?
You may be thinking about weaning baby from the breast. Check with your pediatrician first. He or she will let you know if baby is ready for this step. You'll also learn how to do it. Weaning should be baby's decision. She'll know if she's ready or not.

Note: See also the box above, *Milestones This Week.*

What's Happening This 35th Week?

Answering Baby's Middle-of-the-Night Call
If you have been diligent in your efforts to teach baby to go back to sleep by herself, she should be waking up less often at night. Keep up the good work! When she does wake during the night, which we all do, softly encourage her to go back to sleep. Don't play with her or wake her up further by turning on lights or picking her up, if you can avoid it. Let her learn to fall asleep on her own.

Baby's Reaction to Those She Doesn't Know Can Hurt Their Feelings
Baby can clearly distinguish between voices and faces of people she knows and people she doesn't know. She craves familiarity—it's her

security. She may still be wary of strangers.

Her reactions can dishearten grandparents, other relatives and friends she doesn't see often. To avoid hurt feelings, don't use the word "stranger." Explain to them that she has been a little shy when she encounters anything new, including people. Ask them to give her some time and space. It won't be long before she's ready to make friends.

Insect Bite and Sting

What it is. Any of us can get an insect bite or sting. As baby starts moving around and exploring the little corners of her world, her curiosity may put her at greater risk of bites and stings. If you notice unusual swelling or redness on her skin, accompanied by itching, look for a bite or sting mark in the area. Reactions in infants often are more severe than those in older children and adults.

Prevention. Dress baby appropriately when you go outside. Cover as much of her skin with clothing as you can without overdressing her. Also take the following precautions:

- Avoid when possible areas where insects are commonly found, such as dense woods.
- Don't use strong-scented soaps, lotions or powders on baby or yourself before you go outdoors. The scent attracts insects.
- Do not use insect repellents on a baby under the age of 1. You don't want to expose her to the chemical compound DEET. It's OK to use repellent on yourself to keep insects away when you're holding her.

What to do. If your baby has been stung or bitten, you can use calamine lotion, hydrocortisone cream or a paste of baking soda and water on the area. Check with baby's doctor about using an antihistamine to reduce swelling and discomfort.

If a bee stings your baby, carefully remove the stinger. Hold one end with tweezers and pull it out. Apply ice to relieve pain.

When to call the doctor. Call baby's doctor if baby has trouble breathing or experiences excessive swelling or redness in the area around the bite or sting. Call if she develops a fever or is more irritable than normal.

Your pediatrician may tell you to use an antihistamine to help relieve baby's discomfort. If a secondary infection develops, the doctor may prescribe an antibiotic.

If baby has a severe allergic reaction, she may be hospitalized for further treatment.

Yeast Infection in Baby Girls

What it is. A yeast infection, also called *monilia,* is an inflammation or infection of the vaginal area. It can affect females of any age. A yeast infection can occur at any time, and often occurs following antibiotic use. Symptoms include

- itchiness in vaginal area
- skin in vaginal area is red
- skin in area is dry
- may be burning, pain or discomfort with urination
- thick white discharge from vagina

What to do. If your baby girl has these symptoms, keep the area as clean and dry as possible. Change her diapers as soon as they are wet. Wash the area with mild soap when bathing or cleaning after bowel movements.

When to call the doctor. Call the doctor if you believe your baby has a yeast infection. Your pediatrician will probably prescribe topical antiyeast medications. Call the doctor's office if symptoms don't improve with treatment, if there is bleeding from the vagina or baby experiences persistent pain.

Toys and Play This 35th Week

Big and Small

Stacking games and fill-and-empty games may be baby's favorites now. They address some of baby's current interests: How does a big toy relates to a smaller one? How does the smaller one fit into the larger one? Try these variations!

- Fill a shoe box with plastic or wooden blocks. Empty it in front of baby. Watch her figure out how to put the blocks back in the box.

- Gather together small nesting plastic bowls or plastic spoons. She'll have fun putting them inside one another.
- When baby's taking a bath, give her a couple of plastic measuring cups that nest. She'll enjoy filling them and emptying them with water or putting one inside another.

Catch Me!

This chase game helps baby learn to follow you and keep you in sight.

Sit on the floor with baby. Crawl a little way from her. Turn around, and tell her to come and get you. Let her catch you. Laugh, hug her and crawl away again.

She may play like this for a while, then crawl away from you. If she does, tell her you're going to catch her! Crawl slowly after her. Give her a hug when you reach her to end the game.

Drip, Drip, Drip

In the bathtub or an outdoor play pool, let baby play with dripping water. Use a squeeze bottle or a turkey baster for this game.

When baby is in the water, partially fill the bottle or baster. Squeeze a few drops of water on her arm. Say, "Drip, drip, drip! The water drips on baby" as you let some drops fall on her arm

or leg. Help her squeeze some of the water out so it drips on her or on you.

As you play the game, show her that squeezing a little harder makes the water squirt instead of drip. Explain this to her as you let her feel the water squirting onto her arm or leg.

How Big Is Your Baby This 36th Week?

Baby weighs 19-1/4 pounds and is 28-1/4 inches long this week.

Baby Care and Equipment

Concerns about Poison Ivy

Contrary to popular belief, baby's scratching doesn't spread the irritation associated with poison ivy. New areas continue to break out. These "late-breaking" areas had less contact with the plant oils. They break out later when the oils eventually irritate baby's skin.

To relieve itching, ask your doctor about giving baby an antihistamine. Over-the-counter lotions, such as calamine lotion and those made with camphor or oatmeal, might also be helpful. Check first with your pediatrician. Itching should clear up in a few days. Sometimes it takes longer. Keep mittens or socks on baby's hands so he can't scratch and infect himself. As long as baby's skin itches, use these anti-itch tactics. If he keeps scratching the skin, a secondary infection could develop, which can make the rash even more uncomfortable.

In rare cases, a baby will have a violent reaction when exposed to poison oak or poison ivy. If you notice your baby is having any problems beyond a rash and itching, contact your pediatrician immediately.

Puréeing Protein Foods

If you want to purée a bit of tender beef or chicken for baby, go ahead. Thoroughly cook the meat with broth or water, then purée.

Or mash the yolk of a boiled egg. Serve any of these foods once a day. You can move on to finely minced protein when baby eats mashed food without difficulty.

Baby doesn't need much protein at this point. His needs are still being met with formula or breast milk.

Breastfeeding Babies May Skip Middle-of-the-Night Feedings

By this age, a healthy breastfeeding infant can probably skip his middle-of-the-night feed. He should be able to go from late at night to early morning without much trouble. However, he may resist your efforts to cut out your late-night "drinks date." Baby may accept this change more readily if you let dad go in when baby wakes up. Your baby may fuss for a few nights, but he'll settle down soon. If you have problems getting baby to adjust, contact your pediatrician for advice.

> **Mealtimes may be more pleasurable for the entire family if you let baby feed himself between spoonfuls that you feed him. He likes to practice his independence by feeding himself.**

Offering Baby a Cup

If baby has been bottle-feeding, he may show less interest in the bottle now. Many babies are ready to be weaned from the bottle at about 9 months. Offer him a little formula (not cow's milk!) in a cup. He could just as easily change his mind about drinking from a cup next month, however. If so, his willingness to quit the bottle probably will reappear when he's 1 year old.

Milestones This 36th Week

Baby's Memory Develops

By approximately 9 months of age, a baby can form specific memories from his experiences. He may remember how to push a ball to make it roll or how to shake a toy so it makes a sound. He clearly recognizes his name and responds to it. He also recognizes the names of familiar objects.

Baby can now more accurately judge an object's size, so grasping an object is easier. Improved eye-hand coordination enables him to bang two objects together in front of him. He can also drop things into a container.

Is He Talking to an Object?

If your baby makes certain sounds in connection with a particular object or event, he may be making an attempt at talking. For example, he may say "doh" for dog or "bah" for bottle. It's a good start. He'll probably say some real words in the next few weeks or months.

> Schedule your baby's 9-month well-baby checkup now. See page 97 for any immunizations he may receive at this next visit.

Many Physical Accomplishments!

Your baby can sit steadily for up to 15 minutes. He grasps with his thumb against the side of his index finger and can pick up small items fairly easily. He leans forward while sitting to pick up a toy, and he doesn't lose his balance.

Play habits change. You may notice his play is different, too. He may play with two objects at once. He may sort various items. He may put small toys in a bucket or pan.

Balance improves. He may stand with little support. He may be able to balance well enough to play with a toy while standing. Baby may also be better able to get down to the floor from a standing position. If he hasn't mastered it yet, keep working with him on it.

Cruising? If he hasn't already begun, soon he will begin "cruising." It often starts as a trip up and down the length of

Milestones This 36th Week

Changes in Baby You May See Now

Physical Development
- stands up if he's holding onto something
- sits well in a chair

Senses and Reflexes
- approaches large objects with both hands
- picks up and manipulates two objects, one in each hand

Mental Development
- may remember game that was played the previous day
- responds to his name

Social Development
- wants to play near parent
- imitates play
- objects when something is taken away from him
- feeds himself some foods

Every baby is an individual, and your baby may do some of these things more quickly or more slowly than another baby. If you are concerned about your baby's progress, discuss it with your healthcare provider. Also see page viii.

a piece of furniture, as he holds on to it for support. Next, he will probably flop or stumble from one piece of furniture to another while holding on or leaning.

> **Don't be surprised or concerned if baby seems to be slowing down in his development around this time. He's concentrating on perfecting some newfound skills.**

Be Careful of Spoiling Him

When baby is 9 months old, it is possible to spoil him. You may need to be firm—more so than you have been in the past. He needs to feel your confidence and conviction. It will be hard for him to hear "No," but it is necessary. When you tell him "No" or "Don't," he also needs to be reassured that his world will be OK again. Follow through and offer the reassurance he needs.

Baby Interprets What He Hears

Your baby interprets what he hears. He knows when he hears "Meow," it's coming from the cat. Or he knows that the doorbell means someone's at the door. You can help him make these associations by pointing them out whenever they occur.

> **Don't get frustrated if baby's separation anxiety gets in the way of entertaining himself. Solo play doesn't mean he has to be alone. He can play by himself with you in the room.**

Note: See also the box on page 335, *Milestones This Week.*

What's Happening This 36th Week?

Teaching Baby to Be Calm

If you get upset or angry when things don't go your way, your baby may do the same. He's like a little sponge that absorbs everything around him, including what you do. You may not think he's aware of what's going on around him, but he is!

Be a good role model. If you do the right thing, your child will model that behavior. When he spills juice, clean it up calmly. You'll teach him about dealing with problems in a mature way. If you yell, you teach him to get angry and upset when things go wrong.

Animal Bite

What it is. Animal bites in babies occur most often from household pets. Animal bites can be very serious for a baby. If you have a pet, take extreme care to protect your baby. See the discussion of pets and baby in Week 12. Know where your pet is, if baby is on the floor or within reach of the pet. If you're visiting a friend or when you leave your baby with another person, take care to know that baby will be safe from pets.

Be careful when you and baby are around animals, especially those you don't know. A dangerous situation can develop before you know it. Animal-bite symptoms include

- puncture wounds
- torn or ripped skin
- bruising
- bleeding from skin

Precautions. Never let your child approach an unfamiliar animal. Because children are small and at eye level with many dogs, a dog may feel threatened. Even the nicest dog can react and bite when it feels threatened.

Call the doctor. Call the doctor if you believe an animal has bitten your baby. Baby may need a tetanus shot. A deep or ragged wound may require stitches. Your pediatrician will clean the wound. Animal bites typically contain lots of bacteria, so follow directions for wound care. Antibiotics or antibiotic gels or ointments may be prescribed in some cases. It is important to find out if the animal that bit baby is up-to-date on its rabies shots and other vaccinations.

Tonsillitis
What it is. Tonsillitis, also called *pharyngitis,* is an inflammation and infection of the tonsils. Baby's tonsils are clumps of tissue located at the back of his throat. Infection can occur at all ages but is most common in children between 5 to 10 years old. Symptoms include

- fever
- difficulty swallowing
- swollen tonsils
- listlessness
- poor feeding
- swollen lymph nodes on either side of the jaw
- difficulty breathing

What to do. If your baby develops these symptoms, use a cool-mist humidifier in his room when he's sleeping. See the discussion of humidifiers in Week 13. Increase his fluid intake. Keep him quiet.

When to call the doctor. Call the doctor if your baby displays the symptoms above. Your pediatrician probably will want to see him. If his fever rises or other symptoms worsen or if he has difficulty breathing or difficulty swallowing, call your doctor.

Treatment includes acetaminophen or ibuprofen for fever and general discomfort. Your doctor may prescribe antibiotics, such as amoxicillin or penicillin, to deal with the infection.

Rubella

What it is. Rubella, also called *German measles,* is most common in children, but adults can get it, too. It is caused by a virus passed from human to human in the air we breathe. Symptoms include

- fever
- listlessness
- a fine red rash on the head and body
- swollen lymph nodes (glands) behind the ears and the back sides of the neck

What to do. Immunize your baby against rubella at about 15 months of age. See the immunization schedule on page 97. A rubella titer, a blood test done to see if the baby's mother has antibodies to rubella, is done at the beginning of the pregnancy. If it is positive (most are), it protects baby while he is in the uterus and for a short time afterward.

When to call your doctor. Call your doctor if you believe your baby has rubella or has been exposed to rubella. If your baby has contracted rubella, keep him away from any pregnant women you know. Exposure to rubella is most serious in a pregnant woman during the first trimester. Treatment for rubella includes over-the-counter medications, such as acetaminophen or ibuprofen, for fever or aches. Do *not* give baby aspirin, to avoid the possibility of Reye's syndrome (see Week 37).

Toys and Play This 36th Week

Baby will take the initiative to play games with you more often now. He may grab your hands to play pat-a-cake or try to crawl on your lap if he wants to play "This is the Way the Lady Rides." This is a breakthrough to encourage! The best times for learning occur when the *child* initiates it.

Warm-Breeze Game

Baby will enjoy playing this touch-and-sing game with you. He probably has lots of fun with you when you tickle him. As you sing this song, carry out the actions.

> *A warm breeze*—blow gently on his neck
> *A warm squeeze*—hug him
> *Baby's got the tickles!*—tickle him lightly all over

Make Noise while You Drop Blocks Together

This game is fun because you get to make lots of noise! Choose a metal pan or dish. Drop a few blocks into it and listen to the metallic "clink" sound the blocks make. In addition to entertaining baby, this game helps him improve his ability to release an object.

The clattering sound the pan makes when he drops the block is a positive reinforcement of his new skill.

Pick up a block, show it to him, then turn over your hand. Spread your fingers wide as you drop the block. Let baby see your actions clearly. Let him try next. He may not do it the same way you did. That's OK.

Make it fun! Respond positively even when he misses the pan or dish or bangs the block on the side of the dish.

Stacking Fun

Your baby may enjoy stacking toys higher now. A round plastic spindle with different-sized rings to stack on it is a fun toy. Wide-mouthed plastic containers that he can fill with blocks are good choices too.

Let Him Make Music

Let baby make his own music with a pan and a wooden spoon. An aluminum pie plate can become a musical instrument when you attach bells to it securely. Let baby play with these items when you can interact with him, not alone. You must be present to make sure he doesn't hit himself in the head with the spoon or chew on a bell.

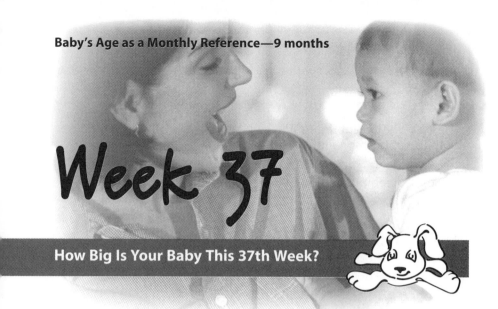

Week 37

How Big Is Your Baby This 37th Week?

Baby weighs 19-1/2 pounds and is 28-1/4 inches long this week.

Baby Care and Equipment

The American Academy of Pediatrics and Child-Rearing Issues
The American Academy of Pediatrics (AAP) is the medical association for pediatricians. The Academy makes current medical information available to members so they may provide the most up-to-date care for patients. The AAP offers advice to parents on many child-rearing issues. To learn more about these issues, contact them for information. See the Resources section. They address the following areas, among others.

Breastfeeding. The AAP believes human milk is best for all infants, with only a few exceptions. Advantages to breastfeeding your baby include health, psychological and economic benefits. A pediatrician will usually promote breastfeeding for the first year.

Pacifiers. Pacifiers do not cause psychological or medical problems. Some babies need to suck more than others. Pacifiers help them meet this need.

Spanking. Spanking is usually an ineffective method for changing a child's behavior. The AAP suggests parents find other ways to discipline a child.

Temper tantrums. Temper tantrums help a child vent frustration and are a normal behavior. Parents are advised to remain calm and to distract the child or to ignore her when she succumbs to a tantrum. Punishing a temper tantrum is not advised. Parents are also encouraged not to give in to a child when she has a tantrum.

Bed sharing. The AAP does not encourage bed sharing. See the discussion of baby sleeping alone in Week 5. Adult beds are not made for babies, and safety is a concern. Sleeping parents can accidentally trap or suffocate a baby.

> Your baby may be taking one or two naps a day. She is probably sleeping about 10-1/2 hours at night.

Peanut Allergy on the Rise

Worldwide, the number of children allergic to peanuts doubled between 1980 and 1994; however, only 1% of Americans have this allergy. Some experts believe the increase has occurred because more children are being exposed to peanut protein before age 3. A child's immature immune system may consider the protein harmful and develop antibodies to it. The antibodies trigger an allergic reaction.

Caution. Researchers advise parents to delay offering peanut butter to children if there is a family history of peanut allergies. Even without the family history, play it safe: Do not offer your child peanut butter or other products made with peanuts until she's 3 years old.

Symptoms. Symptoms of an allergic reaction to peanuts include hives, diarrhea, stomachache, swelling in the throat, wheezing, vomiting and faintness or unconsciousness. Hives or swelling may also appear when the nut comes in contact with the skin. In those who are extremely sensitive to peanuts, 1/44,000 of a peanut kernel can cause a reaction!

Allergy tests. A skin test can be done to determine if a child who has had certain reactions after eating peanut protein is allergic to peanut products. A "direct oral challenge" may determine if a child is allergic. That means the child eats a small amount of the nut in a hospital setting. This kind of testing is the most reliable for detecting a nut allergy. Discuss it with your pediatrician if you are concerned.

Hidden sources of peanuts. Foods made without peanut products can be contaminated and cause allergy problems too. Food mixed or stirred with utensils that were used with peanut-protein foods can be cross-contaminated if utensils are not cleaned thoroughly. If your child has a peanut allergy, ask when you eat out if food might have come in contact with peanuts or peanut products.

Read labels, too. Many commercially produced foods contain peanuts, peanut oil or other peanut products. Check labels closely. Peanuts may appear near the end of the list. Surprisingly, the following foods, among others, may contain peanut protein:

- bakery goods
- potato chips
- packaged cheese and crackers
- many chocolate candies–not only the peanut varieties
- chili sauces at restaurants
- gravies at restaurants
- Asian, Thai, Chinese and African dishes may use peanut butter and peanut oils, among other products

Milestones This 37th Week

She Wants to Read with You!
Around now, baby realizes that books and magazines are fun objects. You may be surprised to find your favorite magazine torn apart or its pages crumpled when your baby investigates it. She enjoys ripping out pages. She may want to handle books that attract her attention—and treat them like magazines. Give her picture books with hinged or spiral bindings made just for babies. She'll pore over the book, and she won't be able to pull it apart.

Baby May Reveal New Fears
Your baby may be getting over her fear of strangers, although for some babies, this phase lasts a little longer. Now she may demonstrate different fears. She may be afraid of things that didn't bother her before, such as visiting a strange place or taking a bath.

Don't be alarmed—this phase is natural. She is becoming more conscious of herself as separate. She's developing concern for her own well-being.

One way to help her overcome some of these fears is to take her shopping or on other errands with you. With you at her side, she'll realize that she has nothing to fear from new situations and experiences.

Sitting Is Comfortable for Baby
Your baby is becoming adept at sitting and all it involves. She can push up into a sitting position when lying down. She can lean over, change positions and go from lying on her stomach to sitting up with ease. She may practice moving from one position to another.

Crawling as Transportation
Out of the way! Baby is probably crawling all over by now. She can turn around and change direction while she crawls. She may even crawl while holding a toy in one hand. She may crawl stiff-legged or with her limbs straight. This is the precursor to walking.

Be careful of stairs. Stairs attract her attention. However, she still can't get down if she crawls up, so keep an eye on her. Stay close when she's near stairs, or block them off. Going down stairs safely is usually too difficult for a baby to learn at this age.

> **You may notice baby sometimes pushes up on all fours. She does this as she gets ready to walk.**

She May Be More Vocal
Is she "talking"? You may notice she is more verbal or babbling a lot. She loves it when you cough or click your tongue against your teeth. She may try to imitate you.

She may be saying more words, too. Sometimes she gets it wrong, but that's OK. She may look at a picture of a cow and say matter-of-factly "Dog!" She'll feel very good about naming the animal. To her, the four-legged cow *does* look like a dog. She's made an important connection between the picture in the book and the concept of an animal.

Curiosity Propels Her
Your baby is extremely curious. Nothing in her environment is off limits—at least to her! She wants to investigate everything.

Her curiosity may get her in trouble. She may empty a trashcan, then dig through it, for example. Keep the bathroom door closed. Your baby may find the toilet is a fun place to put things. You might find all the paper on a roll of toilet tissue, or a box of tissues, ends up in the toilet bowl!

Patience and Firmness
Keep practicing patience and firmness with your baby. For example, if an object or situation is dangerous to baby, handle it quickly

and firmly. Your example will eventually teach her valuable self-management skills and behaviors.

Note: See also the box below, *Milestones This Week.*

What's Happening This 37th Week?

When Baby Is Shy

If your baby is shy, don't worry about it. She may only need a little help exploring a new or different situation. Shy children do not have low self-esteem, nor does shyness affect her ability to make friends.

> **Want to help someone break the ice with baby? Have the adult play peek-a-boo with baby or bounce her gently on the knee when she feels comfortable with that person.**

Let your child take her time approaching others. Ease her into new social situations gradually. Do not to force her into interactions that make her feel uncomfortable.

Pay attention to her cues. If she hangs onto you for dear life, she's not ready to interact yet. Encourage her to play or to get involved. As she gets older, she'll probably be less shy.

Baby Is an Explorer

As we've mentioned, your baby may be exploring more than ever before. She can crawl and stand while holding onto something, often with one hand. This frees her other hand to reach out and grab whatever is nearby. Be diligent about putting treasures out of baby's reach if you don't want her to touch them.

Milestones This 37th Week

Changes in Baby You May See Now

Physical Development
- crawls with one hand holding something
- turns around when crawling

Senses and Reflexes
- bangs objects together at center of body

Mental Development
- uncovers a toy that she saw hidden

Social Development
- deliberately chooses a toy for play
- imitates some sounds, such as cough, hisses
- manipulates and drinks from cup

Every baby is an individual, and your baby may do some of these things more quickly or more slowly than another baby. If you are concerned about your baby's progress, discuss it with your healthcare provider. Also see page viii.

She'll explore at every opportunity. When you are away from home, keep your eyes open to what's around her. A cigarette off the floor can be very interesting, for example. You'll be surprised by what she'll find when she crawls under the bed or behind a chair.

We suggest you make a quick search of an area every time you place her on the floor. We all drop or overlook little things all the time. Usually that isn't a problem, but with an inquisitive baby, it might turn into one.

Falls
What it is. A fall occurs most often in a young child who is learning to walk. It may also occur when she is crawling and climbs stairs. In addition to crying, symptoms include

- bruises
- lacerations
- bumps (from swelling)

The first time baby falls hard can be traumatic for mom and dad, too! No matter how safe you make your home for baby, she'll probably fall now and then and get some bruises.

What to do. If your baby takes a tumble, apply cold to the area for the first 24 hours, then apply something warm. Clean cuts and scrapes right away.

When to call the doctor. Call the doctor if your baby has any serious cuts. They may need to be stitched. If a bruise gets bigger or becomes more painful, call the doctor. If she seems to get bruises without any injury, falls down a lot or bleeds very easily, contact your pediatrician.

Reye's Syndrome
What it is. Reye's syndrome is a rare disease that can occur from infancy through childhood. It usually follows a viral illness, such as chickenpox or flu, and is associated with aspirin used to treat the illness. It occurs more frequently in white babies than in babies of color. Symptoms include

- weakness
- drowsiness
- lethargy
- seizures

What to do. The best treatment is prevention. Don't give your baby aspirin or any other medication (including over-the-counter medications) unless directed to do so by your baby's doctor.

> ### Caution
> **Don't give your baby aspirin for any illness with a fever, unless your baby's doctor specifically says it's OK.**

Call the doctor immediately! Call the doctor immediately if your child has symptoms of Reye's syndrome. **It's an emergency!** Your doctor will probably prescribe rest and increased fluid intake. If your baby has seizures, she may need antiseizure medication. Antibiotics are prescribed if a bacterial infection occurs afterward.

Toys and Play This 37th Week

Mimic the Mirror
Seat baby in front of a large mirror. While she watches you in the mirror, make different gestures with your hands. Wave at her. Blow her a kiss. Make faces: Wrinkle your nose, or stick out your tongue. Nod your head, or shake it. See if she'll imitate your movements.

Ask her to point to the baby. Point to her image in the mirror and say, "There's the baby!"

> ### My Toy!
> **Baby is attached to her toys now. You may notice her choose a toy to play with quite deliberately. She may even fight to keep it away from someone else!**
>
> **Check your baby's toys frequently. Some become worn after months of play. Look for loose parts or sharp edges. When you find worn parts, repair the toy or throw it away to keep baby safe.**

"Hickory, Dickory, Dock"
This tickling game is fun for baby and her play partner. Lightly walk a couple of your fingers over baby, from head to foot, while you sing,

> *Hickory, dickory, dock!*
> *The mouse ran up the clock.*
> *The clock struck one, and down he came.*
> *Hickory, dickory, dock!*

Then reverse the way you tickle her—from foot to head—while you sing the song again.

Your baby will enjoy playfully mimicking your expressions.

Find the Toy

This game helps baby solidify her concept of object permanence.

Find the Toy #1. While she watches you, place one of her favorite toys in a box. Cover the box with one of her blankets. Ask her to find her toy. Help her if she can't find it.

Find the Toy #2. Another way to play the game is to hide a small toy in one of your hands. Ask her to pick a hand. Switch the toy back and forth between your hands. If she doesn't find it in one hand, she'll soon learn to look in the other one.

It's important to encourage baby in her search. Clap when she finds the favorite toy. Exclaim how fun it was to find it. Be enthusiastic, and give her a kiss when the game is over.

Week 38

How Big Is Your Baby This 38th Week?

Baby weighs 19-3/4 pounds and is 28-1/2 inches long this week.

Baby Care and Equipment

Baby Walkers

In recent years, parents have been warned not to put their babies in a baby walker. Baby walkers have been associated with a number of injuries. In 1997, nearly 15,000 children under 15 months old were treated in emergency rooms for walker-related accidents. More children may have been injured who did not seek medical attention. Researchers believe using a baby walker can delay a baby's motor development. Baby's mental development may also be delayed.

Doesn't help baby learn to walk. Contrary to popular opinion, a baby walker won't help your baby learn to walk. He does use his legs to propel himself in a walker. But propelling himself forward doesn't strengthen the muscles he needs to develop for walking.

Safety issues. Baby walkers give baby instant mobility. He can go places quickly in a walker that would take longer to reach if he were scooting or crawling. He can find himself in harm's way *in a moment.* A baby on wheels may be exposed to other serious dangers, such as a tumble down a flight of stairs or access to an area with equipment that is dangerous for baby.

New standards. The Consumer Product Safety Commission (CPSC) has mandated new safety standards for baby walkers. Two of these are especially important: If you do buy a walker, choose one that is too wide to fit through a standard doorway. Be sure it has a gripping mechanism to stop the walker at the edge of a step.

Developmental delays. Researchers found that on average, babies who did not use walkers sat up at about 5 months, crawled at 8 months and walked at 11 months. By comparison, babies who did use walkers sat and crawled at about 7 months and walked at 12 months. Babies who used walkers also scored lower on a battery of tests covering memory, language and perception.

Babies who could see their feet when they were in the walker had closer-to-normal motor development. Researchers believe that a baby needs to see his feet for optimum motor development.

As we've discussed each week, a baby needs to explore his environment to learn. A baby in a walker can't do this as easily or as thoroughly as a baby who crawls. Another theory is that parents pay less attention to a baby placed in a walker. This may mean less parental interaction for baby, which could lead to delays in some aspects of development.

Guidelines. If you choose to put baby in a walker, take care to select one that meets current safety standards. Limit the amount of time he's in a walker. Give him plenty of floor time to develop his motor skills.

Safer alternatives. Consider the stationary chair as an alternative. Stationary chairs have no wheels and cannot move. Baby sits in an upright position and can push up on his legs to a semistanding position while in the chair. These chairs usually include a large tray and some toys to entertain baby.

Finger Foods

If you haven't started feeding baby finger foods, now is a good time to start. "Finger foods" are small, bite-sized pieces of food. Crackers, teething crackers, pieces of toast, pieces of cheese, small bits of meat, pieces of soft tortilla and well-cooked pieces of pasta or macaroni are good finger foods.

The object of giving baby finger foods is to help him learn to feed himself. He can't use a spoon effectively yet; finger food encourages him to practice eating skills.

Offer a variety of foods. Let baby touch, taste and smell them. Remember to be patient. It takes him much longer to eat when he feeds himself.

Milestones This 38th Week

Different Stages of Motor Development

At this time, babies who are the same age may be at radically different stages of motor development. The majority of babies are crawling by 9 months of age. Many are standing but may need help maintaining their balance. Some are cruising around the furniture. Some may take steps all by themselves. In some instances, baby is actually walking!

Development varies because babies are different. If baby is concentrating on one aspect of development, another aspect may lag for a little while.

The important thing to remember is that every baby is an individual. Don't compare your baby with any other baby—even among multiples. Your baby is progressing normally for him. He'll get there (wherever "there" is) in his own good time. As long as he is making forward progress, everything is OK and you don't have to be concerned.

Activities Baby Enjoys

By 9 months of age, baby enjoys many activities. He likes to dance. He likes to pull things apart—probably to your dismay. He loves to play simple games, such as "Where's baby?" or "Chase the baby." He may initiate games more often than ever before. Story time may be his favorite time with you.

> Shaking his head from side to side is easy for baby. However, nodding won't be accomplished for several more months.

His Language Development

His ability to understand words is increasing rapidly. Read to him to improve his comprehension. His responses show he understands a lot. When you ask, "Show me . . ." he can correctly point to an object. When you play the game "So big!" he may smile and shoot his arms into the air to show you how big he is.

When You Say "No"

Your baby may have difficulty obeying when you tell him "No" or "Don't." He may look hurt or get angry. That's OK. Some restrictions are

> Be consistent about putting away magazines and books when you aren't reading them. Your baby loves to pull things apart, and books and magazines are perfect for practicing this skill!

necessary for baby's health and safety, so don't let his dismay or anger keep you from parenting him.

Concepts of "Up" and "Down"

Baby understands concepts of "up" and "down." You may notice this when he is afraid to get down from a chair he climbed on top of. When he turns his sippy cup right side up, he's showing that he knows which end belongs up.

Your baby knows quite a bit about his visual world now. He continues to refine his sense of perspective. He understands how objects appear larger or smaller in relation to how close they are to him.

Let Him Practice Walking Often

Give baby many opportunities to practice walking. Let him hold on to both of your hands and walk in front of you. Don't strain his arms. See if he watches his feet. Letting him practice builds his confidence. Get your camera ready—it won't be too long before he takes his first steps by himself!

Note: See also the box below, *Milestones This Week.*

> **Baby may be practicing some of his new skills at night. Some babies have been found asleep while standing against crib rails! The thrill of learning these activities may interfere somewhat with baby's sleep, but he will settle down soon.**

Milestones This 38th Week

Changes in Baby You May See Now

Physical Development
- takes a few steps if supported; walks with adult holding his hands

Senses and Reflexes
- reaches for small objects with finger and thumb

Mental Development
- grows bored with repetition
- is aware of vertical space

Social Development
- begins to evaluate other people's moods

Every baby is an individual, and your baby may do some of these things more quickly or more slowly than another baby. If you are concerned about your baby's progress, discuss it with your healthcare provider. Also see page viii.

What's Happening This 38th Week?

Restrictions Are Necessary

Baby loves his freedom. As a loving parent, you have to impose certain restrictions on that freedom. When necessary, block off areas you don't want baby to explore, such as entire rooms or cabinets and cupboards.

When you set limits, you help baby understand that he can't always do what he wants, when he wants. That's a fact of life we all face.

Setting some restrictions makes baby feel secure. It's good practice for you, too. It's much easier to begin setting restrictions when baby is young. He'll know you mean business when you follow through consistently. When he gets older, it's harder to make him believe you are serious if you've let him get his way all the time as a baby and toddler.

Burns

What it is. In a baby or an infant, a burn can be very serious. A burn may be caused by contact with fire, electricity or chemicals. It usually occurs due to an accident or the carelessness of those caring for baby. Burn symptoms are categorized in three degrees. (See box.)

What to do. If your baby gets a second- or third-degree burn, go to the nearest emergency-medicine facility.

> **Burn Definitions**
>
> • *First-degree burns* **involve the upper layer of skin. Skin may be red and swollen.**
>
> • *Second-degree burns* **involve deeper skin layers. Skin may have blisters.**
>
> • *Third-degree burns* **involve all layers of skin. Skin may appear white.**

If your baby receives a minor (first-degree) burn, quickly remove any clothing covering the burned skin. Run cold water continuously over the skin or immerse the affected area in cold water for 15 to 25 minutes, if possible. Don't use ice or butter—it makes the injury worse. Loosely cover the burned area with sterile gauze. Call your pediatrician for advice.

Call the doctor. Call the doctor if your baby gets any type of burn, even if it seems minor. Your doctor will advise you how to care for it. If a burn blisters, call your pediatrician. If a burn appears infected, with a discharge, or if it doesn't heal with recommended treatment, notify your pediatrician.

The type of burn dictates the treatment. In a serious burn, IV medication to relieve pain may be administered. Antianxiety medication may be used for procedures that are painful. With a less-serious or minor burn, antibiotics (gels or salves), topical anesthetics and pain relievers may be prescribed. Once the burn begins healing, medication to deal with itchiness may be needed.

Caution: Be extremely careful with anything that might burn your baby. Keep chemicals out of reach. Never leave matches or lighters lying about. If you smoke, don't smoke around baby. Turn handles of pots and pans inward on the stove so baby cannot grab them from below. Cover all electrical outlets, and keep electric cords up high when possible. Turn down your water-heater temperature. Check your entire house periodically to keep your little one safe.

Ringworm

What it is. Ringworm is a fungal infection that can affect many parts of the body, including the scalp, the skin, the nails and the feet. It has different names depending on the body part involved. The most common ringworm infection is *athlete's foot*. A ringworm infection can occur at any age. Symptoms include

- itching
- scaliness
- pain
- lesions are red rings, with a distinct border

What to do. If you believe your baby has ringworm, keep his skin dry. Dress him in loose cotton clothing to allow airflow. Wash clothing, bed clothes and towels in very hot water. Clean the bathroom floors, tub and shower stall with a disinfectant (for athlete's foot).

When to call the doctor. Contact your doctor if your baby appears to have ringworm. He or she may prescribe a topical antifungal medication to deal with the problem.

Strep Throat

What it is. Strep throat is an infection of the pharynx by the streptococcus bacteria. It can occur at any age and can be quite painful. Symptoms include

- fever
- difficulty swallowing or eating
- swollen neck glands
- swollen tonsils
- irritability

What to do. If your baby has symptoms, use a cool-mist humidifier when he's sleeping. See Week 13 for information on humidifiers. Try to increase fluids, although this may be difficult if baby's throat is extremely sore.

Call the doctor. Call the doctor if baby has symptoms of strep throat. Contact your pediatrician during or following treatment if fever persists or rises, or if new symptoms appear, such as an earache or a cough.

Your doctor may prescribe medications to deal with the infection, such as antibiotics. You may also be advised to give baby acetaminophen or ibuprofen for fever or a sore throat.

Toys and Play This 38th Week

Cardboard Megaphone

This is a fun game to play with baby because he listens so closely to your voice. Get a long cardboard tube, like those used with paper towels or wrapping paper. (If you use a very long wrapping-paper tube, trim to make it somewhat shorter.) Sit across from baby, and talk to him through the tube. Make funny noises. Watch his reactions.

Now hand the tube to baby. Help him put it up to his mouth, and show him how to use it. You may be surprised by what he does next!

The tube concentrates the sounds, so speak softly. Leave a small space between the end of the tube and baby's ear.

Where's Baby?

Your baby may start a game of "Find the baby." Play along when he does.

If he puts his blanket over his head or buries himself in it, say in a bewildered voice, "Where's baby?" Pretend to look around, and repeat that you can't find him. He may pull the blanket off himself immediately. When he does reappear, exclaim, "There's baby!"

If he stays hidden for a while, pretend to keep looking. You may discover he is having a wonderful time playing this trick on you. Enjoy it with him.

Week 39

How Big Is Your Baby This 39th Week?

Baby weighs 20 pounds this week and is 28-1/2 inches long.

Baby Care and Equipment

Good Food Choices for Baby

Good choices to offer baby now include bananas and ripe apricots. Well-cooked vegetables, such as carrots, yams, potatoes and peas, are also tasty. If you offer meat, choose soft meats, such as turkey and well-cooked stew beef.

Cut food into small pieces that baby can gum, about the size of her thumbnail. Pieces should be small enough that baby won't choke if she swallows a piece whole.

Your baby may be even less interested in drinking her formula or breastfeeding now. Offer 1 or 2 tablespoons of a protein food every day to help her get the nutrition she needs. In addition to meat, cheese, egg yolk or tofu (microwaved for 15 seconds, then cooled) are acceptable protein choices.

Continue to offer foods of various textures. Slippery spaghetti, sticky mashed potatoes, crunchy oat-circle cereal pieces—each one offers something different.

Citrus Juice

If your baby hasn't had problems with the foods you've offered her already, you might want to try a citrus juice now. Limit the total amount of juice you give her to 4 ounces a day. Dilute the juice with at least as much water—2 ounces of juice to 2 ounces of water. Offer the juice in a cup.

Milestones This 39th Week

Baby's Language Development
Your baby is making many sounds that have the tones of language. Some babies of this age are able to speak short words, such as "hi," "bye," "mama" or "dada." She may imitate a few animal sounds. She usually responds to her name. By stopping an action or behavior when you tell her to stop, she shows she understands what "No" means.

She Learns Well—When She Wants To!
Your baby is willing to cooperate and learn about things, as long as she is interested in them already. She can be stubborn when she's not interested in something. She may want to feed herself (she's interested in that) but not want to help dress herself (she's not interested).

She'll display many moods. Don't get frustrated or upset when she balks at doing something. She may change her mind tomorrow!

Baby Anticipates Events
Your baby can now anticipate events better than she could a short while ago. For example, she associates certain sounds and actions with getting ready for a bath. She knows that when you are in the kitchen making certain noises, she'll eat soon. Learning anticipation helps her learn to wait for something. However, she won't wait long!

She Can Be Emotional
Even babies at this tender age can be emotional. Your baby may object vehemently when you try to take a toy away from her. She may cry copiously when you scold her or tell her "No." But just as quickly, she can be sunshine and smiles if something amuses her. She may show off for an audience, especially if they shower her with attention.

The moods of others may affect her. When a sibling is excited, she may be, too. If she sees another baby crying, she may burst into tears!

Milestones This 39th Week

Changes in Baby You May See Now

Physical Development
- climbs
- crawls up stairs

Senses and Reflexes
- clasps hands

Mental Development
- follows simple instructions
- is becoming afraid of heights

Social Development
- may begin to protect herself and possessions
- performs for audiences; repeats act if applauded

Every baby is an individual, and your baby may do some of these things more quickly or more slowly than another baby. If you are concerned about your baby's progress, discuss it with your healthcare provider. Also see page viii.

Is Your Baby Lagging?

Your baby may be concentrating her efforts on learning skills in certain areas instead of others right now. She may be vocalizing more or involved with studying visual details around her rather than working on crawling or cruising or picking up objects with her hands. She'll probably begin her motor activities soon. You may be pleasantly surprised when she does. Often babies who start later accomplish a task more quickly than babies who started the same task early. Don't despair, and don't push her!

Note: See also the box on this page, *Milestones This Week.*

What's Happening This 39th Week?

Say "No" for Safety

In this book, we've suggested many ways to make your house safe for baby. You may have used some or all of these good ideas. Practically speaking, you can only do so much to make the environment safe for your baby. You don't want to feel as if you live in a dwelling devoid of all comfort or interest. You want to feel like it's home.

At this point, your baby needs to learn there will always be certain areas that are off limits. This understanding will make your life easier when you visit other people's homes. If baby knows she can't have certain things, she won't have a tantrum when you tell her

"No" at someone else's house. Also see the discussion in Week 40 about alternatives to saying "No."

Food Allergy
What it is. A food allergy is hypersensitivity to a particular food. The most common causes of food allergies include cow's milk, wheat, eggs, peanuts, seafood, some fruits, tomatoes and some legumes. It can occur at any age but usually does not occur until a child begins eating solid foods. Occasionally a baby is allergic to formula made of cow's milk and must be given a different type of formula. Symptoms your baby may have a food allergy include

> ## Baby's Bowels May Change with New Foods
>
> You may notice a change in baby's bowels now that she's eating more "grown-up" food. As you vary the foods she eats, there will be a change in the consistency, color and frequency of her bowels. This is normal. It's not a sign of food allergies or food intolerance.

- nausea
- vomiting
- abdominal bloating
- itching
- congestion
- skin rash
- crying or fussing
- fatigue
- feeding problems

What to do. Keep track of every new food you give baby. This is important! Introduce new foods one at a time. Check for a reaction before you offer another new food. As we've discussed earlier, rice products cause fewer allergy problems than wheat products. Don't feed baby any peanut products before she is 3 years old.

If you believe your baby has a food allergy, try to identify the problem food. Don't offer it again without discussing the matter with your pediatrician first. Increase the amount of fluid you give her. Decrease solid food until she feels better.

When to call the doctor. Call the doctor if you believe your baby is having an allergic reaction to formula or food. You will probably be advised to avoid the food. You may be advised to take other measures as well.

Heat Stroke

What it is. In extremely hot conditions, it's not uncommon for a person of any age to suffer from exposure and get heat stroke, also called *heat exhaustion, sunstroke* or *heat prostration* (similar to hyperthermia). Symptoms include

- fever or high body temperature
- hot, dry skin
- little or no urine production (no wet diapers)
- listlessness
- irritability
- poor feeding

What to do. It's best to try to avoid the problem, when you can. When it's very hot, give baby lots of fluids. Keep her hydrated and as cool as possible. Keep her out of the sun. Heat stroke can be a serious problem.

Call the doctor! Call the doctor if you believe your baby is getting or has heat stroke. **It's an emergency.** Baby's body temperature will need to be brought down. This important procedure should be done at the hospital or under the direction of qualified medical personnel.

Ruptured Eardrum

What it is. A ruptured eardrum can occur at any age. It may be a cause of otitis media. See the discussion of ear infections, including otitis media, in Week 28. Symptoms your baby's eardrum may be ruptured include

- earache
- fever
- fussiness
- irritability
- pulling or rubbing the ear
- drainage from the ear

What to do. Your care of baby can sometimes help prevent a ruptured eardrum. Never put anything inside baby's ear, including

cotton swabs—it can rupture her eardrum. Clean only the outside
of baby's ear. If you believe your baby's eardrum may be ruptured,
keep the ears dry. Don't let baby put her head under water. Be
vigilant about objects baby could put in her own ears, such as pens
or pencils lying around.

When to call the doctor. Call the doctor if you believe
your baby has a ruptured eardrum. If her fever rises above
102F (38.8C) or if she shows signs of a middle-ear infection,
contact your pediatrician. Your baby's doctor will prescribe ear
drops or antibiotics to treat an infection, and acetaminophen or
ibuprofen for fever or pain.

Toys and Play This 39th Week

Distraction Game for a Cranky Baby
Sometimes playing this game with a cranky baby will help her forget
why she was cranky. Instead of hiding something, like other games
you've been playing, you find something!

Walk through your home together searching for various familiar
objects. Make it interesting. Holding baby in your arms, ask her,
"Where's the...?" Look for a toy, the doggie, her blanket, a book.
Choose anything she might be interested in. Ask her to find
whatever you name. She can probably point to it quite easily by now.

Exploring Light and Dark
This game encourages baby to explore differences between light
and dark. Find a large cardboard box. Cut an opening on one side.
Place the box so baby can crawl inside through the opening.

Invite her to crawl inside the box. It's darker inside than outside.
Tell her, "It's dark in there." Ask if she can see her hand. Encourage
her to crawl to the box opening. Ask if it's light outside. When she
crawls out of the box, say, "Now you're crawling back outside, where
it's light."

Hammer, Hammer
Your baby is learning to use her fist and extended arm as a tool. This
game helps her develop gross-motor skills in her arms.

Show her how to make a hammer with her fist. Guide her arm
up and down in a hammering motion. While moving her arm up and

down gently, sing

> (Baby's name) *hammers with one hammer,*
> *One hammer, one hammer.*
> (Baby's name) *hammers with one hammer.*
> *Now she hammers with two!* (Make a hammer with her other
>   fist, and alternately move each one up and down.)

Show Me!

Place two familiar toys in front of baby, one at a time. Identify them
for her: "This is your dolly, and this is your ball." Ask her to point to
the one you name. "Which one is the dolly?" Any response is OK,
such as reaching, touching or just looking at the toy. Praise her for
her response. If she doesn't respond, give her the toy you named.
Name it again. Then put it down and try again.

Weekly Milestones at a Glance

Week 40

Physical Development
- stands with little support
- may develop sleep problems caused by practicing standing in the middle of the night

Senses and Reflexes
- voluntarily releases object in awkward manner
- grasps tiny objects with thumb and index finger

Mental Development
- increasingly imitates actions of others
- understands and obeys some words and commands

Social Development
- enjoys playing in water
- prefers one of several toys
- repeats sounds and gestures to get attention
- waves bye-bye

Week 41

Physical Development
- walks holding on with both hands

Senses and Reflexes
- begins to show preference for one hand and one side of the body

Mental Development
- searches for an object if she saw it hidden

Social Development
- shows moods, such as hurt, happy, sad, angry
- imitates facial expressions
- imitates sounds
- enjoys variations of peek-a-boo
- feeds himself some foods

Week 42

Physical Development
- sits down from standing position

Senses and Reflexes
- responds to music by rocking, bouncing, swaying, humming

Mental Development
- may repeat word incessantly, making it an answer to every question

Social Development
- grows aware of self
- imitates gestures

Week 43

Physical Development
- may be able to rise to a standing position

Senses and Reflexes
- can carry two small objects in one hand

Mental Development
- reaches behind her to get a toy without seeing it
- is interested in fitting things together

Social Development
- seeks social approval; seeks companionship and attention
- fears strange places
- can feed herself entire meals

Week 40

How Big Is Your Baby This 40th Week?

Baby weighs 20-1/4 pounds and is 28-3/4 inches long this week.

Baby Care and Equipment

Barefoot Cruising

When baby "cruises," he's not really walking, but he's getting there! He gets around on his feet by using furniture as support. Let him practice cruising barefoot. If it's too cold indoors to go barefoot, dress him in booties or socks that have tread on the bottom. The tread provides some grip so he won't slip on linoleum or hardwood floors. Outside, shoes protect his feet.

Don't Ignore Recalls

By now, you're experienced at the parenting game. You may feel confident dealing with the varied situations parents face. That's great, but don't relax when it comes to baby-product recalls.

If the manufacturer or the Consumer Product Safety Commission (CPSC) determines a product is unsafe, don't ignore it. Pay attention to recalls reported in newspapers or news broadcasts. Return the product or find out if there's an approved way to modify it. You can call the CPSC directly or visit their web site on the Internet. See the Resources section for contact information.

Begin Feeding Lumpier Foods

By this time, baby may be ready to start eating lumpier puréed foods. You may wish to offer new table foods also. You're

probably already giving baby
crackers and bits of cheese.
Add cooked rice and baked
potato removed from its skin.
Be sure pieces are no larger
than a green pea.

Offer baby a spoon, and
let him feed himself. Don't
give him the baby spoons
you've been using to feed
him. Choose a spoon with a

*Baby utensils are sturdy and easy
for baby to hold.*

fairly large handle so he can grasp it more easily. Don't worry about
the mess he creates. He'll need lots of practice before he can get the
spoon and its contents to his mouth.

Milestones This 40th Week

> **It's fun having baby
> join you at the table.
> He may not eat with
> the family, but he can
> interact with you. If
> you're shopping for a
> highchair, consider one
> with a large tray to
> hold baby's toys and
> finger foods.**

He May Stand Alone
Your baby has better control over his legs
and feet now. He's probably cruising around
the furniture with confidence. He may be
able to stand briefly without support. He
may be confident enough to squat to pick
up a toy or turn to his side to reach something. It is easier for him
to go from a standing position to sitting. If another person supports
him, he may walk a few steps.

Baby's Hand Control Improves
Your baby's control over his hands continues to improve. His pincer
grasp is well developed. He can pick up very small objects between
his thumb and index finger. (Stay alert to what's on the floor around
you. Keep the floor picked up so you will easily spot any little fallen
items that shouldn't be within baby's reach.) Releasing an object
gently is still difficult for baby. He drops or throws an object when
he loses interest.

His coordination is improving, too. He may pound one object on
the ground while feeling another with his fingers. He can grip one
item while reaching for another. Or he may carry something in one
hand while leaving the other free to explore.

He uses his little hands and fingers to explore everything around him. He'll stick fingers into just about any opening. Stay vigilant to hazards such as electrical outlets.

He Responds to Simple Requests

By this time, you may notice baby's grasp of language is blossoming. He may do what he is asked, such as wave bye-bye. He may respond to a simple request, such as "Bring me the dolly, please." He can also follow one-step instructions, such as "Go to Grandma."

He may say a few simple words or make animal sounds. He can imitate you when you say "Shhh" by putting his finger over his mouth. By this time, a baby's ear is attuned to his own language. He no longer pays attention to the sounds of a foreign language, although he can still learn a foreign language more easily than an adult can.

Baby Enjoys His World

Your baby may love to play in the water. He'll splash and kick when he takes a bath. The toilet may intrigue him because he can swish things in it. Keep the toilet off limits! Leave the bathroom door closed to keep baby—and the toilet—safe. Now may be the time to invest in a toilet-seat lock if you haven't already. This simple device locks the lid shut so baby cannot open it.

Baby may imitate some things you do, such as combing your hair or brushing your teeth. When you clean up his highchair tray after eating, he may want a cloth so he can clean, too! He thinks this play is lots of fun.

How Much Sleep Does He Need?

> **If baby has trouble sleeping, try giving him a massage. It will help him relax. It also helps lower stress-hormone levels.**

Your baby may not need as much sleep as he's needed in the past. If he's very active, he may sleep about 11 hours at night and need only one 1-hour nap in the afternoon. You can tell whether he's getting enough sleep by his behavior. If he seems fussy and cranky, try putting him to bed a little earlier. If he doesn't seem to need the extra sleep, he can stay up a little longer.

Baby Needs His Own Space

If it's not possible to put baby in his own room, set aside part of a room for his toys. He won't spend much time there, but he'll know it's his space. This is a good idea if you have other children, especially a toddler. Baby needs to know he has a place all his own.

Milestones This 40th Week

Changes in Baby You May See Now

Physical Development

- stands with little support
- may develop sleep problems caused by practicing standing in the middle of the night

Senses and Reflexes

- voluntarily releases object in an awkward manner
- grasps tiny objects with thumb and index finger

Mental Development

- increasingly imitates actions of others
- understands and obeys some words and commands

Social Development

- enjoys water play
- prefers one of several toys
- repeats sounds and gestures to get attention
- waves bye-bye

Every baby is an individual, and your baby may do some of these things more quickly or more slowly than another baby. If you are concerned about your baby's progress, discuss it with your healthcare provider. Also see page viii.

Fearfulness May Reappear

Even if your baby has been confident about doing many activities or daily routines, he may be afraid to do some of them now. It's a stage, and it will pass soon.

He still needs the reassurance your presence provides. He may check often to see if you are near. He wants to break away, yet he needs to hold on. He enjoys his independence but it can also make him a little fearful.

Note: See also the box above, *Milestones This Week.*

Baby's fearfulness may reappear in the ninth month.

What's Happening This 40th Week?

Alternatives to Saying "No"

Now that your baby gets around more easily, you may have to tell him "No" more often than you did in the past. A stern "No" is fast and easy, but you may want to avoid using this negative approach all the time. You can't strip your home completely or put everything out of reach. What else can you do?

Show him the way. Show baby another way to deal with an object. He may want to tear the pages out of one of your magazines. Instead of letting him destroy the magazine, sit down with him and show him the pictures as you turn pages. Point out animals or people. Share the magazine with him, then put it away out of his reach.

Turn baby's attention. Before you tell baby not to touch something, try to redirect him. He may be reaching for a glass object because it's pretty and has caught his eye. Instead, offer something shiny that is also safe, such as a metal spoon or a baby-safe mirror.

Give him "the Look." He may glance at you before he does something. When he does, and it's something you don't want him to do, look at baby sternly. Your look may be enough to divert him.

Restrain baby when necessary. When he does something physical, you may have to get physical yourself—but not in the same way. If he's pulling the cat's tail or hitting the dog, restrain him. Hold his hands in yours and quietly tell him, "Stop pulling the cat's tail," or "It hurts when you hit the dog."

When you have to say "No." Sometimes you have to say "No" to baby. When he's in a dangerous situation, you may not have time to distract him or give him a stern look. At those times, it is quicker and easier to say "No!" But try to reserve "No" for times you really need it. When children hear the same word over and over, they stop paying attention to it.

Serious Baby?

Some babies seem more serious than others. Often, when a baby is serious, it doesn't reflect his personality. It may reflect where he is developmentally. He may study something new intensely.

> Although baby is learning the difference between *before* and *after,* he lives in *right now.* He still expects his demands to be met immediately.

A baby's seriousness may also reflect stranger anxiety, which we've discussed in previous weeks. He may not exhibit classic symptoms of screaming or crying when he encounters someone new. Being quiet and a little withdrawn are also signs he's anxious about this new person.

A serious look on your baby's face may mean he is trying to figure out what you think about a stranger. This is called *social referencing.* It often begins around 9 or 10 months of age. He is looking to someone who is important to him—you—for clues as to how to react to this new person. He may be more comfortable with a stranger after he sees you interact with him or her.

Hand-Foot-and-Mouth Disease

What it is. This disease, caused by the coxsackie virus, is highly infectious. Baby will have painful sores in his mouth and sores on his hands and feet.

The problem can occur anytime from 2 weeks after birth through adulthood. It's more common in children, but parents can become infected when their children do. Symptoms include

- rash of blisters involving hands, feet and mouth (throat)
- rapid onset of fever
- sore throat, with ulcers in throat
- feeds poorly
- irritability

What to do. If your baby shows these symptoms, try increasing fluids, although it may be difficult because his mouth is sore. Boil bottle nipples and any other items used to feed baby.

When to call the doctor. Contact your pediatrician if your baby has any symptoms of hand-foot-and-mouth disease. Because the illness is caused by a virus, antibiotics are not prescribed. Acetaminophen or ibuprofen may be suggested for baby's fever or pain.

Stye

What it is. A stye is an inflammation, with swelling, of one of the eyelid's sebaceous (oil) glands. It is caused by a bacterial infection and can occur at any age. A stye can be spread by contact with someone who has one, if that person touches the infected area, then touches someone else. Symptoms include

- swelling
- redness on the edge of either the upper or lower eyelid
- pain on the edge of either the upper or lower eyelid
- sensitivity to bright lights
- increase in tearing

What to do. If your baby has a stye, apply warm-water soaks for 10 to 20 minutes at a time. Decrease light in baby's room. Everyone should wash hands frequently. Don't share towels. Avoid irritants, such as cigarette smoke and bright sunlight.

When to call the doctor. Call your doctor if your baby has a stye. The doctor will probably prescribe a treatment including topical antibiotics, antibiotic eye drops or oral antibiotics. It may be necessary to treat both eyes.

Toys and Play This 40th Week

All Gone!

To help baby learn the difference between *full* and *empty,* play this game. Use a couple of plastic see-through boxes or two open-weave laundry baskets. Together, fill one of the containers with objects. When you finish, tell baby, "All filled up!"

Next, encourage baby to move all the objects to the other basket or container. If he needs help, move the objects with him. He'll love doing this.

When he's finished, turn over the empty basket. Tell baby the objects are "All gone!"

Bathtime Fun

If baby is having fun playing in the bath, add new activities to his bathtime. Get a large plastic sipping straw, and blow bubbles in the tub. Bring the colander or a strainer to his bath, and pour water into it. Tell him it's raining! Show him how to kick his legs and splash.

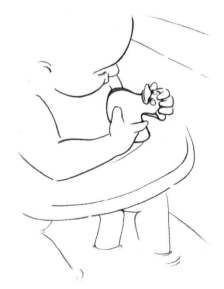

Week 41

How Big Is Your Baby This 41st Week?

Baby weighs 20-1/2 pounds and is 28-3/4 inches long this week.

Baby Care and Equipment

Can Yogurt Help Prevent Diarrhea?

A recent study followed babies between 10 and 18 months old. Some babies in the study were fed yogurt and others were not. Each baby's stool was evaluated during the study. Researchers found that babies who ate yogurt had more "good" bacteria (helpful in digestion) in their intestinal tracts. Too much "bad" bacteria can cause diarrhea.

Yogurt's calcium content is beneficial also. Yogurt contains riboflavin, potassium and magnesium. Baby needs all these minerals in her diet. Yogurt is a good transitional food for your baby.

You don't have to feed baby a lot of yogurt to get the benefits. A few teaspoons of *plain* (not flavored or sweetened) yogurt is enough. Try it—your baby may like it a lot.

Dressing for Snow

Until your baby is walking and playing in the snow, she probably won't need a one-piece snowsuit when she goes outside. A warm jacket may be enough when you just take her in and out of the car while you do errands. A good jacket choice is one with a hood that fastens under the chin. You might look for a jacket with "built-in" mittens. Mittens are attached to sleeves and flip on to cover baby's hands.

If you live in a very cold area or you and baby spend time outdoors when it's cold, your baby may need a snowsuit. Look for a suit that zips from ankle to neck. When baby is walking, don't buy a snowsuit with permanently attached feet. This style makes walking difficult.

Don't Let Baby Have Fruit with Seeds

Caution: An inhaled seed from fruit can be dangerous. Even if your baby's not eating apples, watermelon or grapes yet—or other fruit with seeds—she may soon. Under age 5, a child can easily suck a seed into her airway while she is eating. An inhaled seed can block breathing and cause choking. A seed that remains in the lung may cause an infection.

Remove all seeds before you feed baby a piece of fruit. Don't give her sunflower or pumpkin seeds until she's at least 5 years old.

If your child begins to cough or to wheeze after eating fruit, she may have inhaled a seed. Call your pediatrician; he or she may want a chest X-ray taken. If a seed is found, a specialist with a tool called a *bronchoscope* may have to remove the seed.

Milestones This 41st Week

She "Talks" on Her Toy Telephone

Your baby may be entertaining you by "talking" on a toy phone. At this age, she is beginning "pseudo-conversation," which means her babbling may sound like a real conversation. She's varying the pitch of her voice and changing the rate and volume to echo what she hears every day.

Expressing Her Emotions

Your baby expresses emotions including sadness, anger, happiness and enjoyment. She learns about emotions from her experiences. She also observes how others react when something happens to them, and stores that information. That's one reason for you not to overreact when something happens. Sooner or later, you'll see baby act the same way!

Baby may also act like a baby, which is natural. She may need a reassuring hug or cuddle at these times. Give her a cuddle whenever she asks. When she feels secure, she's ready to learn even more.

Physical Accomplishments Now

Pulling herself to a standing position may be easy for her now. She may refuse your help! She also is capable of sitting down without falling.

Firm grasp. Her grasp is fairly firm. She uses her thumb and fingers with more precision. Don't be surprised when she does something that requires dexterity, such as putting a coin in a slot.

> It may be time to start bathing baby every day. She's getting dirtier from trying to feed herself. She's also crawling, which adds to the dirt. Bathing her in the evening is a good practice. A warm bath helps her relax before she goes to bed.

Loose-jointed? If your baby appears loose-jointed, it may be due to the fact she is less active physically than other babies. Joint looseness gradually disappears as her muscles get stronger. She is probably not walking yet, if she's loose-jointed. She needs support in her hips and knees that stronger muscles offer. But don't be concerned—she'll walk soon.

She's an Explorer

As baby explores the world around her thoroughly, she learns a lot. She will search for an object if she knows it has been hidden. If you hide something that is a bit difficult to find, such as under her blanket, she'll look for it for quite awhile. She is also learning that if a toy or something else is hidden in a second place, it won't be found by looking in the first hiding place.

Milestones This 41st Week

Changes in Baby You May See Now

Physical Development

- walks while holding both of your hands

Senses and Reflexes

- may begin to show preference for one hand and one side of the body

Mental Development

- searches for an object if she saw it hidden

Social Development

- shows various moods, such as hurt, happy, sad, angry
- imitates facial expressions
- imitates sounds
- enjoys variations of peek-a-boo

Every baby is an individual, and your baby may do some of these things more quickly or more slowly than another baby If you are concerned about your baby's progress, discuss it with your healthcare provider. Also see page viii.

She may try to figure out how big her body is. She may crawl into small spaces to see if she fits. Sometimes she doesn't, and you'll need to rescue her.

Note: See also the box on page 374, *Milestones This Week.*

What's Happening This 41st Week?

Repetition Is Important to Baby
Your baby already has favorite stories. She may want to hear them over and over. It's boring for you, but your little one feels more secure hearing a story she knows. Don't fight it. Read the stories she loves, and add a new one occasionally.

Cold Sore (Fever Blister)
What it is. A cold sore, also called a *fever blister,* is a common, contagious viral infection. Cold sores are caused by the herpes simplex virus 1 and affect the lips and mouth, and very occasionally the genitals. A cold sore can occur at any age. Most sufferers have their first infection by age 5. Symptoms include

- eruptions of very small, painful blisters, usually in and around the mouth
- red ring around blisters
- blisters fill with fluid (pus), then dry up and disappear
- pain in and around blister

What to do. Help prevent cold sores by avoiding physical contact with others when they have active lesions. If you have a cold sore, don't kiss baby! If your baby has a cold sore already, the following tips might make your baby more comfortable:

- Offer baby cold liquids to drink, or have her suck on a frozen pop. This helps ease blister discomfort.
- Try to keep baby from scratching or picking at the blisters.
- Zinc oxide on baby's lips when you go outdoors may help prevent a cold sore.
- Give acetaminophen or ibuprofen for discomfort, *after* consulting with your pediatrician.
- With future outbreaks, apply cold to the area when redness appears. Viruses don't like cold, so it may help prevent an outbreak or lessen its severity.

When to call the doctor. Call your baby's doctor if baby develops signs of secondary bacterial infection, such as fever, if pus oozes from blisters instead of clear fluid or if she becomes extremely irritable. If your baby has an eruption of lesions on the genitals similar to those around the mouth, notify your doctor.

Your doctor may prescribe antiviral topical or oral medication. Antibiotic ointment may be used if lesions become infected.

Mumps

What it is. Mumps is a contagious disease that causes inflammation of the salivary glands. It can occur at any age but is most common in children between 2 and 12 years of age. Symptoms include

- salivary glands are inflamed, swollen and painful
- glands feel hard
- pain increases with chewing or swallowing
- mild fever
- chills
- headache
- pain below ears
- sore throat
- saliva may be increased or diminished
- facial features may be distorted by swelling
- in males, testicles may become painful and swollen

Water Alert!

Water in the home and outside poses a serious danger to an infant. Take these precautions at your house to protect your baby.

- **Hot tap water can seriously burn a baby. Set your water heater temperature no higher than 120F (48.8C).**
- **At the tap, always turn off the hot water before you turn off the cold water.**
- **Never leave baby alone around any water. A baby can drown in 1 inch of water.**
- **Fasten toilet seats closed with special fasteners and keep bathroom doors closed.**
- **Keep an eye on pet's water dishes—children love to play in them.**
- **If you have other children, warn them to close the door behind them when they leave the bathroom.**

What to do. Protect your child by having her immunized against the mumps at the appropriate age. See the immunization schedule on page 97. Immunization offers real protection.

If your child gets the mumps before she is immunized, apply heat or ice to the swollen glands. Heat and cold may be alternated. Give acetaminophen or ibuprofen for discomfort. Don't use aspirin, to avoid Reye's syndrome. Offer baby plenty of mild fluids; tart juices may increase the pain.

When to call the doctor. Call your pediatrician if you believe your baby has the mumps. He or she will want to know this important information. Other reasons to call the doctor include

- fever rises above 101F (38.3C) rectally
- vomiting
- abdominal pain
- severe headache not relieved with over-the-counter medication
- swelling or pain in the testicles
- twitching of facial muscles
- seizures
- discomfort or redness in the eyes
- lethargy or extreme irritability

Your baby's doctor may prescribe stronger pain medication to help relieve pain. Cortisone may be used if testicles are involved. Once the disease begins, it must run its natural course. No safe, readily available medicine or treatment is available.

Upper-Respiratory Infection

What it is. The term *upper-respiratory infection* covers almost any kind of infectious disease involving nasal passages, the passageway for air between the throat (larynx) and nasal cavity (pharynx) and the two main passageways to the lungs for air (bronchi). A virus or bacteria may cause such infections, which we often call "colds."

An infection can occur at any age. Infants under 3 months old have a lower infection rate. This rate soars between 3 and 6 months of age. It remains high through the toddler and preschool years. By age 5, respiratory infections occur less frequently. Infants and young children react more severely to acute respiratory tract infections than older children. Symptoms include

- fever, often as the first sign of infection; may reach 103F (39.4C) to 105F (40.5C), even with mild infections
- listlessness and irritability, or euphoria and hyperactivity
- vomiting
- diarrhea—usually mild but may become severe
- nasal blockage due to swelling, which may interfere with breathing and feeding in infants
- nasal discharge, either thin and watery or very thick
- cough
- sore throat

What to do. If your baby has symptoms of an upper-respiratory infection, use a cool-mist humidifier in your baby's room when she's sleeping. See the discussion of humidifiers in Week 13. Warm mist in the bathroom from a hot shower also helps. Offer lots of liquids

Is It the Flu or a Cold?

Sometimes it's difficult to determine if baby has the flu or a cold. Use this comparison chart to help you determine which illness your little one might have.

Cold	Flu
Baby is slightly tired.	She's weak and seems exhausted.
She doesn't seem too uncomfortable.	She seems to feel soreness all over her body.
If fever is present, it is slight.	She has chills and fever.
Nose is runny or stuffy.	She is congested and may have a cough.
She may have a slight sore throat.	Sore throat develops quickly.
Symptoms begin slowly.	Symptoms present quickly.
Vomiting is probably not a problem.	She may vomit.
Diarrhea is probably not a problem.	She may have diarrhea.
She may participate in most regular activities.	She may not feel like doing much.

so she doesn't get dehydrated. Before you put her in her crib, raise the top (head) end of the crib. This is the best position for easier breathing. Give ibuprofen or acetaminophen for discomfort or fever. If your pediatrician says it's OK, you may give over-the-counter cold medications.

Clear baby's nasal secretions with a bulb syringe and saline nose drops. This helps baby if she's having a hard time breathing and eating at the same time.

When to call the doctor. It's important to call baby's doctor if baby is under 3 months of age. Also call if a high fever is not relieved with medication, baby shows signs of dehydration, she has difficulty breathing or rapid, labored breathing, she turns blue or gray, or is extremely irritable and can't be comforted.

Your doctor may prescribe antibiotics, if baby has a secondary bacterial infection. Otherwise your doctor will recommend ways to treat symptoms. If baby is extremely dehydrated, she may be admitted to the hospital to be given fluids. A baby is also hospitalized if she develops other respiratory problems that may need close monitoring or support.

Toys and Play This 41st Week

Brrrr!
When it's warm outside, cool off and have fun at the same time. Fill a plastic or aluminum bowl with water. Place one ice cube in the bowl. Holding baby's hand, touch it to the ice cube for a second. Exclaim, "The ice cube is cold!" then shiver. Holding the ice cube in your hand, briefly (and lightly) touch it to baby's leg, her hand, her arm and her face. Keep remarking that it's cold.

Making Noise
Put a handful of uncooked popcorn or rice into a clear plastic bottle with a screw-top lid, such as a clean, 1-liter pop bottle. After filling the bottle, glue on the top so baby can't remove it. Let her shake it! You may have to show her what to do, but she'll get the hang of it soon.

Point out how the popcorn or rice bounces inside the bottle. Talk about the loud noise the kernels make. Roll the bottle back and forth between you. Shake it in time to music. Play with it in the bathtub. You'll discover many ways to play with this new toy.

Week 42

How Big Is Your Baby This 42nd Week?

Baby weighs 20-1/2 pounds and is 29 inches long this week.

Baby Care and Equipment

Scheduling Solids

By offering your baby more solid food at established mealtimes, you reinforce your baby's milk-feeding schedule. Meals provide some of the nutrition he needs. Because these meals are not large, he will get hungry again fairly soon. Even at this age, when he's eating at least two meals a day, breast milk or formula should still supply much of his nutrition. Offer the breast or a bottle when he's hungry between meals.

A Sunburn with Little Sun Exposure

How is it possible for a baby or child to sunburn when he's outside for only a short time? Check the medication he's taking!

Sun sensitivity from medications. Some medications cause skin to become more sensitive to sunlight. Sun exposure causes a rash or sunburn on exposed skin. It may not be apparent for several days.

Sun-food reactions. At other times, when baby's not taking medication, sun exposure on skin that has touched fresh foods can cause problems. Celery and the juices and oils from lemon or lime rinds can cause a rash. The rash may itch, blister and turn red or dark brown.

If your child experiences any sun-food reaction, treat it as you would a typical sunburn. Cool compresses help relieve irritation, as does fragrance-free lotion. Some products are designed to reduce or relieve sunburn pain. Check with your pediatrician before using them. In some cases, cortisone cream helps relieve discomfort. Again, make sure it's OK with baby's doctor before you apply the cream.

Before giving your child any medication (prescription or over-the-counter), check with the doctor or pharmacist about any possible sunlight reactions. If a reaction is indicated, keep baby completely out of the sun while he's taking the medication. If you have to be in the sun, cover baby completely with long pants, long sleeves and a hat. See the box above regarding common medications that cause sunlight reactions.

Medications and Sun Sensitivity

Common drugs that may increase baby's sensitivity to sunlight include

- **Advil®, Nuprin®, Motrin® (ibuprofen)**
- **Bactrim® (sulfamethoxazole)**
- **Benadryl® (diphenhydramine hydrochloride)**
- **Cipro® (ciprofloxin)**
- **Floxin® (ofloxin)**

Milestones This 42nd Week

Baby May Take only One Nap

At around this age, some babies take only one short nap during the day. They may sleep longer at night to make up for it. Many babies nap in the morning. However, it may be difficult for a baby who naps in the morning to make it all the way through the afternoon in a pleasant mood.

After-lunch nap. Now may be the time to encourage an after-lunch nap. It will help baby retain his good mood through dinnertime. You may have to adjust his routine somewhat to work in the nap. You may have to promote a later waking time, for example. Lunch may have to be fed earlier than normal, such as 11:00 A.M. These changes, and any others you devise, can make the evenings more enjoyable for everyone in the family.

If He Acts Helpless

Sometimes your baby will pretend to be helpless. He will expect you to take care of him immediately. As hard as it may be to do, stand

Baby's First "Real" Shoes

Until now, your baby has probably been wearing cute little shoes to match an outfit or to keep his feet warm. Those shoes weren't made for walking. Now that he's getting ready to walk, you'll want to start thinking about shoes that are made for walking.

When, How to Buy Shoes

When your little one is steady on his feet (leaning or standing on his own), it's time to buy shoes. It's best to go to a shoe store that specializes in children's shoes. Be sure the salesperson is trained in fitting shoes to babies' feet. Have your baby's feet measured while he's standing up. If one foot is bigger than the other, buy shoes to fit the larger foot.

The shoe you choose should have a little room in the toe to allow for growth. Don't buy shoes that are too big in hopes you'll save money and not have to replace them as often. When a shoe is too big, baby has to adjust his stride to keep them on. He could stumble as a result. When you do need to buy a new pair of shoes, probably in 2 to 3 months, have his foot remeasured. You can't just buy the next larger size.

What Kind of Shoe Is Best?

Light and flexible. Your baby's first shoes should be light and flexible so the shoe can conform to the foot more readily. Some parents believe

> When your little one is steady on his feet (leaning or standing on his own), it's time to buy shoes.

a baby shoe must be hard-soled to support the foot, but this idea is incorrect.

Natural materials are best. A natural material, such as soft leather or canvas, lets baby's foot breathe. His feet perspire more than yours do. Avoid vinyl, plastic or synthetics. A shoe should be sturdy but not rigid. Baby should be able to flex his forefoot slightly, which helps him walk better.

Shapes and soles. A round-toed shoe is a good choice because it does not restrict foot movement as much as a pointed-toe shoe does. Check to be sure the soles have some traction but not too much. You don't want soles slippery, but you don't want them to grip the floor too tightly, either. Avoid bulky or platform soles.

High tops? The high-top baby shoes that you might have worn when you were baby's age don't offer any greater support to the ankle or foot than low-cut shoes do. If baby likes to take off his shoes or has trouble keeping them on, high tops may be a good choice for him. If your baby is fairly active and moving around a lot, a sturdy athletic shoe may be a good choice. There are many to choose from.

About dressy shoes. If you want to buy dress shoes, that's OK. Save them for special occasions.

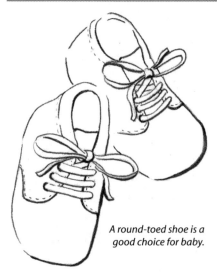

A round-toed shoe is a good choice for baby.

When his toe touches the tip of the shoe, it's time to buy a new pair.

Other Baby-Shoe Tips

Use plain socks. Choose plain socks to wear with shoes. Socks with tread on the bottom make it hard to slide baby's feet in and out of shoes.

Keep toenails short. Clip baby's toenails regularly. Long toenails interfere with a comfortable shoe fit.

Used shoes won't fit properly. If someone offers you a pair of shoes another baby has worn, say "No, thanks." A shoe molds to the shape of a child's foot. A used pair of shoes could mean a poor fit or inadequate support for your baby.

They don't usually offer enough support to wear every day. Be sure laces are not too long. Buckles or straps are good fastener choices.

Checking the Fit

How often? Check the fit of baby's shoes every week. Baby could have a growth spurt at any time. As long as there is adequate space between the end of his big toe and the tip of the shoe, he's OK.

> Check the fit of baby's shoes every week. Baby could have a growth spurt at any time.

Look for changes in baby's walk. If shoes seem to cause discomfort, watch how your baby walks in them. Changes in baby's coordination, balance or walking pattern could indicate a problem. Check feet for blisters and other signs that a shoe adjustment might be necessary. When his toe touches the tip of the shoe, it's time to buy a new pair.

To Practice Walking, Barefoot Is Best

Shoes are necessary in a lot of situations, but remember that most pediatricians recommend that baby practice walking in his bare feet when he's in the house. Walking barefoot helps strengthen foot muscles. Bare feet also allow baby's foot to spread, increasing ground contact. And the bare arch forms a suction with the ground that helps the foot grip. When baby's wearing shoes, his feet can't do these things.

back and let him try to do some things on his own. Baby won't learn what he is capable of doing if you respond to his every demand. You'll do baby a greater favor if you let him learn to think and act for himself.

> **Baby may be doing something new—asking for something by pointing to it.**

When Baby Ignores You

Do you get the feeling sometimes that your baby isn't listening when you talk to him? Don't be upset; he probably isn't ignoring you. He may be concentrating so much on doing something else that he doesn't respond. It may be difficult for him to switch tasks (for example, from concentrating on a toy to concentrating on you). Allow him adequate time to make transitions.

A Free Spirit

At this age, your baby may dislike being confined. He may fight being put in a stroller or his car seat. When you can, give him the freedom to move around. Instead of putting him in a stroller and taking him for a walk, let him crawl around on the grass in your yard.

A word of warning: Even if baby doesn't want to be put in his car seat, you *must* place him in it *every time* he rides in the car. You may have to devise ways to prevent your 10-month-old from undoing the restraints or otherwise getting out of them. He is not safe in a car unless he's in his car seat.

Note: See also the box below, *Milestones This Week.*

Milestones This 42nd Week

Changes in Baby You May See Now

Physical Development
- sits down from standing position

Senses and Reflexes
- responds to music by rocking, bouncing, swaying, humming

Mental Development
- may repeat word incessantly, making it an answer to every question

Social Development
- grows aware of self
- imitates gestures

Every baby is an individual, and your baby may do some of these things more quickly or more slowly than another baby. If you are concerned about your baby's progress, discuss it with your healthcare provider. Also see page viii.

What's Happening This 42nd Week?

Make Mealtime Fun!
Is mealtime with baby a hassle? Is it messy? Make feeding easier on you and baby by trying some of these suggestions.

- *Feed yourself first.* Eat in an exaggerated way. Show how much you like the food. He'll probably want to try it if he thinks *you* like it.
- *Play "Open the door!"* When baby is hungry, but not too hungry, say "Open the door!" and open your mouth wide to demonstrate. Once baby opens his mouth, pop in the food.
- *"Up and in."* When feeding baby, put a spoonful of the food in his mouth as you lift up the spoon. His upper lip will clean off the spoon, which helps food stay in his mouth.
- *Don't push it.* If baby doesn't want to eat a meal, he'll be OK. Sometimes he just doesn't feel like eating. He may be teething, with a little soreness in his mouth. He may be getting a cold. Or maybe he doesn't like what you're offering. Skip solids for a meal or two, then offer them again.
- *Occupy his hands.* Some babies want to reach for and take the spoon themselves. Some like to pour their liquids on the highchair tray. Some want to drop food on the floor. Give baby a spoon of his own when you feed him. Use plates and bowls that attach to the tray so they will stay where you put them. Some highchairs have activity bars that will entertain him. Use whatever methods work best for you.

Food Poisoning
What it is. The term *food poisoning* describes an illness resulting from eating a food that contains poisonous substances. True food poisoning includes poisoning from mushrooms, shellfish, insecticides and milk from cows that have eaten poisonous plants. The rotting process can also poison foods.

Food poisoning usually occurs in those who eat solids. It would be extremely rare in a baby that is not yet eating solid foods to be exposed to contaminated foods. Symptoms of food poisoning include

- nausea
- vomiting
- severe abdominal cramps
- profuse diarrhea

What to do. If your baby exhibits any of these symptoms, offer lots of fluid to help prevent dehydration. Allow baby plenty of rest.

When to call the doctor. Call the doctor if your baby develops a fever or is dehydrated. Medical treatment is usually unnecessary. Symptoms usually improve within 24 hours.

Tick Bite

What it is. Tick bites are serious for two reasons. The first is that the tick can attach itself to the baby (and you must remove it). The second is the chance of contracting various diseases from tick bites, including Lyme disease, Rocky Mountain spotted fever, tick fever, spotted fever or tick typhus.

You may notice a tick attached to baby when you bathe or change him. Or you may notice symptoms of a tick bite, including

- a red rash on the skin
- fever
- lethargy
- nausea
- vomiting
- chills
- difficulty feeding
- irritability

What to do. Examine your baby's body if you have been in a tick-infested area. Look over his entire body, particularly in his hair (if he has any).

If you think a tick has bitten your baby, call your doctor. He or she may prescribe antibiotics, such as chloramphenicol, depending on baby's age. Acetaminophen or ibuprofen may be suggested to treat pain or fever.

Prevention. If you live in an area where ticks are common, take some preventive measures for baby. If he's sitting in the grass, be sure he is dressed in long sleeves and long pants. Keep socks on his feet and a hat on his head. Check him thoroughly each time you undress or bathe him to see if he has any tick bites.

When to call the doctor. If you notice a sore with a bull's-eye appearance, it could be the sign of Lyme disease. Contact your doctor immediately.

Puncture Wound

What it is. A puncture wound occurs when baby's skin is pierced by a sharp, pointed object. If the object is dirty or rusty, there is concern about tetanus infection. Symptoms include

- a hole in the skin
- bleeding from skin
- redness or swelling in the area

What to do. If your baby gets a puncture wound, wash the area with soap and water. Keep the area clean and dry by covering it lightly with a bandage. Apply gentle pressure if the wound bleeds.

When to call the doctor. Call the doctor if bleeding continues, if there is extreme swelling or pain, or if you are concerned about damage to underlying structures or organs. If the wound occurs near the eyes or any other vital structure, call your pediatrician.

Your doctor will probably suggest antibiotic gels or oral antibiotics. He or she will advise you on cleaning and dressing of the wound. Ask about the need for any immunization.

Undescended Testicle

What it is. Before birth, a baby boy's testicles travel down the pelvis, into the scrotum. This usually occurs around the seventh month of gestation. An *undescended testicle* means the testicle did not make this journey. About 3% of all full-term baby boys are born with one or both testicles undescended. By about 6 months after birth, most testicles descend on their own. However, about 1% of all baby boys under 1 year have a testicle that has not descended to the proper position.

What to do. Surgery to correct the problem is not usually performed until after a baby is 6 months old. However, it is considered if a baby's testicles have not descended by then. A testicle that hasn't appeared by 6 months of age is unlikely to descend later. If the testicle remains in the pelvis, it begins to change microscopically at around 1 year of age. These changes could affect fertility later in life.

Performing surgery to correct the problem on a baby around 6 months of age is considered safe. He's old enough to tolerate the surgical procedure and the general anesthesia. Most medical problems that could interfere with surgery have usually been discovered by then.

What surgery involves. A small incision is made in the groin. The surgeon finds the testicle and frees it from tissue that is restraining it. An incision is made in the scrotum. The testicle is pulled down into the scrotum.

Surgery for an undescended testicle is often done as an outpatient procedure. Recovery takes only a couple of days.

Toys and Play This 42nd Week

The Tickle Game

Most babies love to be tickled. Your fingers are the best tickle tools around, but you can use other things, too. If you have long hair, lightly stroke it on his arm. Gently move the fringe of a blanket over his face. A clean feather duster might delight him. A soft tissue or the fingers of a glove can make him laugh. Even the cat's tail can become a tickling tool!

After you tickle him, encourage him to tickle you. Let him start with his fingers (he'll probably need your help). Then show him how to use the other tickle tools. You'll soon be laughing together.

Telephone Talk

As we've mentioned, your baby may enjoy "talking" on his toy telephone by now. He will also be happy when he hears a voice he knows on a real telephone!

He's probably watched you have a phone conversation countless times. He can't hold the receiver himself yet, but he can listen. This helps him concentrate on speech alone. When grandma or daddy calls, let him listen to their voice on the phone.

Creative Toys

These are just some of the many toys that entertain baby and also help his mental and physical development.

- Nesting cups, stacking rings, pails, balls and soft bags— to encourage swatting, stacking, throwing and grasping
- Stable push toys— to encourage walking
- Pop-up toys, reversible dolls or reversible puppets— to help him learn what's out of sight hasn't disappeared forever

Invent Songs

To help your baby recognize parts of his body, make up a song. Sing a song or rhyme that names body parts and what they do. Bathing or changing are good times to sing these songs. You can sing a song about how baby's legs are for walking and his lips are for talking. Or his arms are for waving and his head is for shaving. Anything silly and fun can help him learn.

Indoor Sandbox

When it's rainy or cold outside, bring the fun indoors! Make an indoor sandbox, and your little one will have lots of fun playing in it.

Gather together a large, shallow pan, cornmeal, a tarp or sheet to cover the floor, and some toys. Lay the tarp or sheet on the kitchen floor (the floor is easier to clean than a carpet). Place the container on top of the sheet, and put about an inch or so of cornmeal in it. Sit baby next to the container, and give him a spoon and some other toys with which to "play in the sand." Plastic cups, small strainers and scoops are all fun to use in the "sandbox."

Week 43

How Big Is Your Baby This 43rd Week?

Baby weighs 20-3/4 pounds and is 29 inches long this week.

Baby Care and Equipment

Taking Care of Baby's Hair

At 10 months, your baby may have enough hair to brush and style. If she doesn't have hair yet, don't be too concerned. She'll be getting some soon. Until then, just use a dab of K-Y Jelly or corn syrup to fix a bow on her head. Both wash out with warm water without pulling her sparse hair.

Washing. When you wash her hair, apply a conditioner no more often than once a week—*only* if she needs it. If her hair is fairly manageable, you won't need conditioner.

Styling. The best time to style a baby's hair is after washing, while it's still wet. It should hold its shape while it dries. You can use your fingers to style it during her first 6 months. As baby gets older, use a soft baby hairbrush to brush and to style her hair. Arrange baby's hair in a style that makes sense for its texture and type. If baby has stick-straight hair, for example, ringlets just won't hold.

If baby has a bald spot. Babies sometimes develop bald spots on one side of the head. If your baby has a bald spot, check her while she sleeps. Does she always turn her head to the same side? If so, she may rub the same spot against the sheets every night, resulting in a bald spot. After she goes to sleep, gently turn her head to the other side if this concerns you.

> Avoid using a hair dryer until baby is about 2 years old.

390

Baby hair is fragile. Don't use barrettes or elastic bands too often. When you do use them, be gentle! Don't pull hair too tight, which can damage baby's scalp. If you notice a red rash on her scalp after pulling her hair tight in a band or barrette, her hair follicles are inflamed. If you pull the same area of hair too tightly for too long, it is possible to cause permanent hair loss at that spot. Avoid using a hair dryer until baby is about 2 years old. Heat from a hair dryer can damage baby's hair shafts.

About hair accessories. Your baby may not cooperate with your styling efforts. Like many other babies, she may pull out every hair accessory as soon as it goes on her head. Choose hair accessories very carefully if your baby has this habit. She might pull the accessory out of her hair and put it in her mouth. She could choke on it.

When to Offer Lumpy Foods

Some parents hesitate to add lumpier foods to baby's diet. They are afraid their baby might choke. However, parents may delay baby's chewing and swallowing development by not giving lumpy foods when baby is ready for them.

Lumpy foods help develop tongue control. One goal of feeding solids to a baby during the first year is to teach tongue control, so baby learns how to push food around in her mouth with her tongue. She needs to progress through the different textures of food—from strained to puréed to lumpy, to small bits of "real food," such as well-cooked meats and vegetables. If she doesn't progress through these foods, she may have eating problems later.

> Your baby's weight at this age has nothing to do with her weight in the future. During the first few months, some babies grow very quickly. As they get older, their growth slows. Focus on the height/weight tables. If baby's height stays apace with her weight, she's doing OK!

When to offer lumpy foods. You may not know exactly when to offer the next level of food. Experts suggest offering foods of the next level in manageable bites after she masters a level. For example, when she's eating puréed food without difficulty, slowly introduce lumpier foods.

Gag reflex is natural. Don't be alarmed when baby gags on a food every once in awhile. As she learns to swallow, she gags as a normal way to protect herself. Some babies have a more-sensitive

Fluid–Comparison Chart for Baby

Fluid	Comments
Water	One of the best fluids because it doesn't contain sugar, caffeine or flavorings
Fruit pieces	Contain a lot of water, often as high as 85%
Juice	Often contains a lot of sugar
Soda	Usually high in sugar and caffeine
Ice pops	Often contain flavorings and sugar
Sports drinks	Contain sugar and electrolytes, which are usually unnecessary

gag reflex than others and may gag more easily. However, if baby gags consistently, contact your pediatrician. Consistent gagging may indicate a problem.

Thirst Quenchers

As baby grows, your pediatrician may recommend giving her more fluids. You have lots of choices. Some liquids are better for her than others. See the chart on this page for a comparison of various fluids you might be thinking of offering baby.

Milestones This 43rd Week

Baby on the Move

By this time, your baby is probably moving all over the place. She may be cruising around the furniture with ease. She may crawl into corners and get stuck. She pulls up to a standing position and may hold on with only one hand.

Your baby will fall and have other minor accidents—it's natural. If you don't get upset when she falls, she probably won't either. Of course, when she really hurts herself, take care of her right away. But when she takes a minor spill, react with a laugh, as if it were a little joke. You may be surprised when she falls again—just to hear you laugh!

Her Relationship with Her Parents

Your relationship with your baby is unique. And your partner's relationship with baby is also unique. Each parent expands baby's understanding of her world around her, but in different ways.

She feels a strong attachment to her parents and other caregivers. She will seek the attention of these special people. On the other hand, she is even more likely to be wary of strangers now. She may look to her parents when a stranger approaches.

> Experts believe that family dinnertime is important to rearing happy, well-adjusted children. Sixty-seven percent of all families eat a meal together at least 5 times every week. Make it a habit in your family.

"Please" and "Thank You"

Your baby probably isn't talking much, but she understands quite a bit. She knows the names of as many as a dozen objects (or more). She can follow simple instructions or directions.

You might want to begin saying "please" and "thank you" when you make a request of her. You may be doing this already. If she hears it now, it will become part of her vocabulary.

Baby Likes to Stand

By 10 months of age, many babies like to stand as often as possible. Your baby may want to stand up for baths, diaper changes and even meals. Let her stand whenever it is safe, but don't let her endanger herself by standing up in the wrong place or situation. You may have to be forceful with her if she wants to stand when it is unsafe to do so.

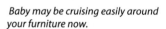

Baby may be cruising easily around your furniture now.

Her Perception Sharpens

You may notice baby moves her toys intently, up and down. Or she may move them closer, then farther away. When she turns her toys upside down, she gets another view. Squinting at them provides a different perspective also. When baby is absorbed in these activities, she is exploring what objects look like.

Note: See also the box below, *Milestones This Week.*

What's Happening This 43rd Week?

Who Should Not Be Immunized?

Children who have special health problems may need to avoid certain immunizations. Your pediatrician will discuss the situation with you if he or she believes your child is in a high-risk group. Your doctor will review your child's health history and discuss the potential risks of immunizing her, including side effects. The Centers for Disease Control (CDC) publishes *Vaccine Information Statements.* Ask your doctor for copies if you are concerned.

Children who may not receive certain immunizations include those with seizure disorders, immune problems and neurological disorders. Some vaccines are safe; others are not. Your doctor will evaluate your child carefully.

If your child suffers from an allergy to a component of a vaccine, such as eggs or yeast, a vaccine may not be recommended. If your child has a food allergy or drug sensitivity, discuss every immunization with your pediatrician *before* it is given.

Milestones This 43rd Week
Changes in Baby You May See Now

Physical Development
- may be able to raise herself to a standing position

Senses and Reflexes
- carries two small objects in one hand

Mental Development
- reaches behind herself to get a toy without seeing it
- is interested in fitting things together

Social Development
- seeks social approval
- seeks companionship and attention
- fears strange places
- feeds herself entire meals

Every baby is an individual, and your baby may do some of these things more quickly or more slowly than another baby. If you are concerned about your baby's progress, discuss it with your healthcare provider. Also see page viii.

A *word of caution:* Some parents may choose not to have a child immunized for personal reasons. However, every unimmunized child puts every other child at risk, especially those who cannot receive immunizations for the reasons stated above. Immunizing your child is a protective measure, and every parent should consider a decision not to immunize very carefully.

Solo Play Is Important

A baby who regularly plays by herself learns a lot. She learns how to entertain herself. By concentrating on a task, she may make developmental advances. Let your baby enjoy solo play, but make sure she's safe, too.

When baby is playing by herself, always stay within hearing range. Be sure the area she's in has been childproofed. To keep your little one extra safe, you may want to take advantage of some of the safety measures listed below.

- When baby can push up on her hands and knees, remove mobiles from her crib. They are health hazards once she can reach them.
- Examine all toys for loose threads and tags. Remove them.
- Keep playpen free of objects baby could use to crawl out of the playpen.
- Use gates or barriers to keep her inside one area or outside of another.
- Give age-appropriate toys only. If you give baby toys that are too old for her, they are likely to contain pieces or parts that could harm her.

Blisters from New Shoes

What it is. A blister is caused by something rubbing on the outermost layer of skin, as new shoes can do. The top layer of skin separates from the under layer. The space between the two layers typically fills with fluid. When your baby starts wearing shoes, she may get a blister or two. Nearly everyone has gotten a blister from a new pair of shoes at some time. Symptoms include

- skin redness
- fluid-filled blister
- baby cries when shoes are put on

What to do. Apply a cold compress to the blister for a few minutes. Wash the area with mild soap and water. Pat dry. Using a sterilized needle (cleaned with rubbing alcohol), puncture the blister at the edge. Gently squeeze out the fluid. Leave the skin in place. Cover with a light bandage. Before you put on baby's shoes again, apply moleskin to the area to protect it from rubbing.

When to call the doctor. Call your baby's doctor if she has a blister that appears infected. If you notice a discharge, or bleeding or swelling at the site, call your pediatrician's office. You may be advised to put antibiotic ointment on the area to deal with any infection.

Prevention. Consult your pediatrician before you buy baby shoes to determine if there is a type of shoe that would be best for your baby. Put socks on baby when she wears shoes. When she's moving around and walking, buy shoes that fit correctly, not ones that just look "cute." Her socks should fit well, too. They shouldn't be too tight, too loose or too heavy.

Gastroenteritis

What it is. Gastroenteritis is really a fancy term for a "tummyache" or "upset stomach." Technically, it is an inflammation or irritation of the stomach and intestinal tract, resulting in the following symptoms. It can occur at any age.

- vomiting
- diarrhea
- irritability, fussiness
- poor appetite
- fever
- bloating or gas

What to do. You can try various treatments at home, but always consult with your pediatrician first. Fluids are necessary, but the bowel also needs to rest. Offer a clear-liquid diet for the first day or two. In very young infants, a commercial electrolyte solution, such as Pedialyte , can be used. In older infants, clear liquid is "anything you can see through." For a child under 1 year, give ½ ounce of fluid every 20 to 30 minutes. For a child over 1 year, give 1 ounce every 30 minutes.

When a child has been free of diarrhea for 1 day, you may offer baby a bland diet known as the *BRATT diet*. This diet includes bananas, rice, applesauce, tea and toast. If diarrhea doesn't recur within 2 hours after eating, continue feeding the bland foods for 24 hours. Gradually work back to a normal diet.

Caution: Do not use nonprescription antidiarrheal drugs without first consulting your baby's doctor.

When to call the doctor. If your baby has symptoms of gastroenteritis, you may be able to take care of the problem at home. However, call the doctor if

- rectal temperature rises to 103F (39.4C) or higher
- child shows signs of dehydration
- symptoms don't improve in 48 hours, despite treatment
- your baby is under 2 months old

Your physician will probably recommend treating symptoms at home. However, hospitalization may occur for IV hydration, if baby is dehydrated. The condition should improve in 48 hours.

Pneumonia

What it is. Pneumonia is an inflammation of the lungs caused by bacteria, viruses or chemical irritants. There are more than 50 known causes of pneumonia. It can occur at any age but is most severe in infants, young children and the very old. Pneumonia symptoms vary, but be alert for the following:

- fever—ranges from mild to high (99F/37.5C to 105F/40.5C)
- cough—slight to severe
- sputum may contain blood or bloody streaks
- rapid breathing
- fatigue
- chills
- pain in the chest
- loss of appetite
- difficulty breathing

What to do. If your baby develops symptoms of pneumonia, use a cool-mist humidifier to increase air moisture when she's sleeping. See the discussion of humidifiers in Week 13. Don't use cough medicine unless advised to do so by your pediatrician. You don't want to suppress the cough with medicine if it produces sputum. Sputum helps the body get rid of lung secretions. Offer lots of fluids. Let baby sleep when she wants to. Give ibuprofen or acetaminophen for discomfort or fever.

When to call the doctor. Call your pediatrician if you are concerned that your baby may have pneumonia. Treatments he or she may recommend can include X-rays to diagnose pneumonia and a sputum culture. Antibiotics may be prescribed to fight the infection. In severe cases, a baby will be hospitalized.

Toys and Play This 43rd Week

To encourage your baby's independence and solo play, clear out a low shelf just for baby in the family room or another room, if you haven't already. Put some of her toys and books on the shelf. Being able to reach her things without your help boosts baby's sense of independence. It means she can play by herself when she wants to.

Finger-Counting Game
This finger-counting play helps baby develop some simple math concepts. Touch each finger of one of her hands while you recite

> *1, 2, 3, 4, 5*
> *I caught a bird alive!*
> *Why did I let her go?*
> *Because she bit my finger so—ouch!* (gently squeeze her thumb)

Repeat the song touching each toe on her foot. Change the last line from "finger" to "toe."

Egg-Carton Delight
Babies love to poke and touch things. Feeling objects helps babies learn about them.

Using an empty egg carton, glue different items in the cups. Choose hard pasta or cereal pieces, fabric, paper or plastic wrap—anything that baby might like to touch and feel. Give her the egg carton, and let her explore the different objects. This game is *not* for solo play. Always stay with baby while she plays with the egg carton, in case small pieces break off. You don't want her to choke on anything.

Obstacle Course
Set up a fun obstacle course in the family room. Put down a blanket, pillows and other objects for baby to climb over or crawl around. Be sure they will support her weight and do not move easily. Encourage her to traverse the obstacle course one way, then another.

Weekly Milestones at a Glance

Week 44

Physical Development
• climbs up and down from chairs

Senses and Reflexes
• may differentiate use of hands

Mental Development
• likes to take things apart and put them back together
• opens drawers and cupboards to explore contents
• experiments with means to a goal, such as using a large wheeled toy for a walker

Social Development
• begins to learn sexual identity
• helps dress himself
• enjoys games, such as hide-and-seek, rolling back and forth on floor
• drops objects for someone else to pick up

Week 45

Physical Development
• cruises furniture

Senses and Reflexes
• picks up extremely small objects
• holds cup and drinks from it

Mental Development
• recognizes words as symbols for objects–e.g., knows cow "moos"
• can imitate speech rhythms, inflections and facial expressions

Social Development
• does not always cooperate
• withdraws from strangers

Week 46

Physical Development
• may lean over while standing against support
• squats and stoops

Senses and Reflexes
• holds out arm or leg to help you dress him
• lifts lid from boxes

Mental Development
• speaks a few intelligible words

Social Development
• asserts himself among siblings

Week 47

Physical Development
• lowers herself from a standing position without falling

Senses and Reflexes
• deliberately places objects
• may untie shoelaces

Mental Development
• may nest objects, such as boxes or cups

Social Development
• tries to avoid disapproval
• shows guilt

Week 48

Physical Development
• may take a step without holding onto anything
• may stand on toes
• may carry spoon to mouth

Senses and Reflexes
• turns pages of book
• may pull off shoes and socks

Mental Development
• speaks long, babbling sentences with full inflection

Social Development
• seeks approval
• engages in parallel play with another child

Week 44

How Big Is Your Baby This 44th Week?

Baby weighs 21 pounds and is 29-1/2 inches long this week.

Baby Care and Equipment

Portable Seating for Baby
A portable baby seat is helpful when highchairs aren't provided at some restaurants, or when you visit relatives' or friends' homes. This device is a hook-on highchair that may fold in half for easy transport. Grippers attach the seat to the edge of the table; baby is suspended at the table. It's handy and works with most tables and many counters. It's safe for children from age 6 months to 3 years or up to 50 pounds.

Keep Minor Cuts and Scrapes Moist
Minor wounds heal faster when they are kept moist and covered. After gently cleaning the area with soap and water, apply an antibiotic ointment to the cut or scrape. Cover with a bandage. The ointment helps protect against infection and keeps the wound area moist so it doesn't form irritating small cracks as it heals. Keep the area covered until a scab forms.

Could Your Baby Have a Rubber Allergy?
An allergy to rubber isn't too common—about 1 person in 100 suffers from it. However, it's good to know about, especially if your baby has unexplained symptoms.

A baby who is allergic to rubber and sucks on a rubber pacifier may have a physical reaction. Common reactions include itching, coughing, wheezing, sneezing and swelling. One study showed that symptoms disappeared for babies with this allergy when they were given a silicon pacifier.

Can Baby Eat a Vegetarian Diet?

Some parents choose to feed their families a vegetarian diet, for religious or personal reasons. Many want to know if a baby can get the nutrients he needs from a vegetarian meal plan.

Yes, a baby can be healthy on a vegetarian diet if he is offered a wide variety of foods. Get your pediatrician's advice first if you want to follow a vegetarian meal plan for your baby. He or she will advise you about any special needs or concerns. Different vegetarian eating plans require special considerations to ensure that baby gets all the nutrients that he needs.

Ovo-lacto vegetarian diet. This diet includes dairy products and eggs. When baby is eating solid foods, he needs to receive adequate amounts of food that contain protein, iron and vitamin B12. However, don't feed baby egg whites until he is at least 1 year old to help him avoid developing an egg allergy.

Lacto-vegetarian diet. Dairy foods are part of this diet, but eggs are not. Adequate amounts of food that contain protein, iron and vitamin B12 are necessary in this diet plan.

Vegan diet. This diet does not include animal products, including dairy foods or eggs. When baby is introduced to solid foods, they must contain adequate amounts of calcium, protein, iron and vitamin B12. You can meet these needs by giving baby iron-enriched grains and cereals. Serve them with vitamin-C foods to enhance iron absorption. Soy products are rich in protein, and many are enriched with calcium and vitamin B12. Soy products baby may like include tofu, textured vegetable protein (looks like ground meat), soy cheese and soymilk. By around 7 months, you can start adding puréed beans, lentils and split peas as other sources of protein to baby's diet.

Milestones This 44th Week

The Great Experimenter

Baby's curiosity leads him to try all kinds
of new activities now. He opens drawers to
explore the contents. He may decide to pull
out everything he can from the drawer. He
pokes, pinches or rolls an object to see what
will happen. He tries to fit objects together.
You may find baby wants to take things
apart, too. He is a fledgling scientist, and
your home is his laboratory!

> **Be Ready!**
> Keep a one-time-use
> camera close at hand,
> in your diaper bag,
> glove box or purse.
> You'll always be
> prepared when baby
> is doing something
> you want to
> remember or show
> someone.

Baby Talk

Baby talk exists all over the world. "Baby words" help a baby
communicate his wishes or express his feelings simply. A word in
baby talk is usually shorter and easier to say than the same word in
adult language. For example, baby can say "mama" and "dada" long
before he can say "mommy" and "daddy" or "mother" and "father."

Your baby has learned that he can say some words that carry
authority. You may hear him say "No," even when he means "Yes." As
he begins to discriminate in his use of the word, he may say "No" and
shake his head at the same time.

Love of Books

Your baby enjoys books at this age because he likes to listen to
you read to him while he looks at the pictures. You may notice him
pointing to and naming pictures in a book.

Choose books that contain words and pictures of objects he
knows. A simple book with a picture of a ball on one page and
a shoe on the other, for example, is a good choice. These are
household items he recognizes.

Let him turn the pages, if he is able. If he wants to turn them
but can't, help him. Spend as much time as he wants on each page
of a book. He may be studying a picture in relation to something
else he is learning.

Cruising and Climbing

He's probably walking around the edges of the furniture a lot now.
When he's comfortable with cruising, he'll begin to let go a little

or hold on less tightly. You'll see him practice standing on his toes or standing on one leg. He is probably comfortable bending over to pick up an object, supporting himself with only one hand.

> **You may find your baby is more cooperative now. He may help dress himself or want to dry himself after his bath.**

Baby may be climbing more. He may try to climb on top of an object as high as 1 foot. You may even see him climb on and off a chair. When he climbs on something, he makes an attempt to get off. He knows about how far away the floor is. He can slowly back down from an object when he wants to. He uses his feet as "feelers." He will call for your help if he gets stuck!

His feet may roll in somewhat at the edges. This condition corrects itself as he learns to balance and his foot muscles get stronger.

Baby Play Now

Your baby may show boredom with some of his toys. If he doesn't seem interested in them, put them away for a while. He'll let you know if he wants them again.

Baby wants to play games with people. But it's a good idea to encourage him in his solo play. Let him play by himself near you.

Note: See also the box below, *Milestones This Week*.

Milestones This 44th Week

Changes in Baby You May See Now

Physical Development
• climbs up and down from chairs

Senses and Reflexes
• may differentiate use of hands

Mental Development
• likes to take things apart and put them back together
• opens drawers and cupboards to explore contents
• experiments with means to a goal, such as using a chair for a walker

Social Development
• begins to learn sexual identity
• helps dress himself
• enjoys games, such as hide-and-seek, rolling back and forth on floor
• drops objects for someone else to pick up

Every baby is an individual, and your baby may do some of these things more quickly or more slowly than another baby. If you are concerned about your baby's progress, discuss it with your healthcare provider. Also see page viii.

Car-Seat Dilemma?

Parents know they shouldn't turn baby's car seat around until he's 1 year old and weighs at least 20 pounds. However, if your child reaches this weight limit well before his first birthday, you may be at a loss as to what to do. The best solution is to switch to a convertible seat that holds a child up to 30 pounds. Keep it in the rear-facing position.

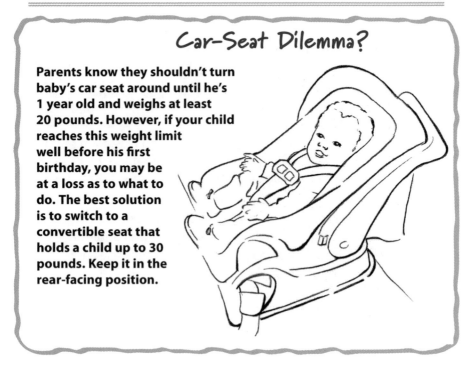

What's Happening This 44th Week?

Play It Safe in Sand

Lots of infectious organisms live and thrive in sandy areas. Some of these include staph, strep and pinworms. These organisms are more prevalent at beaches where wastewater collects near the shoreline. A playground sandbox can also be suspect because cats may use them for litter boxes.

Before you put baby down in the sand, make sure any cuts are bandaged. When he's finished playing in the sand, bathe him thoroughly, especially his hands. If he gets a cut or scrape while playing, wash the area with soap and water, apply antibacterial ointment and bandage.

Making Friends

It's good idea for baby to start interacting with other children, if he hasn't already. If he's not in day care and doesn't have siblings, get him together with a companion of the same age on a regular basis. Two or three times a week is fine. Get together with other parents in your neighborhood or church, or join a play group in the area.

The social interaction your baby has with another baby is different from his interactions with you and other family members, but equally beneficial. Adults usually direct the interaction. Babies often alternate who directs the action. Don't expect babies to "play" together. At this age, they often engage in *parallel play*. This means they play next to each other but do not play together.

If Baby Pulls His Ears

You may notice your baby pulling at his ears. This can occur when he starts to cut his first molars. If he is teething, he may run a low-grade fever. His symptoms should respond to acetaminophen or ibuprofen.

If he runs a higher fever, has obvious pain in his ears and he doesn't feel better when you give him acetaminophen or ibuprofen, he may have an ear infection. Don't ignore these symptoms. Call your pediatrician.

When Your Baby Points at Things

If your baby points at things, it's one way of speaking without words. When a child points, an adult usually responds! You probably name (label) or describe what he's pointing at.

When your baby points, he may be asking you to provide verbal labels to things in his world. His pointing also shows you some of the things that attract his attention.

Asthma

What it is. Asthma sufferers experience recurrent attacks of difficulty breathing with wheezing and shortness of breath. Asthma can occur at almost any age, with the exception of newborn infants. Most cases develop during childhood. Symptoms include

- tightness in the chest
- shortness of breath
- wheezing noise with breathing
- coughing spells, often at night
- coughing or wheezing after activity
- rapid, shallow breathing
- difficulty catching a breath

What to do. If your child suffers from asthma, try to eliminate allergens and irritants in the house. When baby has an attack, hold him upright, in a semisitting position, until he breathes easier.

When to call the doctor. Call the doctor if your baby has symptoms of asthma and has not been diagnosed. Call if any of the following symptoms develop:

- skin color becomes bluish
- baby is exhausted
- he has problems with breathing
- inability to cry

After diagnosis, your baby's doctor may prescribe expectorants to loosen sputum, a bronchodilator to open air passages or cortisone medications by nebulizer. Emergency-room care and hospitalization may be necessary for severe attacks.

Pinworms

What they are. Pinworms, also called *enterobiasis* and *threadworms,* are parasites that cause infection in the intestines and rectum. Infection is transferred by hand-to-hand contact or hand-to-mouth contact with the tiny eggs of the pinworm. Eggs may also be inhaled or swallowed when they float in the air.

Pinworms can occur at any age but are most common in school-age children. Symptoms include

- skin irritation at the anus, especially during sleep
- painful itching around the anus, especially during sleep
- restlessness
- poor appetite

What to do. If you believe your child might have pinworms, wash your hands carefully after changing his diapers and using the toilet. Wash your hands thoroughly before preparing meals. Keep your infant from playing with his genitals. Don't let him scratch his anal area when he's not diapered.

Call the doctor. Call the doctor if your baby has been exposed to pinworms at day care or by older siblings. If your baby has pinworms, your doctor will prescribe an antiworm medication. Pinworms are usually curable in one treatment. All family members should be treated along with baby. Recurrence is common.

If worms reappear soon after treatment, they usually represent a new infection, not a treatment failure. Call your pediatrician. Retreatment may be necessary.

Tear-Duct Infection

What it is. The opening to a tear duct is blocked or infected. This condition is sometimes called a *tear-duct blockage.* Infection can occur at any age but is most common in children. An inherited tear-duct blockage usually appears in infants between 3 and 12 weeks of age. Symptoms of a blocked tear duct include

- tearing or watering of one or both eyes
- drainage of mucus or pus from the eye
- pain, redness or swelling around the eye
- redness of the white of the eye surrounding the tear duct

What to do. Some home treatments include massaging the tear duct twice a day with clean fingertips to open it. Place warm soaks on the eye to relieve pain and to open an eye sticky from discharge.

When to call the doctor. Call the doctor if your baby has symptoms of tear-duct infection or blockage. If he runs a fever or symptoms don't improve, let your pediatrician know. If baby's vision is affected, notify your doctor immediately.

Your doctor may prescribe oral or topical antibiotics for the infection. In extreme cases, surgery to dilate and to probe the tear-duct canal is necessary.

Toys and Play This 44th Week

Scoopy Scoops

Your kitchen drawer and cabinet may provide the best selection of scoops for this game. Gather plastic, metal or wood scoops of various sizes and shapes. You might choose a coffee scoop, various-sized measuring cups, various-sized measuring spoons, plastic teaspoons and some serving spoons.

Place baby on the floor in front of a pan or bowl filled with cotton balls. Place another pan or bowl next to it. Show how to scoop the cotton balls into the second pan with one of the scoops. Encourage baby to scoop cotton balls from one pan into the other, back and forth.

If you feel adventurous, use cornmeal, sand, water or dry beans for scooping. When using various materials, watch baby carefully so he doesn't put these objects in his mouth, nose or ears.

Recognizing Voices

Does baby recognize familiar voices? Test his ability by having different family members record a short message on a tape. Play the tape for baby and watch him closely. He may look up in recognition when he can identify a voice.

Stop the tape after every message. Identify the speaker to baby. Point out anything that's different. For example, you might say, "Uncle John makes funny noises!"

Hide-and-Seek, Baby Style

This is a "training-wheels" version of the more advanced hide-and-seek game baby will play when he gets older. He'll enjoy the fun of finding you. Crouch beside a chair, out of baby's sight. Call his name as you peek around the corner at him. Let him see you.

Duck away so he can't see you, and call to him again. Keep talking and calling to him as he crawls toward you. When he finds you, laugh and say, "Baby found me!" Give him a hug and a kiss. And play the game again.

The Smelling Game

Ever wonder what to do with all those baby-food jars? This activity makes good use of them! Wrap empty jars in foil, leaving an opening at the top, and poke holes in each lid. Put something fragrant in each jar, and replace the lid, screwing it on tightly. Let baby sniff the different scents in each jar. After he's smelled what's inside, show him the contents. Fragrant things you might put in a jar include orange rind, banana peel, flower petals, grass clippings and cotton balls soaked in shampoo or eucalyptus oil.

Week 45

How Big Is Your Baby This 45th Week?

Baby weighs 21 pounds and is 29-1/4 inches long this week.

Baby Care and Equipment

Cruising Clothes

The "cruise wear" we mean isn't resort wear for the high seas—it is comfortable clothing for an active baby in your home.

> If you have to use the footed outfits you already own, put nonskid socks over footed outfits. It's a little bulky, but it does the trick.

Baby needs to wear the right clothes for her safety and protection. Now that she's up and moving, some of the clothes she has been wearing probably need to be put away.

Store outfits with feet, except for bedtime or going out (where she won't be cruising anyway). Keep her feet bare, when possible. If you need to keep her feet covered because it is cold or for another reason, choose socks with rubber treads on the soles. Plain socks may be too slippery.

About Public Changing Tables

Most of the time, public changing tables are not clean. Public restrooms were tested for cleanliness in one recent study. Researchers found that women's restrooms had twice as many germs as men's restrooms. The cleanest rest areas were found in hospitals and fast-food restaurants. The worst were in airport bathrooms. These surfaces are often contaminated with *E. coli* from previous diaper changes.

How to protect baby. To protect baby and you from *E. coli*, always clean a changing surface with a wipe that contains disinfectant before laying baby on it. After you've wiped the surface, put down your own pad or blanket on the changing table. If you don't have one, put down several paper towels before placing baby on the table.

If there's no changing table, look for a toilet-seat lid that you can close. This is often one of the cleanest places in a public restroom. If baby is small enough, close the lid, clean it with a disinfecting wipe, then cover with your pad or paper towels.

The dirtiest places in a bathroom are the floor and around the sink. Never place baby on the floor to change her! You might not want to put your diaper bag down there, either.

Wash hands after changing baby. When you've finished, wash your hands with soap and water. This helps prevent taking germs with you when you leave.

Foods Baby Is Eating Now

Your baby is eating lots of different things by now. She probably eats infant cereal or other grain foods at all three meals. She is eating soft fruits at two meals a day and soft veggies at two meals a day. Baby isn't eating much meat—about 1 to 2 tablespoons at two meals a day. See the chart below for typical portion sizes. Baby is still taking in 6 to 8 ounces of breast milk or formula 3 or 4 times a day.

What Baby Eats at 11 Months

These are typical serving sizes for an average 11-month-old baby.

Food	Portion	Number of mealtimes/day
Cereals, grains	¼ cup cereal, ¼ cup cooked pasta; ¼ slice bread	3 meals a day
Soft fruits	2 to 3 tablespoons	2 meals a day
Soft vegetables	2 to 3 tablespoons	2 meals a day
Meats	1 to 2 tablespoons	2 meals a day

You might prepare nutritious foods in combination for baby. Good choices include macaroni and cheese, a casserole of meat, rice and a vegetable or jarred combination of baby foods. Leave out spices when you cook. At this age, baby may not like them.

Milestones This 45th Week

What a Personality!

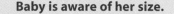

Your baby's personality is evident now. She knows what she likes and doesn't like. She displays a sense of humor. She has a growing sense of self, too. She knows she is separate and distinct from those around her. She is aware of her size.

> **Baby is aware of her size.**

You may notice your baby has better control of her emotions. She may use emotions to persuade those around her to do what she wants. If you take away her toy, she may protest—loudly! When you encounter such displays, remain calm. It's natural for baby to learn that she cannot always have her own way.

Her Vocabulary and Understanding of Words

Baby recognizes words as symbols for objects. When you name something, she may point to it. Or she may point to where she expects to find it. For example, if you say "juice" and she does not see it, she may point to the refrigerator if she knows you keep it there.

Use correct terms, not baby names. She is ready to start learning names for her body parts. When referring to body parts, some people think it is cute to give them made-up names. However, use the correct terms. Refer to a boy's penis as "penis," instead of "bobo" or some other term, from the beginning, for example.

Name objects often. The more words your baby hears, the better her association with words and objects will be. Let her hear the terms often. If you say "spoon" every time you feed her with her spoon, she'll soon make the connection between the spoon and its name.

Practice makes perfect. Your baby continues her patter in baby language. You may be amused by how closely it resembles actual speech patterns. She's practicing the rhythm and intonation of language.

Learning New Tasks Continues

Baby may work very hard to learn a new task. She needs practice to learn to solve a problem on her own. It takes a great deal of repetition, and time, to master a new skill.

She likes to imitate your actions, facial gestures, speech intonations. They all help her process information and continue learning.

> At 11 months of age, your baby may understand the word "No." She also may ignore you completely when you tell her "No"!

A comfort object may help relieve baby's anxiety.

Separation Anxiety and Stranger Anxiety

Your baby may still want you or her other parent to be nearby when she's playing. Separation anxiety may continue to be an issue, especially when you are in an unfamiliar place. She will want and will need you to be close. Baby may react more strongly to strangers when she is away from home, too.

At home, she is more relaxed. Even though you may have thought she had outgrown both of these anxieties, they may reappear around this time. It's normal, so don't be too concerned.

Note: See also the box below, *Milestones This Week*.

Milestones This 45th Week

Changes in Baby You May See Now

Physical Development
• cruises furniture

Senses and Reflexes
• picks up extremely small objects
• holds cup and drinks from it

Mental Development
• recognizes words as symbols for objects–hears "airplane" and points to sky; knows cow "moos"
• can imitate speech rhythms, inflections and facial expressions

Social Development
• does not always cooperate
• withdraws from strangers

Every baby is an individual, and your baby may do some of these things more quickly or more slowly than another baby. If you are concerned about your baby's progress, discuss it with your healthcare provider. Also see page viii.

What's Happening This 45th Week?

Baby's Mobility

Your baby may be an expert cruiser by now. Holding on to furniture for support, she takes little sideways steps to move. Cruising is a safe way for her to practice balance and to strengthen muscles she needs for walking. You may notice she forgets to hold on at times.

> While baby is in the cruising mode, keep her play area free of slippery rugs to help prevent mishaps.

Be sure furniture is stable. When your baby becomes a regular cruiser, be sure the objects she uses for support are not easily pushed or moved. If baby uses the furniture for cruising, pad it or use furniture guards to protect her from the occasional spills she's sure to take.

When Baby Is Tongue-Tied

A baby who is born with an unusually short flap of skin beneath the tongue can't move her tongue very well. When the skin flap, called the *frenulum*, is very short, it pulls the tongue toward the floor of the mouth. When a child with this condition sticks out her tongue, the frenulum pulls on the tongue from below, creating a deep "V" in its center. In layman's terms, this condition is called *tongue-tied.*

Usually by the end of the first year, the frenulum stretches to its normal length and doesn't interfere with baby's speech. However, if it remains short, a child may have trouble making certain sounds. She may have difficulty swallowing.

Many doctors and speech specialists recommend a minor surgical procedure to cut a tight frenulum. If you notice symptoms your baby is tongue-tied, discuss it with your pediatrician. He or she will evaluate your child. You may be referred to a pediatric ear, nose and throat specialist for further evaluation.

Various Developmental Stages

All babies are individuals. You may notice your baby does something that passes over or skips a step in the developmental phases discussed in this book. You may worry that baby isn't developing properly when this happens. For example, some parents worry when a child doesn't go through a crawling phase but goes straight to walking.

Be reassured: If a baby skips one stage and enters another at the appropriate age, there's little cause for concern. For example, if a baby goes straight to walking at the normal age, without going through a crawling phase, it does not indicate a problem. Occasionally a child with developmental delay doesn't go through the crawling stage. In these situations, not crawling is an early *symptom* of delays. It is not a cause of delays.

Babies usually begin walking at between 9 and 15 months of age. If a baby walks without crawling first, she may just be an early walker.

Prickly Heat

What it is. Prickly heat occurs when sweat pores are blocked and perspiration escapes into the skin because baby is overheated or overdressed. It can occur any time of year. Tiny blisters may form, which you may not see. As perspiration goes deeper into the skin, the area becomes painful, accompanied by intense itching.

Prickly heat can occur at any age and is common in infants. Symptoms include

- itchy rash
- clusters of small, fluid-filled skin blisters, which may come and go within a matter of hours
- a red rash without blisters in areas of heavy perspiration, such as the neck, shoulders, back of the head and in skin folds

What to do. When you notice these changes on your baby's skin, expose the affected area to air as much as possible. Change diapers as soon as they are wet. Dress baby in cotton clothing or other cool, breathable attire. Give baby frequent, cool baths. Apply lubricating ointment or cream to the area 4 to 6 times a day.

When to call the doctor. Call the doctor if the rash doesn't improve in 5 to 7 days, despite home care. He or she may suggest a nonprescription steroid cream, which should be applied 2 to 3 times a day.

Blood Poisoning

What it is. Blood poisoning, also called *septicemia,* occurs when bacteria enter the bloodstream and cause an infection. Blood poisoning in most cases follows a localized infection in some other part of the body, such as the appendix, a tooth, a sinus infection, a urinary-tract infection, ear infections or infected wounds or burns. Symptoms include

- high fever, with rapid temperature rise
- rapid, pounding heartbeat
- chills
- warm, flushed skin
- lethargy
- abscesses

What to do. At home, you may be advised to offer acetaminophen or ibuprofen for fever or discomfort. Offer your child lots of fluids.

When to call the doctor. Call the doctor if baby develops a high fever suddenly or has signs of infection anywhere in the body, such as fever, redness or discharge.

Your doctor may prescribe antibiotics to fight infection. Blood cultures are done to identify the bacteria in the bloodstream. A child is hospitalized in severe cases for intravenous antibiotic therapy and IV hydration.

Toys and Play This 45th Week

Continue to select age-appropriate toys. Toys for a particular age group suit a child's intellectual capacity. They are safer for her, too. You may decide to give her objects that are not strictly toys—but she'll love them anyway. Plastic containers that nest inside one another, measuring cups or spoons, an old pan and a wooden spoon—all continue to be stimulating toys for your little one.

Have fun with sound. Put different objects into securely closed containers. Dried beans, uncooked rice or pasta, and buttons are good choices. Let baby shake them as you point out the different sound each makes. Don't leave baby alone with this toy. Check containers frequently to be sure the lids remain securely fastened.

Baby's Own Photo Album
Put pictures of family members doing something they enjoy in a small photo album. Write a simple sentence under each photo to describe what's happening. Look at the album with baby, and talk about the pictures.

Playing in the Sand

Bury your hand in sand while baby watches you. Ask her, "Where's my hand?" She may pat the sand on top of your hand or dig for it. When she finds your hand, hold it up and exclaim, "See, there's my hand! You found it!"

Next, cover your baby's hand with the sand. Talk about how the sand feels. Ask baby where her hand is. To vary the game, together bury a toy. Then ask her to find it. If she has difficulty, help her.

Big, Bigger, Biggest

Use those ever-popular baby toys, nesting plastic measuring cups and plastic measuring spoons, for a new purpose this week—to help baby learn the concept of size. Aluminum bowls that fit inside one another work well, too. Show baby how to nest the bowls, one within the next. As you nest them, talk about their sizes: small, smaller, smallest. Then reverse the game: As you remove the nested bowls or spoons, point out the concept of big, bigger, biggest.

Bathtub Basketball

To help your baby's eye-hand coordination develop, gather a few plastic balls and a plastic container at bath time. While baby sits in the water, show her how to drop a ball into the floating container. Then let her try. This activity helps her develop coordination.

Week 46

How Big Is Your Baby This 46th Week?

Baby weighs 21-1/4 pounds and is 29-1/4 inches long this week.

Baby Care and Equipment

When Baby Is a Picky Eater

A picky eater refuses certain foods, eats only a couple of foods or won't eat at all. Some babies are picky eaters from an early age. These tips may help you deal more effectively with the situation of picky eating. Use what works best for you and your baby.

Give baby enough time to eat. Some babies need more time to eat than you might expect. Try setting aside an extra 15 minutes for mealtime.

Feed him solids first. If he drinks a lot, he may not have room in his tummy for the food. Offer solid foods first, then breastfeed or give him a bottle.

Don't allow too much snacking during the day. If you give your baby snacks whenever he's hungry, he won't want to eat at mealtime. Schedule snacks for certain times. Stick with the schedule.

Keep introducing new foods. Your baby may need time to adjust to a new food, a new taste or a new texture. Wait a few days after he refuses something, then try again. You may have to offer some foods a dozen times before baby will eat them.

Give him the same foods, if he'll eat them. If baby wants to eat only macaroni and cheese for a while, let him! He will tire of it eventually. It's OK to take this approach for a few weeks. It won't hurt him.

417

Set a good example. When you eat a healthful diet and a good selection of foods, so will your baby.

Offer Foods with High Nutritional Value

Some foods offer baby more nutrition than others. If he doesn't get all of his nutrition in one sitting because he's a picky eater, these foods help him "catch up" and get more of the nutrition he needs each day. And most babies like these foods. Offer *yogurt*, which is rich in calcium, protein and vitamin B12. *Egg yolks* contain protein, riboflavin and vitamins A, B12 and K. *Cereals* are loaded with vitamins, zinc, iron, magnesium and folate. *Beans and lentils* are a high-protein source of iron and folate. *Tomatoes* are rich in vitamin C.

If you don't like it, keep it to yourself! We know that certain foods—broccoli, for example—taste great to some and awful to others. Or there may be some foods you just can't stand. Keep your attitudes to yourself. Let your baby try different foods and decide for himself.

His appetite may be small. Not all babies have large appetites. Don't expect yours to eat a lot or to eat often. Let him set some of his eating boundaries. Pushing too much food on him when he can't eat may cause problems. Your baby's stomach is only the size of his fist—it doesn't hold as much as you might expect.

Don't make mealtimes a battle. Conflicts over food can cause lots of problems, now and later. Your behavior may teach him that mealtime battles are a way of gaining your attention. If baby isn't eating what you think he should be eating or all that you think he should, just ignore the situation when you can. Let baby decide what to eat and how much he wants.

Drinking "Old Formula"

Now that baby is moving around and can hold things while he's doing so, you're bound to run across new and perplexing parenting situations. Some parents are concerned about baby drinking old formula—formula that is not fresh. Generally this happens when baby finds a bottle of formula he left someplace and drinks it. Can it hurt him? Probably not, especially if the formula has only been left out a short while.

Over-the-Counter Medication Safety

Most parents use over-the-counter (OTC) medications to help their child feel better when he has a minor ailment. Use these medications as carefully as you would prescription medications! The list below covers some of the most important issues and cautions to keep in mind if you use OTC medications with your baby.

- Ask your pediatrician and pharmacist for advice about OTC medications that are OK to use with your baby.

- Use OTC medications only when your baby is sick or has a condition that requires them (such as allergies).

- Don't use OTCs too much during the day. Many physical symptoms help the body take care of illness. For example, coughing helps clear the lungs.

- Take your baby to the doctor if symptoms don't improve after the recommended time of use found in medication instructions.

- Use a product for its intended purpose only.

- If symptoms worsen while your child is taking a medication, contact your pediatrician.

- If you think your baby needs more than one type of over-the-counter medication (cough syrup and a fever reducer, for example), check with your pharmacist or your pediatrician before giving them to him.

- If your baby is taking a prescription medication, contact your pharmacist or pediatrician before giving him an OTC medication in addition.

- Select "baby" products when possible. Don't use adult-strength medications unless advised to do so by your pediatrician.

- Follow package directions exactly as written for how often and how much to give of each medication.

- When giving any medication, use the proper utensil for measuring. Choose a medication syringe, a dropper, a medicine cup or a dosing spoon. Giving too little of the medication won't help baby much. An overdose could be dangerous.

- Don't give your baby a medication longer than the recommended period.

- Don't use multisymptom medications, such as cold remedies, if your baby doesn't have all the symptoms.

- Be alert for side effects.

- Some OTC baby medications taste good. Keep them out of baby's reach.

If you don't know how long the formula been sitting unrefrigerated, however, you might be concerned about *salmonella* (see page 315). Symptoms of salmonella poisoning usually surface between 2 and 72 hours after baby drinks the formula if they are going to appear. Watch for diarrhea or vomiting, and contact your pediatrician if they occur.

Milestones This 46th Week

Physical Accomplishments

Your baby has accomplished quite a lot in these first 10 months. He may stand alone and turn now. He can climb down backward off a chair without falling. When he stands up, he may do it his own way. He may kneel and push up, or he may squat, then stand.

He still explores and experiments with everything he can. Nearly every object he comes in contact with (or so it seems!) must be touched, shaken, banged, pulled or pushed.

When he masters a task, he may practice it over and over and over. He loves turning switches off and on. He studies anything that moves with great concentration.

It's amusing to see him imitate household chores and tasks. He may imitate actions that deal with self-care. He may brush his teeth, wash his face or comb his hair.

He still needs at least one good rest a day, even though he might not go to sleep. The best time may be right after lunch, although a little later may make the evening hours more enjoyable for everyone in the family.

Water play continues to delight baby.

His Language Skills Increase

Baby understands much about his language now. He knows he can make his wants known with language. His vocabulary is growing. He follows verbal directions after a demonstration. He will "give dolly a hug" after he sees you do it.

> When baby takes a tumble, comment with "Uh-oh" instead of "Oh no!" If you don't show alarm, baby is more apt to take tumbles in stride.

His babbling is more intelligible. He may use a few meaningful words. Or he may repeat a few favorite words quite often. You may recognize some words, such as "dada," "kitty," "mama" or "book." Or he may offer substitutes that sound close. For example, he may say "uce" for *juice* or "gah" for *dog*. He is becoming more of a participant in his world now.

Baby Play

When baby is playing in the house, but not close to you, keep an ear open to what he may be doing. At this age, a long period of quiet may mean he's into something he shouldn't be. Watch him constantly—or at least know where he is and what he's doing at all times.

> A baby learns respect and various social attitudes by watching his parents.

Undressing as a game. A favorite of some babies this age is undressing. He may do it as often as he can. He'll take off his shoes and socks. He'll also take off every stitch of clothes, including his diaper, if he's able. If he revels in this game, put his clothes on backward for a while, to slow him down, until the novelty of undressing wears off.

More complicated interests. The games he likes to play are more sophisticated now. He may try to sing with you. He may spend more time with books and other things you can study together. He likes to look inside things, so curiosity cubes are good choices.

Baby's Cooperation

Baby will cooperate very well sometimes . . . and not so well at other times. One day he may hold out his arms and legs to help you dress him. The next day, he may be totally uncooperative.

> When young children play together, they often take turns being leader. When adults play with babies, they usually direct the play.

Note: See also the box on page 422, *Milestones This Week.*

Milestones This 46th Week

Changes in Baby You May See Now

Physical Development
- may lean over while standing against support
- squats and stoops

Senses and Reflexes
- holds out arm or leg to help you dress him
- lifts lid from boxes

Mental Development
- speaks a few intelligible words

Social Development
- asserts himself among siblings

Every baby is an individual, and your baby may do some of these things more quickly or more slowly than another baby. If you are concerned about your baby's progress, discuss it with your healthcare provider. Also see page viii.

What's Happening This 46th Week?

Giving Twins Attention

When both babies want you, what do you do? How do you tend to each one individually? The tips below can help you give each baby the time and attention he needs. In time, each baby will realize you will meet his needs, even if you can't do it right away.

Alternate attention. One of the best ways to give attention equally is to alternate. Take care of one baby first, then take care of the other baby first the next time.

One baby may need you more. One baby may need you more than the other, perhaps for a significant amount of time. Then the other baby will be more needy for a while. Do the best you can and don't feel guilty putting your attention where it is most needed. The amount of time you spend with each baby usually works out equally in the end.

Involve both babies. You don't have to ignore one baby to take care of the other. Include both in your conversation while taking care of one baby. As best you can, maintain eye contact with the baby who is not being tended to at the moment. Keep him close, if possible.

Teach patience. If one baby is always impatient and wants to be first, be sure you let the other be first sometimes. Tell the impatient one he must wait his turn. This helps the second baby, too. He won't feel second-best.

When Baby Is "Hot-Blooded"

Some babies won't sleep under the covers. Some peel off their clothes at every opportunity. Some refuse to wear sweaters or coats. This is nothing to worry about in most cases. Some children have a higher body temperature, probably due to a higher metabolism. They burn calories more quickly. Often they are more active than other children. They just feel hotter.

When possible, let your hot-blooded baby set his own comfort level. Don't put too many clothes on him. Dress him in layers of clothing that you can peel off during the day if he gets too warm. Dress him comfortably for bed. If he's perspiring a lot at night, dress him in lighter pajamas.

If your baby is overweight, he is more likely to retain heat. He needs to wear cooler clothes and to perspire more to feel comfortable. Overheating may also indicate other health problems, such as an overactive thyroid gland. If you are concerned, discuss it with your pediatrician.

Giardiasis

What it is. Giardiasis is an infection that causes inflammation of the bowel. It is caused by a parasite found in contaminated food or contaminated water. It can occur at any age but is most common in older infants and children. Symptoms include

- diarrhea
- fever
- nausea
- weakness
- flatulence
- belching
- vomiting
- abdominal cramps
- greasy, bad-smelling stools

Prevention is best "treatment." Prevention of this problem is your best bet. Don't let your baby drink water that could be contaminated. Only drink water from normal water supplies. If you don't know if water is safe, boil it for 5 minutes.

What to do. For nausea, vomiting and diarrhea associated with Giardiasis, give your baby lots of fluids to avoid dehydration. Don't use over-the-counter medications for diarrhea or nausea and vomiting unless your pediatrician advises it.

Call the doctor. Call the doctor if your baby has symptoms of Giardiasis. It's important to let your pediatrician know if baby has a fever, severe abdominal pain or is dehydrated.

Your doctor may order laboratory stool studies to detect parasites. Usually tests are done three times before being considered negative. An antiparasitic drug, such as metronidazole, furazolidone or quinacrine, may be prescribed. These drugs are very effective. In severe cases, when baby suffers from dehydration or malabsorption, hospitalization may be necessary for IV hydration and nutrition supplementation.

Nose Injury

A nose injury can occur from a fall, a bump or an accident, such as someone throwing something that hits baby in the face. Younger children and infants have only cartilage in their noses, which does not break but can be badly bruised. Actual fractures usually occur in older children (more than 8 years old). Injury can also occur in young children and toddlers if they put an object in their nose. Symptoms of a nose injury include

- pain in the nose
- nosebleed
- swollen, discolored nose
- inability to breath through the nose
- crooked or misshapen nose

What to do. Keep small objects away from your baby so he can't put them up his nose. If he does stick something in his nose, remove it if you can reach it. If injury occurs from a fall or other accident, apply ice packs to the nose immediately to minimize swelling. Control bleeding by pinching the nostrils tightly together. See the discussion of Nosebleed in Week 48. Give him ibuprofen or acetaminophen for discomfort, if he needs it.

When to call the doctor. If your baby has difficulty breathing or if there are changes in your baby's level of consciousness, call your pediatrician immediately. Call the doctor if a foreign object is lodged in your baby's nose. It's better for a professional to remove it. If baby has a nosebleed, your doctor will want to know if it is heavy or cannot be stopped.

Your doctor may order X-rays of the nose. If an object is stuck in baby's nose and it cannot be removed easily, removal under anesthesia may be necessary. Minor fractures and injuries usually heal in about 4 weeks. Surgery is sometimes necessary to repair severe fractures in older children.

Toys and Play This 46th Week

Baby is interested in many kinds of toys. If you're thinking about a good birthday present for his first birthday, you might shop for a stable riding toy.

Repeating Words

Your baby's vocabulary is increasing. Keep talking to him! To help expand his vocabulary, point out all kinds of things around you—people, pictures, objects, parts of his body or yours—and repeat the name of each several times.

To make a game of it, ask him, "Where is my eye?"—or the cup, the dog, the book or the dolly. If he points to it, praise him. If he doesn't, point it out to him.

Let's Dance!

To help develop baby's sense of anticipation, dance with him. While you're dancing together, have someone else start and stop the music. He'll enjoy the fun of moving with you, and starting and stopping to the music.

"Finger Painting," Baby Style

Dress baby in a diaper, and put on his bib. Place him in his highchair, and put the tray in place. Put a small amount of puréed fruit or some mixed cereal on the tray. Let him "finger paint" with it. You may need to show him what to do to get him started.

Changes Can Be Fun

Add interest to baby's life now by making a few simple changes in his environment. Put his highchair in a new place. Move his crib to another position. Use a new crib sheet with an interesting pattern. Baby may find these changes extremely interesting.

Take baby on a "smelling tour" of the house. Smell things you normally wouldn't. Smell the table, the TV set, a magazine and the telephone.

Making Some Noise

Place a metal pan or bowl on the floor. Place baby next to it, and give him things to drop into the pan. Consider using clothespins, wooden blocks and small plastic balls. Show him how to drop the objects into the pan, and listen to the sounds they make. Stay with him while he plays this game; don't let him put these small objects in his mouth.

*On a nice day, give baby a
"smelling tour" outside.*

How Big Is Your Baby This 47th Week?

Baby weighs 21-1/4 pounds and is 29-1/2 inches long this week.

Baby Care and Equipment

Get to Know Baby's Day-Care Provider

If your baby is in day care, think about stopping in a couple of times each week and talking to the person (or people) who take care of her. Don't just drop off baby and pick her up later. By building a connection with the person who cares for your baby, you'll find it becomes easier to ask questions about how your baby is doing. It also makes it easier for your day-care provider to talk to you about concerns he or she may have. You both have the same goals—making sure your little one is growing and developing as she should.

Stools May Indicate What Baby Has Eaten

Baby is eating many new foods these days. Until her first molars come in, she can't chew very well. As a result, some of what you feed her now may turn up in her stool looking much as it did when she ate it.

Don't be alarmed by this. Nothing is wrong with her digestion. Until her digestive system matures, her stools will reflect the various foods she eats. If you feed her carrots, spinach or beets, you may see yellow, green or red stools. When she eats oat-circle cereal pieces, her stools may be a sandy color. Cucumber and tomato seeds and unchewed raisins may show up in her bowel movements.

427

You can make sure the foods you give your baby are easy to digest. Chop, mash, purée, dice and blend foods she may have difficulty eating otherwise. These prepared foods are also safer for her to eat.

When Baby Refuses Medicine

Medications, especially liquids, don't always taste very good. You can usually reason with older children (or bribe them) to get them to take something they need that tastes bad. With a baby, reasoning doesn't help. When the situation arises, you need to know how to get the medicine inside her, especially if you're by yourself and don't have an extra pair of hands.

Liquid medications. To give liquid medicine to a baby, fill the dropper or syringe with the correct amount of medicine first. Place it next to you on a table. Put baby in your lap, facing you, with her legs on either side of your body. Lean her back on your knees so her head is slightly lower than her body.

Insert the medicine holder between her cheek and her gums (or teeth, if she has any). Give her a little of the medication while gently blowing in her face. Blowing results in a reflex that causes her to swallow. Continue blowing gently while you give her the remainder of the medication.

With a very small baby, use a device that has a nipple similar to a pacifier. Medicine is put in the dosing reservoir, and the nipple is attached. Baby sucks the medicine as if she were drinking from a bottle.

Trust Baby to Eat What She Needs

Unless your baby is sick, trust her to eat what she needs. As long as you offer a variety of nutritious foods, she'll get the vitamins, minerals and calories to help her grow. The best measure of how she's doing is whether she's growing and thriving. If she's doing well, she's probably getting what she needs from the breast milk or formula you give her and from the food she eats.

Milestones This 47th Week

Temper Tantrums

By 11 months, your baby may have occasional temper tantrums. It's one way she expresses frustration. When she has a tantrum, keep your cool. You need to be in control, and your baby needs you to be, too. Walk away from her, or put her in her room when she starts a tantrum. Do it calmly, with no conversation. Without an audience, her tantrum may end quickly.

She Understands "Good" and "Bad" Behavior

Your baby is beginning to understand the differences between "good" and "bad" behavior. Her conscience is beginning to form. She will call attention to her good behavior. She seeks your approval and may repeat an activity if she is praised for it.

She tries to avoid your disapproval. If she feels guilty, she may hide from you.

Try not to be after baby constantly about what she's doing. Let her have time to play or to explore safely by herself, or she'll stop listening to you. If you must correct her behavior, do so when she does something that truly needs correction. These situations involve her own safety and the safety and rights of others.

If She's Very Active

If she's very active, your baby may be climbing out of her crib or playpen by now. Check every so often to make sure she can't climb out of these confining spaces—or to make sure that she can climb out *safely*. If you are fine with baby getting out of her crib, leave one side down so she can do so easily and safely. If you don't want her getting out, use a mesh cover (made for this purpose) to cover the top of the crib or playpen so she remains confined. Another tactic is to keep her out of her playpen and crib as much as possible. Set up a safe place that you've babyproofed for her to play by herself.

Baby's Activities

Baby can bend over halfway and peer through her spread legs. It's fun to view the world upside down!

She likes to put small objects into a large container, and she likes to stack blocks too. She may arrange objects by color and size. These activities involve problem solving and demonstrate her developing skills in this area.

Your baby may be able to stand by pushing up from the floor with her hands. She may take some tentative steps. She gets frustrated sometimes when she can't do what she sets out to do.

Your baby may have a favorite stuffed animal now.

A Favorite Stuffed Animal

At this age, many babies choose one or two stuffed animals as favorites. Experts believe they serve as a comfortable way for baby to transition from waking to sleeping. A stuffed animal could also be a substitute for a parent. You may notice her playing "parent" with her stuffed toys.

Her Physical Growth Slows

Around this time, baby's physical growth slows down. She gains weight at a slower rate. One reason for this is her activity level. As her activities increase, she burns more calories.

The range of foods baby eats may be limited, too. She may eat only one good meal a day. She may refuse a lot of foods. However, her digestive system is maturing, so her body is utilizing the food more efficiently. That's a plus. Note: See also the box below, *Milestones This Week.*

What's Happening This 47th Week?

Reasons to Wake the Doctor

Parents may hesitate to call their pediatrician in the middle of the night. No one wants to be a bother. However, your physician wants you to call about certain problems, no matter what time it is! If your baby experiences any of the signs or symptoms listed in the box on the opposite page, call your doctor immediately or go to the nearest emergency-medicine facility.

Milestones This 47th Week

Changes in Baby You May See Now

Physical Development
• lowers herself from a standing position without falling

Senses and Reflexes
• deliberately places objects
• may untie shoelaces

Mental Development
• may nest objects, such as boxes or cups

Social Development
• tries to avoid disapproval
• shows guilt

Every baby is an individual, and your baby may do some of these things more quickly or more slowly than another baby. If you are concerned about your baby's progress, discuss it with your healthcare provider. Also see page viii.

Reasons to Wake the Doctor

Signs of choking. Difficulty breathing, coughing for no apparent reason and/or turning blue around the lips can be signs of choking on an object. **Call 9-1-1,** and ask for an ambulance. Never do the Heimlich maneuver on a baby if she can cough, cry or make noise.

Breathing difficulty. If baby is breathing noisily or rapidly (more than one breath a second), it could be a sign of croup, asthma, bronchiolitis or pneumonia.

Severe lethargy or unresponsiveness. This could be caused by a serious reaction to a drug, or it may follow a seizure.

Change in skin color. Skin that has turned blue or gray may indicate baby is not getting enough oxygen. Blue skin may also indicate poisoning.

Convulsion or seizure. May be caused by fever or another medical problem.

Diarrhea in an infant under 3 months. In a baby this young, diarrhea can increase the risk of dehydration.

Severe vomiting. In addition to dehydration, severe or persistent vomiting can indicate poisoning. If the vomit contains blood or green bile, a serious problem may be the cause, such as a blocked intestine.

Baby cannot be comforted. If baby is crying incessantly and cannot be soothed, even after you've tried everything in your bag of tricks, it might indicate serious pain.

High fever. Any fever over 103F (39.4C) can mean a serious bacterial infection. Call the doctor if your baby, no matter what her age, has a temperature this high. If baby is younger than 3 months old, call if her temperature is 100.2F (37.8C) or higher. If baby is between 3 and 6 months of age, call if her temperature is 101F (38.3C) or higher.

Signs of dehydration. Dehydration can be a serious matter for baby. A dry mouth, sunken fontanelle, sunken eyes, little urine production and no tears can mean she needs fluid fast. In serious cases, fluids must be given intravenously in the hospital.

Tummy pain. If pain in the tummy seems to worsen when you press on it, especially on the right side, it could mean appendicitis. Baby may cry and put her hands near her tummy, if she can.

Purple or deep-red rash. If baby has a rash like this, press your fingers into it. If it doesn't fade when you press it, it could mean a serious bacterial infection.

Sudden groin pain in a boy. A tender testicle can cause groin pain. This can occur if the testicle is twisted. Surgery must be performed within 8 hours to save the testicle.

Signs of bacterial meningitis. When baby has a fever and a stiff neck, it can be serious. To test for a stiff neck, hold a toy she likes in front of her. While she's looking at it, lower it so she has to look down. If she can't bring her chin to her chest, she may have a stiff neck.

Serious fall. Call your pediatrician if a fall results in loss of consciousness or bleeding that cannot be stopped.

Begin Teaching Responsibility

You can begin teaching baby this important social concept now. By the end of her first year, your baby is beginning to understand cause and effect. She is beginning to realize that her actions have consequences.

Based on these understandings, how do you begin teaching responsibility? Try "baby" responsibilities. For example, ask her to give daddy the napkin when you hand one to her or to throw away a tissue in the garbage can. As she grows older, match tasks to her growing capabilities.

At 11 months, baby may be learning to feed herself with a spoon.

Self-Reliance

Teaching a child self-reliance is an important goal for most parents. You can reinforce your child's sense of self-reliance by giving her certain age-appropriate tasks. An appropriate task right now may be learning to feed herself with a spoon. As she grows, these tasks will change.

Make the tasks as easy as you can for now, and help her when necessary. She'll learn she can do things for herself. The older she gets, the less help she'll need from you.

Hyperthermia (Overheating)

What it is. A baby with hyperthermia creates more heat in her body than she can eliminate. Hyperthermia may be caused by external conditions or something happening within her body. Hyperthermia is most common in hot summer months. If your baby becomes hyperthermic, you will notice these symptoms:

- fever
- crankiness
- bright red cheeks
- loss of consciousness
- seizures

- weakness
- sunken eyes
- dry, hot skin
- rapid heartbeat
- lack of perspiration

Prevention. To help avoid the problem, limit outdoor activities in hot weather.

What to do. Give her lots of fluids. Dress baby in light, loose-fitting clothing. By increasing ventilation, you promote sweat evaporation, which cools her skin. Reduce baby's temperature by wiping her down with a cool, wet sponge or towel.

Call baby's doctor immediately if you see signs of dehydration or if baby loses consciousness. If your baby has a seizure, is weak and listless, feverish, cranky or doesn't respond to cooling off, contact your pediatrician. The condition can be serious.

Your pediatrician will probably suggest cool applications to the skin to help reduce baby's temperature. A tepid (cool) tub bath may also be suggested. Begin with warm water and gradually add cold water to it. This prevents chilling. The bath should last 20 to 30 minutes. Squeeze water over baby's back and chest. If these measures don't work, hospitalization to lower body temperature and to provide intravenous replacement fluids may be required.

Hay Fever

What it is. Hay fever is the body's allergic response to substances in the air. The throat, mouth, nose, upper air passages and lungs are involved. It can occur at any age. Symptoms of hay fever include

- watery discharge from the eyes
- itchy eyes
- sneezing
- headache
- stuffy nose
- clear nasal discharge
- sneezing
- postnasal drip, which can cause bad breath
- coughing from postnasal drip

What to do. Eliminate as many allergens (things that cause allergic reactions) as you can from baby's environment. Clean your home thoroughly to remove allergens and to keep dust at a minimum. Do this regularly. Change furnace filters often. Install an air-purification unit in your home. Treat symptoms as your doctor advises. *Don't* give baby over-the-counter allergy medications without your doctor's advice.

When to call the doctor. Call the doctor if your baby has severe hay fever symptoms. If she displays symptoms of infection, such as fever or a thick, discolored nasal discharge, call your pediatrician. It's possible for a sinus infection to complicate an allergy.

Your doctor may prescribe antihistamines or decongestants to reduce the body's allergic response. Medication can relieve symptoms, but they don't cure the hay fever. If your baby suffers from severe allergies, your pediatrician may refer you to an allergy specialist.

Toys and Play This 47th Week

> It may be fun to let baby play in mud and water, or with clay. But watch her reactions. Some babies don't like playing in gooey messes. Other babies love it!

When you read to your baby and show her storybook pictures, you help her develop an understanding of two dimensions. When you point to objects, people and animals in books, repeat over and over again what they are. You are teaching her to connect the two-dimensional pictures she sees in a book with the three-dimensional objects she knows in her world.

Baby's First Puzzle
To help her eye-hand coordination, make a "puzzle" for baby. Place a muffin tin on the floor in front of her. Put a container with a few tennis balls in it next to her. Show her how the tennis balls fit in the muffin tin. Then let her try to put the puzzle together.

S-T-R-E-T-C-H
This game helps baby exercise her large muscles. Sit on the floor across from her. Gently roll a ball toward her so she has to stretch a little to reach it. Tell her to stretch to get the ball.

If it's nice outside, you can accomplish the same thing by blowing soap bubbles over her head. Encourage her to reach up and grab the bubbles. Make sure she is able to reach most of the bubbles.

It's a Present!
When baby's taking a bath, wrap one of her favorite bath toys in a face cloth. Give her the wrapped toy, and tell her to open the

present. She will enjoy the element of surprise in finding the toy more than the toy itself!

Sprinkle, Sprinkle
You can do this activity in the bathtub or outside in the garden. Fill a small sprinkling can with water. If you don't have a sprinkling can, punch holes in the bottom of a plastic soda bottle, either the 1- or 2-liter size.

Show her how the water sprinkles from the holes into the bathtub or onto the flowers or grass. Sprinkle a little of the water on her. Have fun!

When the can is empty, show her and tell her that all the water is all gone. Put more water in the container, and play this game again.

Week 48

How Big Is Your Baby This 48th Week?

Baby weighs 21-1/2 pounds and is 29-1/2 inches long this week.

Baby Care and Equipment

Planning for Baby's First Birthday

It's getting close to baby's first birthday. As you make plans for a small celebration, keep in mind your child's personality. How does he react in various situations? Some babies love lots of stimulation. Others are shy and don't enjoy a lot of activity.

Time the event to occur when baby is rested and alert. A late afternoon or early-evening party may be perfect, if baby has just gotten up from his nap. Keep the party short. Two hours is the maximum. Consider keeping the guest list short if the party will end after a short time.

Will you invite other babies and children, in addition to adults? Some parents invite only adults to their child's first birthday party. If you do invite children, you'll need to provide activities for them. Set up a safe activity area with age-appropriate toys if other babies are invited. Don't invite a clown or other dressed-up individual, who may only frighten your baby.

Baby's Food Needs Evolve

Your baby's nutritional needs change somewhat as he nears the end of his first year. In a few weeks, he will be drinking whole milk. If your pediatrician says it's OK to offer whole milk, you will no longer offer formula. Your baby's nutritional plan may closely resemble the one listed in the chart below.

Feeding Tips for Your Older Infant

Don't force food. At this age, it's common for baby to eat heartily at one meal, then not want to eat much at the next. Never try to force baby to eat. Offer small portions. If he doesn't like something, you can offer it again later. Vary the tastes and textures of the foods you feed your baby. It makes meals more fun and interesting for him.

Snacks are necessary. Your growing baby needs regular meals and snacks. Give him at least three small snacks a day, in addition

What Baby Eats at 12 Months

These are typical serving sizes for an average 1-year-old baby.

Food	Portion size	Number of servings/day	Notes
Dairy products, including yogurt, cheese and cottage cheese	1/4 cup to 1/2 cup	4 servings	Offer a little plain vanilla ice cream as a special treat.
Grain products, including cereal, pasta, rice, bread, muffins, rolls and crackers	1/4 cup of cooked grains, 1/2 slice bread or a couple of crackers	6 servings	
Fruit or fruit juices	3 ounces	2 servings	Fruit is preferable to fruit juice.
Vegetables	3 ounces	3 servings	
Protein foods, including fish, turkey, chicken, beef, pork, eggs or lentils	1 ounce of meat, 1 egg or 1/4 cup of lentils	2 servings	You can try giving baby egg whites at 1 year.

to his regular meals. He is extremely busy and uses a lot of energy. Snacks provide him the energy he needs to keep going.

Travel snacks; restaurant eating. When you travel with baby, take foods and snacks that don't need to be kept cold. Crackers, oat-circle cereal pieces, juices, bread and fruits are good choices. When you eat in a restaurant, share part of your food with baby. It's a good change for him, and in a new environment he may be more interested in eating something different.

Block That Sun!

It may be hard to believe, but even the short, cool days of winter can present sun hazards to baby. By being vigilant about sun protection, you can prevent sun damage to his skin. As we've already discussed, don't use sunscreen on a baby younger than 6 months. See the box on this page about using sunscreen properly.

In addition to applying sunscreen as protection, dress baby in a sunhat with a good brim. Clothe him to protect his skin. Keep him out of the sun as much as you can. Sunscreen offers a degree of protection, but it can't protect a baby completely.

Applying Sunscreen

If your baby (6 months or older) will be outside longer than 15 minutes, apply sunscreen to any skin that will be exposed to sunlight. Apply sunscreen at least 30 minutes before going outside, for the greatest protection. Choose a sunscreen with a rating of at least 15 SPF (sun protection factor). Be sure it also blocks ultraviolet A and B rays. Read and follow package directions for application.

Milestones This 48th Week

Baby May Feed Himself

By this time, your baby should be able to feed himself fairly well. He may hold a cup steadily and drink from it all by himself. He may be able to carry a spoonful of food to his mouth without much trouble. However, he may spill a lot because his wrist action is not yet fully developed. If you try to help him eat, he may resist you, even if it's something he likes. He really does want to do it himself!

Allow him to practice eating and drinking without much interference from you. He needs to master these important tasks. Stand by with cleaning cloths to clean up the mess afterward.

His Understanding and Curiosity Increase

Because his memory has improved, your baby remembers many things. He knows where to put certain objects. He can group various items by color, size or shape. He studies how fast an object falls. His attention span is longer, which is the reason he will study something for a fairly long time.

> As your baby gets older, he begins to distinguish between good and bad smells. You may notice a definite reaction from him when he smells something unpleasant.

He may love books and has favorites he wants to read many times. He may want to turn the pages of a book. He can do it if you let him try.

Instead of taking things apart, baby may now try to put them back together. He tries to use an object the way he sees you or others use it. By imitating your actions, he gains valuable information about it.

He may be confused by glass and mirrors. He may try to reach through a piece of glass to get something. He may believe he can pick up an object in a mirror. He may even look behind a mirror to see if something is hiding there.

These accomplishments demonstrate that baby is learning to think and to solve problems.

Baby's Muscle Control

Your baby is close to walking, if he isn't already. When he's cruising the furniture, he may take a step without holding on to anything. He may be taking steps while holding your hands. It may be awhile before he wants to sit down again!

Even if he's cruising and taking a few steps, he will often revert to crawling. For the time being, crawling is a quicker, more efficient means of getting somewhere.

Offer Nongender Toys

Some parents mistakenly believe if they offer their son only "boy toys," he won't be interested in anything else. Don't discourage your baby from playing with any type of toy, if it interests him. Let a boy have a doll and household items. Give a girl a truck or baby tool kit. Every toy a child plays with offers a new experience. Every new experience contributes to your baby's overall grasp of his world.

Coping with Inconsistencies

A baby needs consistency in his environment. It makes him feel secure. However, his experiences in the "outside" world are not consistent at times. That's what the real world is like. Now that baby is getting older, it will be easier for him to cope with some inconsistency in his world. Relax when it happens. His growing maturity will help him deal with the changes he encounters.

Note: See also the box below, *Milestones This Week*.

What's Happening This 48th Week?

When Baby Gets Frustrated

As hard as this may be, your job as a parent is to let baby try to do things for himself. Baby will be frustrated at times, but he will also earn a feeling of accomplishment when he succeeds.

Don't ignore him when you see he is frustrated. Assess the situation. Is he frustrated because he's tired? Is the task beyond his abilities? Has he tried too many times without success? If he's frustrated for these reasons, help him out.

However, if you've demonstrated a way to do something that is within his abilities, let him try it on his own. He should be able to work it out eventually. These lessons are important now and later. For now, he learns how to do something for himself. Later, he'll have the confidence to work out a problem without expecting someone else to do it for him.

Milestones This 48th Week

Changes in Baby You May See Now

Physical Development
- may take a step without holding onto anything
- may stand on toes
- may carry spoon to mouth

Senses and Reflexes
- turns pages of book
- may pull off shoes and socks

Mental Development
- speaks long, babbling sentences with full inflection

Social Development
- seeks approval
- engages in parallel play with another child

Every baby is an individual, and your baby may do some of these things more quickly or more slowly than another baby. If you are concerned about your baby's progress, discuss it with your healthcare provider. Also see page viii.

A Swollen Testicle

A swollen testicle in a baby boy, also called a *hydrocele,* results when fluid collects in one or both scrotal sacs. The condition is painless and harmless. It occurs fairly often—about half of all newborn males have it.

A male's testicles migrate from inside his abdomen into the scrotum, just before or just after birth. (See the discussion of undescended testicles in Week 42.) Testicles travel down a very small opening in the muscle wall. This opening usually closes, but occasionally it remains open. When this happens, fluid from inside the abdomen accumulates in the scrotal area, causing swelling.

The situation usually goes away when the passage closes by the end of baby's first year. However, if the passage doesn't close and lasts longer than a year, surgery may be necessary to close the passage. The surgical procedure is fairly safe and is often done on an outpatient basis.

Comment on Baby's Activities

When you describe your baby's activities to him, you help him focus on what he's doing. When he's doing something, such as playing with blocks, tell him how long the block wall is or how big it is. Comment on other aspects of his life, too, such as the blue shirt he is wearing or how nicely he's patting the dog.

When you show baby how to do something, you help him learn. Your baby learns to recall activities by watching you perform them. Show him how to wash his hands without soap and water, or how to comb his hair without a comb or brush. Make a game of it.

You may also notice your baby's sense of humor and originality are emerging. He may change the rules of some games you've been playing, making them uniquely his own. His creative side is beginning to appear.

Head Injury

Every parent is concerned when his or her baby falls and bumps his head. Such accidents are fairly common while baby is learning to walk. You don't have to be too concerned about most tumbles, yet it's smart to be aware of the symptoms that indicate baby has more than a little bump on the head. Symptoms of a head injury that needs immediate care include

- sleepiness, difficulty arousing
- confusion
- difficulty feeding
- vomiting
- nausea
- pupils are different sizes
- loss of consciousness
- fussiness
- bleeding
- an actual lump or bump on his head, large bruise or discoloration

What to do. After your baby falls, examine his head. If he has a bump, apply ice to control swelling. If there is bleeding, clean the area as best you can. Examine the wound. If it is deep, it may need stitches. Apply pressure to the wound with a clean cloth to stop the bleeding, and go to the emergency room. Call your pediatrician's office and advise them of the situation. Your baby's doctor may also want to examine him or follow up later.

When to call the doctor. If you believe your baby has had a serious fall, call your doctor or go directly to the emergency room. An infant with a head injury will need to be evaluated and the seriousness of the head injury checked carefully. After your doctor examines baby, he or she will advise you about the action to take next. You may have to observe your baby closely for 24 hours. If the situation is serious, your pediatrician may recommend further testing.

Nosebleeds
What they are. A baby with a nosebleed can be an unsettling sight for his parents. Nosebleeds occur for all sorts of reasons. A nosebleed may occur because of dried mucous membranes in the nose, or it may be caused by an accident. Infections, such as scarlet fever or sinusitis, may also cause nosebleeds. Picking the nose too aggressively or picking it over a prolonged time can cause bleeding. Evidence of a nosebleed includes

- blood from the nose
- nausea or stomach upset (from swallowing blood)
- vomiting (might be bright red from swallowed blood)
- dark stools (from swallowed blood)
- blood is bright red in color, if nosebleed is close to the nostril
- blood may be dark in color, if nosebleed is deeper in the nose

What to do. When baby has a nosebleed, sit him upright. Bend his head forward slightly. Clamp his nostrils closed for 5 to 10 minutes. Do not lessen pressure during that time! Holding the nose tightly seals the blood vessels. Blood has time to clot. You may also apply pressure across or under the upper lip to help control bleeding. Applying cold compresses over the nose or to the nape of the neck may help stop bleeding.

If bleeding stops, then starts again, repeat the above procedures. If bleeding doesn't stop, take baby to the nearest emergency-care facility. Blood vessels may have to be cauterized (sealed by applying heat or a chemical to the area).

If your baby gets a lot of nosebleeds, his mucous membranes may be dried out. When he is sleeping, run a cool-mist humidifier in his room. See Week 13 for information on humidifiers. Apply a small amount of petroleum jelly to a cotton swab. Put some in each nostril to help moisturize the area.

When to call the doctor. If your baby has frequent nosebleeds, tell your pediatrician. It's important information. Call your doctor if baby has trouble breathing after a nosebleed or a nose injury. If you can't get the nosebleed to stop, or stay stopped, take baby to the emergency room.

Toys and Play This 48th Week

What's Making the Noise?
Help baby make some discoveries. Gather together objects that make noise, such as keys, measuring spoons on a ring, a bell, a rattle or beans in a sealed plastic container. Show him these objects, then put them in separate small brown-paper bags. Shake each bag so he can hear the different sounds. Tell him what is in each bag. Mix up the bags, shake one again, and ask him if it's the keys (or whatever object you have in the bag). He may be able to identify it. If he doesn't, let him look inside the bag to see what's there.

You and Your Shadow
You can play this game together indoors or outside. With the sun behind you both, sit next to baby. Wave your arm so baby can see it

moving on a wall or the ground in front of you. Tell baby to look at the shadow waving at him.

Next move the shadow so it falls on baby's arm or leg where he can see it. Ask him to catch it or touch it. Show him how to wave his hands and create a shadow, too. Holding his hand in yours, talk about what the shadow looks like. If you know how to make shadow puppets, entertain him with those. Hold up an object and talk about how its shadow shape compares to what you're holding.

Puzzle Balls

A toy you may want to buy for baby is a puzzle ball. These balls separate into different wedges—each wedge has its own sound. These are great tools to help baby learn about the part-to-whole relationship.

> Baby's sense of humor enables him to appreciate the things you do that are funny to him. He laughs when you entertain him.

Bath Bubbles

Using a commercial product or a homemade one, blow bubbles onto baby's skin while he's in the bath. Because his skin is wet, the bubbles may not break immediately. Encourage him to pop them when he can. Try to land bubbles on his legs, his arms and his tummy. Name each body part a bubble lands on.

Building Blocks

Give your baby a few large plastic blocks to play with. He may stack them or arrange them. If he doesn't stack them, show him how. Help him arrange the blocks in different ways. Talk about how the arrangement changes by moving one block to a different position.

Get Out the Photo Album

Bring out the photo album you made for baby. Let him look at it. He's getting old enough to turn the pages by himself. If he doesn't seem to recognize a familiar face, tell him who it is. Holding the album and turning the pages all by himself is a big accomplishment for him!

Weekly Milestones at a Glance

Week 49

Physical Development
- may take a step or two without holding onto anything
- may walk with help of wheeled toy

Senses and Reflexes
- prefers to use one hand over the other (left-handed or right-handed)

Mental Development
- identifies animals in pictures
- remembers events for longer periods

Social Development
- gives attention to humans and favored objects
- gives a kiss on request
- reacts sharply to separation from parents
- may resist being fed
- fears strange people and places
- insists on feeding herself

Week 50

Physical Development
- may walk without help
- lowers himself easily to the floor

Senses and Reflexes
- takes covers off containers

Mental Development
- responds to directions
- may speak two or three words

Social Development
- gives and takes a toy
- may refuse to eat new foods

Week 51

Physical Development
- climbs up and down stairs
- may get to standing position by pushing up from a squatting position

Senses and Reflexes
- is learning correct use of a toy, such as pegboard and hammer, telephone

Mental Development
- searches for hidden object if she hasn't seen it but remembers last location

Social Development
- resists napping
- may demand more help from others than is necessary because it is easier
- gives affection to humans and objects
- may undress herself

Week 52

Physical Development
- displays some combination of standing, walking and cruising
- may climb out of a crib or playpen

Senses and Reflexes
- may put two objects in his mouth or under his arm to grasp another

Mental Development
- understands much of what is said to him

Social Development
- may have tantrums
- cares for doll or soft toy by hugging, cuddling, feeding
- takes only one afternoon nap

Week 49

How Big Is Your Baby This 49th Week?

Baby weighs 21-1/2 pounds and is 29-3/4 inches long this week.

Baby Care and Equipment

Herbal Medications

Some parents use herbal medicine to treat themselves for various problems and want to know if it is OK to give herbs to baby. Before you consider giving any herbal substance to your baby, ask yourself these questions:

Has baby's illness or condition been diagnosed? You may be tempted to treat a problem yourself because you believe you know what the problem is and an herb is readily available. Never make a diagnosis on your own. You may unknowingly ignore a potentially serious condition.

Have you checked first with your pediatrician about giving baby herbal medication? Before you give your baby anything your doctor hasn't recommended, check with him or her. Never medicate your child without advice from your physician.

Is the herb effective for the problem? Don't give an herb because it "might" help baby. It might cause more problems.

Know the side effects of the herbal medication. Many people consider herbs "natural substances," and they believe the herbs are therefore harmless. However, even a mild herbal treatment can create side effects in a baby.

Is baby taking other medications? If your child is taking any prescription or over-the-counter medications, think twice about adding an herbal preparation to the mix. Some herbs have an adverse effect when taken with other medicinal substances. Check with your pharmacist or pediatrician before you give baby any herb.

Does the herb contain other ingredients? Some herbs are made with high concentrations of alcohol. Often the same herb comes in many forms. Some forms are more potent than others.

Where is the herb manufactured? Some herbs made outside the United States and Canada can be contaminated with dangerous substances.

What's the correct dosage for a child the size of your baby? The use of herbal medications in children has not been studied to any great extent. The proper dosage for children of various sizes has seldom been established. A smaller amount of an adult dose of an herb *doesn't* mean it's safe.

Safety from Glues and Fingernail Primers

Two substances to keep out of reach of a curious baby include super glue and nail primers. These are dangerous household items.

Super glue. Super glue is dangerous because it adheres so quickly. If baby gets into it, it can bond her skin together in such a way that you might have to go to the emergency room to get her unstuck. If you have super glue at your house, keep a can of acetone on hand in case of an accident. Acetone helps dissolve the bond, but it may not work in all cases (for example, if a lot of glue was spilled). Keep super glue in a locked cabinet when you're not using it. Keep the acetone locked up too!

Nail primers. Nail primers prepare fingernails to bond with acrylic nails. These substances contain methacrylic acid, which causes burns if touched, inhaled or swallowed. Nail primers may not carry warning labels, despite the danger. Keep these out of baby's reach also.

Milestones This 49th Week

Baby May Be More Emotional

As the end of baby's first year draws near, she may cling to you more, and separation anxiety may reappear. Her motor skills have improved, so she is more independent physically. She also understands she is separate from you. It unsettles baby somewhat to comprehend that she can separate from you and others. She may need more reassurance of your love and attention than she has needed in the recent past. She depends a great deal on you for love and affection. You may notice her seeking you quite often.

Stranger anxiety may be evident when you're away from home. Reassure her by giving her attention when she seems to need it, and stay close if she needs you to.

What makes her cry? Now that your baby is approaching "toddlerhood," her crying may become more predictable. You are probably finding ways to deal with her tears *and* save your sanity. First, determine what makes her cry. If your baby always cries when you put her in her stroller, for example, distract her with a toy she likes and she will probably stop crying. If she cries when she can't have your car keys, put them away, out of her sight, and her attention will probably shift rapidly to something else.

> Provide lots of opportunities for your baby to make simple choices. Let her practice now so she'll have experience with decision making when choices become more important.

Baby needs a routine. Knowing what comes next makes her feel secure. When it's necessary to depart from your normal routine, tell her what to expect. She'll be less emotional about the change. Don't let her get too tired. When she's exhausted, she'll go to pieces. Save long outings for times when she's rested and can deal with them.

Milestones This 49th Week

Changes in Baby You May See Now

Physical Development

- may take a step or two without holding on to anything
- may walk with help of wheeled toy

Senses and Reflexes

- may prefer to use one hand over the other (be left-handed or right-handed)

Mental Development

- identifies animals in pictures
- remembers events for longer periods

Social Development

- gives attention to humans and favored objects
- gives a kiss on request
- reacts sharply to separation from parents
- may resist being fed
- insists on feeding herself
- fears strange people and places

Every baby is an individual, and your baby may do some of these things more quickly or more slowly than another baby. If you are concerned about your baby's progress, discuss it with your healthcare provider. Also see page viii.

She's Mobile and Active

Baby is crawling, cruising and may be walking. She probably walks quite well while holding your hands. She may seem as if she never stops moving.

Movement excites her, so provide toys that move. If you put her on a baby tricycle and push her gently, she'll enjoy the ride.

She is demonstrating better eye-hand coordination. She has enough muscle control to put a spoon into her mouth. She may be using her left hand or her right hand more now. This preference can change: It's not unusual for her to switch back and forth between hands for a few more years.

Note: See also the box on page 448, *Milestones This Week*.

What's Happening This 49th Week?

Staying Connected to Baby When You Work

Do you work outside your home? If you do, you may feel the need to spend more quality time with your child to feel "connected" to her. Make the most of your time together. Try these suggestions.

- Spend extra time with baby. Get up earlier in the morning so you and baby can cuddle or play. Quality time together before the day begins benefits both of you.
- Learn about baby's routine at day care. When you're home together, do some of the same things she does at day care. This helps make baby's transition from home to day care, or day care to home, go more smoothly.
- When you get home, forget about chores and cooking for a while. Set aside time to spend with baby alone. Even if she can't talk, you can hold her and tell her about your day. Read a story together, or get out some toys and play. You'll both appreciate having time to unwind. Establish the same interactive routine for both parents.
- If possible (and if it doesn't upset her), call your child during the day to say hi. Even if she can't talk on the phone, she can listen to your voice and will feel connected to you.

Baby May Be Walking

As baby's confidence in her walking ability grows, she'll let go of her support occasionally. She'll grab it again when she feels herself wobble. Pretty soon she'll venture out on her own.

Usually baby will take only a step or two before sitting down. When you encourage her, she'll try again. Soon she'll be able to take quite a few steps.

When your baby starts to walk, her stance is wide legged. She holds out her arms to protect herself. She doesn't know how to stop efficiently, so she may fall when she stops.

> **Your baby is a real ham now. She'll repeat an action if it makes you laugh. She loves it when an audience appreciates her!**

When your baby starts walking, you may be concerned about the way she walks. Is she pigeon-toed? Do her legs look bowed? Does she walk on tiptoe?

Your baby's walking style is probably common for babies this age. You may be concerned that she may need treatment, but don't worry. These situations usually correct themselves by the time baby is 5 years old. However, if you are concerned, discuss it with your pediatrician. He or she will advise you.

Sunburn

What it is. Sunburn occurs when a person is exposed to the sun or other ultraviolet light source for a prolonged time. Sunburn symptoms include

- inflammation of the skin
- redness of the skin
- swelling of sunburned area
- nausea or vomiting with serious burns
- skin may blister later
- skin may peel later

Prevention is best. Prevention is the best protection you can offer your baby. Avoid placing her in direct sunlight for any length of time. It doesn't have to be hot outside to get sunburned. Overcast clouds do not block harmful ultraviolet rays, which cause the skin to burn. Ultraviolet light also reflects off water, snow and sand. If your baby is more than 6 months old, protect her with sunscreen if she will be outdoors for an extended period, and dress her in loose long-sleeved clothing and a sun hat. If she's younger than 6 months old, keep her out of direct sunlight and away from reflected sunlight.

What to do. If sunburn does occur, give your baby lots of fluid to prevent dehydration. Cool her off with damp towels on sunburned skin to reduce heat and pain. After swelling decreases, use creams, aloe vera or lotions to keep skin moist. Acetaminophen or ibuprofen may help relieve pain. Over-the-counter burn remedies that contain local anesthetics may be useful, but check with your pediatrician before using any. Don't pop blisters or peel skin, which could lead to a secondary infection.

When to call the doctor. Call your baby's doctor if baby has severe sunburn or if she develops a fever higher than 101F (38.3C). If she experiences vomiting or diarrhea, becomes extremely lethargic or irritable, or if pain persists longer than 48 hours, contact your pediatrician. Your doctor may prescribe pain medication or cortisone drugs to use briefly.

Hookworm or Roundworm

What it is. A hookworm or roundworm infection can affect the intestines and the rectum. Hookworms and roundworms are commonly found in dogs and cats. An infection can occur at any age. Symptoms include

- fine skin rash or very small blisters that progress to a narrow, raised line on the skin
- poor appetite
- weight loss
- fussiness
- abdominal cramps
- diarrhea

What to do. The best course of action is prevention. Keep your baby away from contact with pets, kitty litter, sand or any other area where there is a risk of exposure to an animal's urine or feces. Always wash your own hands thoroughly after cleaning the cat's litter box or after contact with pets.

When to call the doctor. Call the doctor if your baby has hookworm symptoms. Your doctor may prescribe topical creams or ointments. The prescription will depend on your child's age. Oral medication is prescribed for serious cases.

Whooping Cough

What it is. Whooping cough, also called *pertussis,* is a contagious bacterial infection. Onset of the problem may appear to be a cold. It is less common today because of the vaccine that protects children who have taken it.

With whooping cough, the lungs, bronchial tubes and larynx are involved. It can occur at any age but is most common in children. Symptoms include

- dry cough that gradually becomes more severe
- several short coughs, followed by the "whooping" cough
- the whooping sound comes at the end of a coughing spell, as the child gasps for breath
- fever
- runny nose
- loss of appetite
- irritability

Call the doctor. Call your doctor immediately if you believe your baby has whooping cough. Treatment includes increased liquids and rest. Antibiotics are usually prescribed. Ibuprofen or acetaminophen may be suggested to reduce fever and discomfort.

Prevention. If you know someone has whooping cough, keep baby away from him or her. The best way to avoid the problem is to have your baby immunized. An immunization for whooping cough, diphtheria and tetanus (DTaP) is given in a series of injections. The first is given at around age 2 months.

Toys and Play This 49th Week

Your baby may be walking now. If she is walking, she may combine it with another skill. For example, she may enjoy pulling an object behind her or pushing something ahead of her. Toys she might like now include a pull-along toy (remember the little dog you used to pull behind you?) or a push toy that she can steer. If they make noise while she pulls or pushes them, all the better!

Paint with Water

For outdoor fun, turn baby into an artist. Fill a pail with water. Give baby a few real paintbrushes that aren't too big for her to hold. Seat her in the shade on the grass or the porch. Place a large piece of dark construction paper in front of her, and show her how to paint it with water. You can also place her next to a piece of furniture, and let her

Baby may be walking with just a little outside support.

paint that. Show her how to dip the brush in the water and paint on
something. She'll have fun while she keeps cool—the water will go
everywhere! *Caution:* Never leave baby alone with the water. Keep
an eye on her. This isn't an activity to let her do alone.

Walking Barefoot
To increase your baby's awareness of different textures, let her walk
barefoot. She can walk in sand or soft grass, or on the carpet or
bare floor. By experiencing the way things feel on her feet, she will
become more aware of the various textures around her. And it feels
good, too!

Let Her Be the "Big Girl"
When you're out for a walk, take baby out of her stroller and let her
push it for a while. She'll enjoy the responsibility while improving her
stability and balance. Keep one hand on the stroller to keep it from
going too fast or from heading into the street. Let her ride again
when she gets tired.

Week 50

How Big Is Your Baby This 50th Week?

Baby weighs 21-3/4 pounds and is 29-3/4 inches long this week.

Baby Care and Equipment

Calorie Check

Do you know how many calories your baby should be eating now to get all the nutrients he needs? Use the formula in the box below to figure out how many calories he needs each day. See Week 48 for a discussion of foods to offer your baby now.

What about snacks? Your baby may be eating less than he has in the past. He's busy with activities and more interested in them than in eating. He needs snacks to help balance his diet. Snacks provide the energy he needs to play and to grow. The box on page 455 identifies nutritious snack foods that are good to offer your baby right now.

Baby's Calorie Needs

The American Academy of Pediatrics (AAP) recommends using the following simple formula to determine how many calories your baby needs each day by age 1. Multiply baby's height in inches by 40:

[baby's height in inches] x 40 = [his calorie needs per day]

For example, if baby is 31 inches tall, he should consume approximately 1,240 calories every day (31 x 40 = 1,240).

Feeding Baby Food

Some babies love baby food. Parents may wonder if they should stop offering baby food at any particular age and switch to "adult food." As long as you've introduced your baby to finger foods by this time (and he can eat them), it's OK for him to eat some baby food as well.

At this age, you might want to offer him a grown-up version of his baby food. For example, if he loves baby applesauce, switch to regular applesauce that is fairly smooth.

When you offer your baby "grown-up foods," choose those that do not contain sugar or other additives, when possible. He doesn't need these "extras" in his food. Formula or breast milk may still be part of his diet but may be decreasing in amount at this time.

Snacks Are Important

In addition to his regular meals, offer your baby three snacks a day. Make them nutritious and delicious! Choose snacks from the following options:

- yogurt—plain is best
- cheese, thinly sliced
- baby teething crackers
- saltine crackers
- graham crackers
- small pieces of easily chewed fruit, such as bananas
- a half slice of bread
- fruit juice, diluted one to one with water
- pretzels
- frozen juice pops
- pudding
- a small piece of bagel
- a milkshake
- oat-circle cereal pieces
- cut-up raisins

Is Cow's Milk the Only Option?

In just a few weeks, when he turns 1, baby probably will be ready to stop drinking formula and begin drinking milk. You may wonder if you are limited to offering cow's milk only.

Other milks are OK. You may give him other kinds of milk. Some of what is labeled as "milk" contains no dairy product at all; for example, soy milk and rice milk. Check with your pediatrician before you offer your baby anything beyond formula. He or she may have specific advice in regard to your baby. In addition to cow's milk, your choices include the following.

- **Goat's milk.** It has a tangy taste. It is deficient in vitamin B12 and folacin. It may cause an allergic reaction in a child who is sensitive to cow's milk.
- **Soy milk (also called *soy beverage*).** It can be used as an alternative to cow's milk. Use milk fortified with vitamin D and calcium.

- **Rice milk (also called *rice beverage*).** It can be used as an alternative to cow's milk. Use rice milk fortified with vitamin D and calcium.

Party-Planning Update

With 2 weeks to go, it's time to double-check on refreshments, the guest list and party decorations for your baby's first-birthday party. Have as much organized in advance as possible so you can enjoy the party as much as your baby and your guests.

Keep one significant point in mind: No matter what you've planned or what you anticipate, this is your baby's party. Be prepared to adapt *your* plans to *your baby's* needs.

> Involve Dad in planning baby's party. Let him help choose the guest list. Ask him to help you keep the celebration simple. He can be cameraman for the day. Baby's first birthday will create memories you'll both cherish for a long time.

Milestones This 50th Week

Playing Together

Playing with your baby is a lot of fun, especially now that he's getting older. When you play together, let him show you what he can do. He's rolling, spinning, pushing and pulling his toys now. You may be surprised by how sophisticated his play may be.

He enjoys reading with you. He may want to read books by himself. As long as he is gentle with books (it's better if they're fairly indestructible), let him do this grown-up activity on his own.

Milestones This 50th Week

Changes in Baby You May See This Week

Physical Development
- may walk without help
- lowers himself to the floor easily

Senses and Reflexes
- takes covers off containers

Mental Development
- responds to directions
- may speak some words

Social Development
- gives and takes a toy
- may refuse to eat new foods

Every baby is an individual, and your baby may do some of these things more quickly or more slowly than another baby. If you are concerned about your baby's progress, discuss it with your healthcare provider. Also see page viii.

Baby will probably enjoy climbing inside a box or cabinet to see if he fits. Provide him with the opportunity to make these explorations.

For play activities, talk, sing and read together. Change some of your favorite songs to reflect a particular activity as you are doing it.

His Sleep Patterns

By this time, your baby stays up for longer periods. He sleeps less during the day and longer at night. He is probably still napping up to a couple of hours every afternoon. He may continue to need an afternoon nap for quite a while. Some children nap fairly consistently until they are 4 or 5 years old.

His Efforts to Walk

Your baby may be standing alone. This is a big accomplishment for him. He loves standing, so don't be surprised when he resists sitting.

Perhaps your baby has already taken his first independent steps. Don't be alarmed by how often he falls while he's mastering this new skill. If he's not walking by himself yet, he's probably still cruising the furniture. Soon he'll be walking on his own!

He Imitates Actions

He is very interested in what you are doing. He will study what you do so he can imitate the way you and other family members use an object.

Other Accomplishments

Baby may be talking and saying a few words. Keep talking to him, telling him stories and talking about everything that happens each day.

He may demonstrate other things he has learned through actions if he can't express himself verbally. He may use a stick as a tool to get a toy that he can't reach. He may pull a blanket toward him if a book he wants is lying on it. He can reach for an object while looking at something else in another direction.

Note: See also the box on page 456, *Milestones This Week.*

What's Happening This 50th Week?

Coping with Curiosity

Your baby is curious—it's a natural inclination at his age. You may not be thrilled when he empties your purse. You may not be happy when he takes your shoes out of the closet or tips over the dog's food dish. To help keep your cool, remember that when your baby gets into things, he's learning about them.

It is possible to encourage baby to explore yet keep the mess to a minimum. The most important thing to remember in all of this is baby's safety. Try the following tips.

Keep acceptable alternatives at hand. If you make certain items available that will occupy baby, he may leave other things alone. Provide plastic containers, bowls and boxes. Put lots of different objects in them, such as tennis balls, measuring spoons, empty large thread spools, cut-up cardboard paper-towel tubes and empty plastic jars. (Be sure objects are large enough so he won't choke on them. They should *not* fit through a toilet-paper tube.) These "fun boxes" should keep him entertained for quite a while.

Teach him to pick it up. At this age, part of the fun of playing is picking up afterward. It's not too early to begin teaching him this valuable concept. He'll probably enjoy helping you put things back where they belong. Make a game of it when you can.

Eliminate dangerous situations, when possible. You might not think of the garbage can as a very dangerous place for baby—but it is. Take care what you throw away, such as razor blades, broken glass, balloons, egg shells, metal lids from cans, string and twine. Don't put them in a container that baby might get into. If necessary, put them directly in the outside garbage can to keep them out of his reach.

His Possessions

Before age 1, most babies have not yet developed a sense of ownership. It's easy for babies to share toys. However, by this age, your baby may be showing signs of possessiveness. He will begin to feel strongly about what belongs to him. Sharing will be more difficult for him. Soon you may start hearing him say, "Mine!"

Even empty containers can fascinate baby for a while.

Is Halloween Coming Up?

If you're getting ready to celebrate Halloween, you might want to leave baby out of the festivities. He may be upset to see someone he knows made up as a monster or another unknown figure. He's not ready to go trick or treating, and probably won't be until he's about 3 years old. He'll feel safer at home with you.

Roseola Infantum

What it is. Roseola infantum, also called *exanthem subitum,* or simply *Roseola,* is a skin disease that occurs most often in infants and children up to 3 years old. Symptoms include

> If baby doesn't have a full head of hair yet, don't worry. Many babies don't grow luxurious locks until they are 2 or 3 years old.

- high fever
- red skin rash that appears as the fever subsides
- fussiness
- irritability
- enlargement of the spleen

What to do. The problem occurs most often in the spring or autumn. Avoid large crowds during this time because the condition is contagious. Take measures to reduce baby's fever. Give him cool baths or fever-reducing medications, such ibuprofen or acetaminophen, as directed by your physician.

When to call the doctor. Call the doctor if baby appears listless, has seizures, runs a consistently high fever (102F, 38.8C) or if he refuses to eat or drink. Treatment includes medications to reduce fever and increased fluid intake.

Cuts and Scrapes

What they are. Cuts and scrapes, also called *abrasions* and *lacerations,* can occur because of an accident, a fall, roughhousing or other household incident. As your baby becomes more active and adventurous, he'll experience the normal cuts and scrapes all kids do. Cuts or abrasions may cause

- bleeding
- swelling
- opening of the skin
- bruising

What to do. When baby gets a shallow cut, gently wash the area with warm water and mild soap. Apply pressure to the area to

stop any bleeding, Use ice to help reduce swelling and bruising. If
the cut or scrape is minor, wash well with soap and water. Apply
triple antibiotic ointment and a bandage. With a cut, clean it up
first, then examine it to determine if stitches are required. Have a
doctor examine larger or deeper cuts and scrapes. If there is a lot of
bleeding, apply firm, gentle pressure.

Prevention. Avoid hazardous situations by providing baby with
a safe environment. Regularly check cups, utensils and toys for any
sharp surfaces. Keep stairs and other dangerous areas blocked off.

When to call the doctor. Call the doctor if your baby has a cut
that you believe may require stitches. If a cut continues to bleed,
does not heal or appears infected (area turns red or leaks yellow
or green fluid), contact your pediatrician. He or she will close a
cut when necessary with stitches (sutures) or a "butterfly" bandage.
Baby's doctor may prescribe antibiotics or antibiotic gels.

Obesity
What it is. Obesity is defined as being at least 20% above a person's
desirable weight for his or her height. Although a child of any age
can be extremely overweight, the term "obese" is used rarely to
describe a newborn, infant or young baby. Most babies do not
become extremely overweight in their first year, except for certain
medical reasons.

Doctors rely on a chart that shows a range of average weights
and heights for infants and young children to determine whether
a young patient is the right weight for his size. At each office visit
with your pediatrician, he or she will weigh your baby. Your doctor
will tell you how your baby's height and weight compare to other
children of the same age. As we've discussed throughout the book,
babies develop, grow and gain weight at different rates. Your baby's
doctor will help you understand what's normal for your baby.

What to do. *Do not* restrict your baby's food and formula or
breast milk if you think he's too big. Even if you believe his weight
is out of proportion, he needs the vitamins, minerals and other
nutrients from the food he eats to develop physically and mentally.

Follow the instructions your pediatrician has given you with
regard to feeding and vitamin supplements. If you are concerned,
discuss the matter with your baby's doctor at one of baby's regularly
scheduled well-baby visits. Your pediatrician will provide you with
specific instructions regarding your child's diet.

Toys and Play This 50th Week

Do Some Bath-Math

For this activity you need three small plastic containers. Poke a small hole in one container and a large hole in another. With the third container, show baby how to pour water into the first container with the small hole. Let it leak into the container with the larger hole. Next, let your baby pour water into the first container while you hold a container in each hand. Adding more holes to one or both containers adds to the fun! These "additions" and "subtractions" are the basics of mathematical understanding.

Serious Cruising

Help baby practice cruising skills. In a carpeted area, line a few chairs against a wall. (The chairs shouldn't slip when placed on a carpeted floor.) Place baby next to the chair at one end of the row. Show him how to propel himself down the row, moving from one chair to the next for support.

If he holds back, entice him with a favorite toy. Put it on a chair in the middle, then move it to the chair at the end. When he reaches the end, let him hold the toy for a minute. Then put the toy at the other end, and begin again.

Unwrap the Presents

For the joy of discovery, wrap a few of baby's favorite toys in newsprint. Bright Sunday comics are a good choice. Don't use tape or string. You can wrap a small toy a couple of times loosely in a large sheet of comics. Give him the "presents," and let him unwrap them. He'll enjoy discovering what's inside each one. Let him play with the paper when he's finished—he may like that better than the toys.

Baby Basketball

To help baby develop his coordination, place a laundry basket on the floor near him. Give him a tennis ball or other small object to toss. Show him how to throw the ball or other object into the basket. Begin close to the basket, then move it a little farther away. Be prepared to run after some stray balls!

Week 51

How Big Is Your Baby This 51st Week?

Baby weighs 21-3/4 pounds and is 30 inches long this week.

Baby Care and Equipment

Baby's Interest in Food

Your baby's interest in eating may be almost nonexistent. Concentrate your energies on other activities, such as playing with her and helping her learn about her world.

> Your baby may have tripled her birth weight by her first birthday.

Don't expect her to eat three well-balanced meals every day. If she skips a food group on one day, offer her more of that food group the next. Provide nutritious meals and snacks each day. Over the long run, she'll get the nutrition she needs. And before long, she'll probably begin eating again. If you continue to be concerned, discuss it with your baby's doctor at her next well-baby checkup.

Safety at Mealtimes

As baby grows, safety issues involving eating become important. Keep in mind these safety considerations now.

- She's not ready for a fork yet, so don't give her one to feed herself or to play with.
- Don't let her walk or run when she's eating.
- Don't let her walk or run while she's carrying utensils.
- Use plastic for safety–plastic spoons, plastic dishes, plastic cups.

Milestones This 51st Week

When Baby Repeats Herself

A child's repetitive behavior can try an adult's patience. Baby will do something over and over—and over! Her behavior simply reflects her limited experience and understanding of the world. She is not trying to annoy or "test" you.

Repetition is baby's way of testing her world. Repeating an action helps develop baby's motor skills. It also enhances her memory.

Actions Linked to Goals

Your baby's actions are linked to her goals. She knows that by bringing the spoon to her mouth she can take a bite of cereal and feed herself. When she wants a toy, she crawls to get it. Her coordination and dexterity improve a little every day.

She'll climb on top of furniture or to the top of the stairs to see what is going on around the room. She uses her improved mobility to explore wherever she can. Watch closely to keep her safe. She moves quickly!

Help increase her sense of independence by continuing to encourage her to do things for herself. If it takes a little effort to get a toy, tell your little one she can get it if she wants it. Let her do as much as possible for herself. She'll be very proud when she accomplishes what she set out to do.

Her Perception of Her World

Your baby is quite mobile now, and this fact has changed her view of the world and made it more complex. All the climbing and standing she's done has sharpened her perception. Among other discoveries, she realizes that one object can be used or played with in different ways. She understands that objects exist separately from her. She begins to see herself as part of the world around her.

Baby Play

At this age, your baby is extremely active in her play. She loves to open and close cabinet doors. Emptying cabinets is lots of fun, too. She pounds pegs into a wooden holder with enthusiasm. Playing with blocks—stacking or arranging them—entertains her.

Emptying cabinets keeps baby busy!

When you sing a familiar song, she may supply a word that you intentionally leave out. She is affectionate with people and favorite toys. She may scribble with crayons.

She's a Social Being
As she gets older, she's becoming more sociable. Her stranger anxiety is easing. She still speaks in gibberish, but now she speaks a few recognizable words.

Note: See also the box on the opposite page, *Milestones This Week.*

What's Happening This 51st Week?

When Baby Acts Out
When your little one repeats negative or unpleasant behavior, you can help her get back on the right track. The suggestions below can make life happier for her and for you!

She has a short attention span. When she's being unpleasant, distract your little one. Show her something else she can do that's fun and acceptable to you. She may be glad to switch activities.

Keep reactions under control. When she's acting in a negative way, control your response. If you respond strongly, it teaches her she does some things that make you react. She likes to get your attention, even if it's negative attention. When you don't react, she may lose interest in what she's doing and move on to something else.

Milestones This 51st Week

Changes in Baby You May See Now

Physical Development
- climbs up and down stairs
- may get to standing position by pushing up from a squatting position

Senses and Reflexes
- is learning correct use of a toy, such as pegboard and hammer

Mental Development
- searches for hidden object if she hasn't seen it but remembers last location

Social Development
- resists napping
- may demand more help from others than is necessary because it is easier
- gives affection to humans and objects
- may undress herself

Every baby is an individual, and your baby may do some of these things more quickly or more slowly than another baby. If you are concerned about your baby's progress, discuss it with your healthcare provider. Also see page viii.

Explain changes ahead of time. A young child may be unsettled by an abrupt change in activities. By telling her what's going to happen in advance, you smooth the transition. Sometimes her negativity is only a reaction to a change.

Keep the environment calm when necessary. You can't expect your baby to settle immediately after she's been roughhousing with her siblings or a parent. When you want her to be calm and quiet by a certain time—for example, at bedtime—offer only quiet activities for a period of time leading up to bedtime. Reserve stimulating games and activities for appropriate times of day.

Portable Baby!

Your baby is compact and portable at this age. It's fairly easy to take her just about anywhere you go. When you buckle her in, she probably can't unbuckle herself (yet). She may be interested in looking around and going places with you.

The drawback is that your baby may not always cooperate when you have errands to run or social gatherings to attend. She wants to do things her way and maintain her own comfort level. But bring her along anyway. She has to experience different situations to learn how to react properly—so you can take her with you again.

Fractures and Broken Bones

What it is. A fracture or broken bone is an unusual injury for a newborn or infant. At birth, a baby's bones are relatively "soft"— more like cartilage than bone. The collarbone (scapula) or bones in the arm (humerus) can be broken during a difficult delivery. When this occurs, usually no treatment is required. Within a few months, a break heals so completely that even an X-ray does not reveal evidence of it.

> **A bulge or bump in baby's navel area, where the cord fell off, should have disappeared by now. If it hasn't, bring it to your pediatrician's attention at baby's 1-year well-baby visit.**

Broken bones in newborns and infants may result from an automobile accident or some other type of accident. Children crawling or learning to walk occasionally fracture a bone when they take a serious tumble or fall down stairs. Symptoms your child has suffered a broken bone include

- pain
- redness
- bleeding
- tenderness
- swelling
- bruising

What to do. If you believe your baby has a broken bone, apply ice to the area, then immobilize it. Take your baby to the emergency room.

When Baby Hurts

A toddler's experiences are based on what she can see and hear. When she gets hurt, she may not be able to express herself to you in words. Ask her where it hurts. She may be able to point to it. Ask how much it hurts.

Watch her for physical and behavioral changes, too. Note whether she moves normally. Do you notice changes in her eating or sleeping habits? Whining, listlessness or the inability to settle may indicate a problem. If she favors one arm or protects a leg, it could mean an injury.

Trying to decipher a child's nonverbal clues is sometimes difficult, but you do have an advantage—no one knows your baby better than you do. You have to be a master detective to figure out what she is telling you sometimes. By staying alert and involved with your baby, you will always be prepared to protect her health and well-being.

When to call the doctor. If you aren't sure whether baby has suffered a broken bone or if an injury is serious, call your pediatrician. He or she will advise you.

Fractures are usually immobilized with a cast or splint made of plaster or fiberglass. Surgery may be required in certain serious cases. Your doctor will prescribe pain medication, if it is needed. Following treatment, call your pediatrician if the dressing or cast appear too tight or if part of the body "below" the cast is pale or cool to the touch.

Laryngitis

What it is. A baby with laryngitis may have a very hoarse cry. Laryngitis may be related to a cold or other upper-respiratory problem and can occur at any age. Symptoms include

- change in voice or cry
- fever
- poor feeding
- hoarseness of voice or cry
- difficulty swallowing

What to do. When you hear baby crying hoarsely, use a cool-mist humidifier in her room when she's sleeping. See Week 13 for information on humidifiers. Offer liquids frequently.

When to call the doctor. Call the doctor if symptoms persist and don't improve within 1 or 2 days. If baby has difficulty swallowing, shows signs of dehydration, if she's not feeding well or other symptoms worsen, such as her fever rises, contact your pediatrician. Treatment for the problem may include antibiotics, ibuprofen or acetaminophen for relief of pain or fever.

Sprains and Strains

What they are. Most people use the terms "sprain" and "strain" interchangeably, but they do not mean the same thing in medical terms. A *sprain* is a stretched or torn ligament (which holds a joint in place). A *strain* is a stretched muscle. These aren't common occurrences in babies. However, they can occur in active infants over 6 months of age and children learning to walk. Symptoms of a sprain or strain include

- pain
- bruising
- swelling
- tenderness

What to do. If your baby gets a sprain or strain, apply a cool compress to the injured area for the first 24 hours. Apply warm compresses after that. When applying a compress, place a washcloth or towel between the baby and the hot or cold compress. Protect the injured part of the body by immobilizing it when necessary.

> In the next few months, your baby will be getting a few more teeth. You'll see her first four molars come in, then her four canine teeth.

When to call the doctor. Call the doctor if swelling gets worse after home treatment. If other symptoms worsen, such as bruising, tenderness or pain, baby could have a fracture. Call your pediatrician. Baby's doctor may prescribe pain medication. In severe situations, a cast or splint may be necessary.

Toys and Play This 51st Week

Fun in the Tub
Playing in the tub is always fun. Try these ideas together when baby's in the tub.

- Create a crazy hairdo for baby when you shampoo her hair. While her hair is still soapy, arrange it in funny styles. Hold up a hand mirror so baby can see how she looks.
- Make washing her hair more fun by using a big soup ladle to wet and to rinse her hair. Let her pour water out of it, too.
- Buy a bathtub hand puppet or make one out of a couple of washcloths. The puppet can tickle baby and "talk" to her while it washes her!

Crawl the Plank!
Baby can improve her balance when she plays this game. Place your ironing board flat on the floor. Stabilize it (it might be wobbly because of the stand collapsed underneath) with bath towels on both sides. Put a toy at one end. Set baby at the other end, and encourage her to crawl along the plank to get the toy.

Backward down the Stairs

Now is a good time to begin teaching baby the important skill of climbing safely down the stairs. This game helps. Place baby on the stairs on her tummy, with her feet pointing toward the bottom of the stairs. Gently pull her legs out so she learns how it feels to slide downward on her tummy, stairstep by stairstep. This skill also contributes to her gross-motor coordination. *Note:* Even when she learns to master this "backward slide," don't let her on stairs without your supervision.

Climb the Mountain

Baby wants to climb, so let her be a mountaineer! Pile pillows and cushions on the floor in the middle of the room. Move furniture out of the way. Put the biggest pillows from the sofa on the bottom, then add smaller chair pillows and then throw pillows. Help baby climb the "mountain" to the top. *Note:* Never leave her alone while she's playing this game. Put away all the pillows when you have finished playing together.

First-Birthday Gift Ideas

Toys your baby will enjoy at this age, which you can suggest as gifts for a first birthday if she doesn't already have them, include building blocks made of wood or plastic, stuffed animals or dolls, riding toys, pounding sets, balls and simple puzzles.

Week 52

How Big Is Your Baby This 52nd Week?

Baby weighs 22 pounds and is 30 inches long this week.

Baby Care and Equipment

Baby's First Birthday
Happy birthday to baby! No matter how you celebrate, have a wonderful day with your 1-year-old.

Car-Safety Vest
If your child is fairly large at 1 year (between 25 and 40 pounds), you may want to consider using an alternative to his car seat called *the safety vest*. It is lightweight and has shoulder, hip and crotch straps to secure him in the car. Some vests require an additional tether strap be installed in a vehicle.

If baby's birthday falls on or near a major holiday, such as Christmas or Hanukkah, consider throwing a "half-birthday" party when she's older. When she can understand the concept, have her party 6 months away from her birthday, when she'll be the center of attention at least once during the year. For example, if her birthday is on December 28, celebrate her "haffy birthday" on June 28.

A vest like this is great for travel. You can stick it in your carry-on bag and be ready to buckle up baby when you hail a cab or are picked up by friends or relatives. Car-safety vests are sold in baby-product stores.

Needed Nutrients

Fat. During your child's first 2 years, he needs to get a significant percentage of his daily calories from fat sources. At 6 months of age, baby gets a little more than 40% of calories from fat. By age 1, this percentage drops to about 30%.

Baby needs more fat than you do. It is unhealthy for baby to eat too little fat in his diet. Often a toddler eats what his parents eat. Parents who eat low-fat foods may believe the same foods are OK to feed baby. They aren't! Parents who drink low-fat or fat-free (skim) milk may give these products to their child. As a result, baby gets a less-than-desirable percentage of fat in his diet.

Don't limit your child's fat intake until after he turns 2. At that point, decrease it gradually. By age 5, your child should get about 30% of his calories from fat sources. Until he's quite a bit older, don't feed him fat-reduced foods.

Offer whole milk for now. Your baby should drink whole cow's milk for the next year, until he's 2. He needs the fat and calories to grow and to develop. After he turns 2, until he is 5, you can gradually change what you offer from whole cow's milk to low-fat or fat-free milk. Don't make the transition too abruptly.

Vitamin D. Many babies don't get enough vitamin D or zinc. Some products you might think would contain vitamin D, don't—for example, cheese and yogurt. Parents who do not realize this may feed their baby these foods without offering others that do contain vitamin D. Good sources of vitamin D include eggs, fortified milk and butter.

Zinc. Zinc is found in beef, pork and poultry. Some children may resist eating these foods. Encourage your child to eat them. Two or 3 tablespoons a day of beef, pork, poultry or eggs provide him with enough zinc. If you are a vegetarian, discuss this concern with your pediatrician.

> ## Why Did We Wait to Give Cow's Milk?
>
> Your pediatrician advised you not to give your baby cow's milk until your child reached 1 year of age. His kidneys and digestive system could not safely process the proteins and minerals in whole milk because his digestive system was not yet mature. If you had given him milk before this time, the milk might have caused mild damage to the lining of his intestines.

> At this time, if your baby hasn't had a problem with egg yolks, you may want to consider adding egg whites to his diet.

Milestones This 52nd Week

Your baby may be very affectionate now.

Baby's Emotions

More expressive! By the end of this first year, you may see baby begin to express his emotions in new ways. He may be very affectionate with you and other family members. Baby may give a kiss on request. He may hug and kiss a favorite stuffed animal or doll. He outwardly expresses his feelings.

Good sense of humor. He has a sense of humor and readily displays it. He laughs and plays little jokes on you.

Temper tantrums, too! Baby has temper tantrums because it is difficult for him to express frustration, especially about communicating his needs. When he's angry, he'll let you know it. He is learning acceptable behavior and may test you often. Tell him when you disapprove of his actions.

Baby on the Move

If baby isn't walking yet, he will be soon. Even if he is toddling, he may revert to crawling when he wants to get somewhere quickly. He may also crawl when he engages in certain activities, such as pushing a truck across the floor. He needs both hands for this task. This type of play helps him learn to coordinate the use of his legs, his arms and his eyes.

> When you turn around baby's car seat, install the seat exactly according to the manufacturer's instructions. You will probably have to move harness straps to the top slot.

He sits easily in a child-sized chair. He can hold an object in each hand and has figured out how to pick up a third. He'll put one of the objects he was holding in his mouth or under his arm to free one hand.

He may carry a toy when he walks. This lends him a feeling of support, although it doesn't truly offer any. He may have trouble going around corners or stopping when he wants to. These are skills he'll perfect in the next few months.

Changes in Baby

During this first year, your baby has undergone incredible changes. In this first year, his brain has grown to nearly 60% of its adult size.

Milestones This 52nd Week

Changes in Baby You May See This Week

Physical Development
- displays some combination of standing, walking and cruising
- may climb out of a crib or playpen

Senses and Reflexes
- may put an object in his mouth or under his arm to grasp another

Mental Development
- understands much of what is said to him

Social Development
- may have tantrums
- cares for doll or soft toy by hugging, cuddling, feeding
- takes only one afternoon nap

Every baby is an individual, and your baby may do some of these things more quickly or more slowly than another baby. If you are concerned about your baby's progress, discuss it with your healthcare provider. Also see page viii.

His vision is nearly mature. Baby's sense of spatial relationships is excellent, but he still has trouble judging distance and speed.

He has matured enough to tell the difference between adults and children. He may now seek out other babies.

Note: See also the box above, *Milestones This Week*.

What's Happening This 52nd Week?

Baby's Undesirable Behaviors

Your baby may display behavior that you find undesirable. He may begin hitting, biting, pinching, pulling hair, throwing food or doing other things you don't want him to do.

When baby misbehaves, usually it isn't out of defiance. He's just experimenting. However, if you overreact when he misbehaves, you reinforce his behavior because you give him attention, even if it is negative attention. Stay calm, and the next time your baby is unpleasant, try the following tactics.

Ignore him. Sometimes it's best to ignore baby's behavior. If he

Baby may throw a tantrum if he doesn't feel understood.

doesn't get a reaction from you or others, he'll stop soon and move on to something else.

Don't overreact. When you react strongly, you give baby attention for his negative behavior. He may interpret your reprimand as a reward because he has caught your attention. This situation can reinforce his negative behavior, and he'll repeat the action.

Be consistent. Handle the same problem in the same way every time. Ask others to handle it the way you do. If you tolerate a problem behavior sometimes, but not always, or if some family member thinks it's "cute" and encourages it, it's harder to make baby stop.

Baby is curious. It's his nature to explore. He wants to learn more about his environment. While he is satisfying his curiosity, he will show little regard for anyone else. For example, when you wear a brightly colored necklace, he may grab it to learn more about it by touching and tasting it. He will be so absorbed in his discovery, he won't notice you telling him not to touch it. If you don't want him to pull the necklace, put it inside your blouse while you're holding him. Keep the number of items or situations that are off-limits as low as you can.

> Keep the number of items or situations that are off-limits as low as you can.

React quickly. When baby displays an unacceptable behavior, tell him "No" immediately and firmly. If he does it again, distract him or remove him from the situation. The longer you wait to react, the more likely he is to forget what he did that was unacceptable.

Praise him when his behavior is acceptable. If you always focus on the negative, baby will repeat those actions to get your attention. When you ignore the negative and focus on the positive, he'll change his behavior accordingly to keep your attention focused on him.

Frostbite

What it is. Frostbite occurs when a part of the body is exposed to extreme cold and suffers the effect of freezing. Affected areas usually involve the nose, cheeks, ears, fingers and toes. Frostbite symptoms include

- white or pale appearance of affected area
- exposed area is numb or tender to the touch

- tingling in exposed area
- tissue may feel firm
- color may change from pale or white to red, then to purple, then black
- exposed area blisters

What to do. If your baby experiences frostbite, get him to emergency care as soon as possible. Do not rub or massage the area. Remove clothing covering the affected area, then cover the skin with loose clothing or gauze. Get medical help as soon as possible.

Call the doctor. Call the doctor if you believe your baby has suffered frostbite. After baby has been treated, call your pediatrician if there is an increase in swelling, tenderness or pain, if there is a discharge of liquid or pus from the area or if other symptoms develop.

Baby's doctor will prescribe pain medication if needed. Sometimes the affected body part is placed in warm water (100F; 37.7C), but only qualified personnel should do this.

Conversations with Baby

Whisper to get baby's attention. When you want your baby to pay attention, don't yell at him. Get down to his level or pick him up, and speak quietly. A raised voice sounds a bit angry, even when you don't mean it to be. Baby may think he's being disciplined for something and may ignore you.

Use the correct words. Save baby talk for occasional interactions. He needs to hear you pronounce words correctly. Use real words for the made-up words you may have used with baby when he was younger.

Speak clearly, and use short sentences. Baby doesn't comprehend long explanations or big words. If he doesn't understand you, he may stop listening.

Gently correct mispronunciations. It's common for baby to mispronounce words. He has a lot of words to learn! Instead of correcting him constantly, model the correct word or the correct use of the word for baby. For example, if he says "googie" for "cookie," ask, "Would you like a cookie?"

Stay positive. It's no fun to be corrected all the time. Provide baby with a positive environment in which to learn.

Lactose Intolerance

What it is. A person who suffers from lactose intolerance—also called *lactase deficiency* or *milk intolerance*—has a problem digesting cow's milk or other milk products. A deficiency in, or a lack of, the enzyme lactase causes the condition. Lactase is necessary for the digestion of all milk products other than breast milk.

Lactose intolerance is possible at any age. Some infants are born with this disorder. Symptoms your baby has lactose intolerance include

- diarrhea
- failure to thrive
- failure to gain weight
- diaper rash
- gas
- stomach pain
- nausea
- vomiting

Lactose intolerance is more common among some people than others. Asians, Blacks and Native Americans have a higher incidence of lactose intolerance. It also runs in families. While you are pregnant, seriously consider breastfeeding your baby if either parent has a family history of lactose intolerance. If there is no family history, be alert for problems with formula, especially if it is cow-milk based. When baby turns 1 year old, look for signs of lactose intolerance when he switches to drinking regular cow's milk.

If lactose intolerance does not run in your family, you may have to become a detective to identify it. Start by identifying what substances might be causing your baby's problem.

Call the doctor. Call your pediatrician if you believe your baby has lactose intolerance, especially after switching to cow's milk from formula or breast milk. If baby suffers from persistent diarrhea or vomiting, or if he doesn't gain weight, let his doctor know.

What to do. The best treatment is to change baby's diet. Do not give cow's milk or any products that contain, or are made from, cow's milk. A supplement (lactase) can be added to milk and milk-containing foods to help deal with the problem. If the condition is present at birth and you choose not to nurse, you may be advised to give baby a soybean-based formula.

Toys and Play This 52nd Week

Most 1-year-olds love action. When your baby plays with toys that move or ones that he can manipulate, he's learning about make-believe, improving his motor skills and indulging in physical play. He especially likes pushing or pulling toys. He'll have fun with toys he can ride on. Toys he can turn into his own creations, such as blocks and other shapes, or ones he can pretend with, such as dolls, stuffed animals and hand puppets, are also favorites.

Learning Teamwork
It's time to start teaching baby about teamwork. In addition to helping baby learn to take turns, this game helps develop his muscle coordination. Sit facing baby on the floor. Touch your feet to his feet. Roll a ball to him within the "corral" your feet have created, and ask him to roll it back to you. Continue until he tires of this game.

Meeting Strangers
Stranger anxiety has abated for now. Make a game out of meeting strangers. Before introducing your little one to someone new, hold him securely in your arms. Shake hands with the new person. Ask the visitor to hand baby one of his toys. Later, ask baby to hand something to the person. Let him move along at his own pace—don't force him to interact.

"Loving" His Toys
Encourage baby to hug and to love his toys and stuffed animals. This helps him learn to express affection. Show baby how to give the toy or doll "a love and a hug." Be sure you demonstrate by giving him lots of loves and hugs, too!

Encourage your baby to hug his stuffed toys.

Appendix

Emergency Situations

This section provides you with information for dealing with emergency situations. We urge you to read it thoroughly and to become knowledgeable about the various responses and treatments to emergencies you might face with a child.

We also suggest every parent take a CPR course to learn how to perform this lifesaving technique correctly. Contact your local hospital or the American Red Cross for information on classes they may offer in your area.

Anaphylactic Shock

Anaphylactic shock, also called *allergic shock,* occurs when the body has a severe allergic reaction to something it has become sensitized to, such as a drug or foreign protein. A reaction can occur at any age. Symptoms of anaphylactic shock include

- loss of consciousness (fainting)
- convulsions
- itching or hives
- sneezing or runny nose
- numbness or tingling around the mouth or on fingers
- itchy or runny eyes
- difficulty breathing
- tightness of chest
- fever
- violent cough
- rapid heartbeat (palpitations)

This is an emergency! Anaphylactic shock is a severe reaction. Get help immediately. It may be necessary to perform CPR or mouth-to-mouth resuscitation on your baby.

Try to identify a possible cause. Your observations will help emergency personnel treat your baby. Medications, such as Adrenalin or antihistamines, may be given. It is necessary to identify the causative medicine or agent for future safety.

> It's easy to forget important information in an emergency. Write down your street address and telephone number. Keep it near the phone. It's handy for baby-sitters, too.

Bleeding

How much blood is lost, and how quickly, is a good indicator of how severe bleeding is. Babies have a much smaller volume of blood, so they can't afford to lose as much blood as an older child or an adult.

If serious injury results in bleeding from the arteries, a baby can die in minutes, if left untreated.

If your baby has a small cut or abrasion that bleeds slightly, clean the area with mild soap and water. Dry the area, then apply triple antibiotic ointment and a bandage.

If your baby sustains a wound with a lot of bleeding, immediately apply steady, firm pressure to the wound with a clean cloth, clean disposable diaper or your hand until bleeding stops. Do not attempt to clean the wound first or remove any embedded objects. Call 9-1-1, or take your child to the nearest emergency-medicine facility.

Cardiopulmonary Resuscitation (CPR)

Parents and others who care for children benefit from knowing how to administer CPR correctly. You can learn the technique by reading about it, but it's better to take a course. There you can ask questions and be checked on your technique. Certified courses are held in most communities. Contact the American Red Cross, the American Heart Association or your state or county medical society. It may be necessary to perform CPR if baby

- is not breathing
- is having difficulty breathing (lips or skin turn blue)
- has no pulse or heartbeat
- is unresponsive

Seven steps to perform CPR. Study this section, or review these steps after you take your CPR course. *The first four steps of CPR comprise the four steps of mouth-to-mouth resuscitation.* The steps are as follows.

Step 1. See if baby is responsive or conscious. Nudge, tap or gently shake baby. **If he does not respond, call for help.** Put your ear next to baby's mouth and nose. Listen for breathing, and watch to see if his chest rises and falls. Don't shake baby hard. It could cause further injury.

Step 2. Place baby on his back on a firm, flat surface. Move baby carefully. Support his head and neck.

Step 3. Open the baby's airway by gently tilting his head back with one hand on his forehead. At the same time, lift his chin up with your other hand. The baby's nose should point toward the ceiling. Again, check to see if he's breathing.

Step 4. If baby is not breathing, make a tight seal with your mouth over baby's mouth and nose. Give him two slow breaths. Watch to see if his chest rises and falls. Don't blow with too much force. If baby's chest does not rise and fall, reposition him. Try again. It may be necessary to check baby's airway again and start over. Also see *Choking,* below.

Step 5. Check baby's pulse. Feel on the inside of his upper arm, between his shoulder and his elbow. Count for 15 seconds, and multiply by 4. If there is a pulse and baby is not breathing, continue breathing for baby at a rate of 1 breath every 3 seconds.

Step 6. If there is no pulse, begin chest compressions. Place two or three of your fingers on the lower portion of baby's breastbone, one finger's width below the nipple line. Gently press down ½ to 1 inch. Give 5 compressions, at a rate of 100 per minute, then a rescue breath. It helps to count aloud: "One, two, three, four, five, breathe."

Step 7. After 20 cycles (1 minute), check for pulse and breathing. If both have returned, place baby on his side and watch him. If he is not breathing but his pulse has returned, give one rescue breath every 3 seconds, and monitor his pulse. If both pulse and breathing are absent, continue CPR. Check for pulse and breathing every few minutes. Continue until help arrives.

Choking

One of the many things new parents discover is that everything (except the food you feed baby) ends up in his mouth, often with at least one visit to the floor! Any item baby can put in his mouth presents a danger of choking— *anything!* The information in this section may be lifesaving for your baby.

Babies choke on many small objects, such as toy parts, buttons, coins, plastic bags, balloons, pillows and blankets. Toys with removable small parts are dangerous. Food is also a frequent cause of choking. Those that are particularly

Phone Numbers

Keep the following numbers close to your phone, or put them on your speed dial:

- **your pediatrician's office**
- **the nearest Poison Control Center**
- **the closest hospital**
- **the closest emergency-medicine facility**
- **the telephone number of your neighbor or a close relative**
- **your work number or your partner's work number**
- **9-1-1**

dangerous include:
- candy and gum
- nuts
- popcorn
- hot dogs
- popcorn

- pieces of hard vegetables
- grapes and raisins
- peanut butter
- small food pieces
- any "sticky" or "gooey" food

When baby chokes, he usually can't make any sound. He will turn blue and appear to stop breathing. Coughing or gasping may come before choking. It may be baby's way of trying not to choke. *Don't* use the adult Heimlich maneuver on an infant because it can injure baby. Use the method described below.

If baby is coughing, don't try to stop it. It's a normal reaction and often solves the problem. Use care when trying to remove an object in baby's mouth. You don't want to push it deeper into his throat. It's OK to sweep your finger across or through baby's mouth to remove the obstruction.

When to Call 9-1-1

Sometimes you know you have to call 9-1-1; there's no question in your mind. At other times, you might not be sure whether you should call 9-1-1 or your pediatrician. Below is a list of situations that indicate you should call 9-1-1 first, then your baby's doctor.

- **When bleeding is heavy and you can't stop it after 15 minutes. If a cut appears to be large or deep.**

- **If baby is burned, and the burn looks charred (black) or white. If a burn covers at least 5% of his body (5% means the burn is 5 times or more larger than his hand).**

- **When baby is choking. Try to dislodge the object while someone else calls for help.**

- **If baby falls from a high place and/or hits a very hard surface.**

- **If baby has any trouble breathing.**

- **When baby eats or drinks anything you believe might be poisonous. Call the nearest Poison Control Center but also get emergency help.**

- **If baby has been seriously injured in an accident.**

- **When baby has been submerged in water.**

- **Anytime baby loses consciousness.**

If baby is choking, have someone else call 9-1-1. Put baby face down on your forearm. Support his head and neck, and hold his jaw. His head should be lower than the rest of his body. Using the heel of your other hand, give him four or five blows between his shoulder blades.

If baby doesn't breathe, keep his head lower than the rest of the body. Using two or three fingers, give four or five chest thrusts on the lower half of baby's breast bone. If baby is still not breathing, it may be necessary to repeat the above steps. Also see *CPR*, above.

Concussion

A concussion is an injury that results from the body colliding with an object. Most concussions involve the head or the spine. Symptoms of a concussion to the head include

- drowsiness or confusion
- vomiting
- nausea
- pupils of different sizes
- loss of consciousness
- irritability
- headache
- bleeding of the scalp, if the skin is broken
- bump on the head
- inability to recognize familiar people or objects
- staggering gait or loss of coordination
- weakness, tingling or an uncontrollable twitching of one side of the body, an arm or a leg
- bleeding or drainage of clear fluid from the ears or nose
- seizures

If your baby suffers a head injury, apply pressure to the wound with a clean cloth or diaper. If the wound won't stop bleeding, or if it is deep or large, go to the nearest emergency-medicine facility. If the wound is not serious, after bleeding stops, put ice on th   to reduce swelling. Apply triple antibiotic ointment and a bar

Keep child quiet. After a hard blow to the head, kee
quiet for the next 12 to 24 hours. Keep him awake for a
hour, then let him sleep if he wants to. Awaken the ch
2 hours to see if you can awaken him easily and if he

Determine if his pupils are of equal size and if they constrict when you shine a light in his eyes.

Notify your pediatrician if your child receives a head injury. Your doctor may want to see him for evaluation. The extent of an injury can be determined only by careful examination and observation. If you suspect your baby has suffered a severe head injury, notify your doctor immediately.

Observe carefully for 24 hours. After examination by your doctor, your baby may be sent home with you. He must be carefully observed for the next 24 hours. Report to your doctor immediately if you are unable to awaken or rouse your baby. You will be given other specifics to watch for. Hospitalization may also occur for studies, such as X-rays, CT scan and MRI, and for observation.

Electric Shock

Electric shock occurs when the human body comes in contact with electricity. Electric-shock injury in babies occurs most often when they put metal objects into electrical outlets or when they put electrical cords in their mouth and bite down.

Shut off power. If your baby sustains an electric shock, immediately shut off the power. Determine if he is touching any wires. Remove the wires with a nonmetal object before giving him aid.

Yell for help. Yell for help if baby is unconscious and not breathing. Begin mouth-to-mouth resuscitation immediately. If there is no pulse, begin CPR. Continue these emergency treatments until baby is revived or until help arrives.

Seek help immediately. If baby receives an electric shock severe enough to cause injury, such as burns, notify your pediatrician immediately. Or go to the nearest emergency room.

Mouth-to-Mouth Resuscitation

Mouth-to-mouth resuscitation is an aspect of CPR. See that entry for detailed information.

Nosebleed

When baby has a nosebleed, you'll see blood oozing from his nostril. If bleeding is close to the nostril, blood is usually bright red. If it _deeper in the nose, blood may be bright or dark. Nausea from _wed blood may cause vomit to be bright red. Stools may be __ swallowed blood.

Sit baby upright in your lap, with head forward slightly. If your baby has a nosebleed, sit baby upright in your lap, and bend his head slightly forward. Clamp his nostrils closed with your fingers for 5 uninterrupted minutes. When you hold the nose tightly closed, it allows the blood to clot and to seal the damaged blood vessels. If bleeding stops and recurs, repeat the above procedures. If bleeding does not stop, take your baby to the nearest emergency-medicine facility.

Cool-mist humidifier could help prevent some nosebleeds. A lot of nosebleeds may indicate that baby's mucous membranes are dry. Run a cool-mist humidifier to moisten the air when he's sleeping. Apply a small amount of petroleum jelly to a cotton swab, and apply the petroleum jelly inside each nostril.

Call your pediatrician if your baby suffers from frequent nosebleeds. If your baby is having difficulty breathing through his nose after a nosebleed, let your pediatrician know. Go to the nearest emergency-medicine facility for a nosebleed that won't stop after administering care as described above.

Poisons

Keep the telephone number of your local Poison Control Center near your phone.

Poisons in the eye. A poison can get into the eye when liquid splashes into it. Many substances can damage your baby's eyes, but your infant can't tell you about the problem. Potency of a poison, and the length of exposure to it, may determine how severe damage is. Acting quickly may make the difference between a temporary problem and a long-term disability.

Flood baby's eye with tap water. If any poison splashes into your baby's eyes, use a large glass or pitcher filled with cool tap water to flood your baby's eye for 10 to 20 minutes. Try to get baby to blink frequently by blinking at him. Keep his hands out of his eyes. You may need to wrap him in a blanket to keep his hands out of the affected eye.

Call your nearest Poison Control Center for advice and information.

Inhaled poisons. Many substances are toxic when inhaled. Toxic substances include carbon monoxide, smoke and fumes from fires, propellants, gasoline, kerosene, turpentine, cigarette lighter fluid, glue, paint remover and lamp oil.

A baby's reaction to inhaling a poisonous substance can vary, depending on the amount of the substance inhaled and the substance. Inhaling a poisonous substance can cause various reactions, including

> **When applying a compress to any part of baby's body, place a washcloth or towel between baby's skin and the compress.**

- nausea
- vomiting
- decreased consciousness
- loss of consciousness

- headache
- breathing difficulties
- coughing
- lethargy

Call 9-1-1 immediately if your baby is in obvious distress, such as difficulty breathing, showing a decreased level of consciousness, lethargy, convulsions or lack of a heartbeat. Remove your baby from the source of the poison. Take him into the fresh air or to a well-ventilated area. Call your nearest Poison Control Center for specific instructions.

Poison on the skin. If you suspect your baby has come in contact with a poison, search for evidence. Spilled household cleaners would probably leave the baby's skin looking red and irritated.

Remove contaminated clothes. Call your local Poison Control Center for specific treatments.

Swallowed poison. The incidence of poisoning in children has been greatly decreased since the passage of the Poison Prevention Packaging Act of 1970. This act provides that certain potentially hazardous drugs and household products be sold in child-resistant containers. However, poisoning remains a significant health concern. Most cases occur in children under 6 years old. The most frequently ingested poisons are cosmetics, personal-care products, cleaning products and household plants.

If you find your infant with an open or empty container of a toxic substance, you must suspect poisoning. Watch for behavioral differences, burns or redness of the lips, mouth or hands, unexplained vomiting, breath that smells like chemicals, breathing difficulties or convulsions. If poisoning occurs and your child is in obvious distress (unconscious, convulsing, experiencing breathing difficulties), call 9-1-1 immediately.

Empty mouth of pills, plant parts or any other material.
Identify the poison. Look for clues that may indicate what baby
swallowed, if it is unknown. Save all evidence of poison (container,
vomit, urine), and take them with you to the nearest emergency-
medicine facility.

**Call the nearest Poison Control Center for immediate advice
about treatment.** Be prepared to read the labels on the container
and to describe the substance, the amount ingested and any
physical changes you detect.

Often treatment is to remove the ingested poison by inducing
vomiting. It is important to have a bottle of syrup of ipecac in
your home for this purpose. Keep it in an accessible spot in the
refrigerator. Periodically check the expiration date. Many pharmacies
give syrup of ipecac free of charge to customers who have small
children.

Do *not* induce vomiting on your own. Always check with the
Poison Control Center first. They will advise you as to what action to
take. In some instances, inducing vomiting can cause more damage.
There is a high risk of aspiration in children under 1 year. If vomiting
is necessary to rid the body of a poison, it should only be induced
in a health-care facility.

Medical Glossary

A

acetaminophen. Nonprescription medicine used to reduce fever and to relieve minor pain. Available in children's strength. Tylenol is a common brand name.

acute. Situation that begins suddenly. May also mean severe or intense but of short duration.

airways. Passageways for air to pass to the lungs. Includes *bronchi, bronchioles* and windpipe *(trachea)*.

allergen. Any substance that causes an allergy.

allergy. Acquired sensitivity to a substance that doesn't normally cause a reaction.

analgesics. Various medicines used to relieve pain.

anaphylactic shock. Sudden, severe reaction to an allergen; it is so severe that death may result in a short time.

anaphylaxis. Severe allergic hypersensitivity to a substance. Can result in *anaphylactic shock.*

anemia. Condition in which the oxygen-carrying substances in blood (red blood cells or hemoglobin) are insufficient.

antibiotics. Medicine used against bacteria and to fight bacterial infection; not used against viral infections.

anticonvulsant. Medications that help control or relieve *convulsions* (seizures).

antihistamines. Medication used to relieve allergy symptoms.

arrhythmia. Variation in heart beat; irregular heart beat.

B

bacteria. Germ or microorganism that can cause infection or disease.

balanitis. Penis inflammation.

benign. Harmless.

bilirubin. Waste product of red blood cells found in bile that causes urine to be yellow; can cause jaundice if it builds up in the blood.

biopsy. Removal of a small amount of tissue or fluid for laboratory study.

blepharitis. Inflammation of the edges of the eyelid.

blood cells, red. Cells in the blood that carry oxygen throughout the body.

blood cells, white. Cells in the blood that fight infection.

bronchi. The two main passageways from the *trachea* to the lungs that allow air to enter the lungs.

bronchioles. Smaller air passageways of the *bronchi.*

bronchoscope. Tool that passes through the *trachea* to remove a foreign body or to provide a view of the area.

C

cardiopulmonary resuscitation (CPR). Emergency measures for a person who has stopped breathing and whose heart has stopped beating.

cartilage. Dense connective tissue, with some flexibility, that enables joints to move smoothly.

cauterization. Destroying tissue by means of heat, chemicals or freezing.

chronic. Condition that is long-term and continuing.

circumcision. Surgical removal of the foreskin, or fold of skin, that covers the head of the penis.

colic. Spasm accompanied by pain. When an infant has colic, he or she suffers from bouts of pain, accompanied by crying and gas.

compress. Cloth applied to skin to relieve discomfort.

congenital. Condition or abnormality present at birth.

conjunctivitis. Inflammation of the mucous membrane that lines eyelids.

contagious. Disease that can be spread from one person to another.

convulsions. Involuntary muscle contraction and relaxation.

D

dehydration. Loss of body fluids from the body; occurs when output of body fluids exceed intake of fluid.

dermatitis. Inflammation of the skin accompanied by itching, redness and lesions.

diarrhea. Frequent passing of unformed, watery stools.

discomfort. Physical problems that cause a person to feel uncomfortable.

disease. Condition in which a group of signs or symptoms are present; usually with an adverse effect on health.

E

electrolyte. Chemicals in the body involved in all body functions; may be lost through dehydration, diarrhea, vomiting or other means.

esophagus. Passageway that extends from the *pharynx* to the stomach.

Eustachian tube. Tube that extends from the middle ear to the *pharynx*.

F

family medical history. Information about medical conditions and illnesses that have occurred within a family.

fecal. Relating to the waste products the body eliminates.

feces. Undigested food that passes through the gastrointestinal tract to the colon, where it is eliminated as a bowel movement.

fever. Elevated body temperature, at least 1 degree above normal, which is 98.6F (37C). It is a sign of disease; it is not a disease itself.

fiber. Ingredient of many carbohydrates that increases bulk in the diet.

fissure. Break in the skin or the lining of an organ.

folliculitis. Inflammation of hair follicles.

fontanel (fontanelle). Soft spot on baby's head where skull bones have not grown together.

G

galactosemia. Inherited disease in infants in which they cannot digest milk.

gastroenteritis. Inflammation of the stomach and intestinal tract.

germ. Organism that causes infection; can be *virus*, fungus or *bacteria*.

gluten. Protein in wheat that is indigestible by some people; gluten intolerance is an inherited problem.

H

hernia. Protrusion of part or all of an organ through the wall of the space that usually contains it.

hiccups. Spasm of the diaphragm that causes a short, sharp cough.

hives. Itchy welts caused by an allergic reaction.

hypersensitivity. Extreme sensitivity to a substance.

hyperthermia. Raised body temperature.

hypothermia. Lowered body temperature.

I

IV. Intravenous—into the vein.

immunity. Protection against.

immunization. Vaccine given to produce immunity against a particular germ that causes a disease.

incubation period. Time between exposure to a germ and the onset of symptoms of the infection caused by the germs.

infant. Child from birth to 1 year.

infection. Disease caused by a germ.

intestinal blockage. Blockage in the intestinal tract.

intestine, large. Part of the intestinal tract that lies below the small intestine; processes waste products into *feces.*

intestine, small. Located just under the stomach, it is the largest part of the intestinal tract.

-itis. Inflammation of.

J

jaundice. Disease of the liver and blood resulting in yellow skin, yellow in the white of the eyes and dark urine.

joint. Site in body where two or more bones meet.

L

lactose intolerance. Intolerance to milk and milk products.

larynx. Enlarged upper end of the *trachea,* below base of tongue.

laxative. Medication used to relieve constipation.

lethargy. Tiredness, fatigue or lack of energy.

M

malabsorption. Inadequate absorption of nutrients by the body.

medical history. See *family medical history.*

mucous membrane. Thin tissue that lines an organ; produces *mucus.*

mucus. Fluid produced by the body to protect organs.

N

nasogastric tube. Tube passed through the nose into the stomach for feeding and draining secretions.

nausea. Stomach upset that usually occurs before vomiting; a person can experience nausea without vomiting.

newborn. Baby from birth to 1 month old.

nodule. Lump or swelling beneath the skin.

O - P

oral. Relates to the mouth.

pain. Unpleasant feeling in the body associated with tissue damage caused by disease or injury.

palate. Roof of the mouth.

parasite. Organism that lives within or feeds upon another organism.

pharynx. Passageway for air from the nose to the larynx and for food from the mouth to the *esophagus.*

phlegm. Thick *mucus,* especially from the respiratory areas.

physical therapy. Rehabilitation to restore functions following disease or injury. Involves exercise, massage, heat, cold and other treatments.

pulmonary. Relates to the lungs.

R

rectum. Lower end of the large intestine.

regurgitate. To spit up, or to vomit.

relapse. Person with a disease or illness gets worse after improvement.

rotavirus. Group of viruses that causes enteritis in babies and children.

rubella. German measles.

ruptured eardrum. Break in the eardrum.

S

scaling. Flakes of dried skin.

septic. Infected.

serum. Watery portion of the blood after it coagulates.

shock. Blood flow is inadequate to return enough blood to the heart for normal functioning of the body.

SIDS. Sudden infant death syndrome.

soaks. Application of moisture, by soaking in water, to an inflamed part of the skin.

spore. Reproductive cell produced by plants and fungi.

sputum. Matter coughed up or cleared from the throat.

sterilize. To make completely free of germs. May be done by chemicals, heat and other methods.

stool. See *feces*.

suture. Thin, fibrous material used to hold tissue or skin together.

symptoms. Change in the body or the body's function from a disease.

T

tenderness. Soreness or sensitivity.

testicles. Male sex glands.

trachea. Passageway from the *larynx* to the bronchial tubes.

trauma. Outside force that injures or damages the body.

tube feeding. See *nasogastric tube.*

U

upper-respiratory system. Upper part of the breathing system consisting of nose, throat, larynx, pharynx and bronchial tubes.

urinary tract. Organs and ducts that produce and eliminate urine—made up of kidneys, ureters, bladder and urethra.

V

vaccine. Medication that provides protection from (immunity to) a disease.

virus. Germs responsible for some diseases.

vitamins. Substances needed for healthy growth and body function.

vomiting. Ejection through the mouth of stomach contents.

W - X

wheezing. Whistling sounds produced during periods of difficult breathing.

X-rays. Test that uses high-energy electromagnetic waves to make "pictures" that can be used to diagnose a problem.

Resources for Readers

At-Home Moms

F.E.M.A.L.E. *(Formerly Employed Mothers At the Leading Edge)*
P.O. Box 31
Elmhurst, IL 60126
800-223-9399
www.femalehome.org
International nonprofit organization supports women who stay home and care for their children.

Miserly Moms
www.miserlymoms.com
Money-saving tips for cooking, shopping, decorating and gardening.

MOMS Club International (Mothers Offering Mothers Support)
25371 Rye Canyon Road
Valencia, CA 91355
www.momsclub.org
email: momsclub@aol.com
For at-home mothers.

Moms Online
www.momsonline.com
Mothers created this site for those involved in nurturing children, such as moms, dads, grandparents.

Mothers at Home
800-783-4666
www.mah.org
Nonprofit organization to support mothers who stay at home to care for children.

"Back to Sleep" Program

National Institute of Child Health & Human Development
P.O. Box 29111
Washington, DC 20040
800-505-2742 (Hotline)
www.nichd.nih.gov/

Breastfeeding

Avent
800-542-8368
www.aventamerica.com
Information on breastfeeding, bottle-feeding or a combination.

Beechnut Nutrition Hotline
800-523-6633

Best Start
3500 E. Fletcher Ave., Suite 519
Tampa, FL 33613
800-277-4975
email: beststart@beststartinc.org

Breastfeeding National Network
800-TELL-YOU

La Leche League
1400 North Meacham Road
Schaumburg, IL 60173-4048
847-519-7730
www.lalecheleague.org/

Medela, Inc.
1101 Corporate Drive
McHenry, IL 60050
815-363-1166, 800-435-8316
www.medela.com

National Center for Education & Maternal Child Health
703-524-7802
www.nce.mch.org

Wellstart
4062 First Avenue
San Diego, CA 92103
619-295-5192

Child Care

Au Pair Care
Information from the
U.S. Department of State
www.usembassy.state.gov/legal/gc/aupair/org.html

Child Care Aware Hotline
800-424-2246

Dept. of Health and Human Services
Nat. Child Care Information Ctr.
800-616-2242
www.nccic.org

Kids in Distressed Situations
(K.I.D.S.)
800-266-3314

National Association of Child Care
Resource and Referral Agencies
202-393-5501
www.childcareer.org
Dedicated to providing the most
up-to-date information to parents
and others seeking child care.
Also serves child-care professionals
and child-care advocates.

National Resource Center for Health
and Safety in Child Care
800-598-5437 (KIDS)
nrc.uchsc.edu
Dedicated to promoting health and
safety in out-of-home child care
situations throughout the United
States.

Support Kids
800-801-KIDS
www.supportkids.com

Working Mother
www.workingmother.com
Online magazine devoted to working
mothers and other working women.

Children with Special Needs

Asthma and Allergies
Allergy and Asthma Network
3554 Chain Bridge Road
Suite 200
Fairfax, VA 22030
800-878-4403

American College of Allergy, Asthma
and Immunology (ACAAI)
800-842-7777
allergy.mcg.edu
Informative news services for parents
and patients. Site is maintained by
allergists and ACAAI.

Asthma & Allergy Foundation of
America
3301 New Mexico Ave.
Washington, DC 20016-3302
202-966-2222

Autism
Autism Society of America (ASA)
www.autism-society.org

Families for Early Autism Treatment
(FEAT)
www.feat.org

Birth Defects
March of Dimes
1275 Mamaroneck Ave.
White Plains, NY 10605
914-428-7100
www.madimes.org

Blindness
American Foundation for the Blind
11 Pennsylvania Pl., Suite 300
New York, NY 10001
212-502-7600
www.afb.org

Helen Keller National Center for
Deaf-Blind Youths and Adults
111 Middle Neck Road
Sands Point, NY 11050
516-944-8900

Cancer
Association for Research
of Childhood Cancer
P.O. Box 251
Buffalo, NY 14225-0251
716-681-4433

Candlelighters Childhood Cancer Foundation
USA: www.uway-austin.org/candlelighters.html
Canada: www.candlelighters.ca/

National Childhood Cancer Foundation
www.nccf.org/

Cerebral Palsy
National Easter Seal Society
230 W. Monroe St., Suite 1800
Chicago, IL 60606-4802
312-726-6200
www.easter-seals.org

United Cerebral Palsy Association
1660 L Street, NW, Suite 700
Washington, DC 20036
www.ucpa.org

Cleft Palate
Cleft Palate-Craniofacial Center
University of Pittsburgh
317 Salk Hall
3501 Terrace St.
Pittsburgh, PA 15261
800-408-7390; 412-648-8779
www.cpc.pitt.edu
e-mail: cleft@cpc.pitt.edu

Cystic Fibrosis
CF-WEB
cf-web.mit.edu/
Online information about cystic fibrosis.

Cystic Fibrosis Foundation
6931 Arlington Road
Bethesda, MD 20814
301-951-4422; 800-344-4823
www.cff.org

Down Syndrome
Association for Children with Down Syndrome
4 Fern Place
Plainview, NY 11803
516-933-4700
www.acds.org

National Down Syndrome Society (NDSS)
666 Broadway
New York, NY 10012-2317
800-221-4602
ndss.org

Epilepsy
Epilepsy Foundation of America
4351 Garden City, Suite 500
Landover, MD 20785
301-459-3700
www.epilepsyfoundation.org

Fragile X Syndrome
National Fragile X Foundation
P.O. Box 190488
San Francisco, CA 94119-0488
800-688-8765
www.fragilex.org

General Health Information
CARESS
(Information on services for parents of children with disabilities)
P.O. Box 1492
Washington, DC 20013-1492
800-695-0285
www.nichcy.org

Internet Resources for Special Children
www.irsc.org/
Site set up by a parent with links to other sites.

National Association for Rare Disorders
P.O. Box 8923
New Fairfield, CT 06812
203-746-6518
www.rarediseases.org

Hearing Problems
American Speech-Language-Hearing Association
10801 Rockville Pike
Rockville, MD 20852
301-897-5700
www.asha.org

Helen Keller National Center for
Deaf-Blind Youths and Adults
111 Middle Neck Road.
Sands Point, NY 11050
516-944-8900

Heart Problems
American Heart Association
7272 Greenville Ave.
Dallas, TX 75231-4596
800-242-8721
www.americanheart.org

Congenital Heart Anomalies—
Support, Education, Resources
(CHASER)
2112 North Wilkins Road
Swanton, OH 43558
419-825-5575
www.csun.edu/~hfmth006/chaser/
e-mail: chaser@compuserv.com

Hemophilia
National Hemophilia Foundation
116 W. 32nd St., 17th Floor
New York, NY 10001
212-328-3700
www.hemophilia.org

World Federation of Hemophilia
Suite 1010
1425 René-Levesque Blvd., W.
Montreal, Quebec H3G 1T7 Canada
514-875-7944

Leukemia
Leukemia & Lymphoma Society of
America, Inc.
600 Third Ave.
New York, NY 10016
212-573-8484
www.leukemia-lymphoma.org

Liver Disease
American Liver Foundation
75 Maiden Lane, Suite 603
New York, NY 10038
800-GO-LIVER (465-4837)
liverfoundation.org

Children's Liver Alliance
3835 Richmond Ave., Box 190
Staten Island, NY 10312
718-987-6200
livertx.org/
e-mail: livers4kids@earthlink.net

Mental Retardation
(also see *Down Syndrome*)
The Arc
P.O. Box 1047
Arlington, TX 76004
817-261-6003
817-277-0553 (TDD)
TheArc.org/
e-mail: thearc@metronet.com

Phenylketonuria
Children's PKU Network
1520 State St., #111
San Diego, CA 92101-2930
619-233-3202

Psoriasis
National Psoriasis Foundation
6600 SW 92nd Ave., Suite 300
Portland, OR 97223-7195
503-297-1545
www.psoriasis.org

Reye's Syndrome
National Reye's Syndrome
Foundation
426 North Lewis St.
P.O. Box 829
Bryan, OH 43506
800-233-7393
www.right.net\~reyessyn

Sickle Cell Disease
Sickle Cell Disease Association of
America, Inc.
200 Corporate Pt., Suite 495
Culver City, CA 90230
800-421-8453; 310-216-6363
sicklecelldisease.org

SIDS
SIDS Alliance
1314 Bedford Ave., Suite 210
Baltimore, MD 21208
800-221-SIDS (7437)

Spina Bifida
Spina Bifida Association of America
4590 MacArthur Blvd., NW, #250
Washington, DC 20007-4226
800-621-3141
www.sbaa.org

Tay-Sachs Disease
National Tay-Sachs & Allied Disease Association (NTSAD)
2001 Beacon St., Suite 204
Boston, MA 02135
800-906-8723
e-mail: ntsad-boston@worldnet.att.net

Dads
A Man's Life
www.manslife.com
Many topics of interest to a man.

A Daddy's Home
www.daddyshome.com

At-Home Dad (newsletter $15/year)
Peter Baylies, Editor
61 Brightwood Ave.
North Andover, MA 01845-1702
www.athomedad.com

BabyCenter
www.babycenter.com/dads
Lots of information for men about taking care of a baby.

Boot Camp for New Dads
www.newdads.com
Information and resources for new dads. Lots of stuff for first-time dads. Men learn from each other.

Father's World
www.fathersworld.com
Promotes and celebrates fatherhood and family. Information for resources, support and education for fathers. Multiple links.

Full-Time Dads
193 Shelley Ave.
Elizabeth, NJ 07208
908-355-9722; Fax 908-355-9723
www.fathersworld.com/fulltimedad
Information with open forums. (Linked from Father's World.)

The Single & Custodial Father's Network
www.single-fathers.org
For fathers who are primary caregivers; to connect with other fathers in similar situations.

Help and Information for Parents

Adoptive Parents
www.adoption.com
Handy resource for adoption information.

American Academy of Pediatrics (AAP)
141 Northwest Point Blvd.
Elk Grove Village, IL 60007-1098
847-434-4000
www.aap.org

Family.com
www.family.com
Much of interest to a family, with many jump sites.

First Years
firstyears.excite.com
Follow development of a child.

National Organization of Single Mothers
P.O. Box 68
Midland, NC 28107-0068
704-888-5437
singlemothers.org

Parent Soup
www.parentsoup.com
Plentiful information for parents on numerous child-rearing subjects.

Parent Time
www.parenttime.com
Information for parents on different aspects of rearing a baby.

ParenthoodWeb.com
www.parenthoodweb.com
Find answers to common childrearing problems.

Parenting Questions & Answers
www.parenting-qa.com/
Good place to go with questions on childrearing.

Parents.com
www.parents.com
Great deal of information for parents, including advice, single parenting, toy safety, travel with kids.

Parents Place
www.parentsplace.com
Parents communicating about their experiences of rearing children.

StorkSite
www.storksite.com
Information on babies from birth to 1 year.

Women.com
www.women.com/

Zero to Three
www.zerotothree.org
Great resource for information on a child's first 3 years of life.

Multiples
Center for Loss in Multiple Birth (C.L.I.M.B.)
P.O. Box 91377
Anchorage, AK 99509
907-222-5321
www.climb-support.org
e-mail: climb@pobox.alaska.net

National Organization of Mothers of Twins Clubs, Inc.
P.O. Box 438
Thompson Station, TN 37179-0438
877-540-2200
www.nomotc.org
Information for parents of twins.

Triplet Connection
P.O. Box 99571
Stockton, CA 95209
209-474-0885
www.tripletconnection.org

Twin Services
P.O. Box 10066
Berkeley, CA 94709
510-524-0863
www.twinservices.org

Twin to Twin Transfusion Syndrome (TTTS) Foundation
Mary Slaman-Forsythe, Executive Director
411 Longbeach Parkway
Bay Village, OH 44140
440-899-8887; Fax: 440-899-1184
www.tttsfoundation.org

Twinnet
www.ghg.net/4dee/index.html
Information for parents of twins.

The Twins Foundation
P.O. Box 6043
Providence, RI 02940-6043
401-729-1000

Twins Magazine
5350 S. Roslyn St., Suite 400
Englewood, CO 80111
800-328-3211
www.twinsmagazine.com

Safety for Baby
Auto Safety Hotline
888-327-4236

Centers for Disease Control
www.cdc.gov
The Centers for Disease control
provides information on diseases and
vaccine information when traveling
abroad.

The Danny Foundation, Crib Safety
Checklist
12901 Alcosta Blvd., Suite 2C
San Ramone, CA 94583
800-833-2669
www.dannyfoundation.org
Information on crib dangers.

General Motors Safety &
Communications Hotline
"Precious Cargo: Protecting the
Children Who Ride with You"
(program)
800-247-9168

The International Association of
Chiefs of Police
Operation Kids
800-843-4227

Juvenile Products Manufacturers
Association (JPMA)
Public Relations office
236 Route 38 West, Suite 100
Moorestown, NJ 08057
856-231-8500
www.jpma.org
e-mail: jpma@ahint.com

National Highway Traffic Safety
Administration
800-424-9393 (Hotline)
www.nhtsa.dot.gov
Transportation safety issues,
including safe cars and car-seat safety.

The National SAFE KIDS Campaign
800-441-1888
www.safekids.org
Educate adults and children about
safety for those 14 years and under.
Nissan's Quest for Safety Campaign
"The What to Expect Guide to Car
Seat Safety" (free booklet)
800-955-4500

SafetyBeltSafe U.S.A.
P.O. Box 553
Altadena, CA 91003
www.carseat.org
Provides accurate, authoritative
information about car seats for
infants and children.

U.S. Consumer Products Safety
Commission
800-638-2772
www.cpsc.gov

Miscellaneous
BabyCenter
www.babycenter.com
An online baby store, with many
products to choose from.

Consumer Information
www.deja.com
Consumers can learn about products
and services from other consumers.
Good for first-time parents purchasing
baby equipment.

The Dollar Stretcher
www.stretcher.com
Dollar-stretching ideas; not just for
use with babies.

Internal Revenue Service
(for information on deductions
regarding child-care expenses)
800-829-1040
ww.irs.gov

National Center for Nutrition and
Dietetics' Consumer-Nutrition Hotline
800-366-1655
To speak with a dietitian.

On-line announcements
www.senada.com
Place to send on-line announcements
and invitations for almost every occasion.

Social Security Administration
800-772-1213
www.ssa.gov

Index

About the Authors

Glade B. Curtis, M.D., is board-certified by the American College of Obstetricians and Gynecologists. He is in private practice in obstetrics, gynecology and infertility in Sandy, Utah.

Dr. Curtis has written several books especially for pregnant women, including *Your Pregnancy Week by Week, Your Pregnancy Questions & Answers, Your Pregnancy after 30, Your Pregnancy: Every Woman's Guide* and *Your Pregnancy Recovery Guide.*

Dr. Curtis is a graduate of the University of Utah and the University of Rochester School of Medicine and Dentistry in New York. He was an intern, resident and chief resident in Obstetrics and Gynecology at the University of Rochester Strong Memorial Hospital.

Judith Schuler, M.S., has worked with Dr. Glade Curtis for over 18 years, as his co-author and editor. They have collaborated together on nine books dealing with pregnancy, women's health and children's health. Ms. Schuler earned a Master of Science degree in Family Studies from the University of Arizona in Tucson.

Before becoming an editor for HPBooks, where she and Dr. Curtis first began working together, Ms. Schuler taught at the university level in California and Arizona. She has one son. She divides her time between Tucson, Arizona, and Laramie, Wyoming.